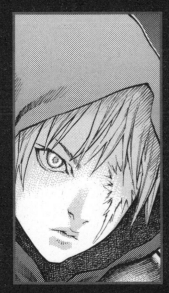

Norihiro Yagi won the 32nd Akatsuka Award for his debut work, *UNDEADMAN*, which appeared in *Monthly Shonen Jump* magazine and produced two sequels. His first serialized manga was his comedy *Angel Densetsu* (Angel Legend), which appeared in *Monthly Shonen Jump* from 1992 to 2000. His epic saga, *Claymore*, is running in *Monthly Jump Square* magazine.

In his spare time, Yagi enjoys things like the Japanese comedic duo Downtown, martial arts, games, driving, and hard rock music, but he doesn't consider these actual hobbies.

CLAYMORE VOL. 12
The SHONEN JUMP ADVANCED Manga Edition

STORY AND ART BY
NORIHIRO YAGI

English Adaptation & Translation/Arashi Productions
Touch-up Art & Lettering/Sabrina Heep
Design/Izumi Evers
Editor/Leyla Aker

Editor in Chief, Books/Alvin Lu
Editor in Chief, Magazines/Marc Weidenbaum
VP of Publishing Licensing/Rika Inouye
VP of Sales/Gonzalo Ferreyra
Sr. VP of Marketing/Liza Coppola
Publisher/Hyoe Narita

Printed in the U.S.A.

Published by VIZ Media, LLC
P.O. Box 77010
San Francisco, CA 94107

SHONEN JUMP ADVANCED Manga Edition
10 9 8 7 6 5 4 3 2 1
First printing, July 2008

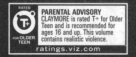

www.viz.com

THE WORLD'S MOST
CUTTING-EDGE MANGA

SHONEN
JUMP
ADVANCED

www.shonenjump.com

SHONEN JUMP ADVANCED Manga Edition

クレイモア

Claymore

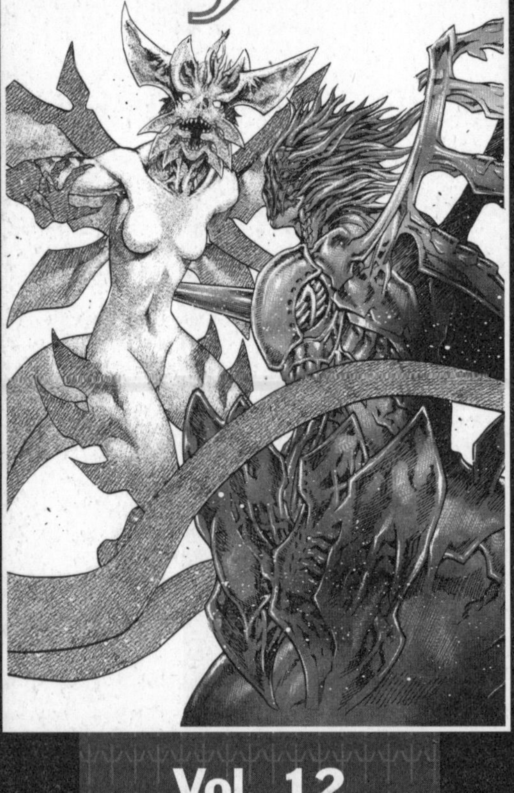

Vol. 12
The Souls of the Fallen

Story and Art by Norihiro Yagi

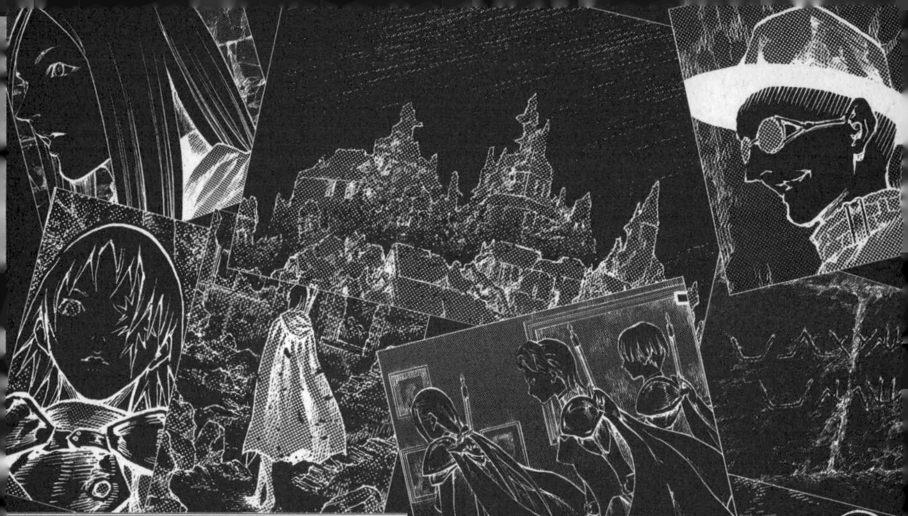

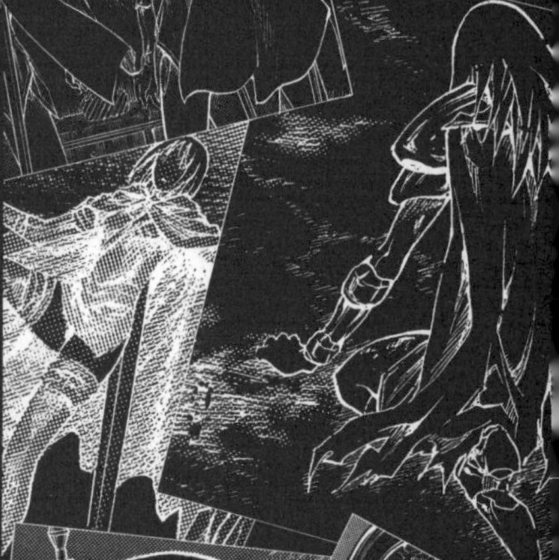

broadswords that they carried.

After sacrificing his awakened underlings as pawns, Isley, one of the Three Great Awakened Ones, goes to battle Luciela of the South. But warrior number 5, Rafaela, suddenly appears. What is her intention? And what of the disappearance of Clare and her comrades?!

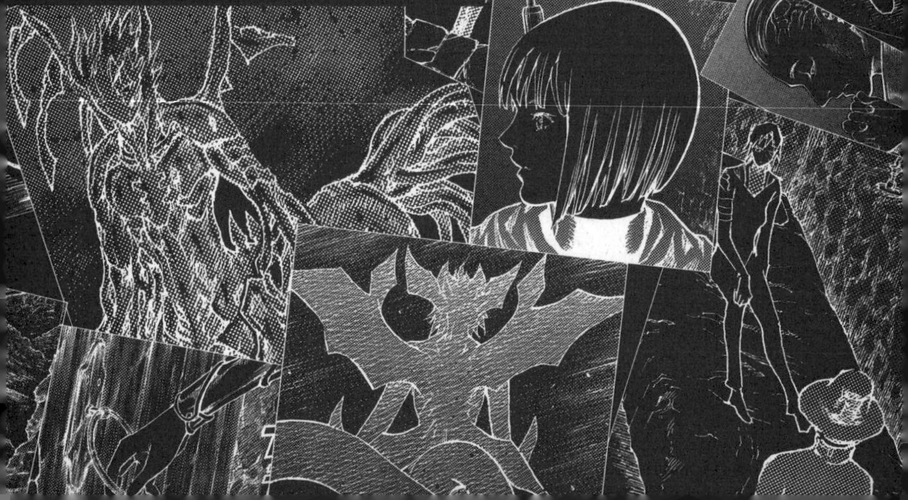

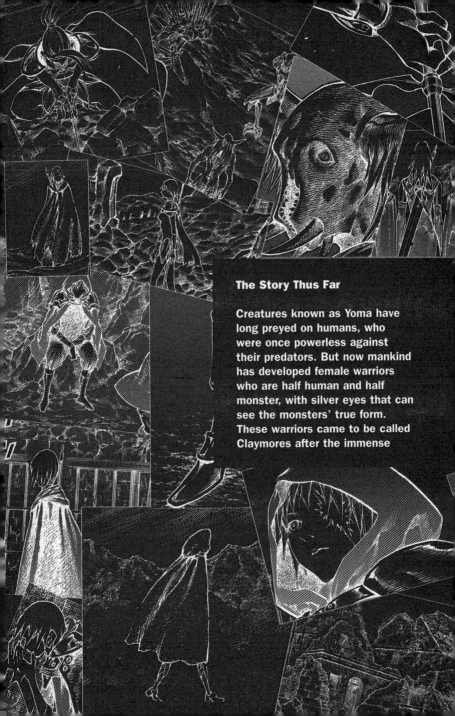

The Story Thus Far

Creatures known as Yoma have long preyed on humans, who were once powerless against their predators. But now mankind has developed female warriors who are half human and half monster, with silver eyes that can see the monsters' true form. These warriors came to be called Claymores after the immense

クレイモア

Claymore

Vol. 12

CONTENTS

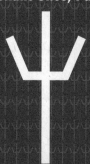

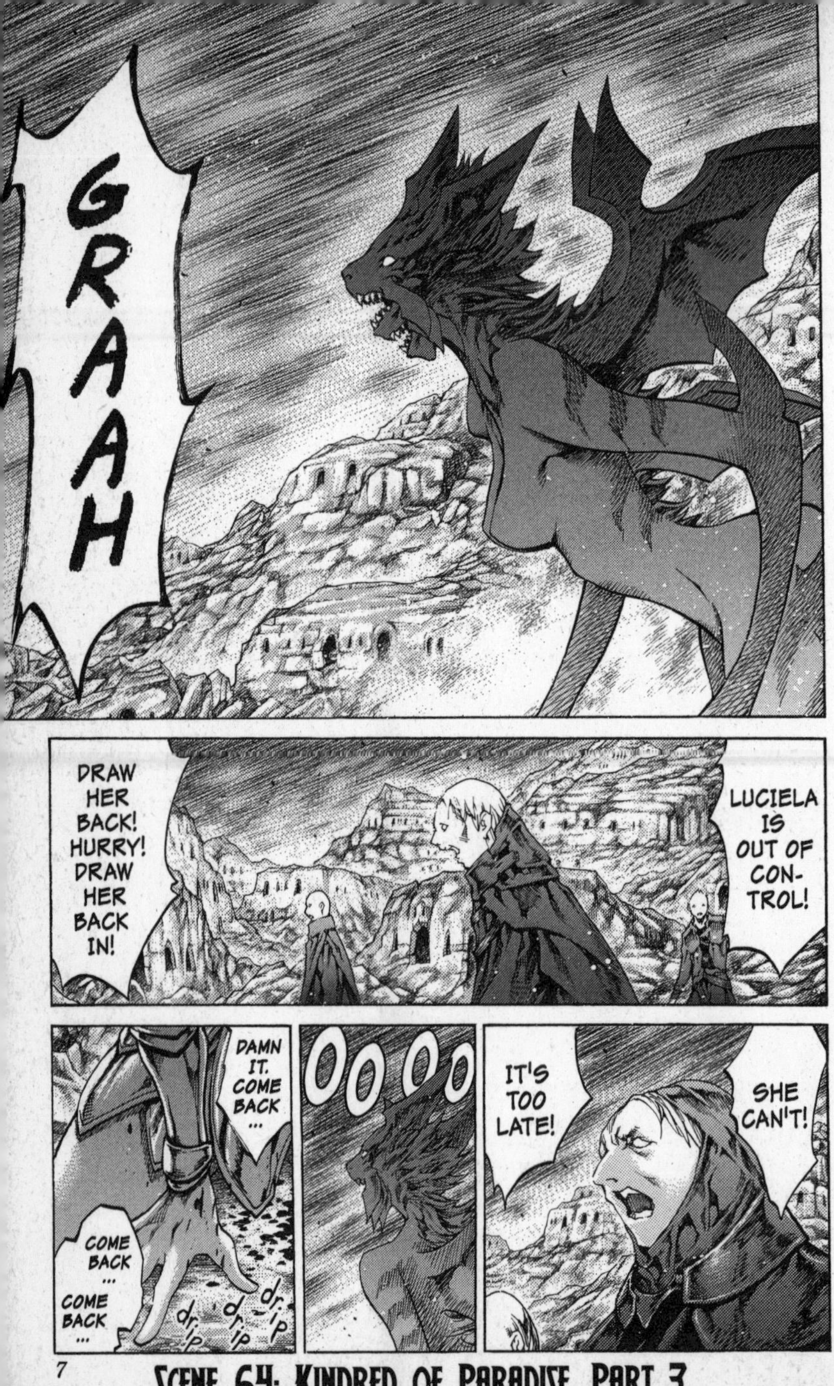
GRAAAH
LUCIELA IS OUT OF CON-TROL!
DRAW HER BACK! HURRY! DRAW HER BACK IN!
SHE CAN'T!
IT'S TOO LATE!
OOOO
DAMN IT. COME BACK ...
COME BACK ... COME BACK ...
drip drip drip

Scene 64: Kindred of Paradise, Part 3

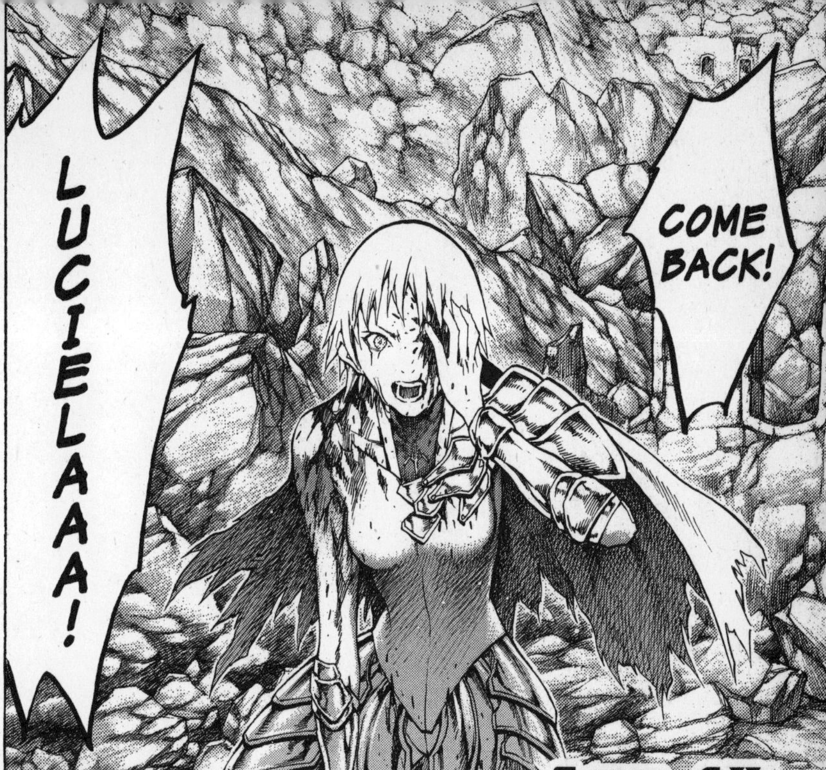
COME BACK!
LUCIELLAAA!

Scene 64: Kindred of Paradise, Part 3

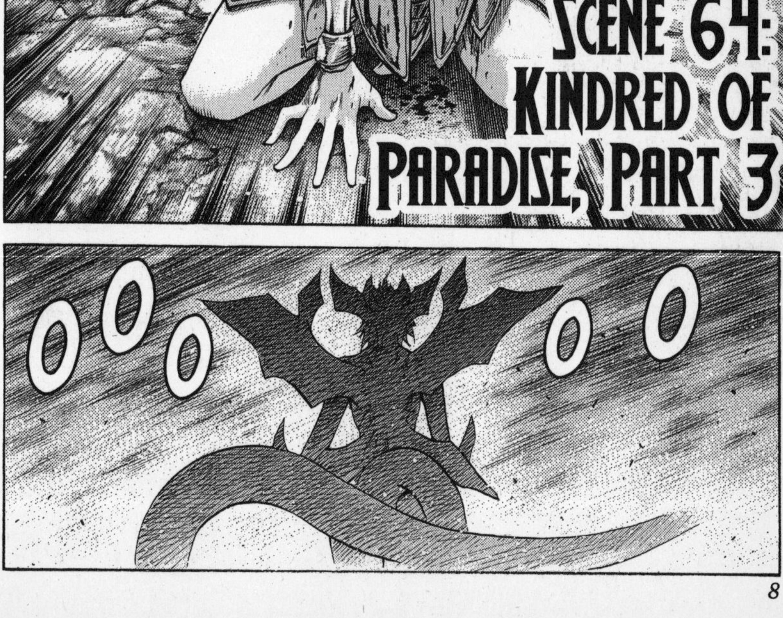
OOO
OO

READ THIS WAY

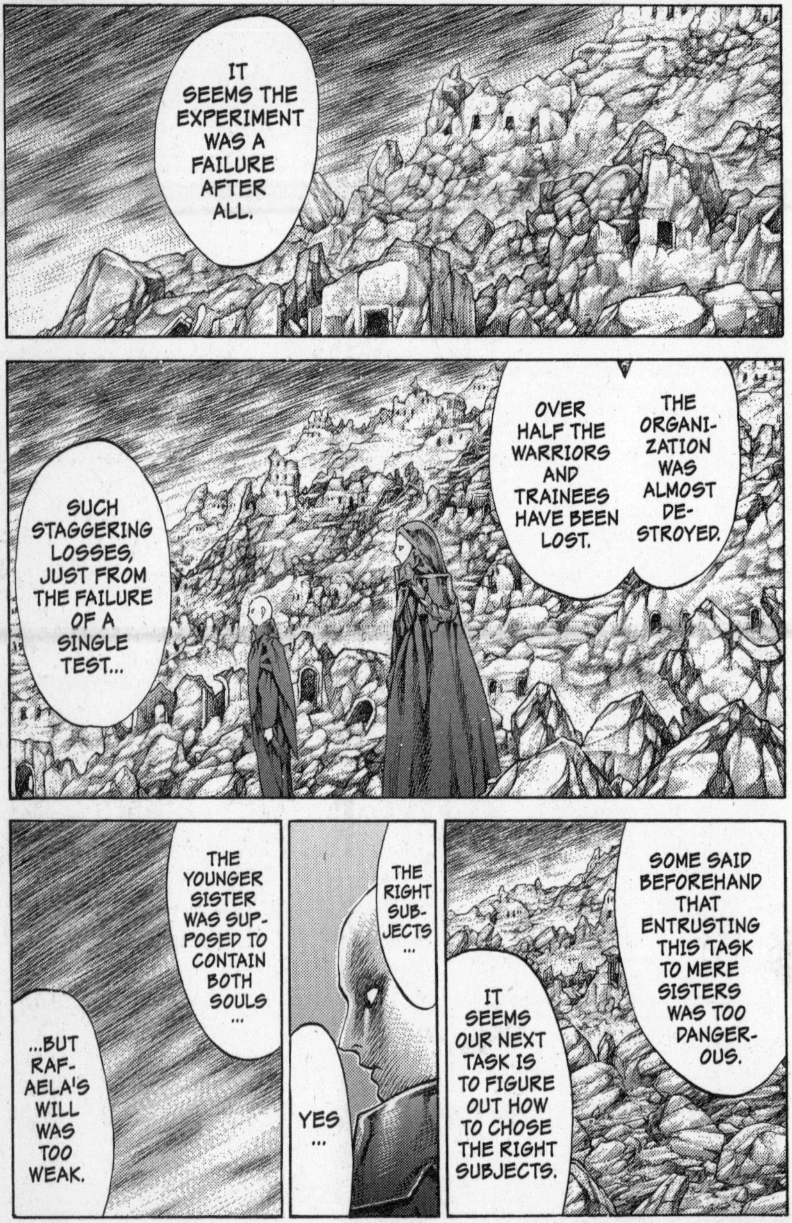
IT SEEMS THE EXPERIMENT WAS A FAILURE AFTER ALL.
THE ORGANIZATION WAS ALMOST DESTROYED.
OVER HALF THE WARRIORS AND TRAINEES HAVE BEEN LOST.
SUCH STAGGERING LOSSES, JUST FROM THE FAILURE OF A SINGLE TEST...
SOME SAID BEFOREHAND THAT ENTRUSTING THIS TASK TO MERE SISTERS WAS TOO DANGEROUS.
IT SEEMS OUR NEXT TASK IS TO FIGURE OUT HOW TO CHOSE THE RIGHT SUBJECTS.
THE RIGHT SUBJECTS...
YES...
THE YOUNGER SISTER WAS SUPPOSED TO CONTAIN BOTH SOULS...
...BUT RAFAELA'S WILL WAS TOO WEAK.

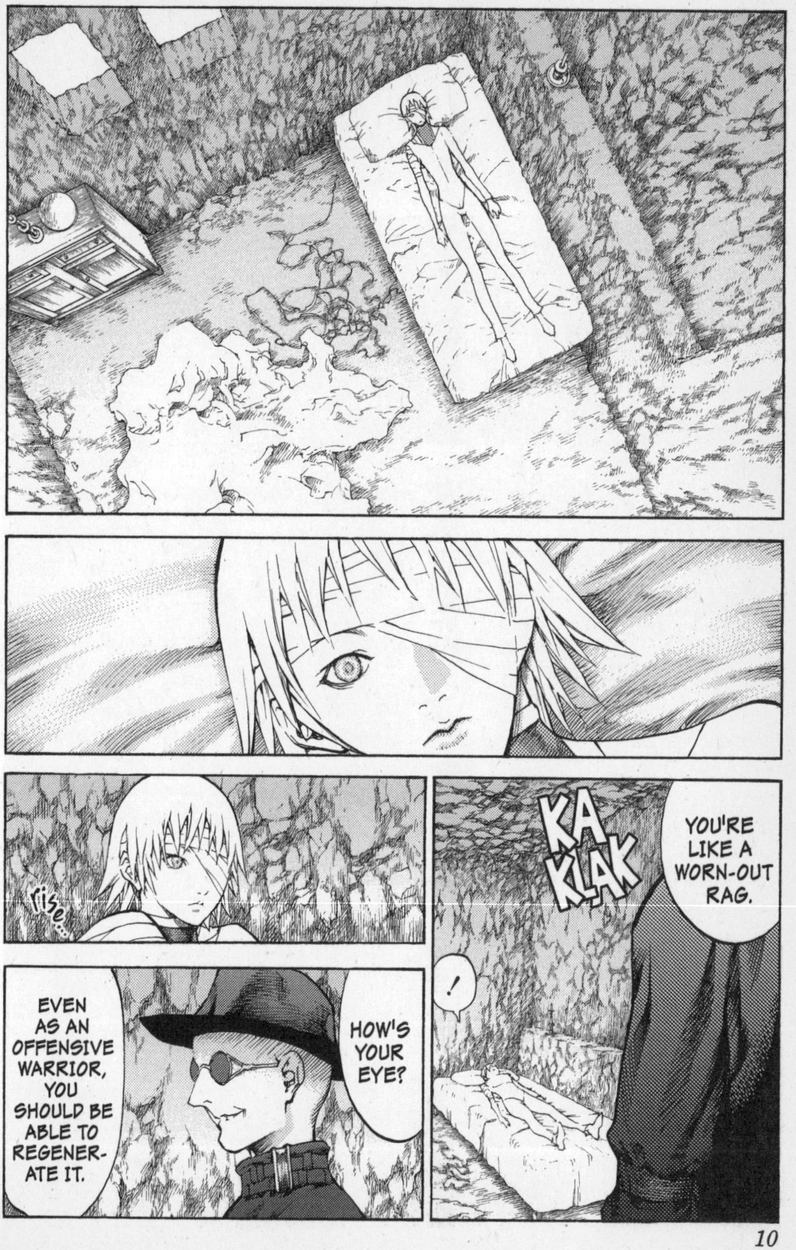
YOU'RE LIKE A WORN-OUT RAG.
KA KLAK
!
rise...
HOW'S YOUR EYE?
EVEN AS AN OFFENSIVE WARRIOR, YOU SHOULD BE ABLE TO REGENER-ATE IT.

READ THIS WAY

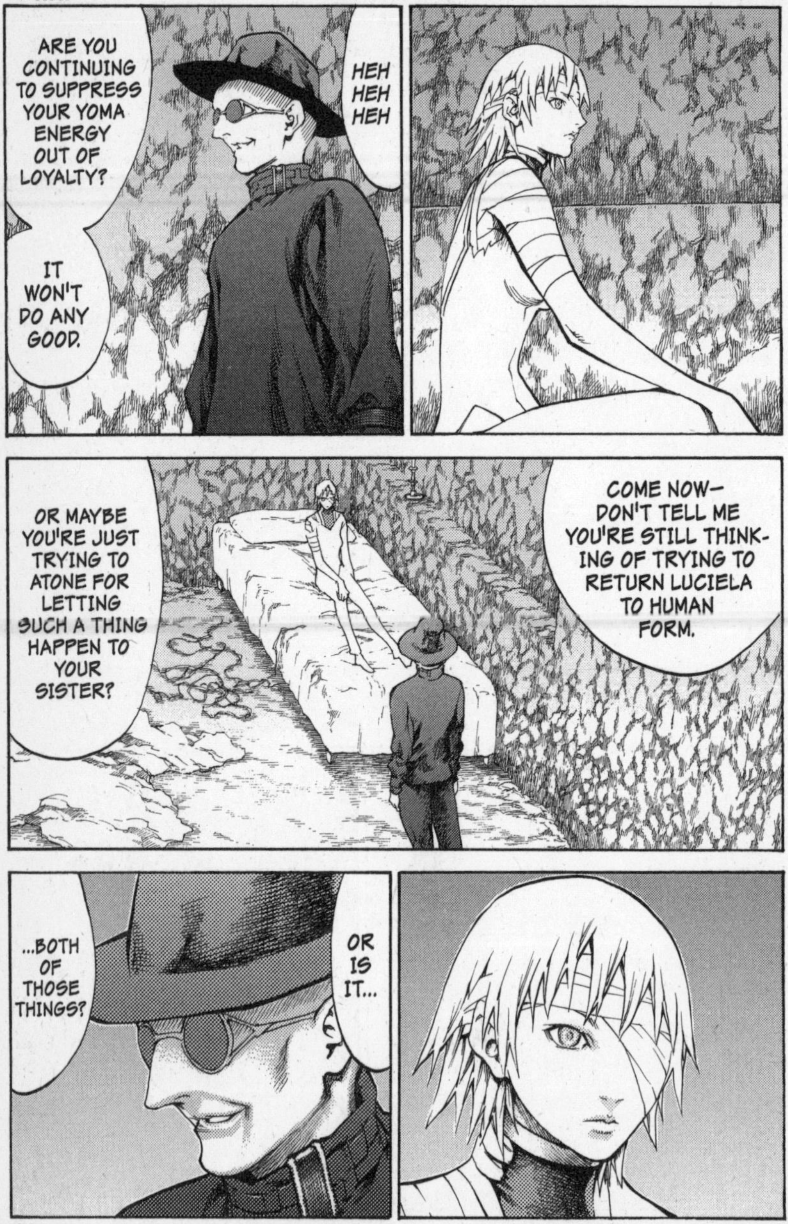

HEH HEH HEH
ARE YOU CONTINUING TO SUPPRESS YOUR YOMA ENERGY OUT OF LOYALTY?
IT WON'T DO ANY GOOD.
COME NOW— DON'T TELL ME YOU'RE STILL THINKING OF TRYING TO RETURN LUCIELA TO HUMAN FORM.
OR MAYBE YOU'RE JUST TRYING TO ATONE FOR LETTING SUCH A THING HAPPEN TO YOUR SISTER?
OR IS IT...
...BOTH OF THOSE THINGS?

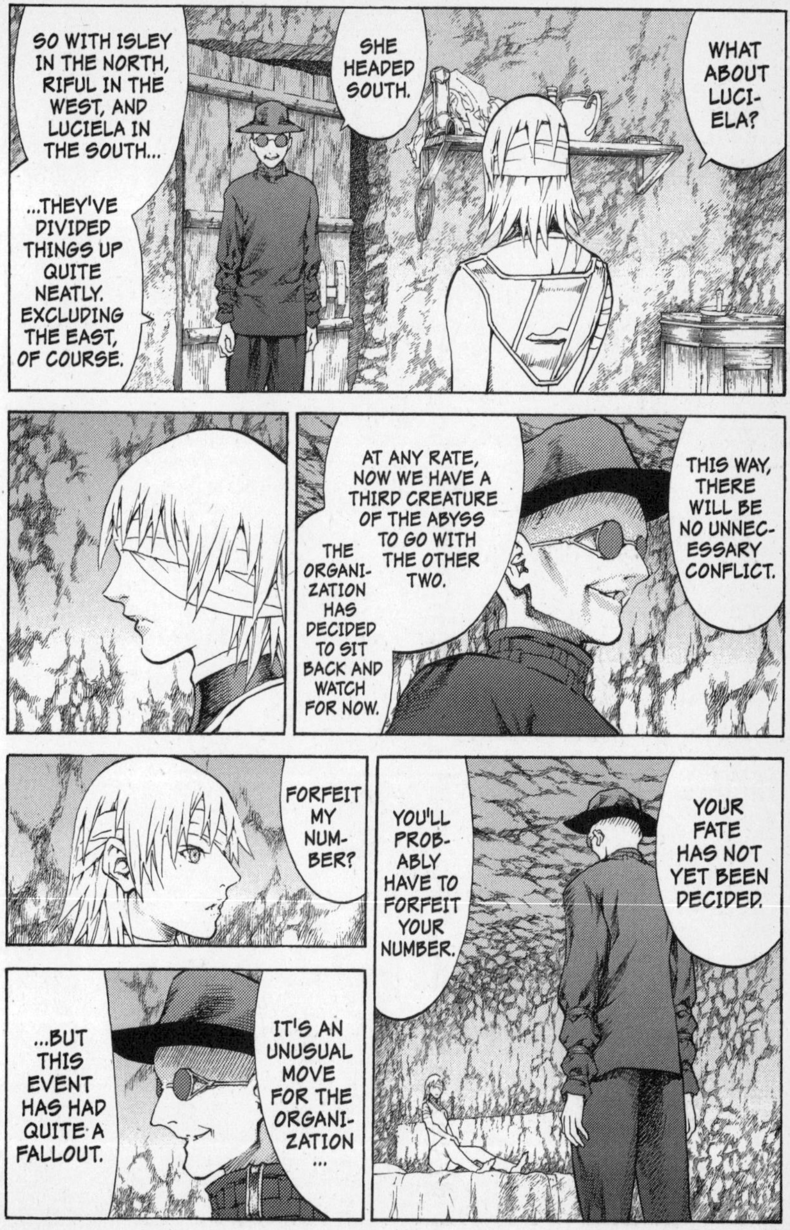
WHAT ABOUT LUCIELA?
SHE HEADED SOUTH.
SO WITH ISLEY IN THE NORTH, RIFUL IN THE WEST, AND LUCIELA IN THE SOUTH...
...THEY'VE DIVIDED THINGS UP QUITE NEATLY. EXCLUDING THE EAST, OF COURSE.
THIS WAY, THERE WILL BE NO UNNECESSARY CONFLICT.
AT ANY RATE, NOW WE HAVE A THIRD CREATURE OF THE ABYSS TO GO WITH THE OTHER TWO.
THE ORGANIZATION HAS DECIDED TO SIT BACK AND WATCH FOR NOW.
YOUR FATE HAS NOT YET BEEN DECIDED.
YOU'LL PROBABLY HAVE TO FORFEIT YOUR NUMBER.
FORFEIT MY NUMBER?
IT'S AN UNUSUAL MOVE FOR THE ORGANIZATION...
...BUT THIS EVENT HAS HAD QUITE A FALLOUT.

READ THIS WAY

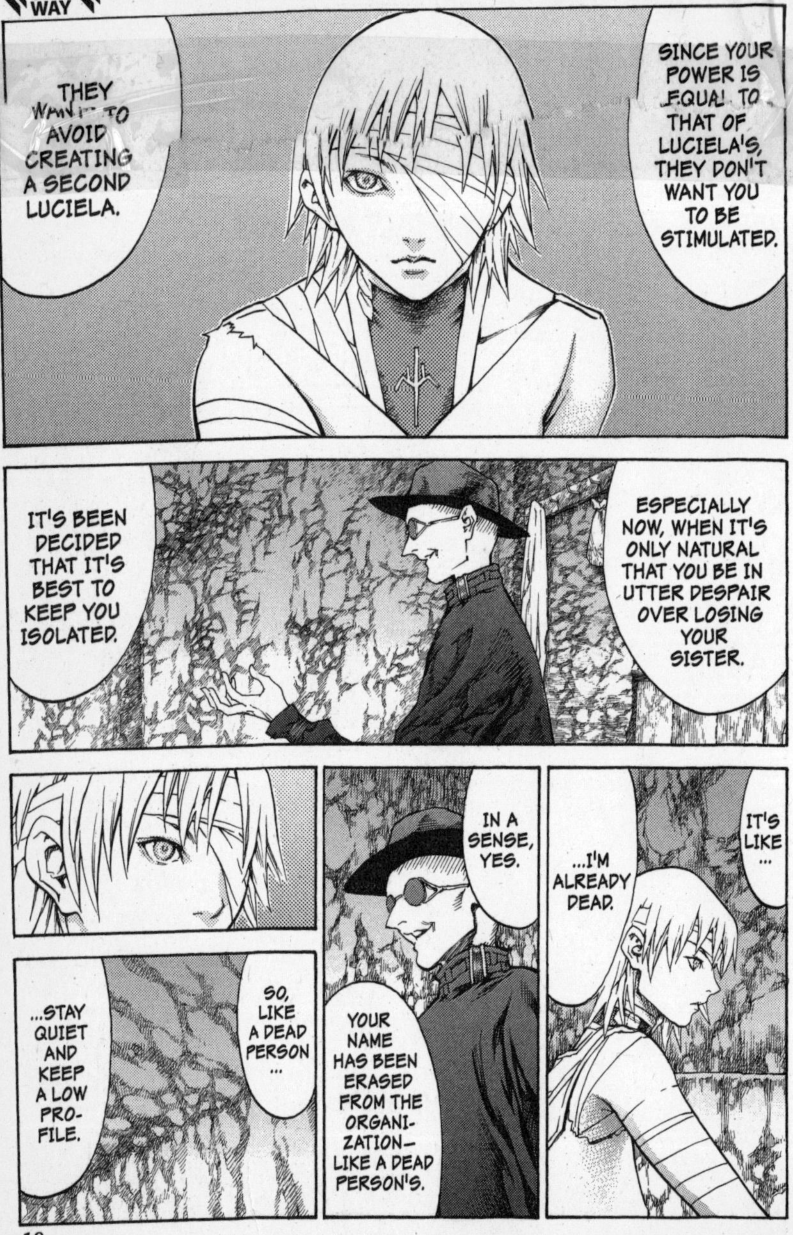
SINCE YOUR POWER IS EQUAL TO THAT OF LUCIELA'S, THEY DON'T WANT YOU TO BE STIMULATED.
THEY WANT TO AVOID CREATING A SECOND LUCIELA.
ESPECIALLY NOW, WHEN IT'S ONLY NATURAL THAT YOU BE IN UTTER DESPAIR OVER LOSING YOUR SISTER.
IT'S BEEN DECIDED THAT IT'S BEST TO KEEP YOU ISOLATED.
IT'S LIKE...
...I'M ALREADY DEAD.
IN A SENSE, YES.
YOUR NAME HAS BEEN ERASED FROM THE ORGANI-ZATION—LIKE A DEAD PERSON'S.
SO, LIKE A DEAD PERSON...
...STAY QUIET AND KEEP A LOW PRO-FILE.

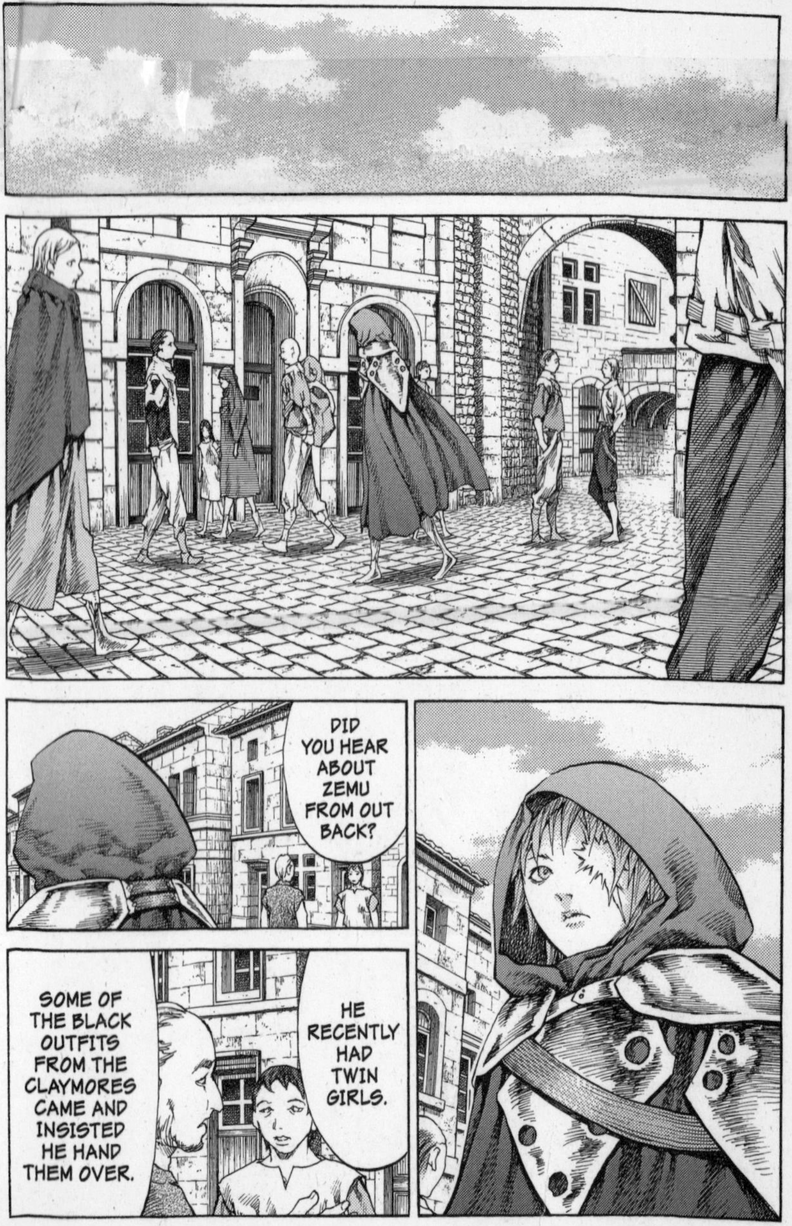
DID YOU HEAR ABOUT ZEMU FROM OUT BACK?
HE RECENTLY HAD TWIN GIRLS.
SOME OF THE BLACK OUTFITS FROM THE CLAYMORES CAME AND INSISTED HE HAND THEM OVER.

READ THIS WAY

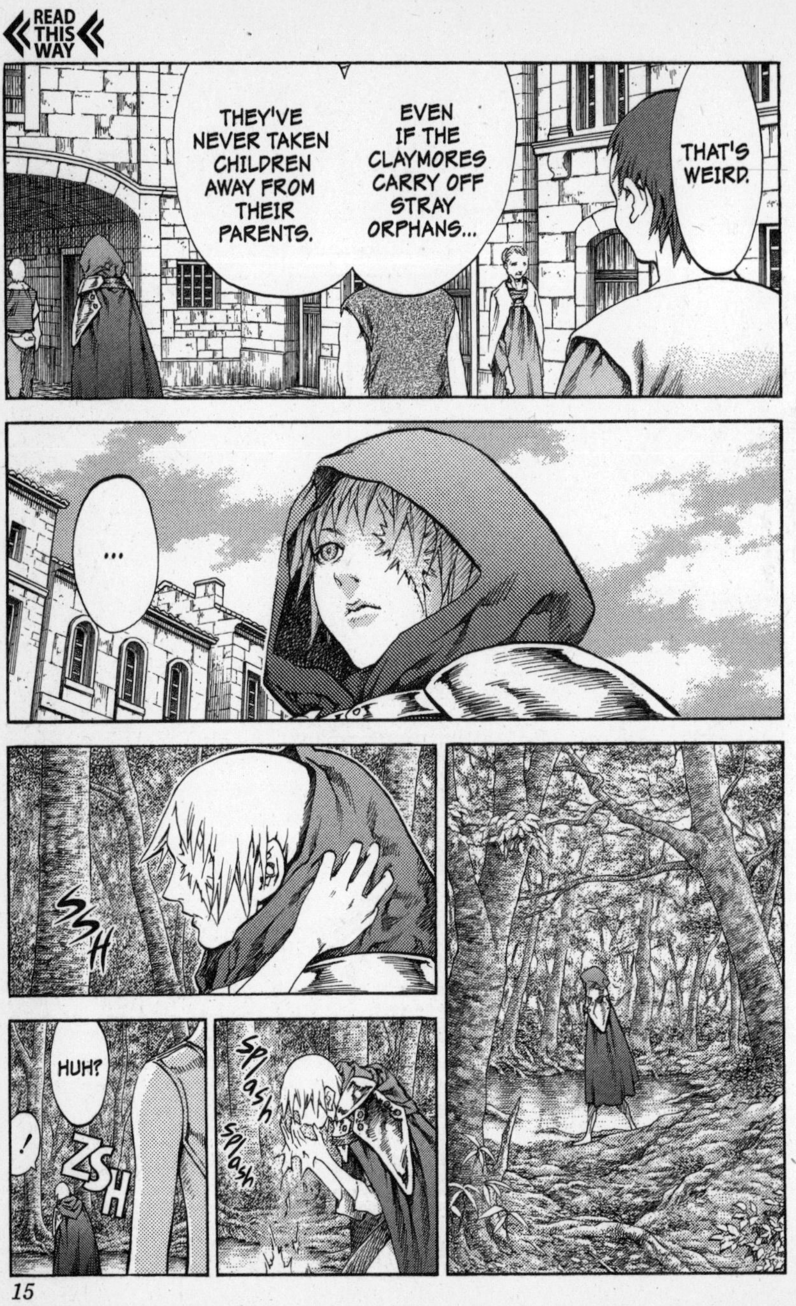
THAT'S WEIRD.
EVEN IF THE CLAYMORES CARRY OFF STRAY ORPHANS...
THEY'VE NEVER TAKEN CHILDREN AWAY FROM THEIR PARENTS.
...
SSH
SPLASH
SPLASH
HUH?
!
ZSH

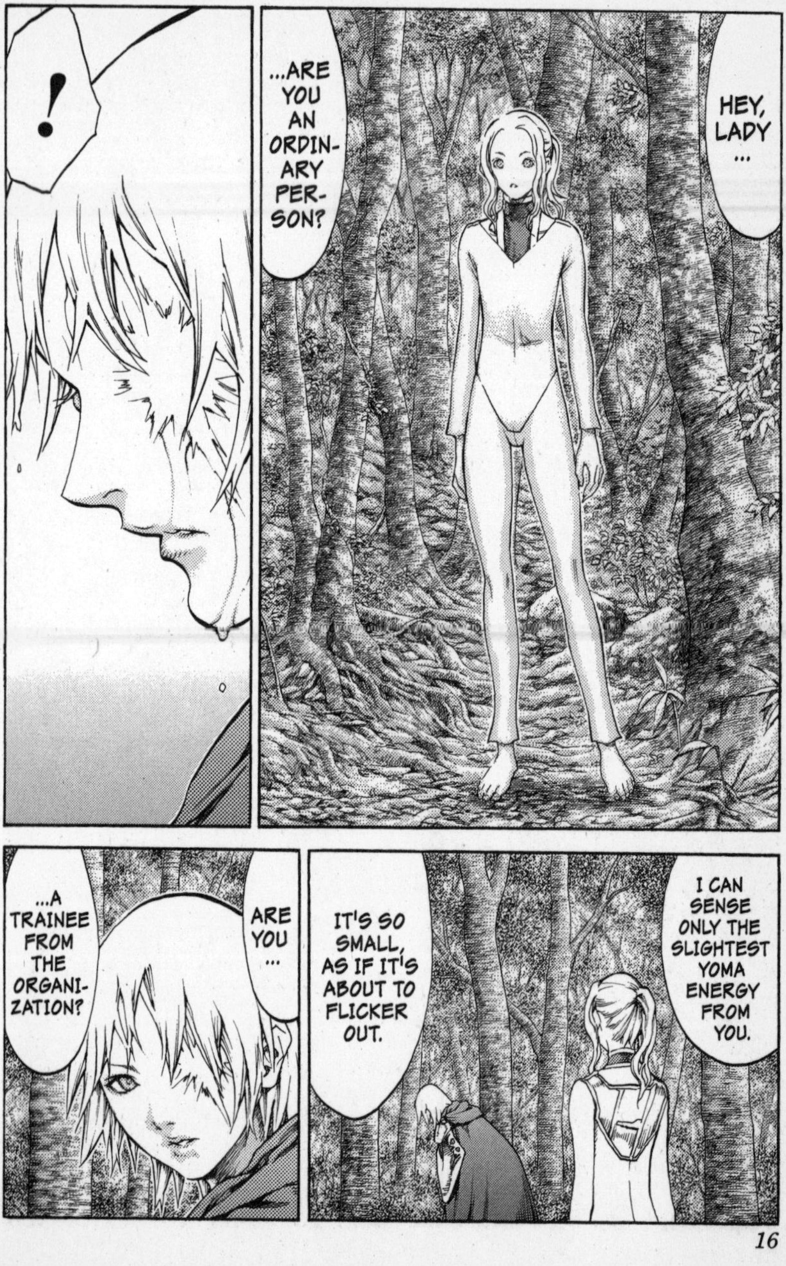
HEY, LADY ...
...ARE YOU AN ORDINARY PERSON?
!
I CAN SENSE ONLY THE SLIGHTEST YOMA ENERGY FROM YOU.
IT'S SO SMALL, AS IF IT'S ABOUT TO FLICKER OUT.
ARE YOU ...
...A TRAINEE FROM THE ORGANIZATION?

READ THIS WAY

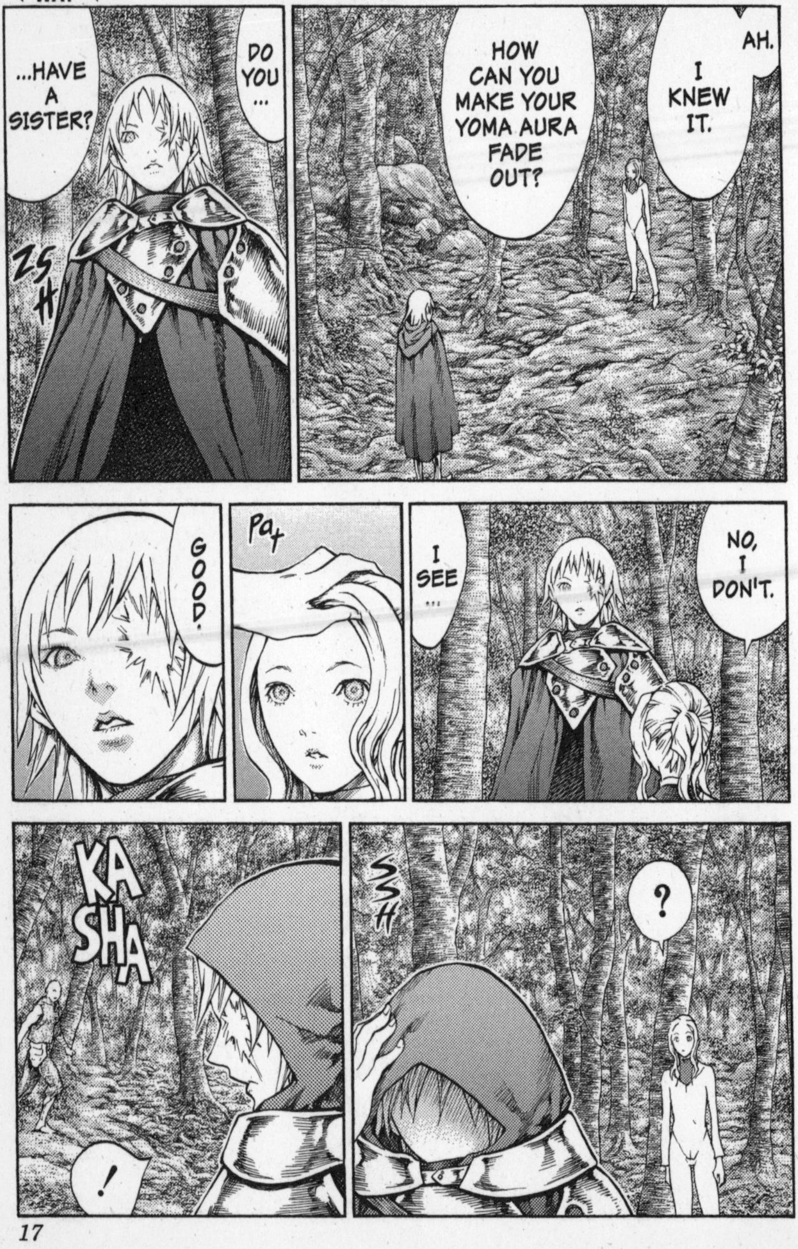
AH.
I KNEW IT.
HOW CAN YOU MAKE YOUR YOMA AURA FADE OUT?
DO YOU ...
...HAVE A SISTER?
ZSH
NO, I DON'T.
I SEE ...
PAT
GOOD.
?
SSH
KA SHA
!

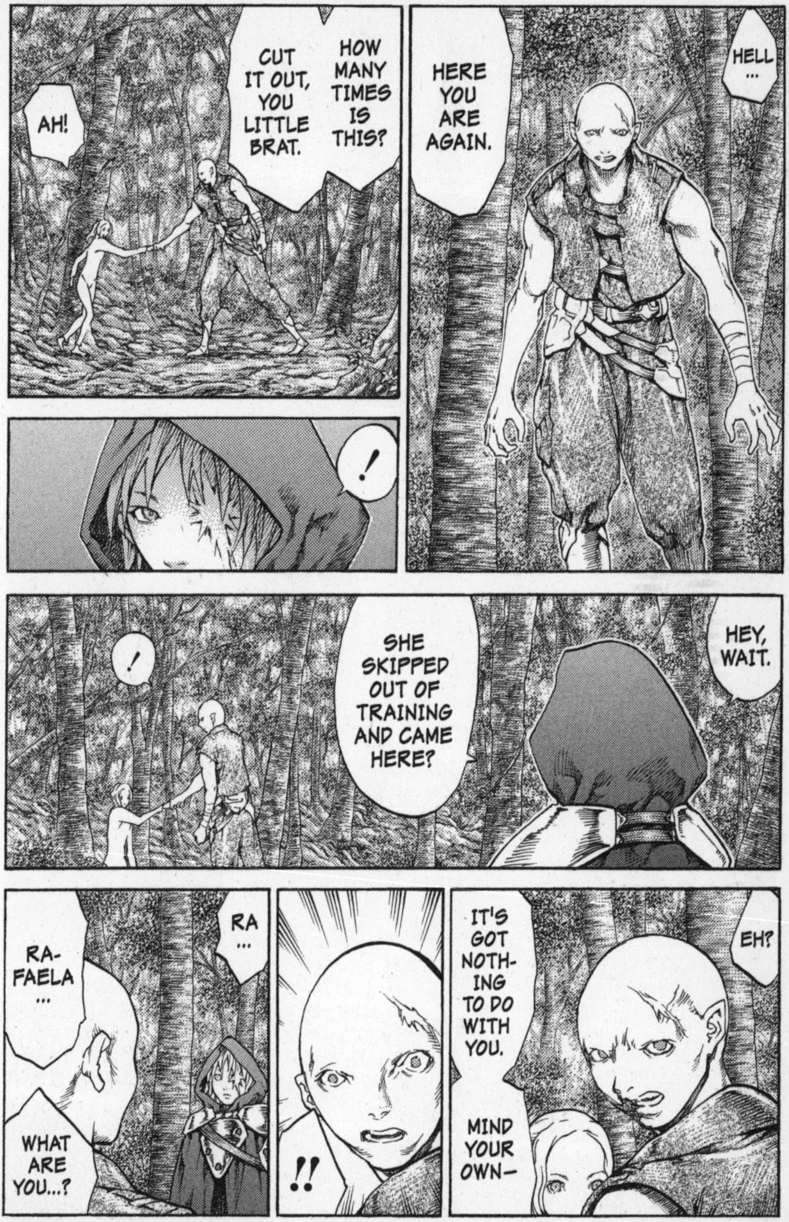
HELL...
HERE YOU ARE AGAIN.
HOW MANY TIMES IS THIS?
CUT IT OUT, YOU LITTLE BRAT.
AH!
!
HEY, WAIT.
SHE SKIPPED OUT OF TRAINING AND CAME HERE?
!
EH?
IT'S GOT NOTHING TO DO WITH YOU.
MIND YOUR OWN—
!!
RA...
RA-FAELA...
WHAT ARE YOU...?

READ THIS WAY

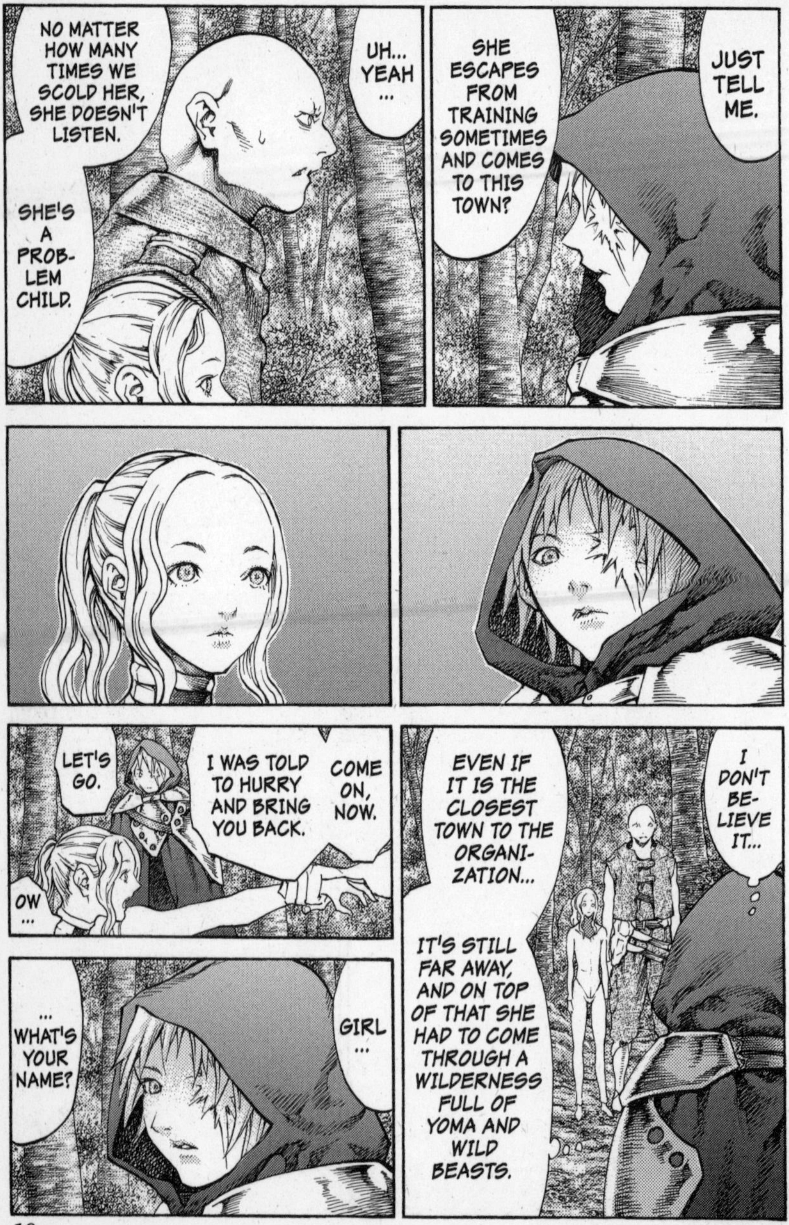
JUST TELL ME.
SHE ESCAPES FROM TRAINING SOMETIMES AND COMES TO THIS TOWN?
UH... YEAH ...
NO MATTER HOW MANY TIMES WE SCOLD HER, SHE DOESN'T LISTEN.
SHE'S A PROB-LEM CHILD.
I DON'T BE-LIEVE IT...
EVEN IF IT IS THE CLOSEST TOWN TO THE ORGANI-ZATION...
IT'S STILL FAR AWAY, AND ON TOP OF THAT SHE HAD TO COME THROUGH A WILDERNESS FULL OF YOMA AND WILD BEASTS.
COME ON, NOW.
I WAS TOLD TO HURRY AND BRING YOU BACK.
LET'S GO.
OW ...
GIRL ...
... WHAT'S YOUR NAME?

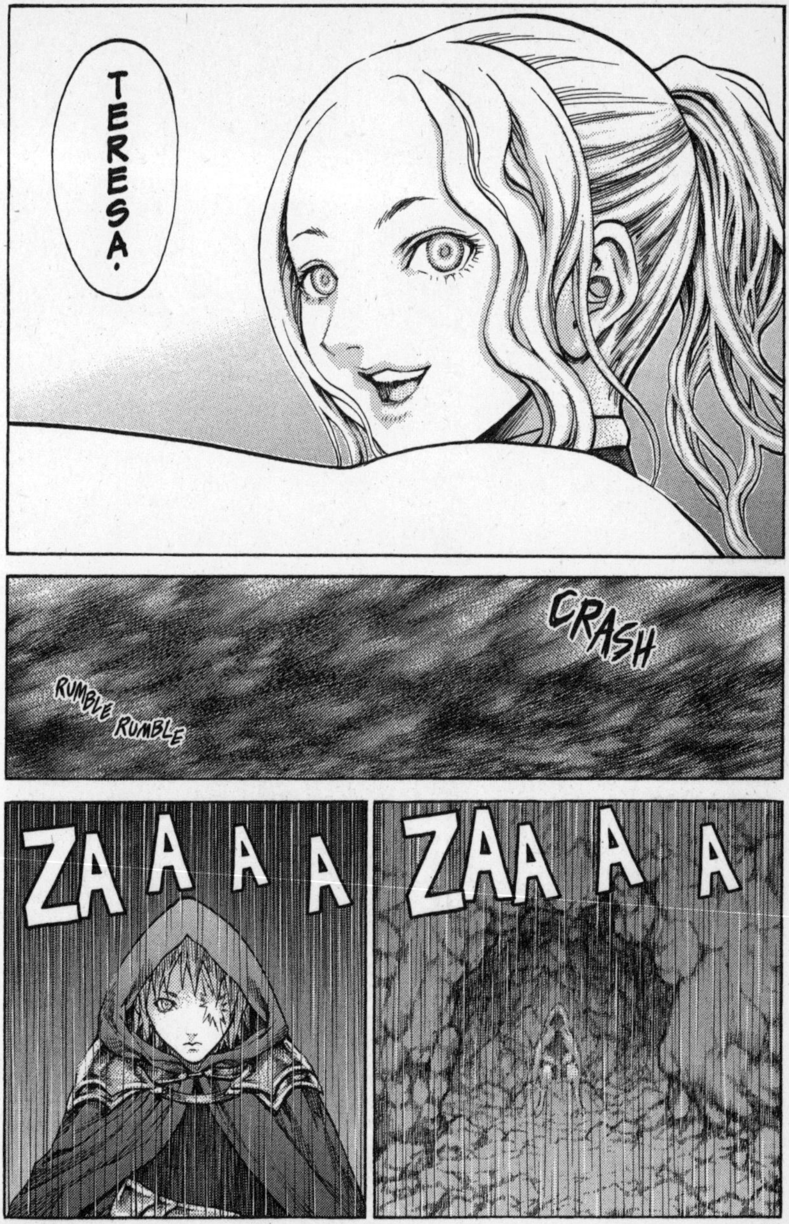
TERESA.
CRASH
RUMBLE RUMBLE
ZAAAA
ZAAAA

READ THIS WAY

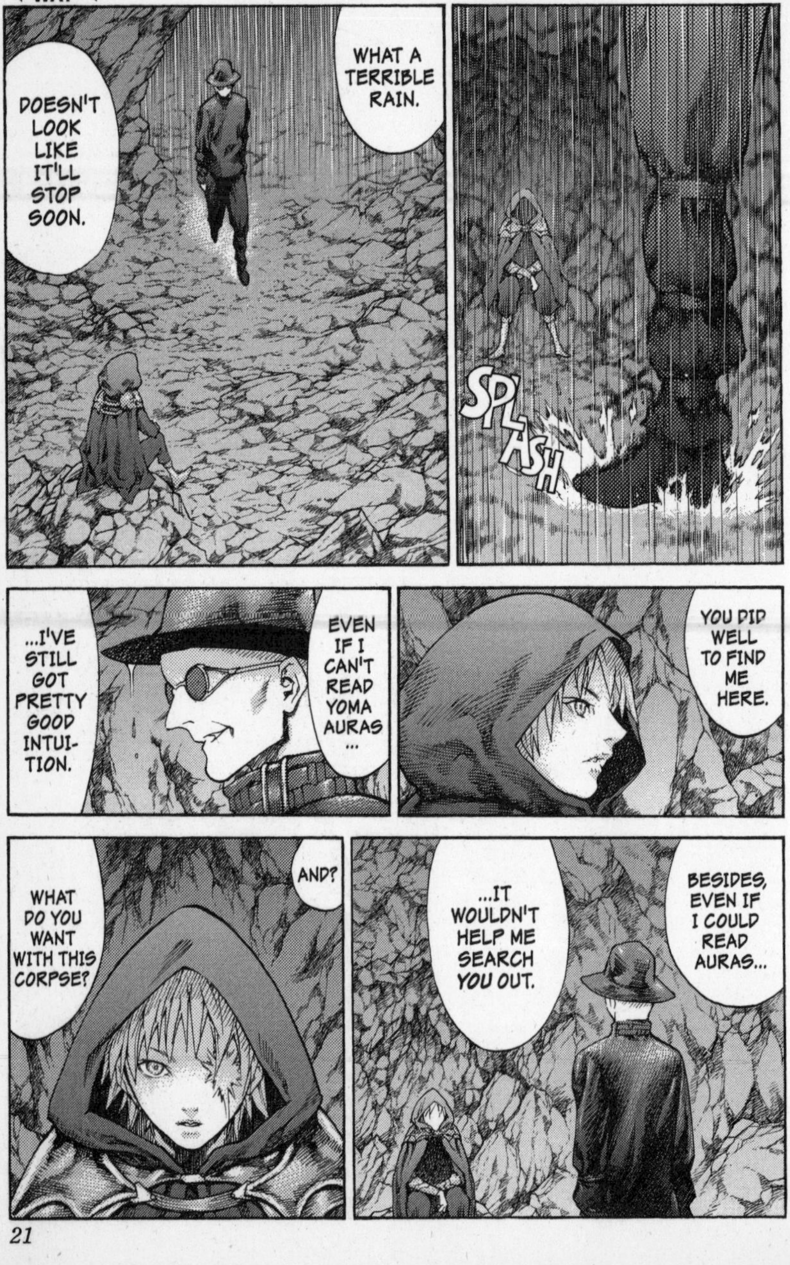
SPLASH
WHAT A TERRIBLE RAIN.
DOESN'T LOOK LIKE IT'LL STOP SOON.
YOU DID WELL TO FIND ME HERE.
EVEN IF I CAN'T READ YOMA AURAS...
...I'VE STILL GOT PRETTY GOOD INTUITION.
BESIDES, EVEN IF I COULD READ AURAS...
...IT WOULDN'T HELP ME SEARCH *YOU* OUT.
AND?
WHAT DO YOU WANT WITH THIS CORPSE?

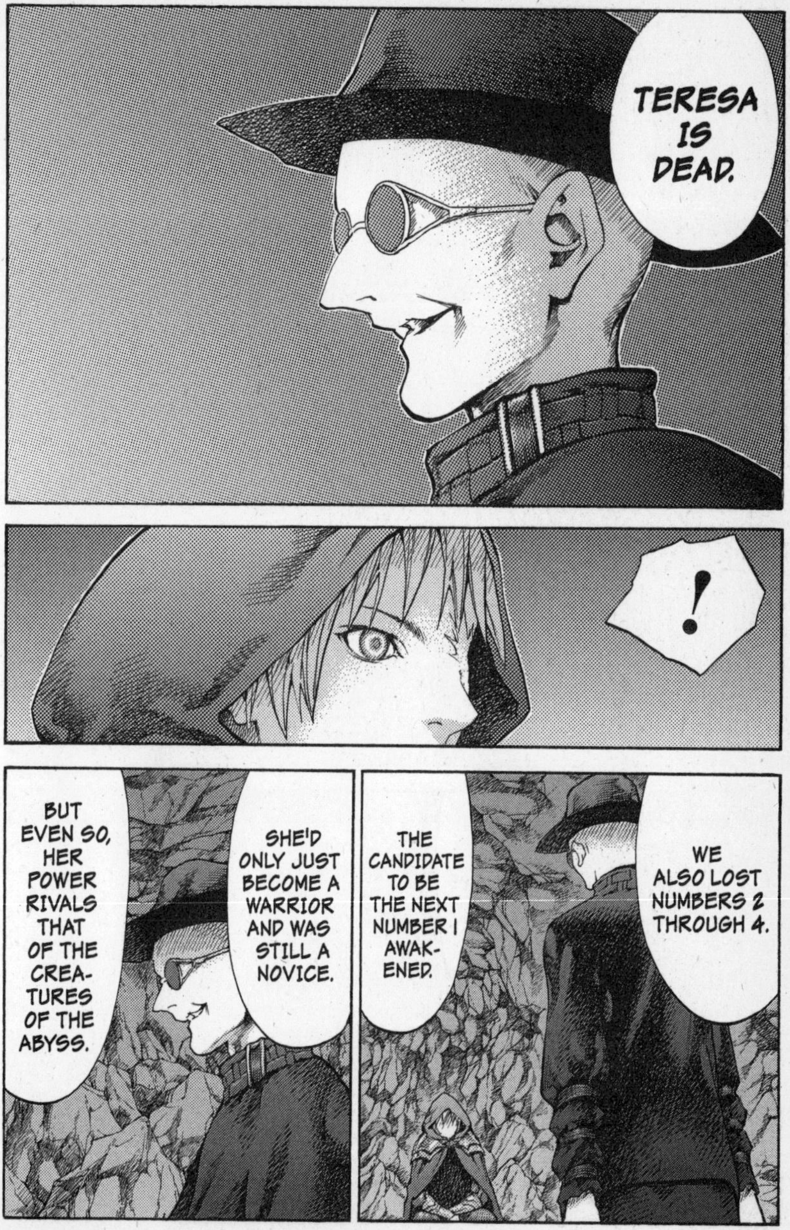
TERESA IS DEAD.
!
WE ALSO LOST NUMBERS 2 THROUGH 4.
THE CANDIDATE TO BE THE NEXT NUMBER 1 AWAKENED.
SHE'D ONLY JUST BECOME A WARRIOR AND WAS STILL A NOVICE.
BUT EVEN SO, HER POWER RIVALS THAT OF THE CREATURES OF THE ABYSS.

READ THIS WAY

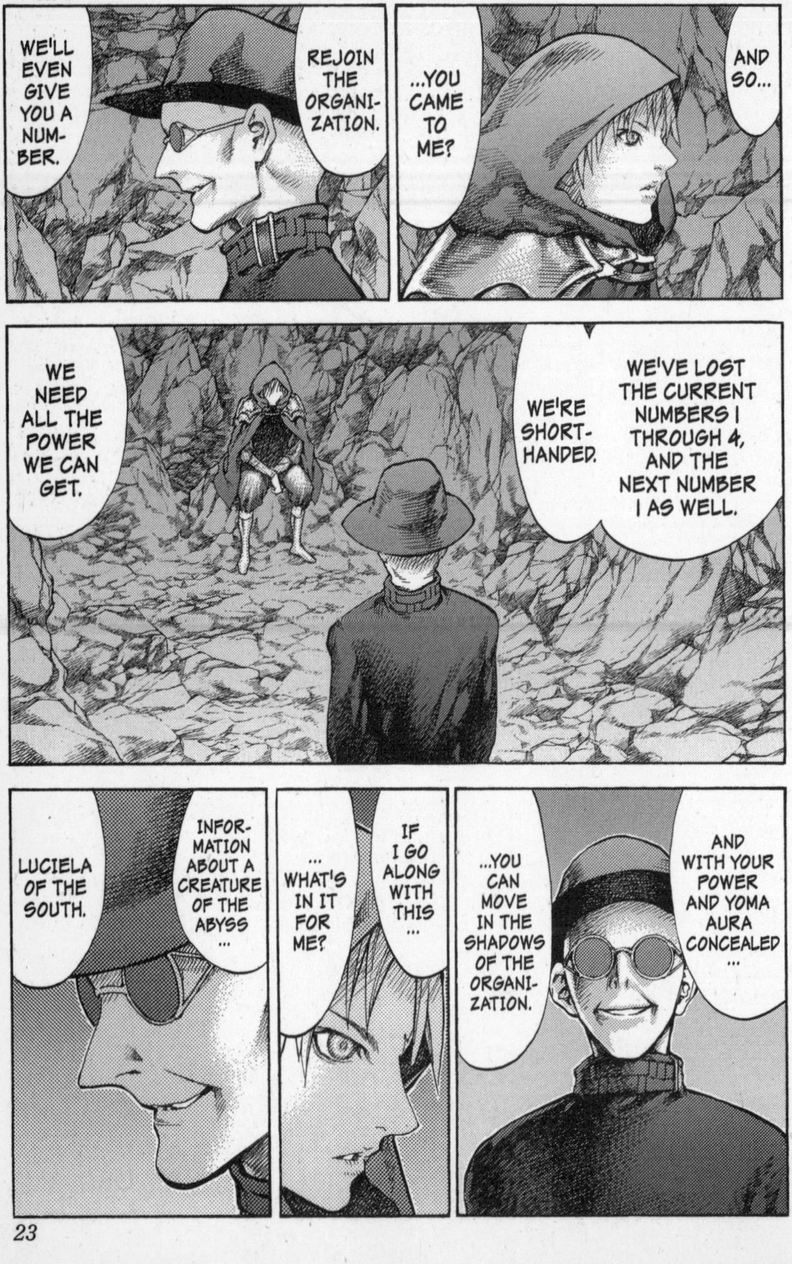
AND SO...
...YOU CAME TO ME?
REJOIN THE ORGANIZATION.
WE'LL EVEN GIVE YOU A NUMBER.
WE'VE LOST THE CURRENT NUMBERS 1 THROUGH 4, AND THE NEXT NUMBER 1 AS WELL.
WE'RE SHORT-HANDED.
WE NEED ALL THE POWER WE CAN GET.
AND WITH YOUR POWER AND YOMA AURA CONCEALED...
...YOU CAN MOVE IN THE SHADOWS OF THE ORGANIZATION.
IF I GO ALONG WITH THIS...
...WHAT'S IN IT FOR ME?
INFORMATION ABOUT A CREATURE OF THE ABYSS...
LUCIELA OF THE SOUTH.

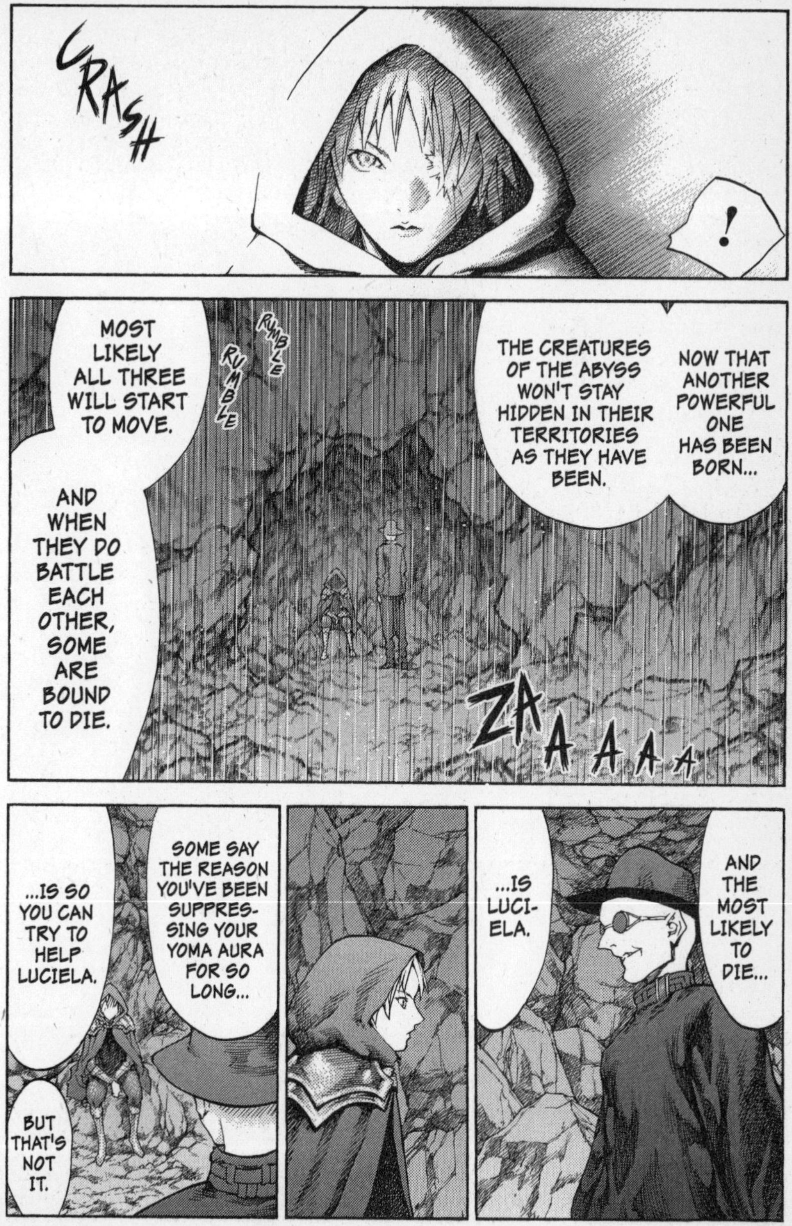
CRASH
!
NOW THAT ANOTHER POWERFUL ONE HAS BEEN BORN...
THE CREATURES OF THE ABYSS WON'T STAY HIDDEN IN THEIR TERRITORIES AS THEY HAVE BEEN.
RUMBLE
RUMBLE
MOST LIKELY ALL THREE WILL START TO MOVE.
AND WHEN THEY DO BATTLE EACH OTHER, SOME ARE BOUND TO DIE.
ZAAAAA
AND THE MOST LIKELY TO DIE...
...IS LUCI-ELA.
SOME SAY THE REASON YOU'VE BEEN SUPPRES-SING YOUR YOMA AURA FOR SO LONG...
...IS SO YOU CAN TRY TO HELP LUCIELA.
BUT THAT'S NOT IT.

READ THIS WAY

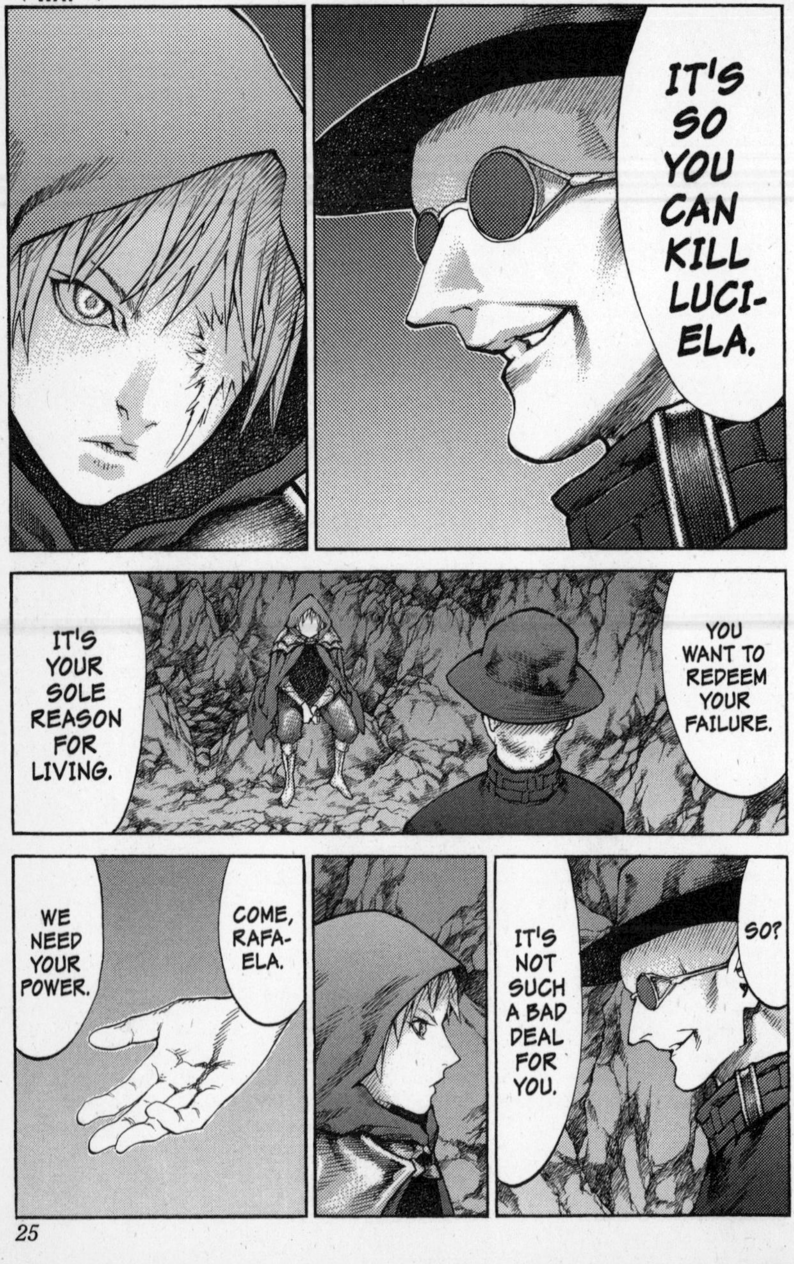
IT'S SO YOU CAN KILL LUCI-ELA.
YOU WANT TO REDEEM YOUR FAILURE.
IT'S YOUR SOLE REASON FOR LIVING.
SO?
IT'S NOT SUCH A BAD DEAL FOR YOU.
COME, RAFA-ELA.
WE NEED YOUR POWER.

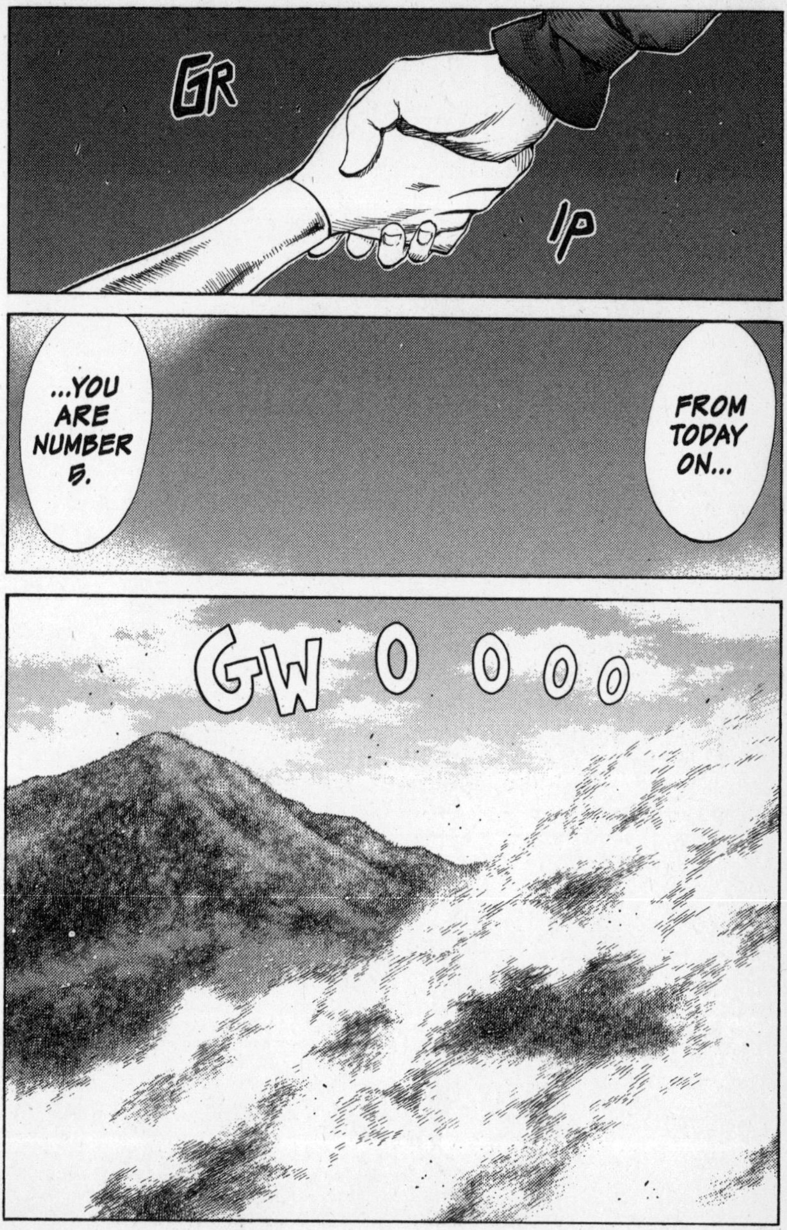
GR
IP
FROM TODAY ON...
...YOU ARE NUMBER 5.
GWOOOO

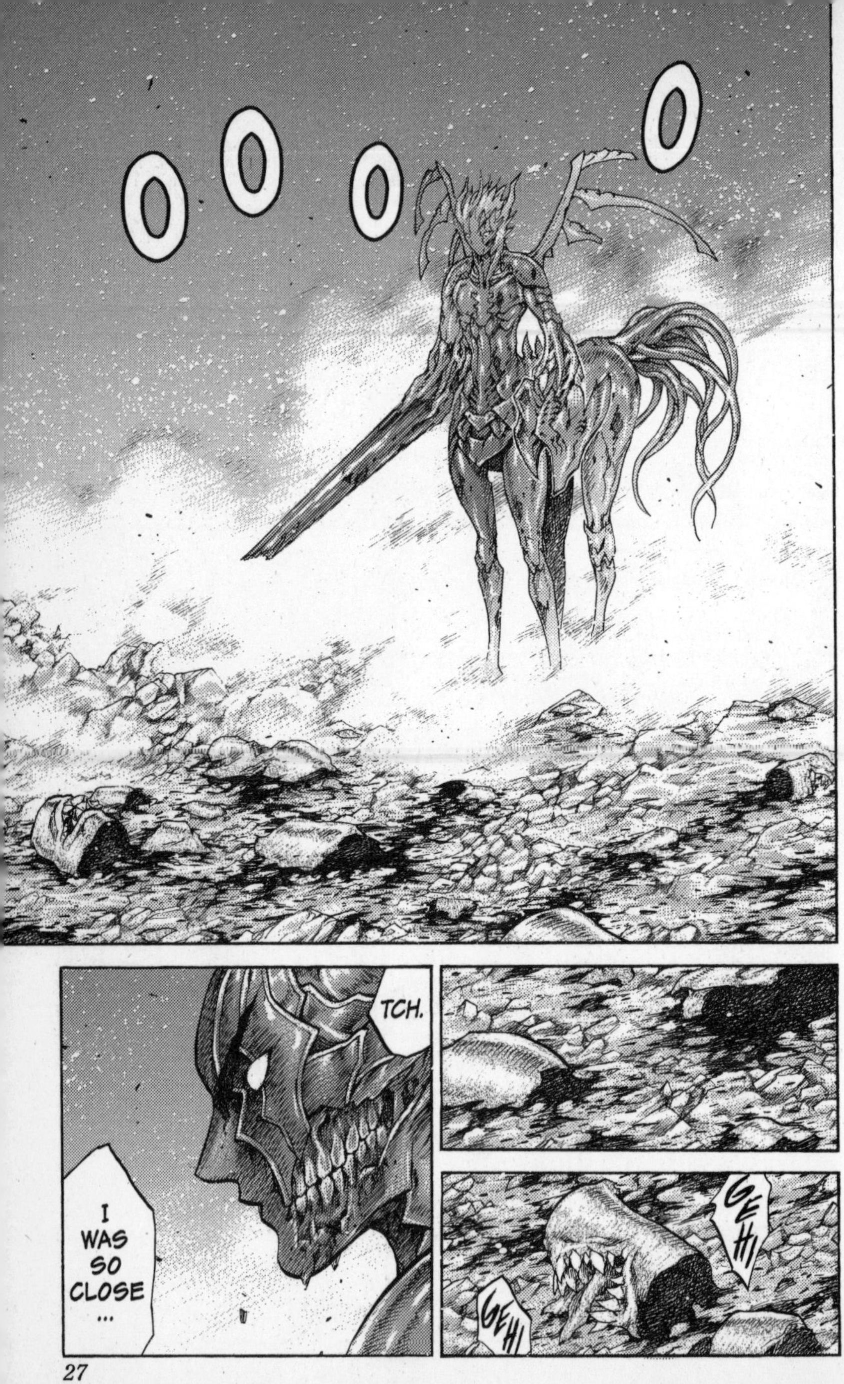
OOOO
GEHI
GEHI
TCH.
I WAS SO CLOSE ...

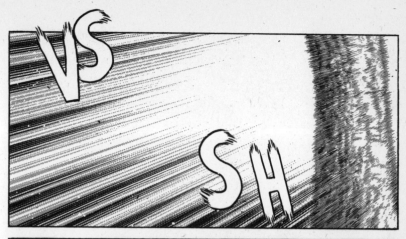

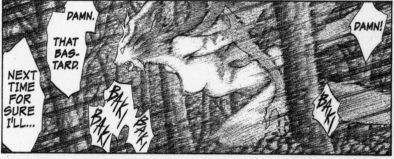

DAMN.

THAT BAS-TARD.

NEXT TIME FOR SURE I'LL...

DAMN!

BAKI BAKI BAKI

BAKI

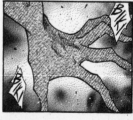

BIKI

BIKI

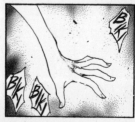

BIKI

BIKI BIKI

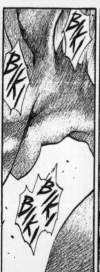

BIKI

BIKI

BIKI BIKI

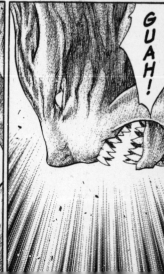

GUAH!

READ THIS WAY

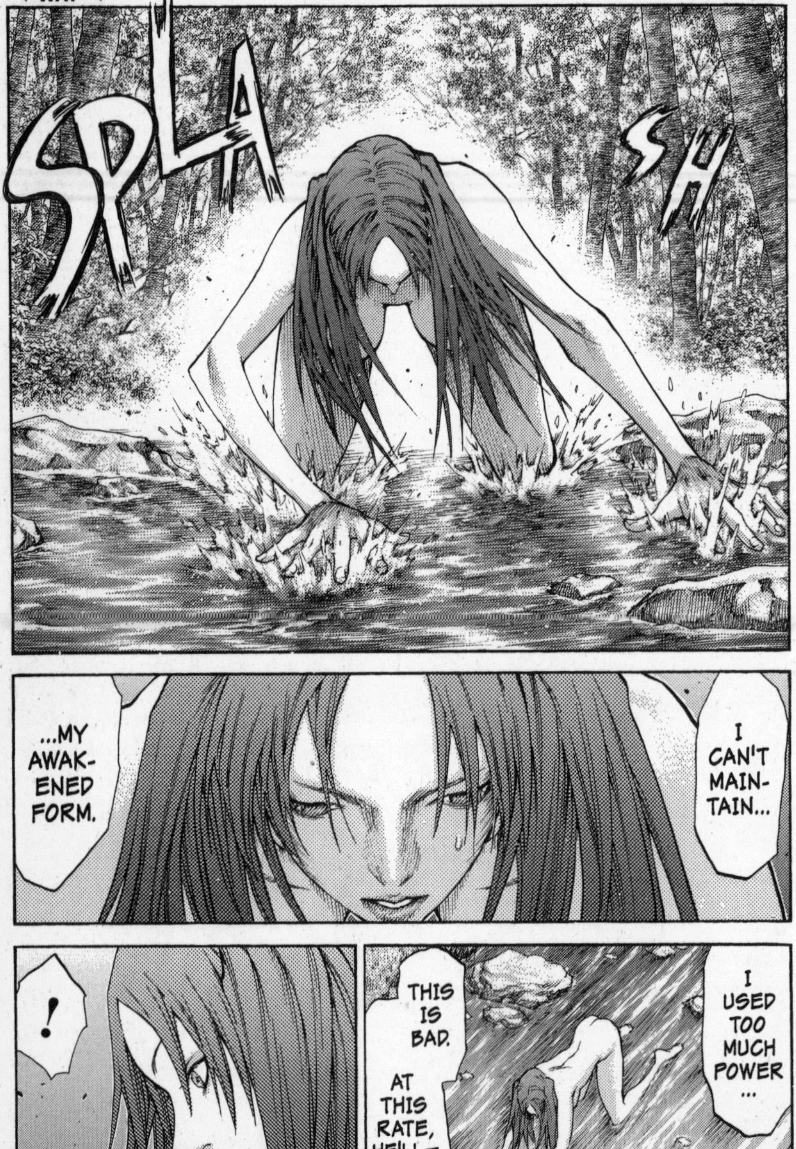
SPLASH
I CAN'T MAINTAIN...
...MY AWAKENED FORM.
I USED TOO MUCH POWER...
THIS IS BAD.
AT THIS RATE, HE'LL—
!

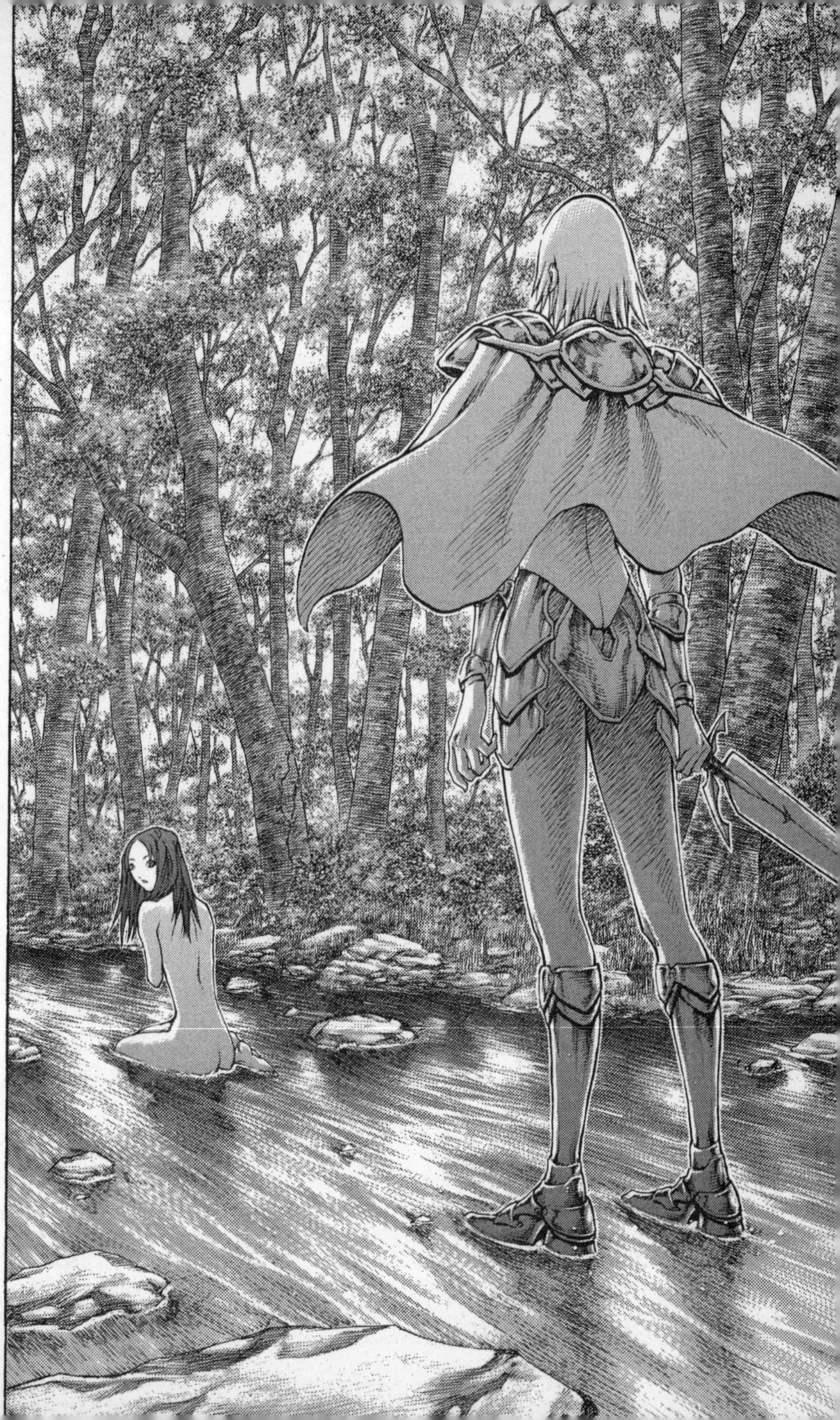

READ THIS WAY

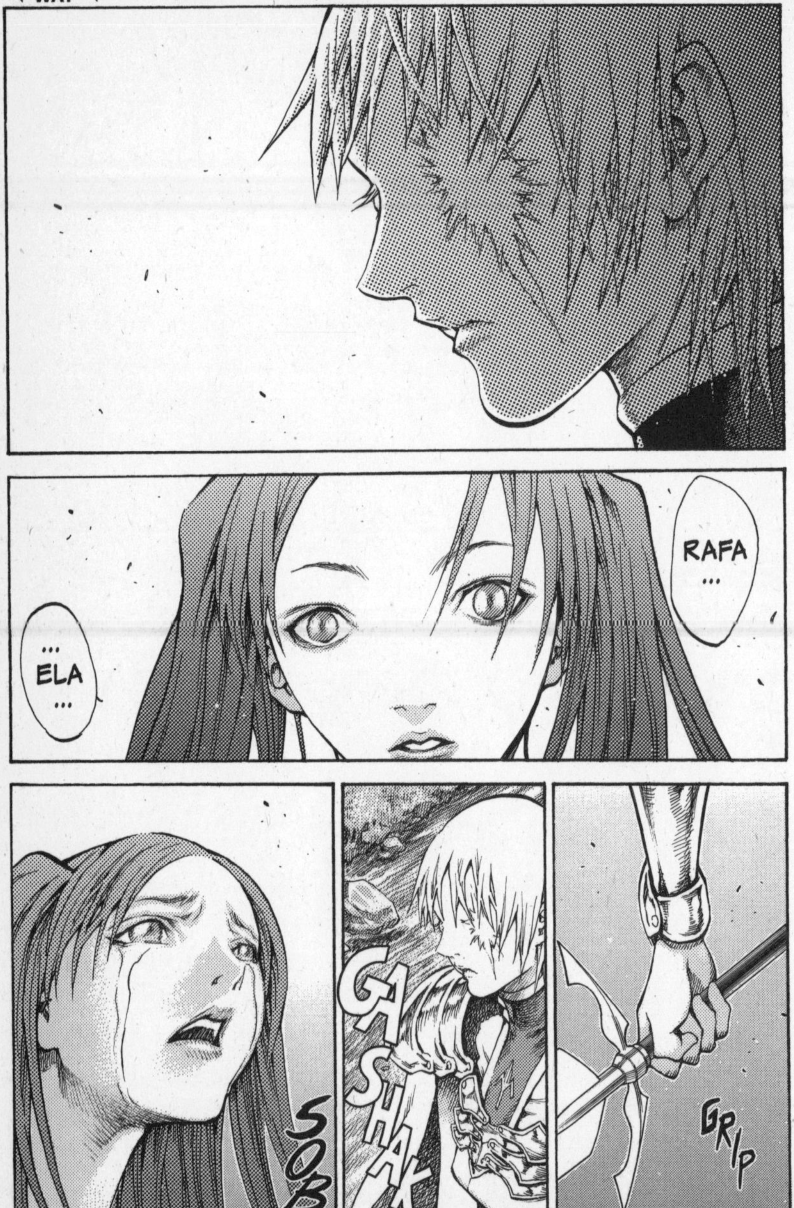
RAFA ...
... ELA ...
GRIP
GASHAK
SOB

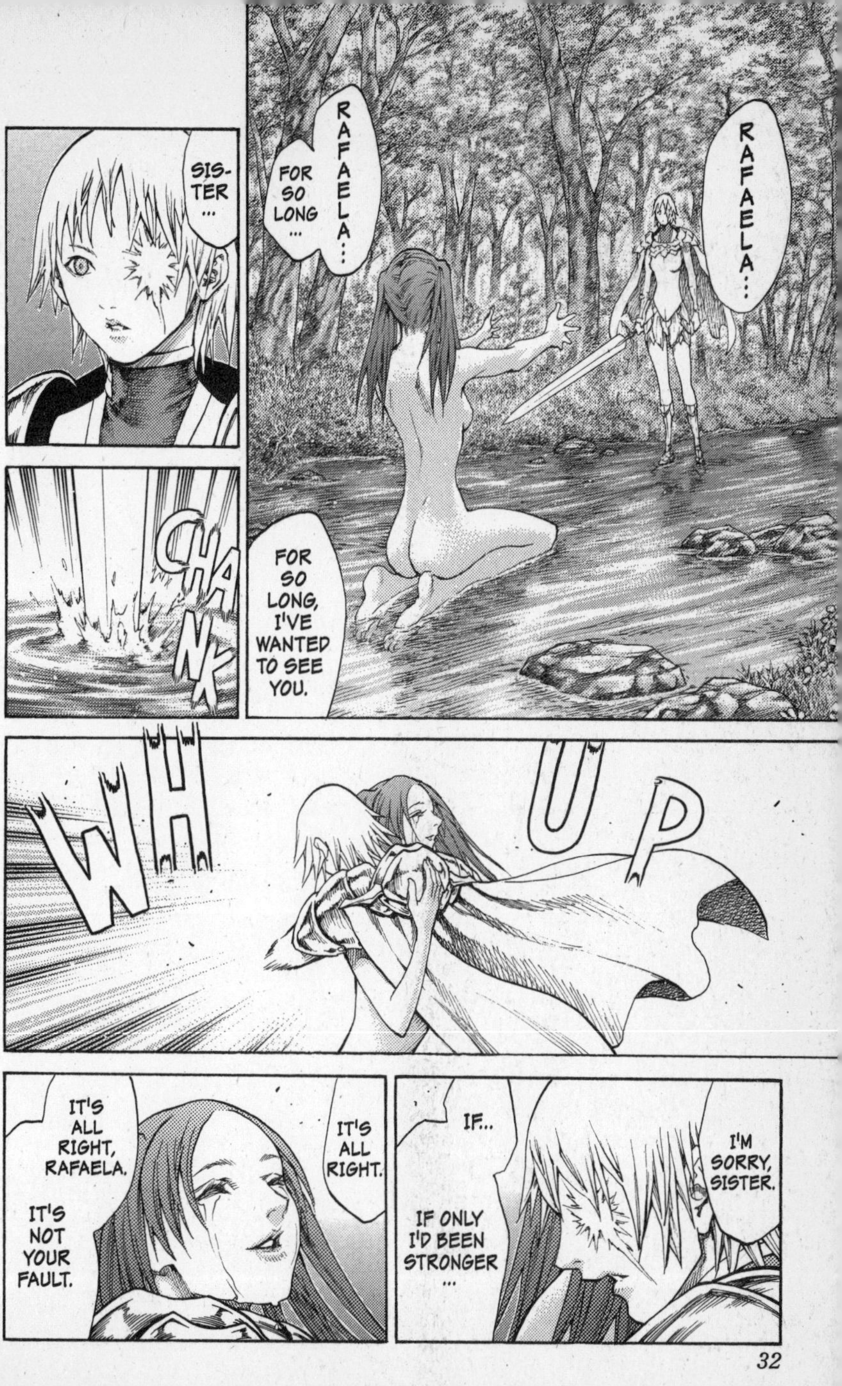
RAFAELA...
RAFAELA...
FOR SO LONG ...
FOR SO LONG, I'VE WANTED TO SEE YOU.
SIS-TER ...
CHANK
WHUP
I'M SORRY, SISTER.
IF...
IF ONLY I'D BEEN STRONGER ...
IT'S ALL RIGHT.
IT'S ALL RIGHT, RAFAELA.
IT'S NOT YOUR FAULT.

READ THIS WAY

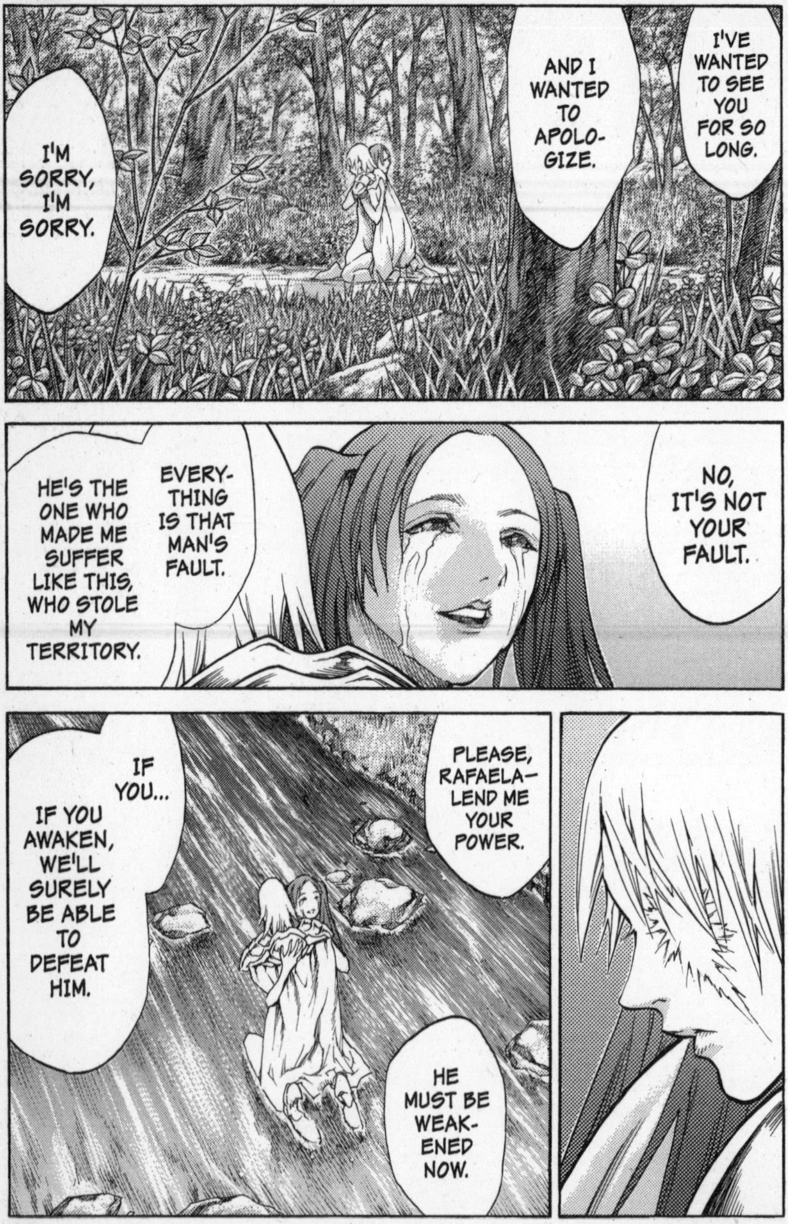

I'VE WANTED TO SEE YOU FOR SO LONG.
AND I WANTED TO APOLOGIZE.
I'M SORRY, I'M SORRY.
NO, IT'S NOT YOUR FAULT.
EVERYTHING IS THAT MAN'S FAULT.
HE'S THE ONE WHO MADE ME SUFFER LIKE THIS, WHO STOLE MY TERRITORY.
PLEASE, RAFAELA— LEND ME YOUR POWER.
IF YOU...
IF YOU AWAKEN, WE'LL SURELY BE ABLE TO DEFEAT HIM.
HE MUST BE WEAKENED NOW.

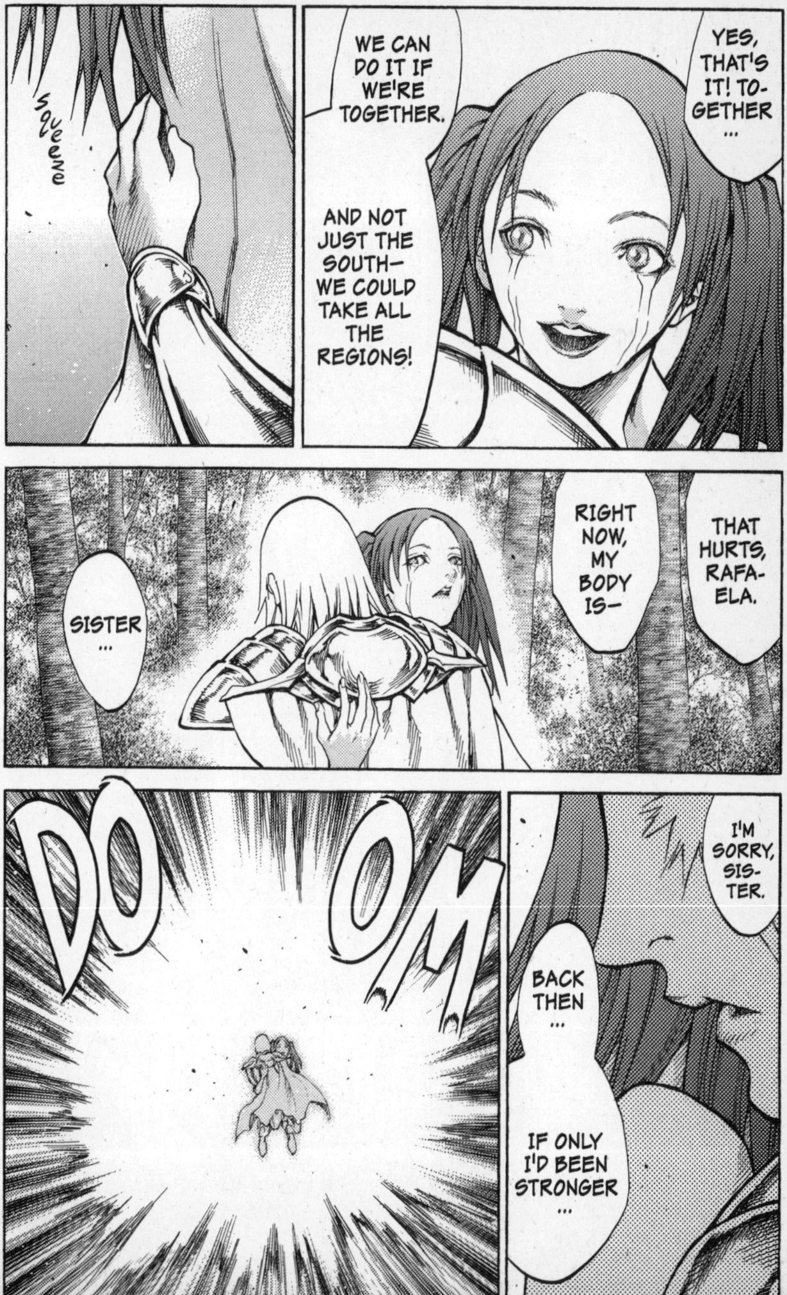
YES, THAT'S IT! TO-GETHER ...
WE CAN DO IT IF WE'RE TOGETHER.
AND NOT JUST THE SOUTH— WE COULD TAKE ALL THE REGIONS!
squeeze
THAT HURTS, RAFA-ELA.
RIGHT NOW, MY BODY IS—
SISTER ...
I'M SORRY, SIS-TER.
BACK THEN ...
IF ONLY I'D BEEN STRONGER ...
DOOM

READ THIS WAY

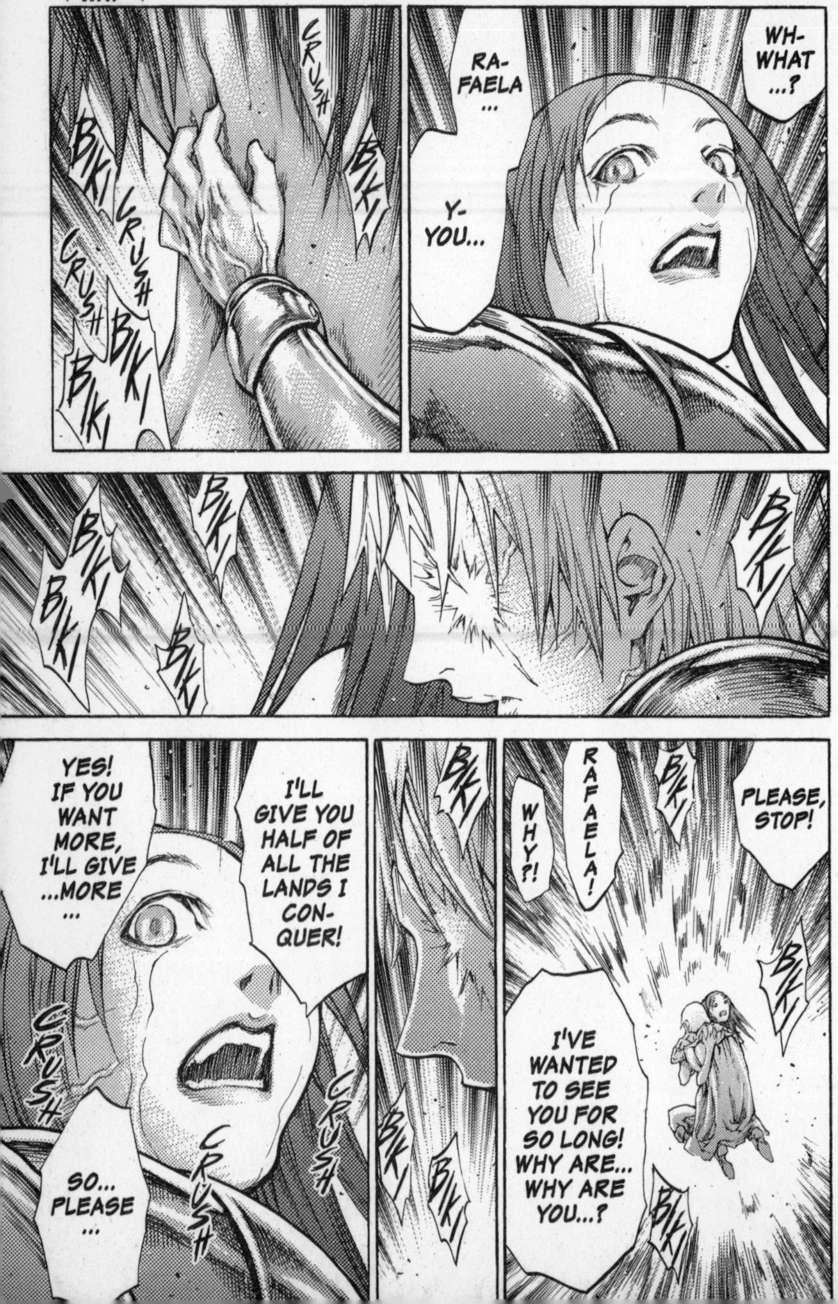
WH-WHAT ...?
RA-FAELA ...
Y-YOU...
CRUSH
BIKI
BIKI
CRUSH
CRUSH
BIKI
BIKI
BIKI
BIKI
BIKI
BIKI
BIKI
PLEASE, STOP!
RAFAELA!
WHY?!
BIKI
BIKI
I'VE WANTED TO SEE YOU FOR SO LONG! WHY ARE... WHY ARE YOU...?
BIKI
BIKI
BIKI
BIKI
I'LL GIVE YOU HALF OF ALL THE LANDS I CONQUER!
YES! IF YOU WANT MORE, I'LL GIVE ...MORE ...
CRUSH
CRUSH
SO... PLEASE ...
CRUSH

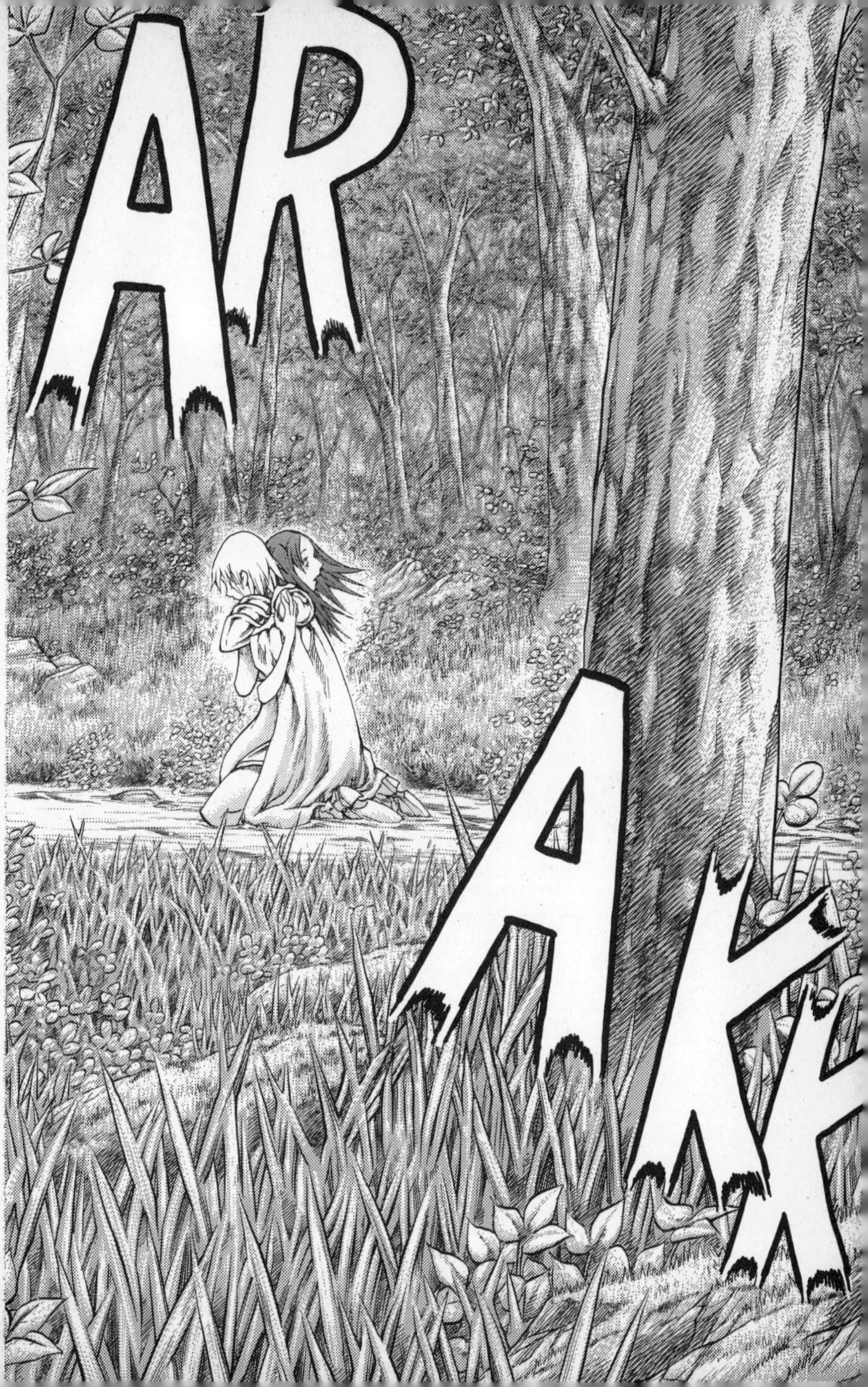

ARAAX

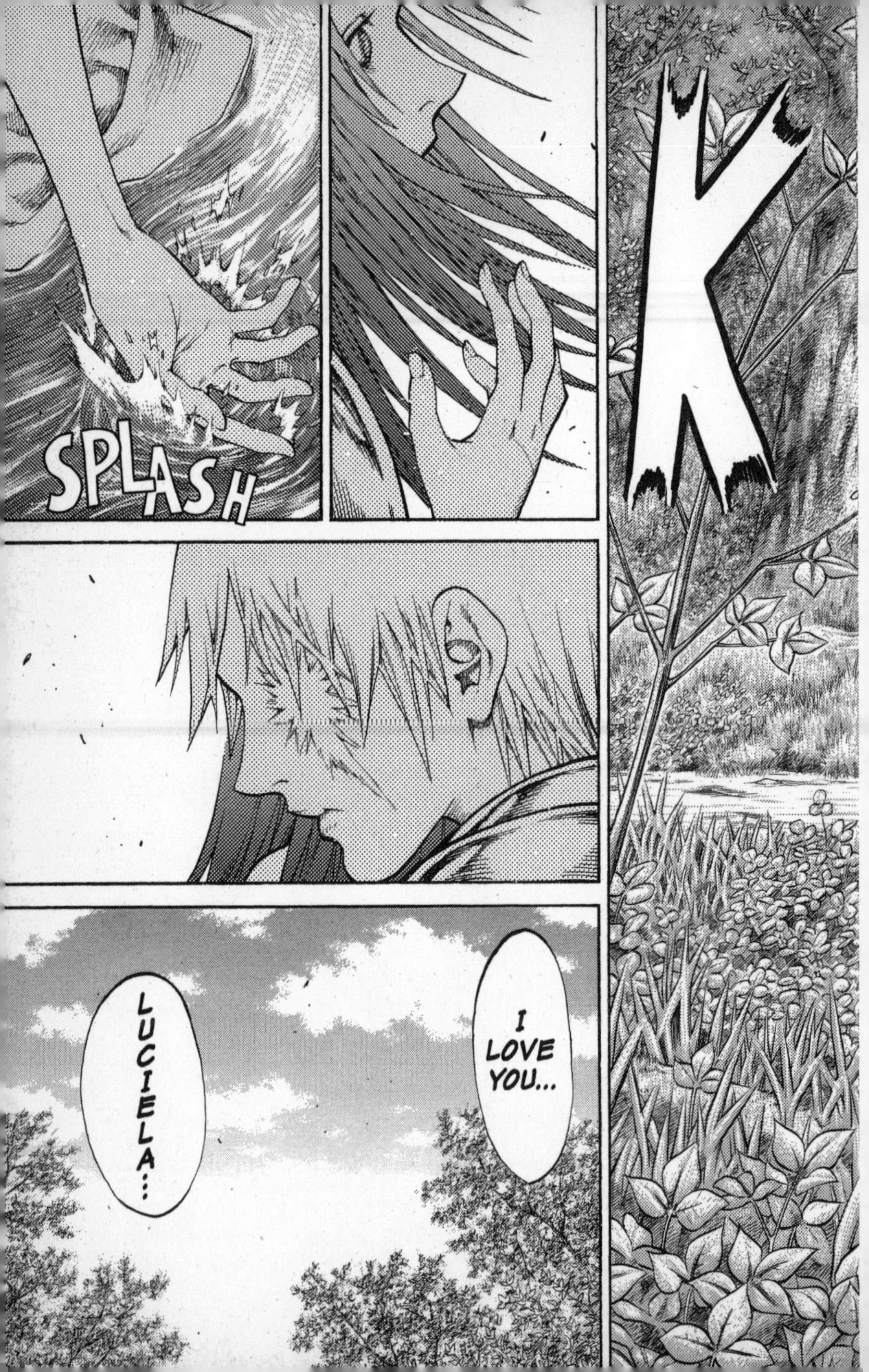
SPLASH
I LOVE YOU...
LUCIELA...

クレイモア
Claymore

Scene 65: The Souls of the Fallen, Part 1

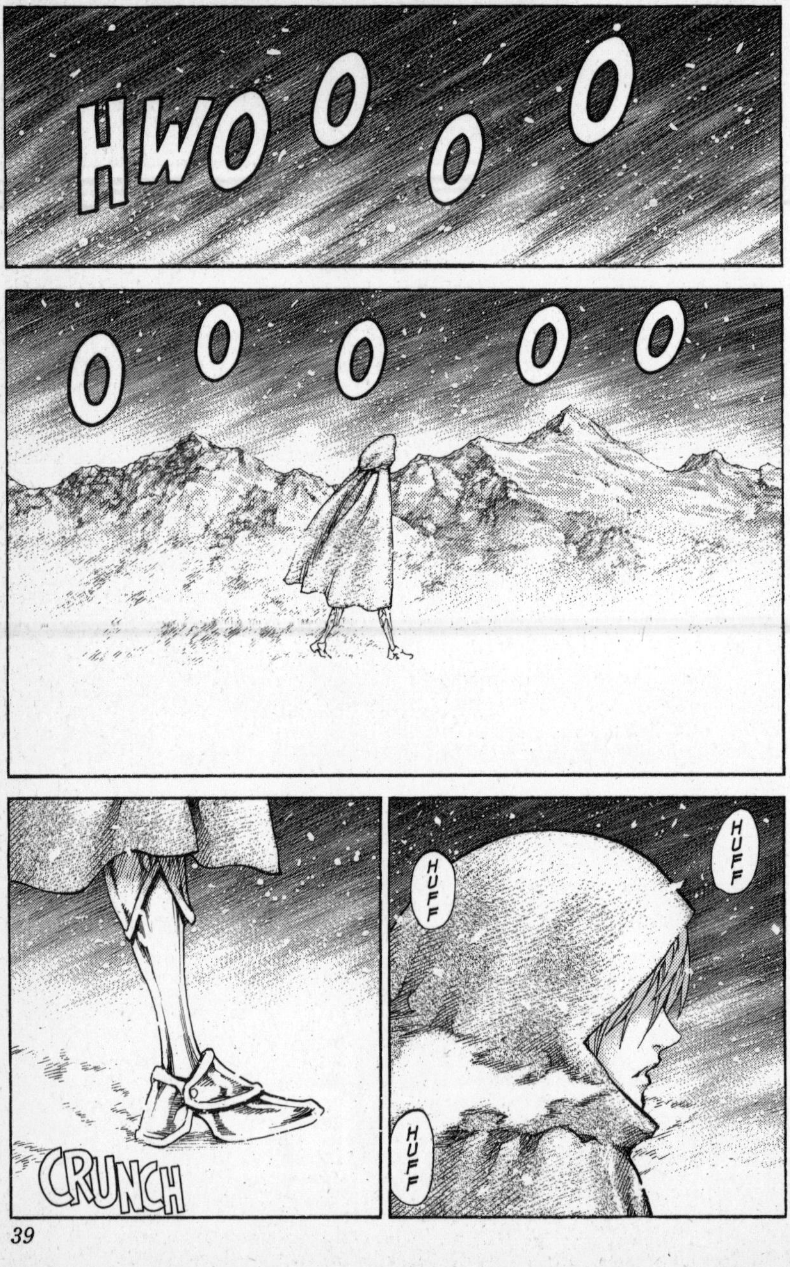
HWOOOO
OOOOO
HUFF
HUFF
HUFF
CRUNCH

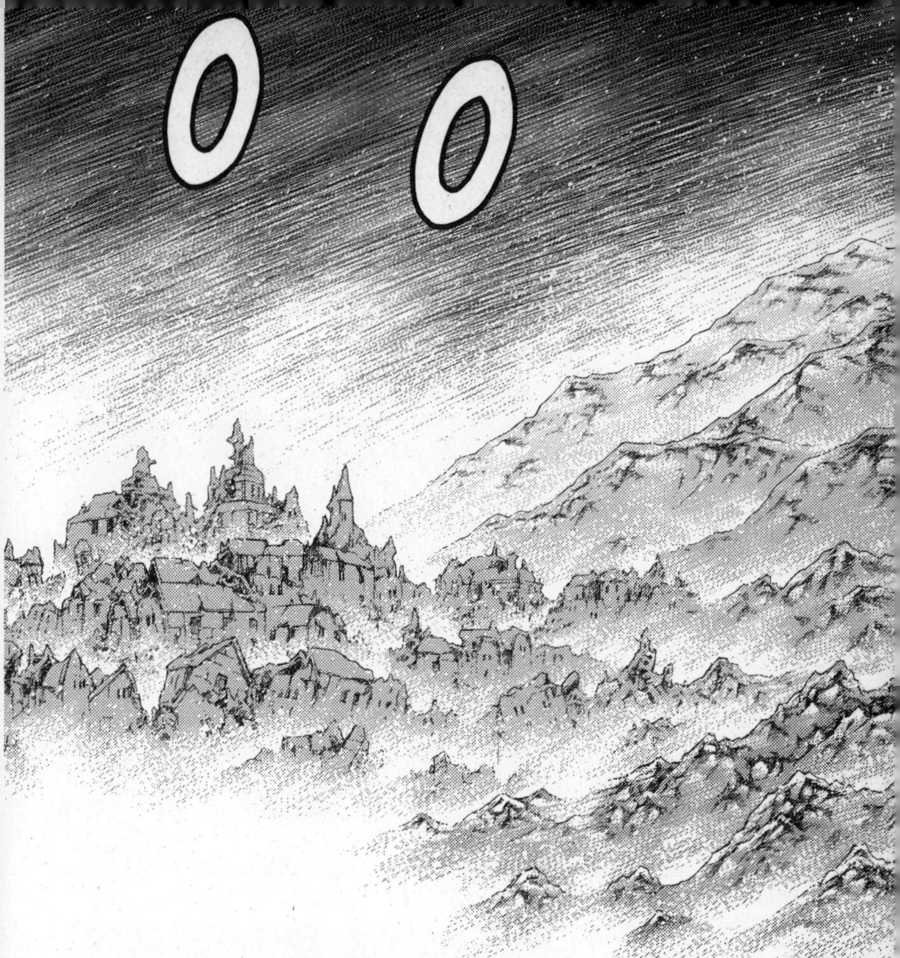
OO

Scene 65: The Souls of the Fallen, Part 1

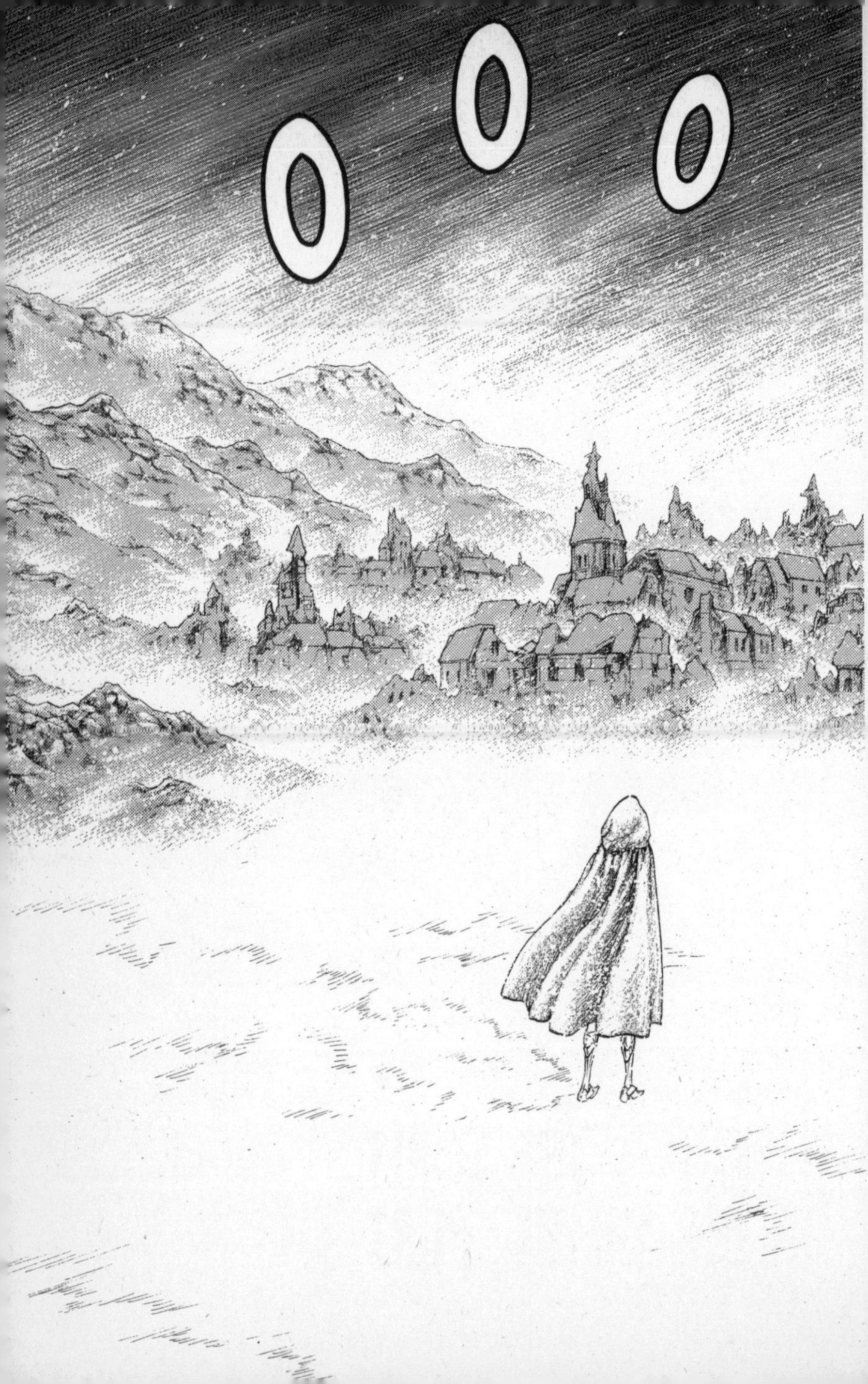
O O O

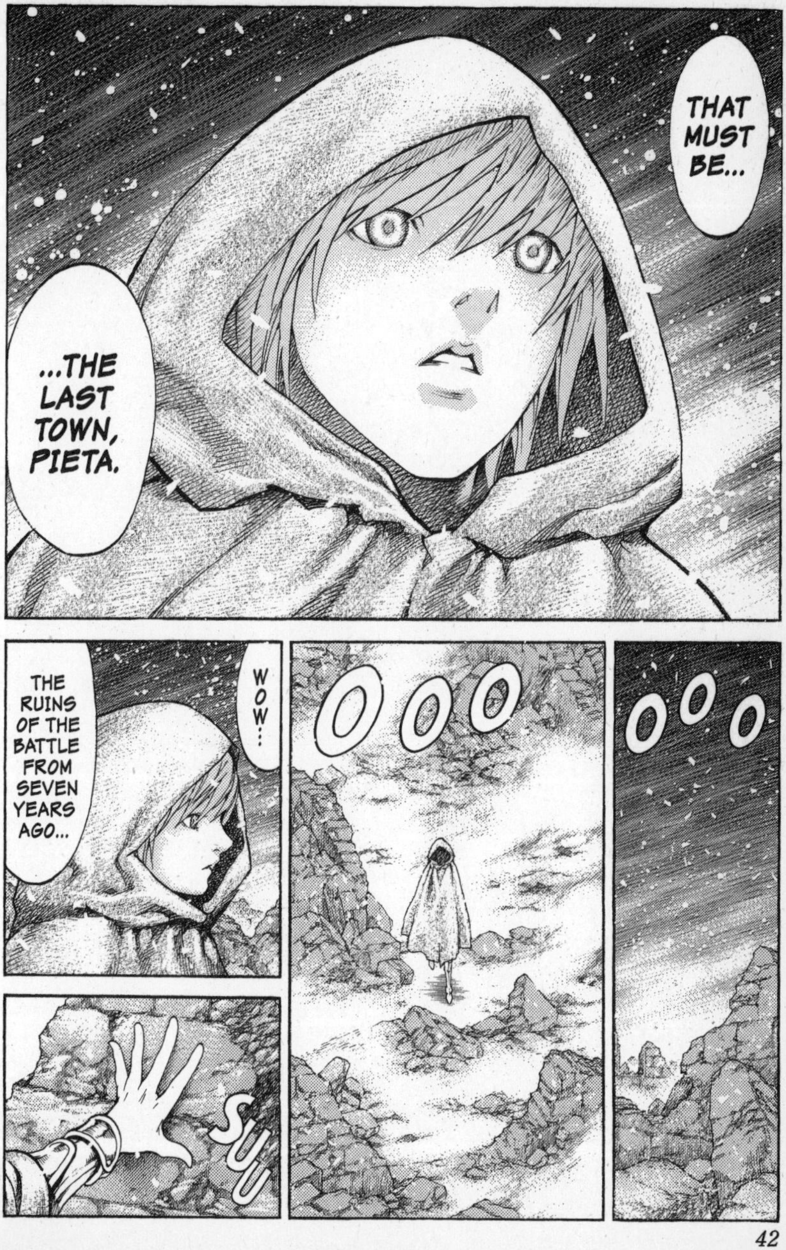
THAT MUST BE...
...THE LAST TOWN, PIETA.
OOO
OOO
WOW...
THE RUINS OF THE BATTLE FROM SEVEN YEARS AGO...
SUU

READ THIS WAY

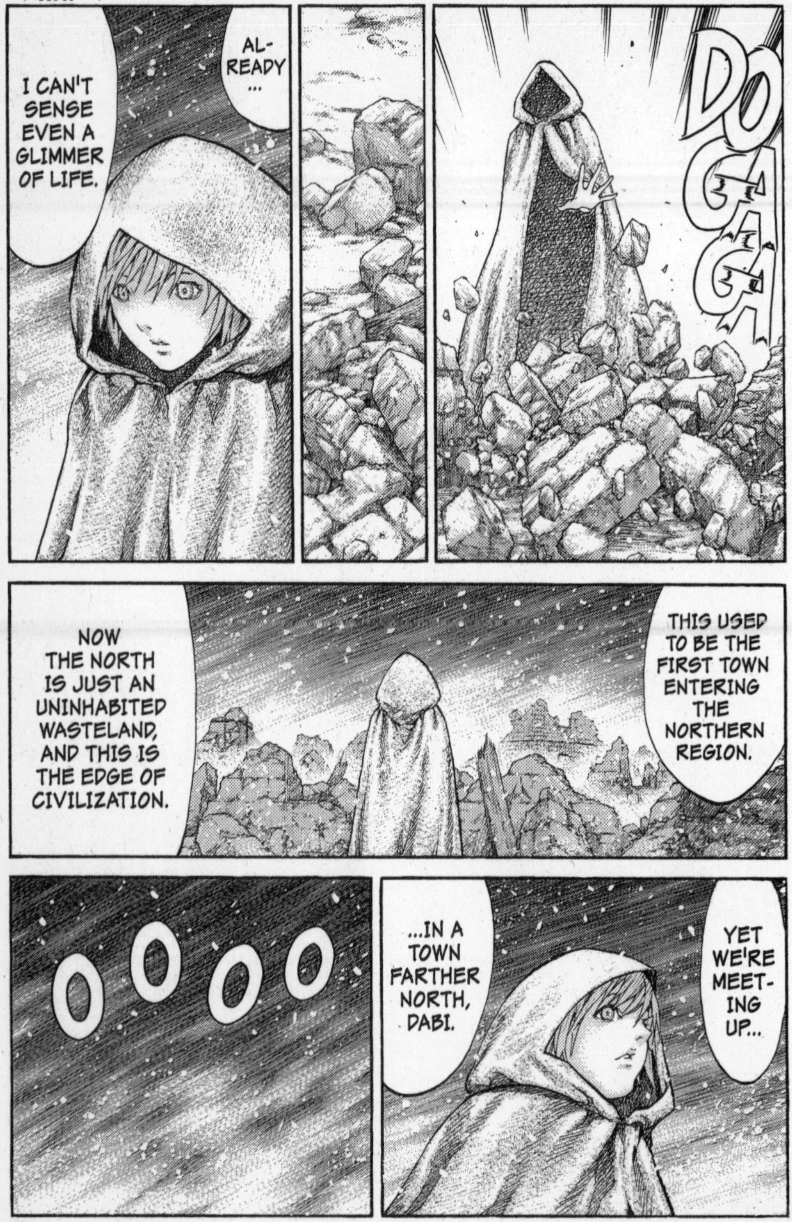

DOGAGAGA
AL-READY...
I CAN'T SENSE EVEN A GLIMMER OF LIFE.
THIS USED TO BE THE FIRST TOWN ENTERING THE NORTHERN REGION.
NOW THE NORTH IS JUST AN UNINHABITED WASTELAND, AND THIS IS THE EDGE OF CIVILIZATION.
YET WE'RE MEETING UP...
...IN A TOWN FARTHER NORTH, DABI.
OOOO

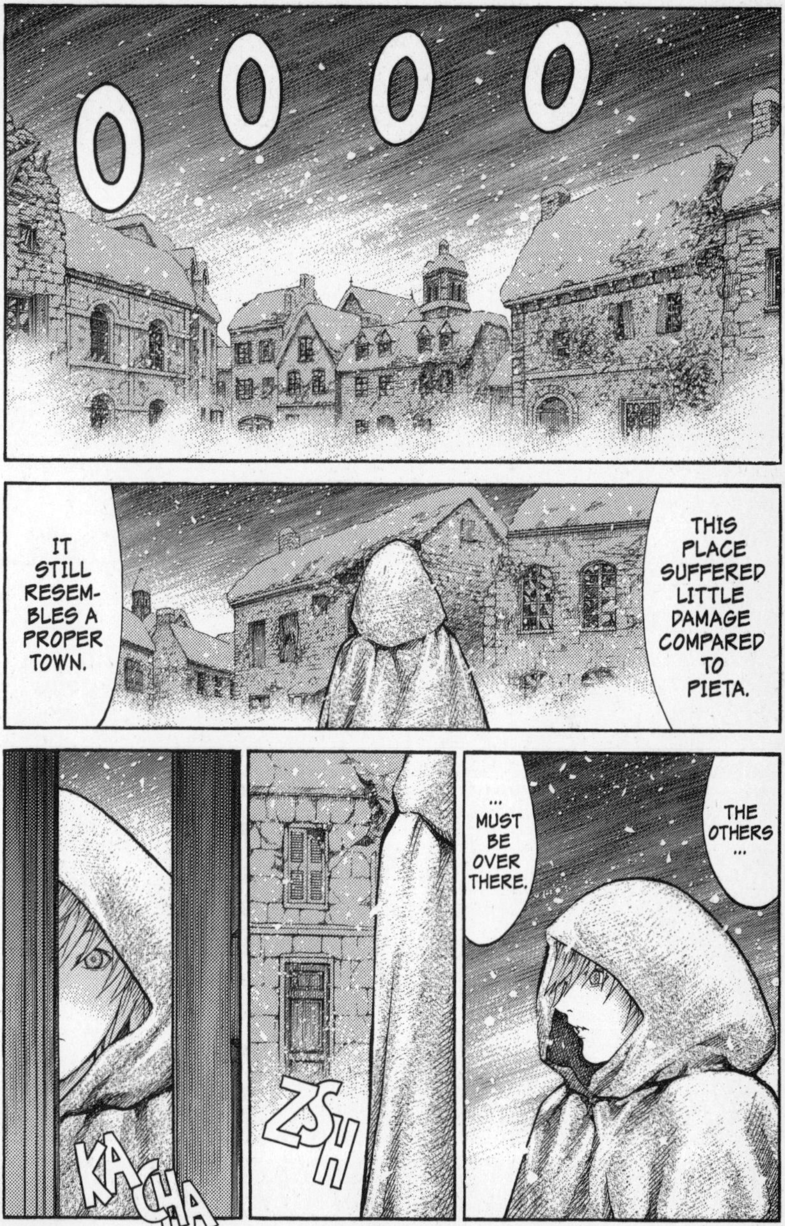
OOOO
THIS PLACE SUFFERED LITTLE DAMAGE COMPARED TO PIETA.
IT STILL RESEMBLES A PROPER TOWN.
THE OTHERS...
...MUST BE OVER THERE.
ZSH
KACHA

READ THIS WAY

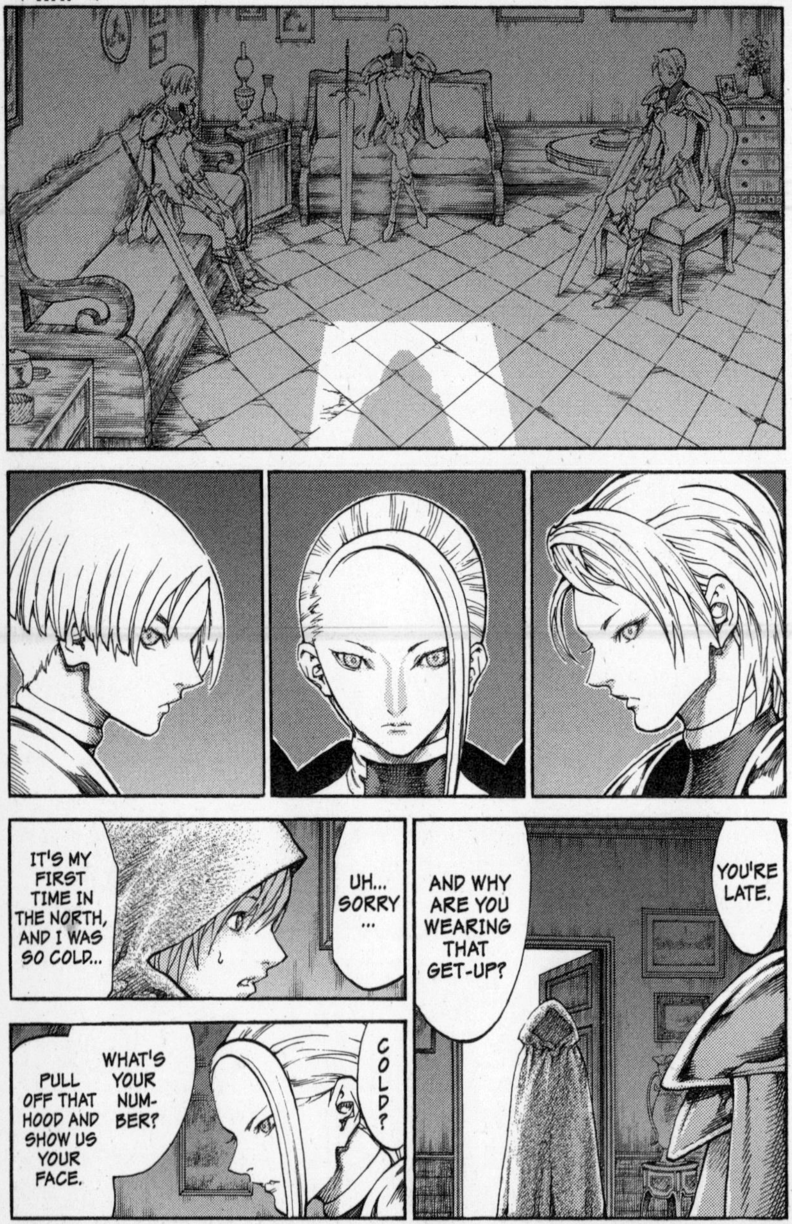

YOU'RE LATE.
AND WHY ARE YOU WEARING THAT GET-UP?
UH... SORRY...
IT'S MY FIRST TIME IN THE NORTH, AND I WAS SO COLD...
COLD?
WHAT'S YOUR NUMBER?
PULL OFF THAT HOOD AND SHOW US YOUR FACE.

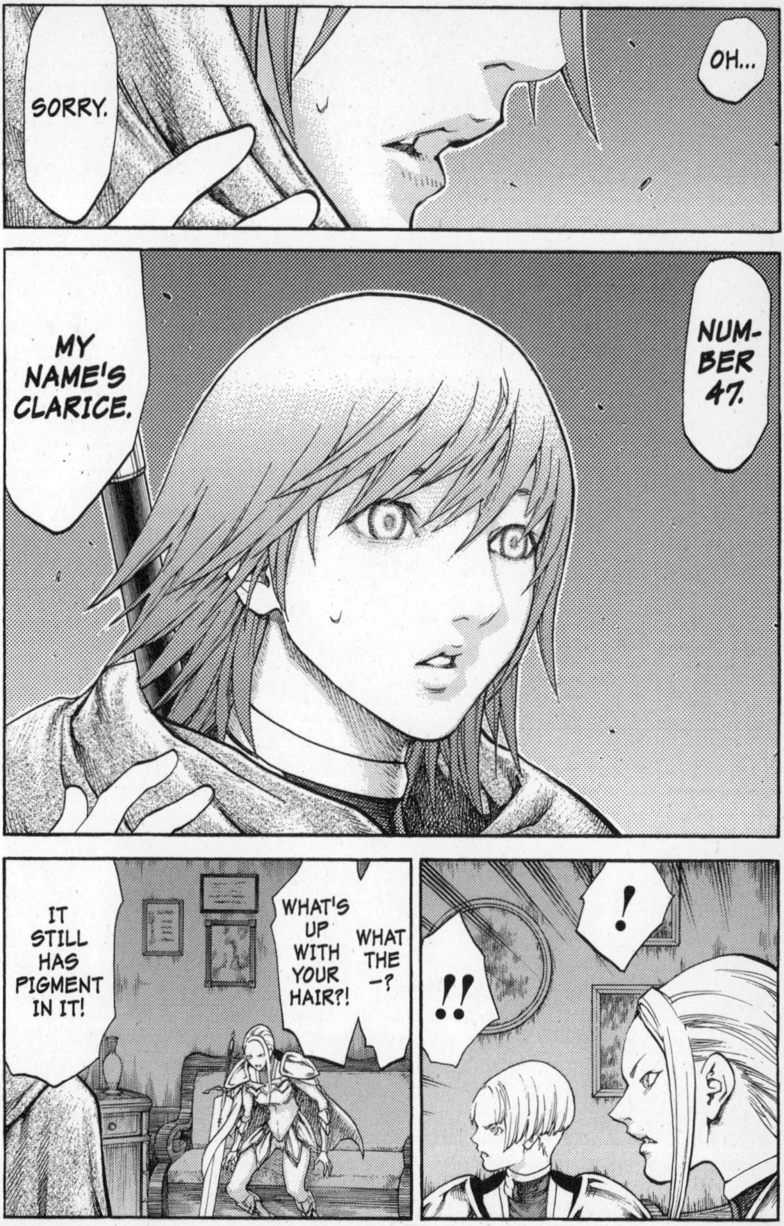
OH...
SORRY.
NUM-
BER
47.
MY NAME'S CLARICE.
!
!!
WHAT THE —?
WHAT'S UP WITH YOUR HAIR?!
IT STILL HAS PIGMENT IN IT!

READ THIS WAY

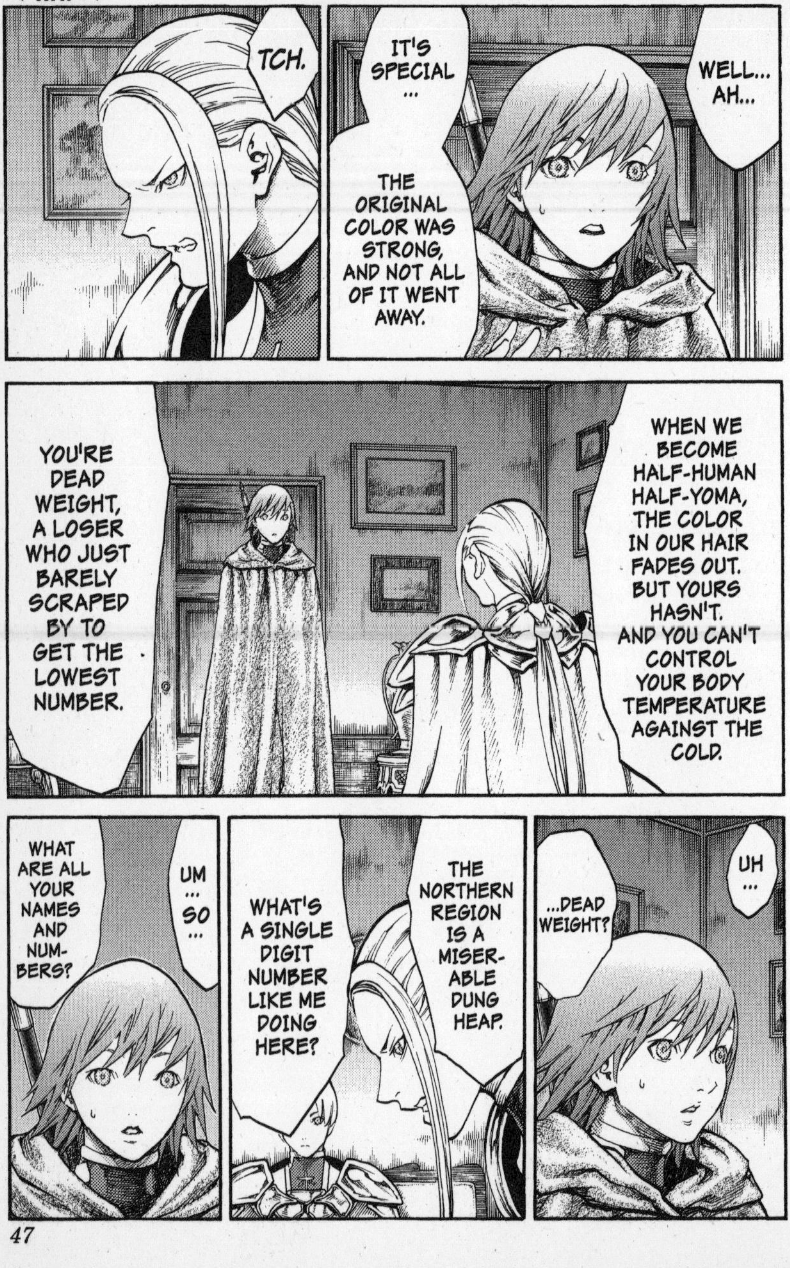
WELL... AH...
IT'S SPECIAL ...
THE ORIGINAL COLOR WAS STRONG, AND NOT ALL OF IT WENT AWAY.
TCH.
WHEN WE BECOME HALF-HUMAN HALF-YOMA, THE COLOR IN OUR HAIR FADES OUT. BUT YOURS HASN'T. AND YOU CAN'T CONTROL YOUR BODY TEMPERATURE AGAINST THE COLD.
YOU'RE DEAD WEIGHT, A LOSER WHO JUST BARELY SCRAPED BY TO GET THE LOWEST NUMBER.
UH ...
...DEAD WEIGHT?
THE NORTHERN REGION IS A MISER-ABLE DUNG HEAP.
WHAT'S A SINGLE DIGIT NUMBER LIKE ME DOING HERE?
UM ... SO ...
WHAT ARE ALL YOUR NAMES AND NUM-BERS?

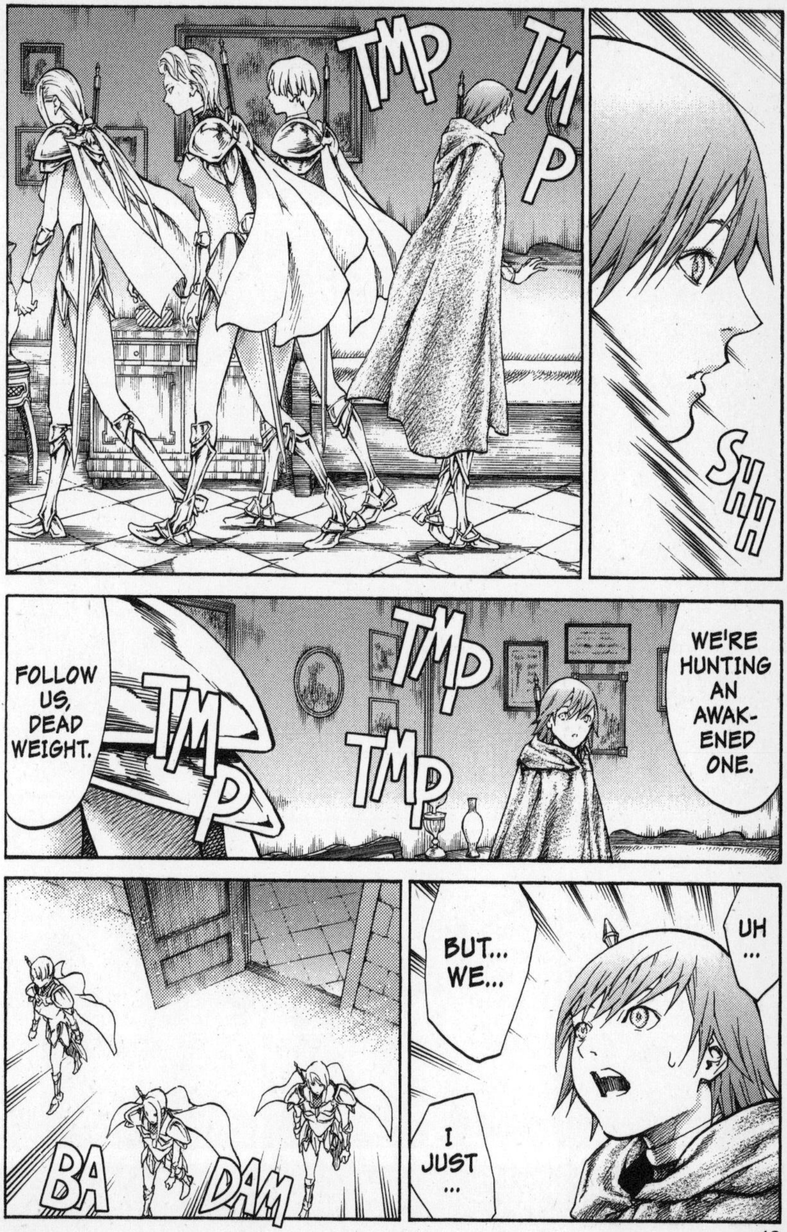
SHHH
TMP
TMP
WE'RE HUNTING AN AWAK-ENED ONE.
TMP
TMP
TMP
FOLLOW US, DEAD WEIGHT.
UH ...
BUT... WE...
I JUST ...
BA DAM

READ THIS WAY

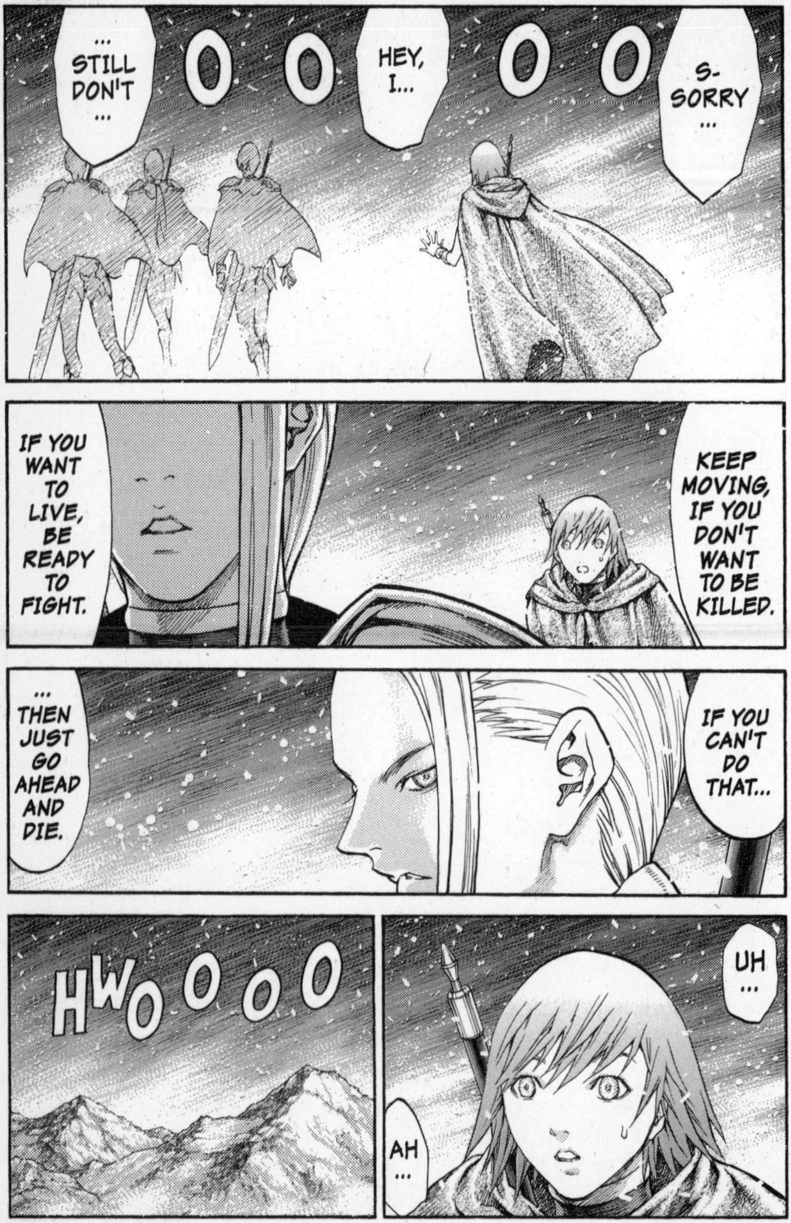
S-SORRY...
O O
HEY, I...
O O
...STILL DON'T...
KEEP MOVING, IF YOU DON'T WANT TO BE KILLED.
IF YOU WANT TO LIVE, BE READY TO FIGHT.
IF YOU CAN'T DO THAT...
...THEN JUST GO AHEAD AND DIE.
UH...
AH...
HWOOOO

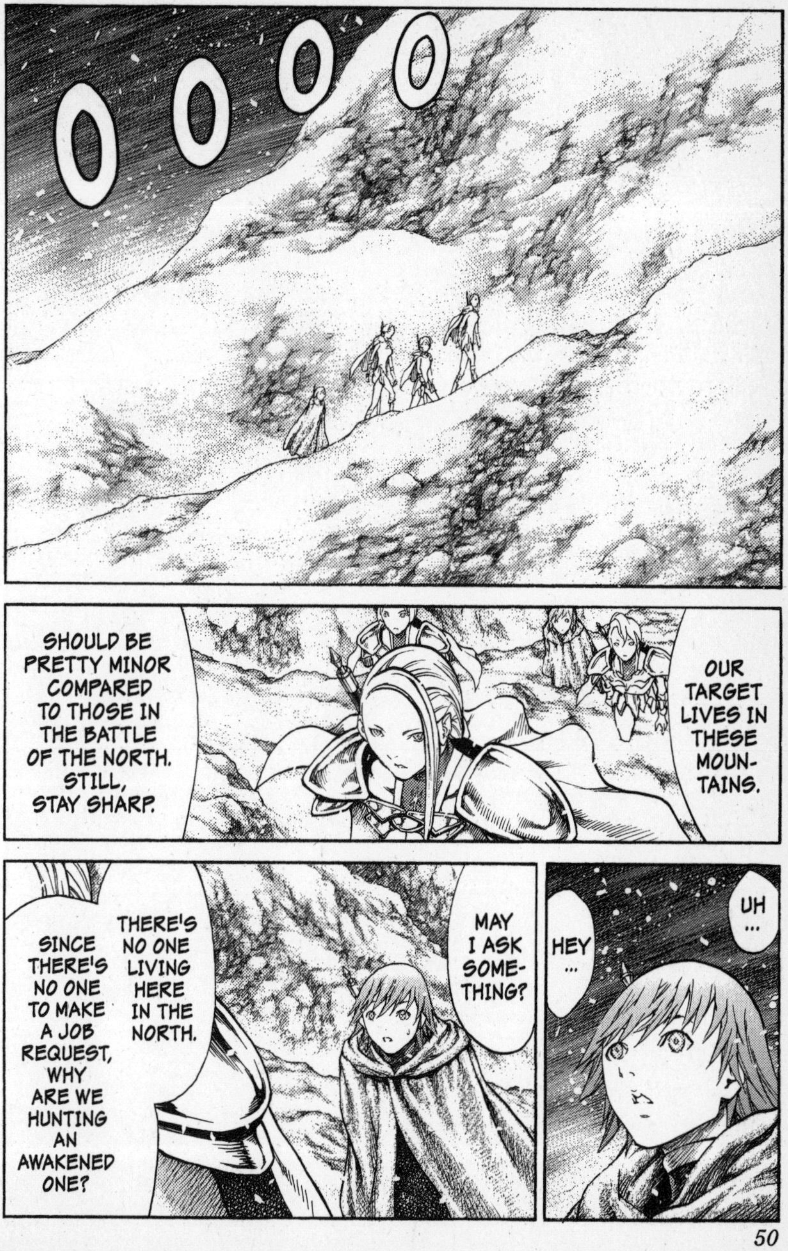
OOOO
OUR TARGET LIVES IN THESE MOUN-TAINS.
SHOULD BE PRETTY MINOR COMPARED TO THOSE IN THE BATTLE OF THE NORTH. STILL, STAY SHARP.
UH ...
HEY ...
MAY I ASK SOME-THING?
THERE'S NO ONE LIVING HERE IN THE NORTH.
SINCE THERE'S NO ONE TO MAKE A JOB REQUEST, WHY ARE WE HUNTING AN AWAKENED ONE?

READ THIS WAY

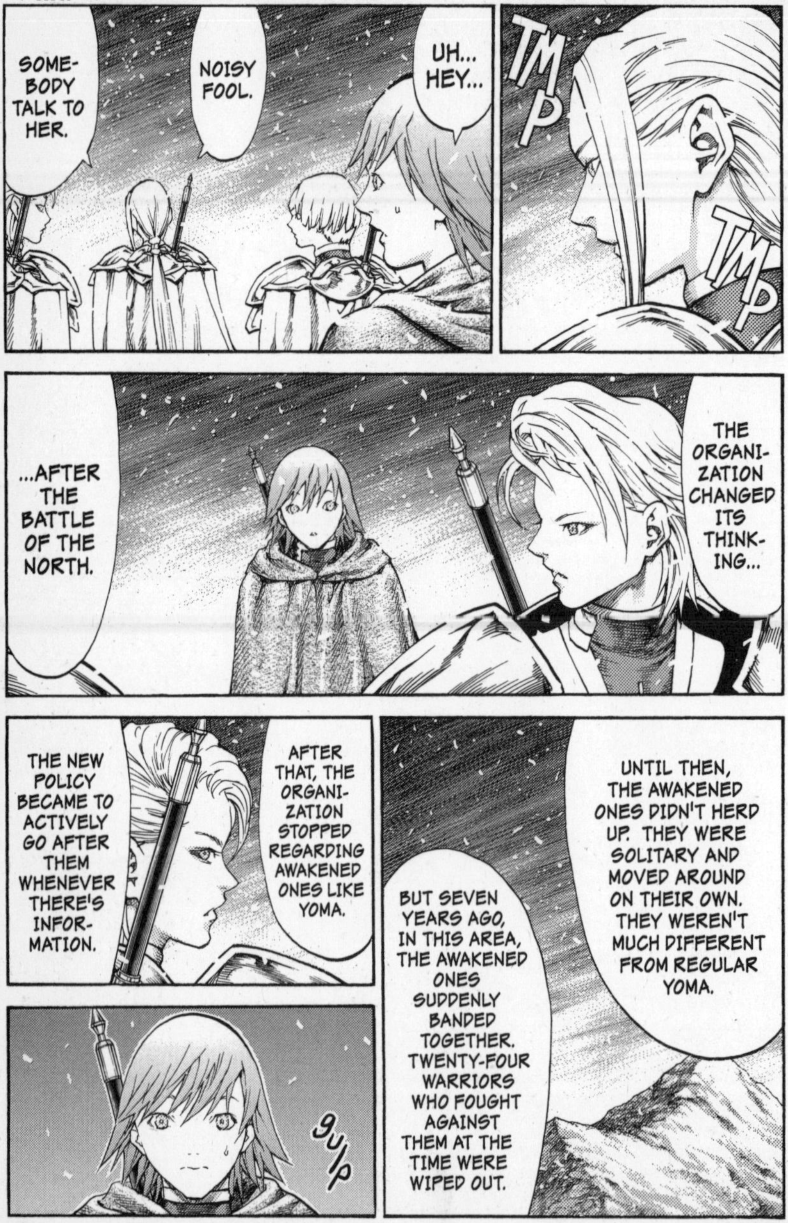
TMP
TMP
UH... HEY...
NOISY FOOL.
SOMEBODY TALK TO HER.
THE ORGANIZATION CHANGED ITS THINKING...
...AFTER THE BATTLE OF THE NORTH.
UNTIL THEN, THE AWAKENED ONES DIDN'T HERD UP. THEY WERE SOLITARY AND MOVED AROUND ON THEIR OWN. THEY WEREN'T MUCH DIFFERENT FROM REGULAR YOMA.
BUT SEVEN YEARS AGO, IN THIS AREA, THE AWAKENED ONES SUDDENLY BANDED TOGETHER. TWENTY-FOUR WARRIORS WHO FOUGHT AGAINST THEM AT THE TIME WERE WIPED OUT.
AFTER THAT, THE ORGANIZATION STOPPED REGARDING AWAKENED ONES LIKE YOMA.
THE NEW POLICY BECAME TO ACTIVELY GO AFTER THEM WHENEVER THERE'S INFORMATION.
gulp

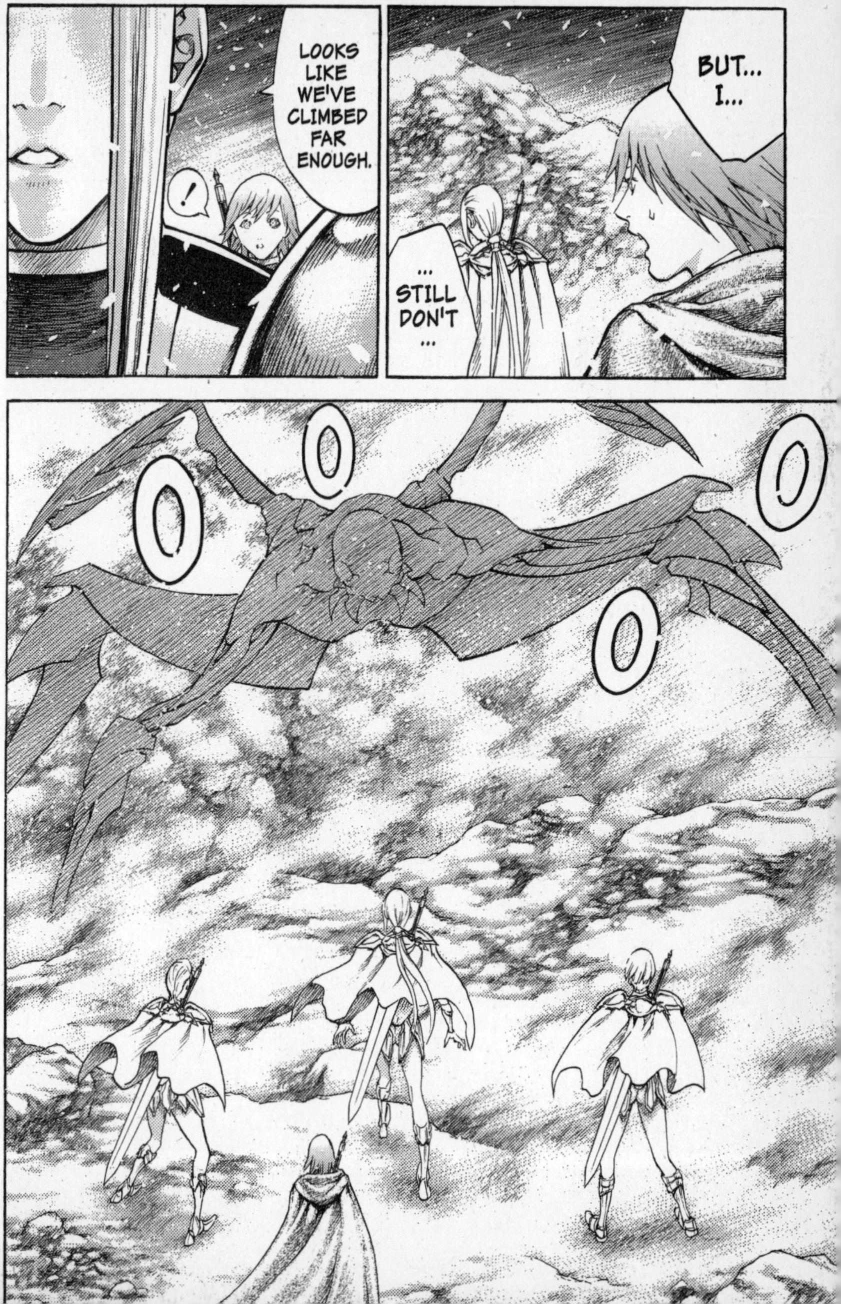
BUT... I...
... STILL DON'T ...
LOOKS LIKE WE'VE CLIMBED FAR ENOUGH.
!
O
O
O
O

READ THIS WAY

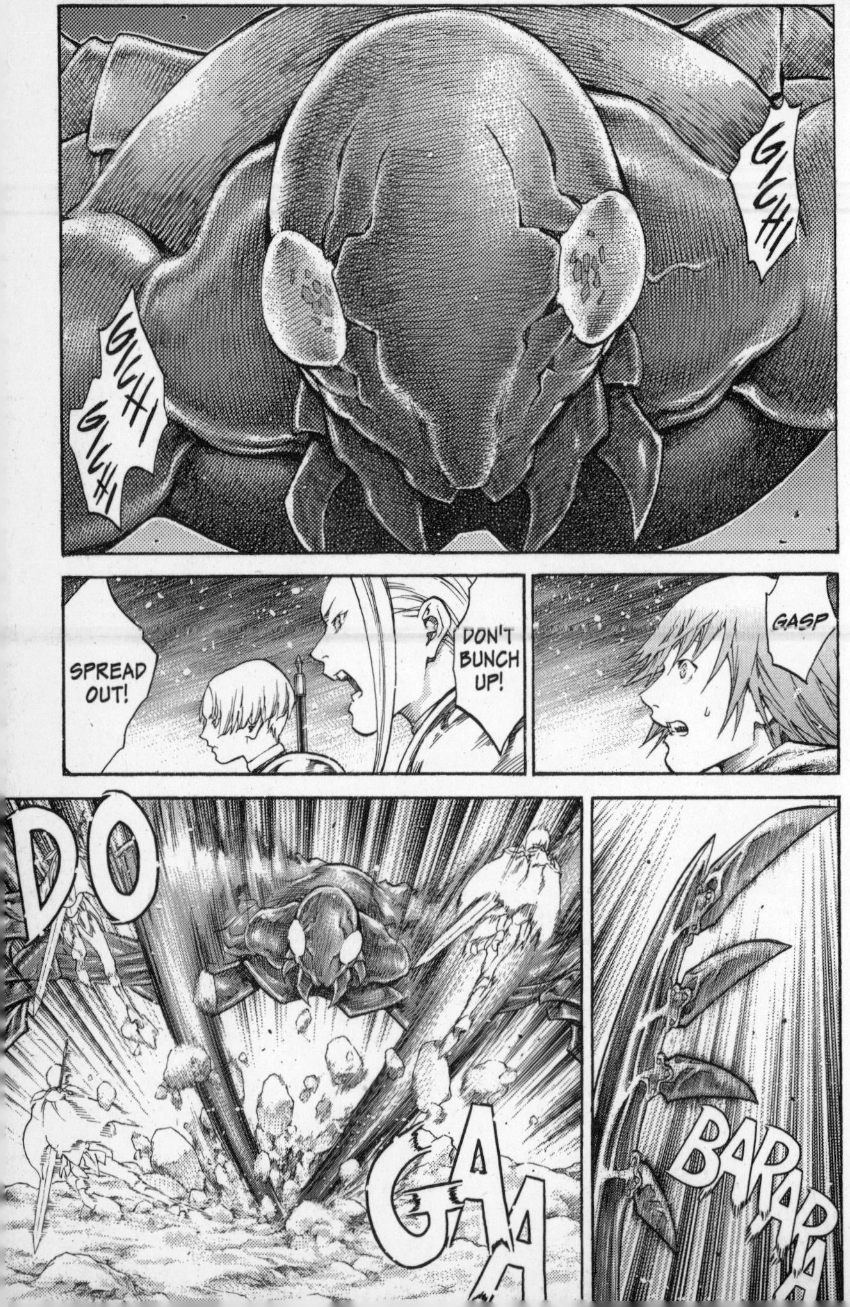
GICHI
GICHI GICHI
GASP
DON'T BUNCH UP!
SPREAD OUT!
BARARA
DO
GAAA

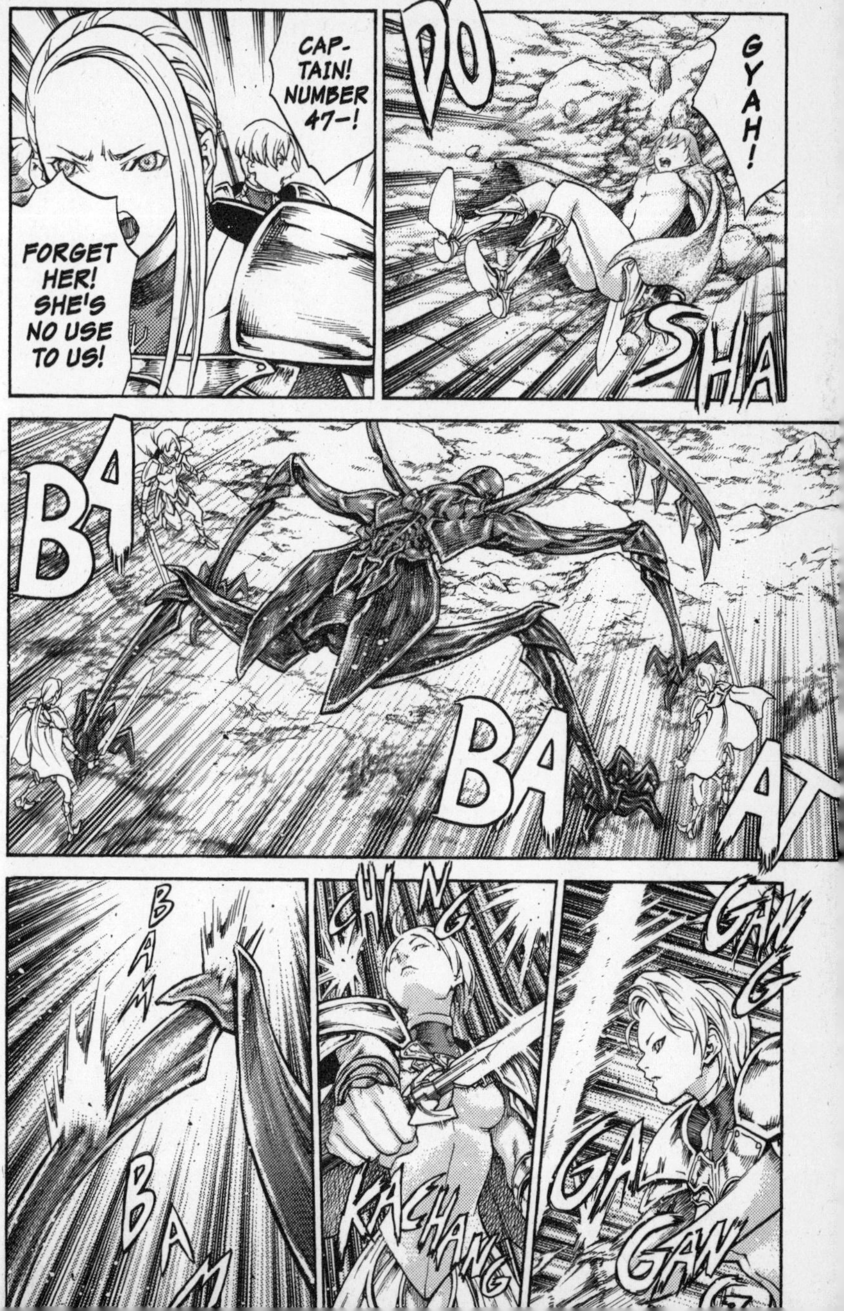
DO
GYAH!
SHA
CAP-TAIN! NUMBER 47—!
FORGET HER! SHE'S NO USE TO US!
BA
BAAT
BA
GAWG
GAGAW
CHING
KACHANG
BAM
BAM

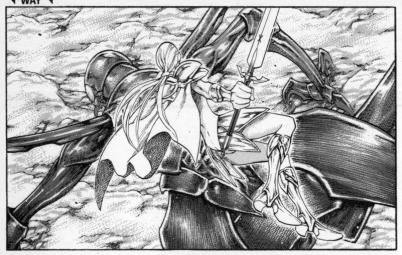

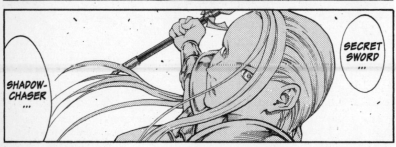

SECRET SWORD ...

SHADOW-CHASER ...

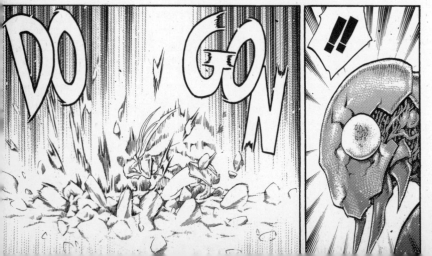

DO

GON

!!

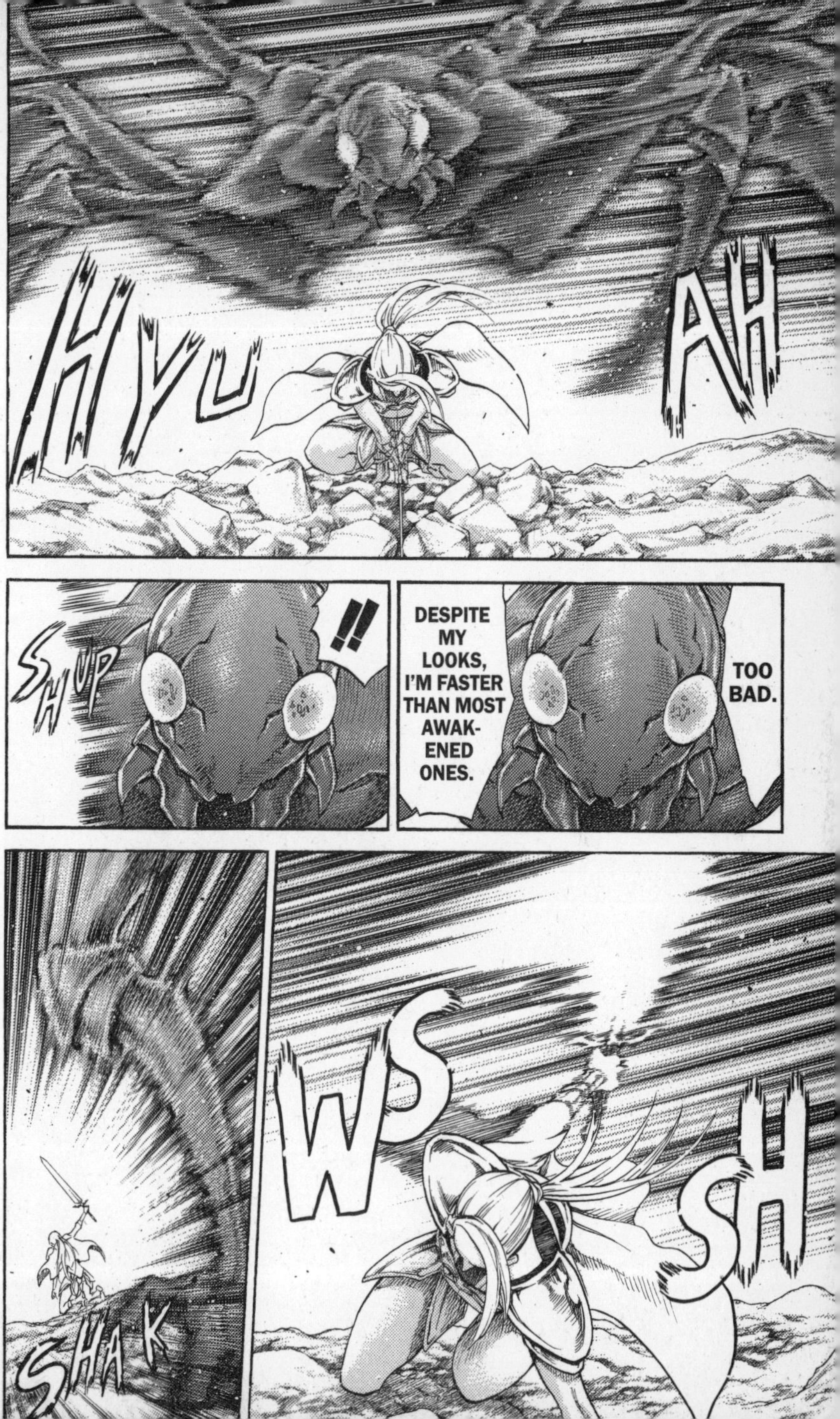
HYU AH
TOO BAD.
DESPITE MY LOOKS, I'M FASTER THAN MOST AWAK-ENED ONES.
!!
SHUP
WSSH
SHAK

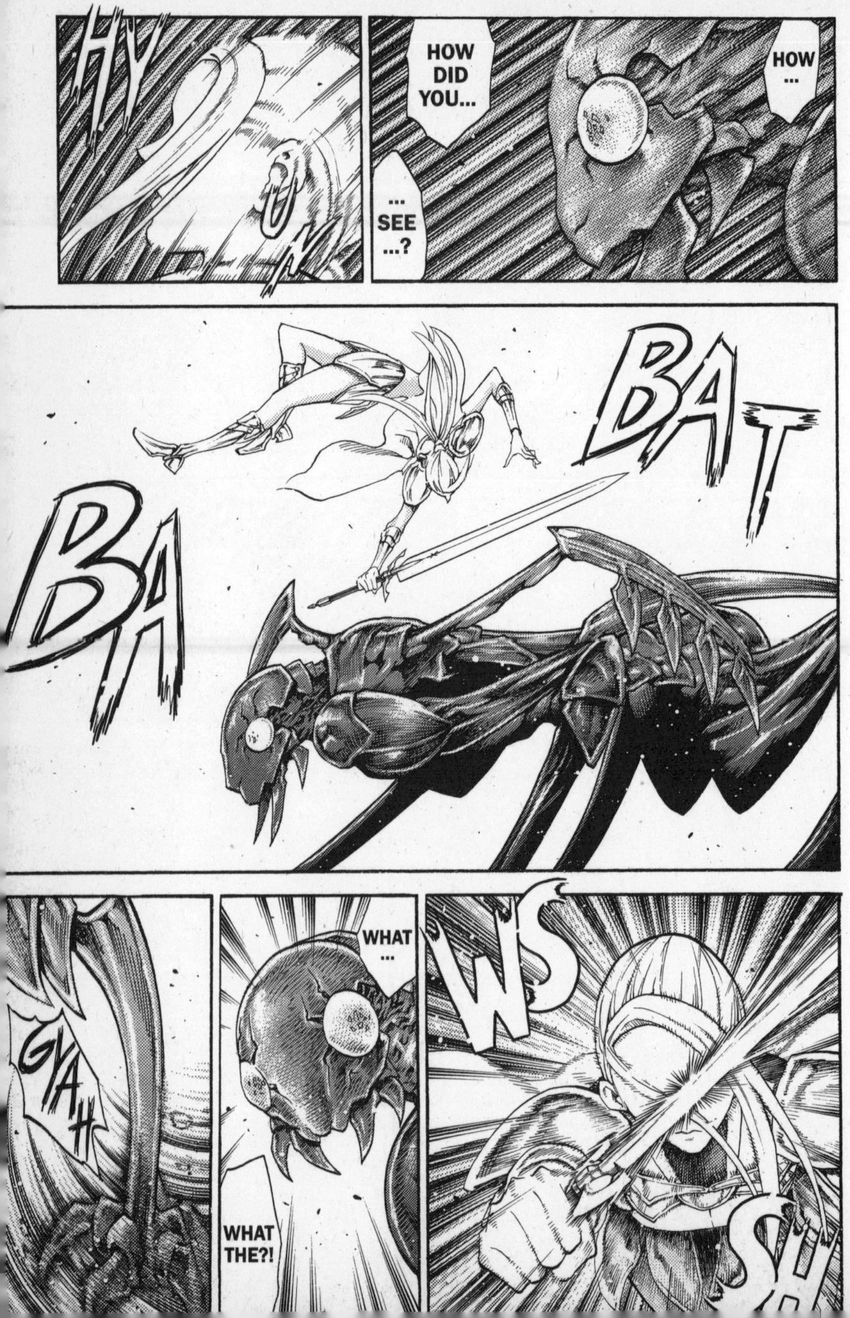
HOW ...
HOW DID YOU...
... SEE ...?
HYUN
BAT
BA
WS
SH
WHAT ...
WHAT THE?!
GYAH

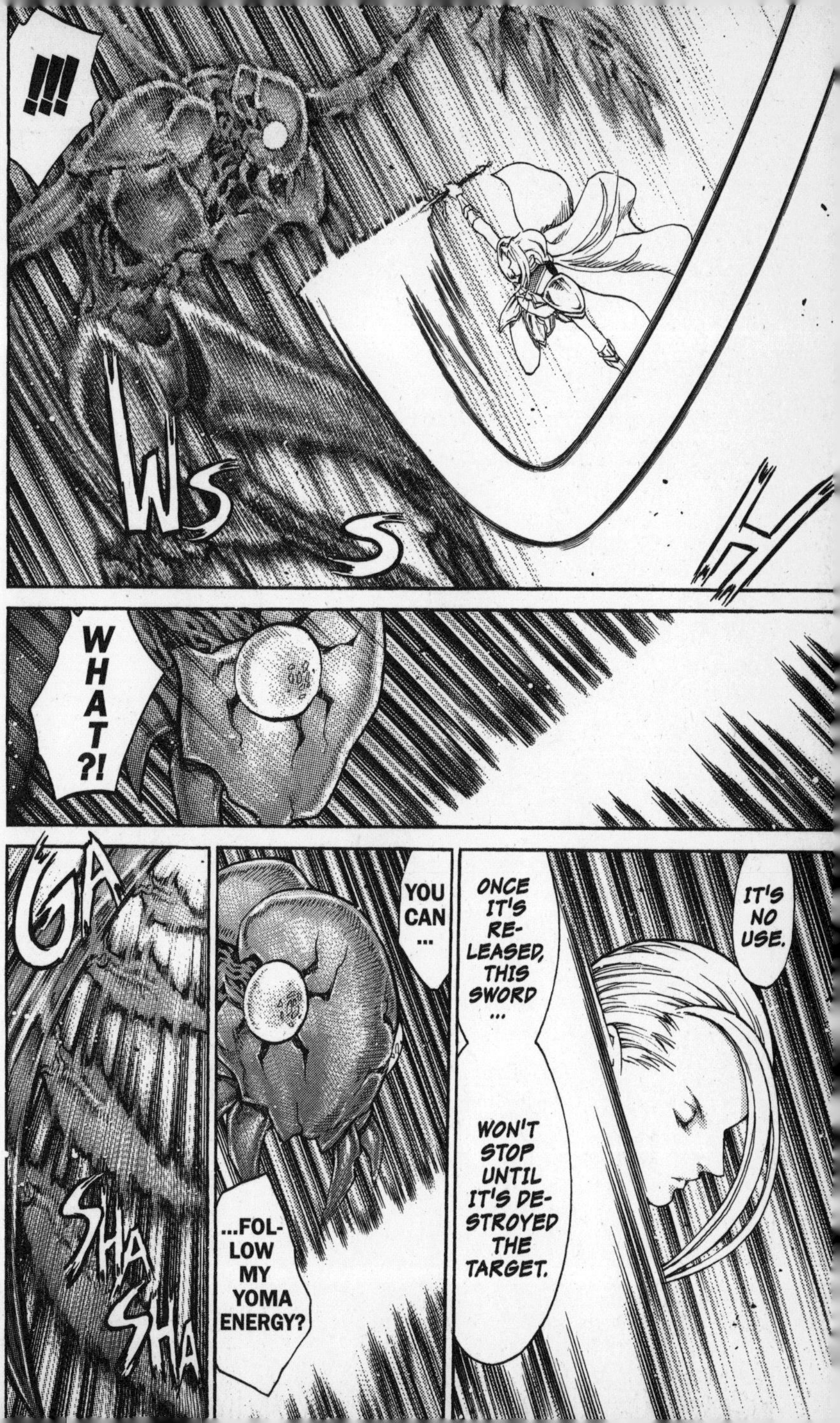
!!!
WSSH
WHAT?!
IT'S NO USE.
ONCE IT'S RELEASED, THIS SWORD...
WON'T STOP UNTIL IT'S DESTROYED THE TARGET.
YOU CAN...
...FOLLOW MY YOMA ENERGY?
GA
SHA SHA

READ THIS WAY

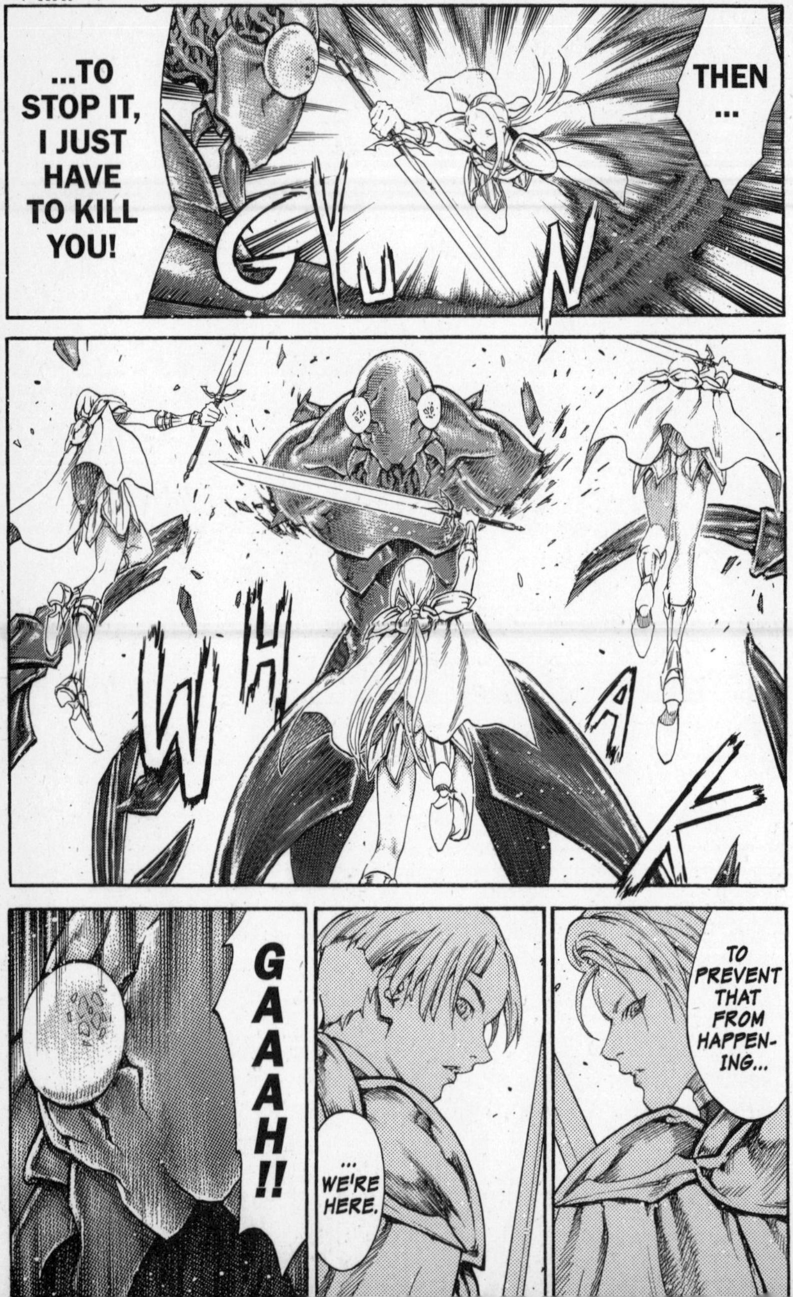
THEN ...
...TO STOP IT, I JUST HAVE TO KILL YOU!
GYUN
WHAK
TO PREVENT THAT FROM HAPPEN-ING...
... WE'RE HERE.
GAAAH!!

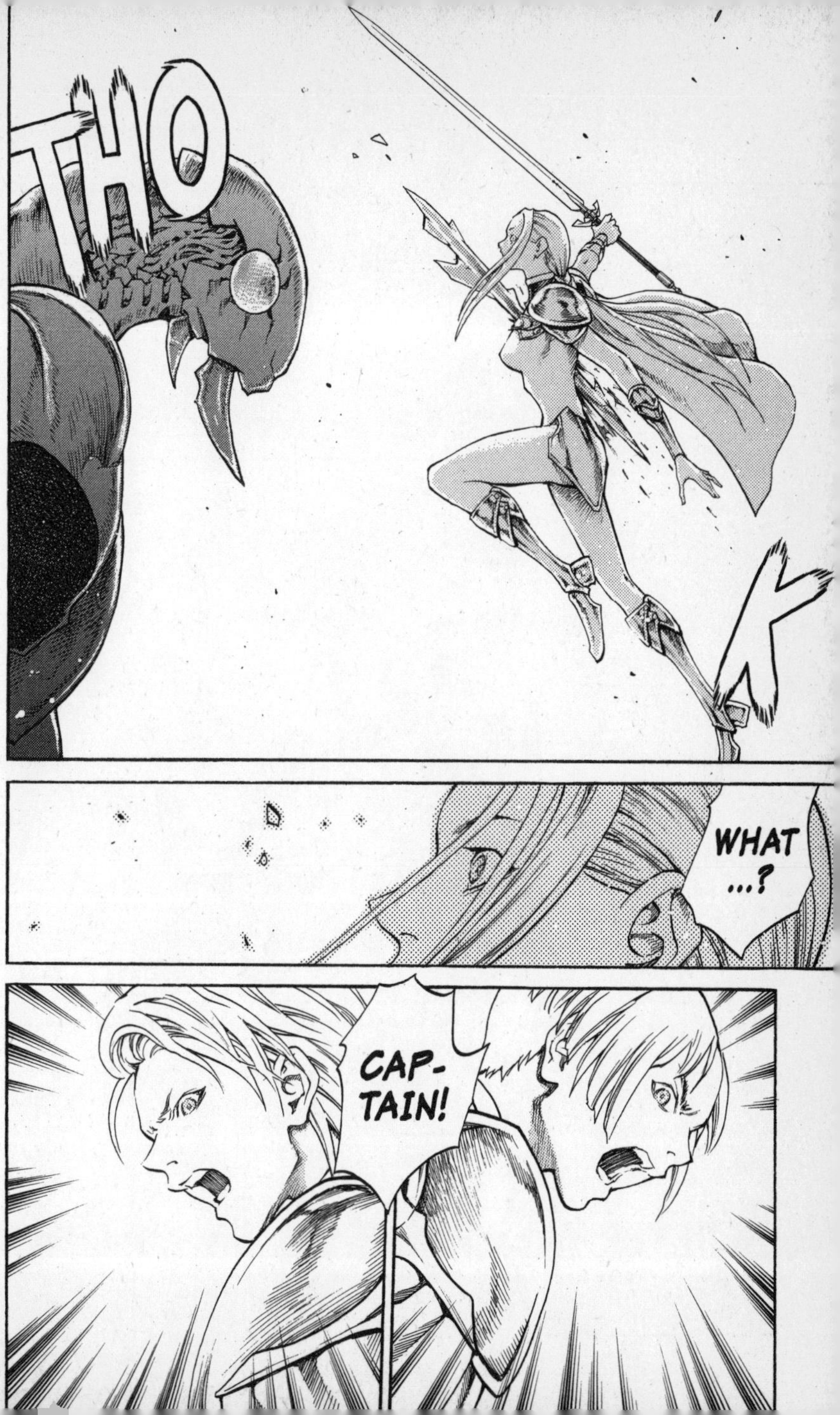
THO
WHAT ...?
CAP-
TAIN!

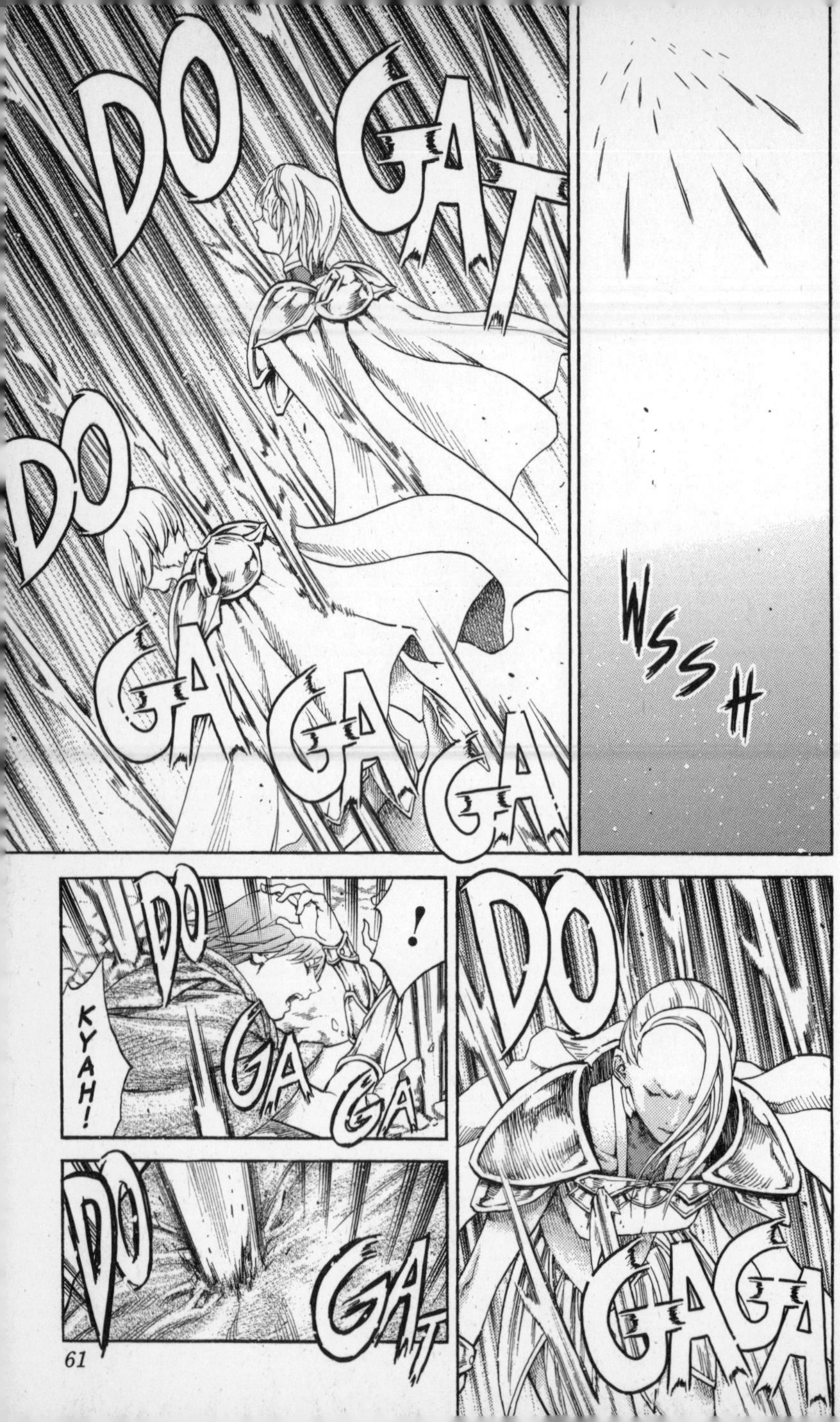
WSSH
DO GAT
DO GA GA GA
DO GAGA
!
DO GA GA
KYAH!
DO GAT

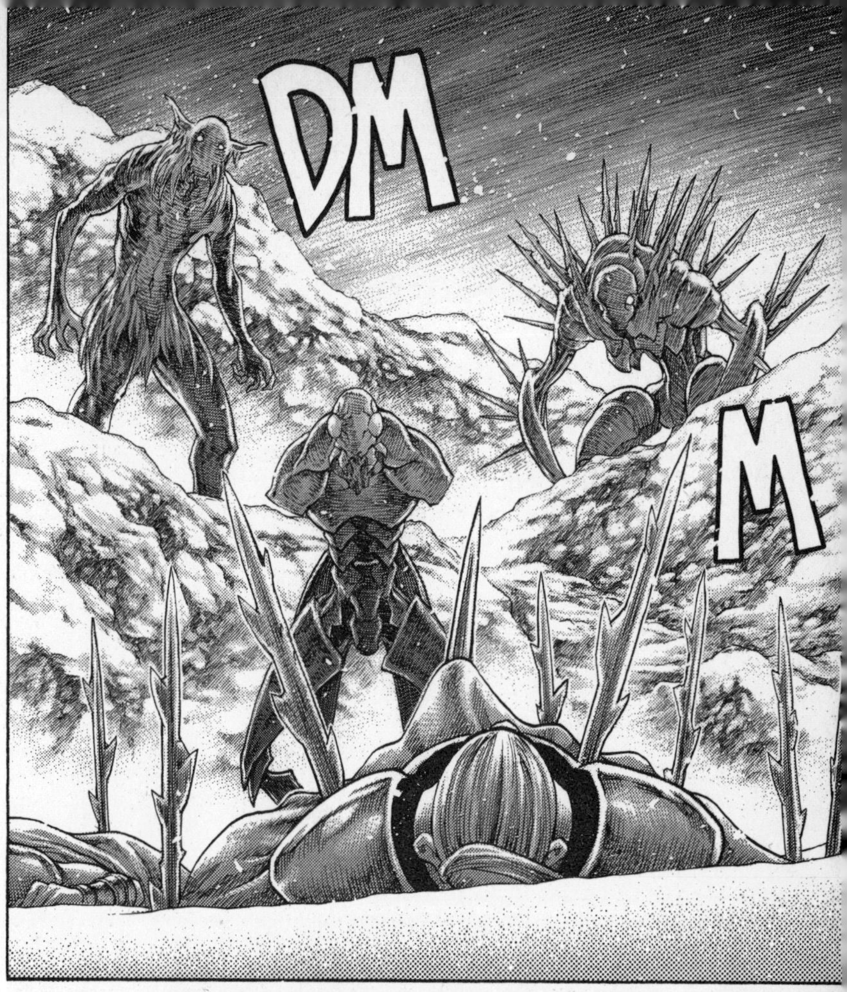
DM
M

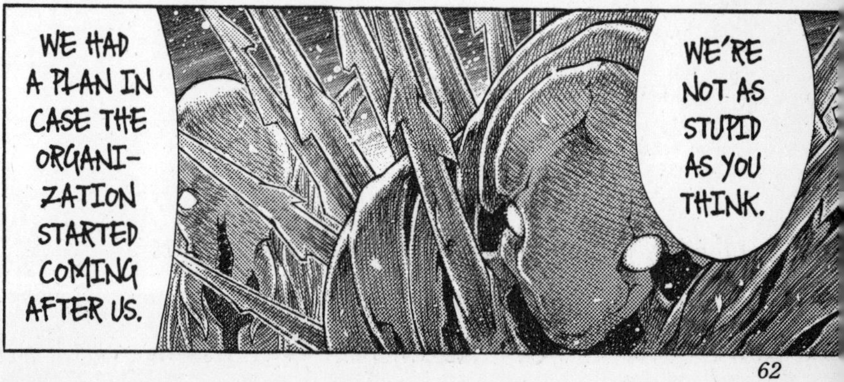
WE'RE NOT AS STUPID AS YOU THINK.
WE HAD A PLAN IN CASE THE ORGANI-ZATION STARTED COMING AFTER US.

READ THIS WAY

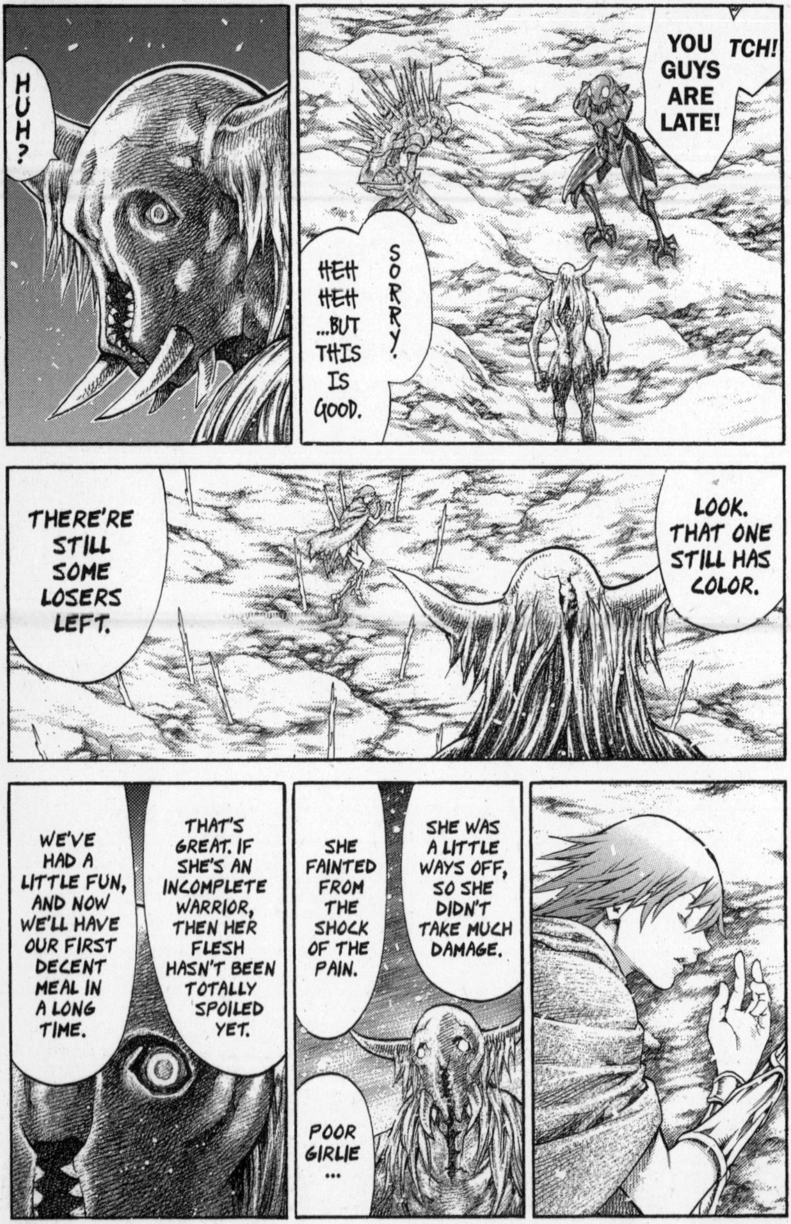
TCH!
YOU GUYS ARE LATE!
SORRY.
HEH HEH ...BUT THIS IS GOOD.
HUH?
LOOK. THAT ONE STILL HAS COLOR.
THERE'RE STILL SOME LOSERS LEFT.
SHE WAS A LITTLE WAYS OFF, SO SHE DIDN'T TAKE MUCH DAMAGE.
SHE FAINTED FROM THE SHOCK OF THE PAIN.
POOR GIRLIE ...
THAT'S GREAT. IF SHE'S AN INCOMPLETE WARRIOR, THEN HER FLESH HASN'T BEEN TOTALLY SPOILED YET.
WE'VE HAD A LITTLE FUN, AND NOW WE'LL HAVE OUR FIRST DECENT MEAL IN A LONG TIME.

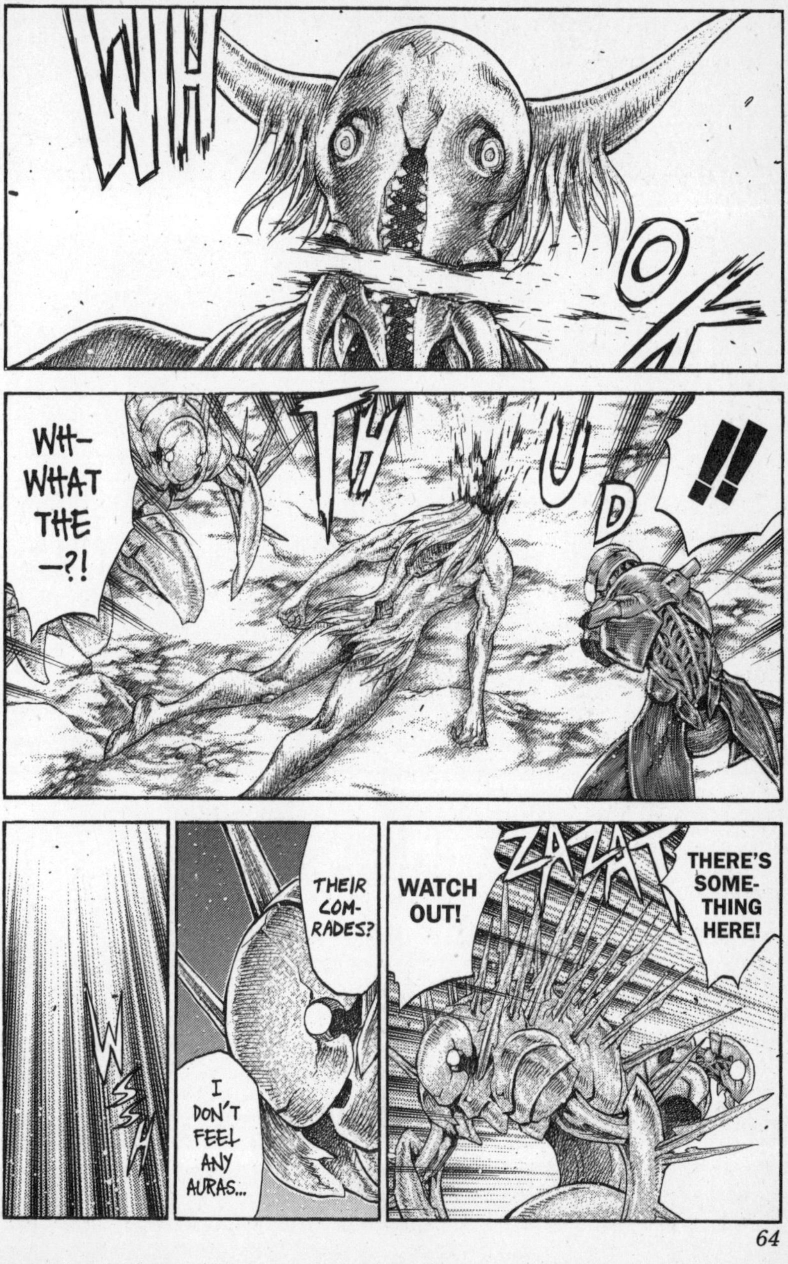
WH
THUD!!
WH-WHAT THE—?!
ZAZAT
THERE'S SOME-THING HERE!
WATCH OUT!
THEIR COM-RADES?
I DON'T FEEL ANY AURAS...
WSSH

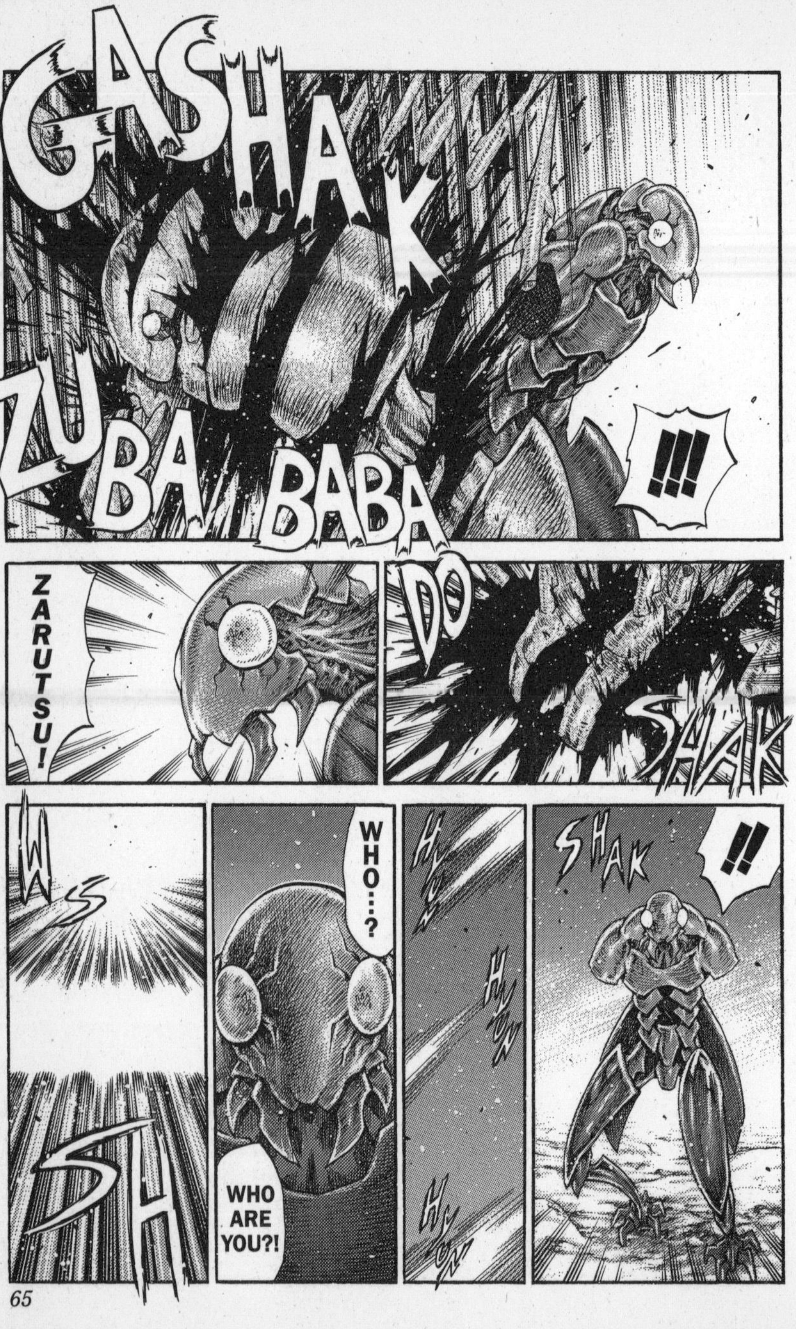
GASHAK
!!!
ZUBA BABA
DO
SHAK
ZARUTSU!
SHAK
!!
WHO…?
WHO ARE YOU?!
SH

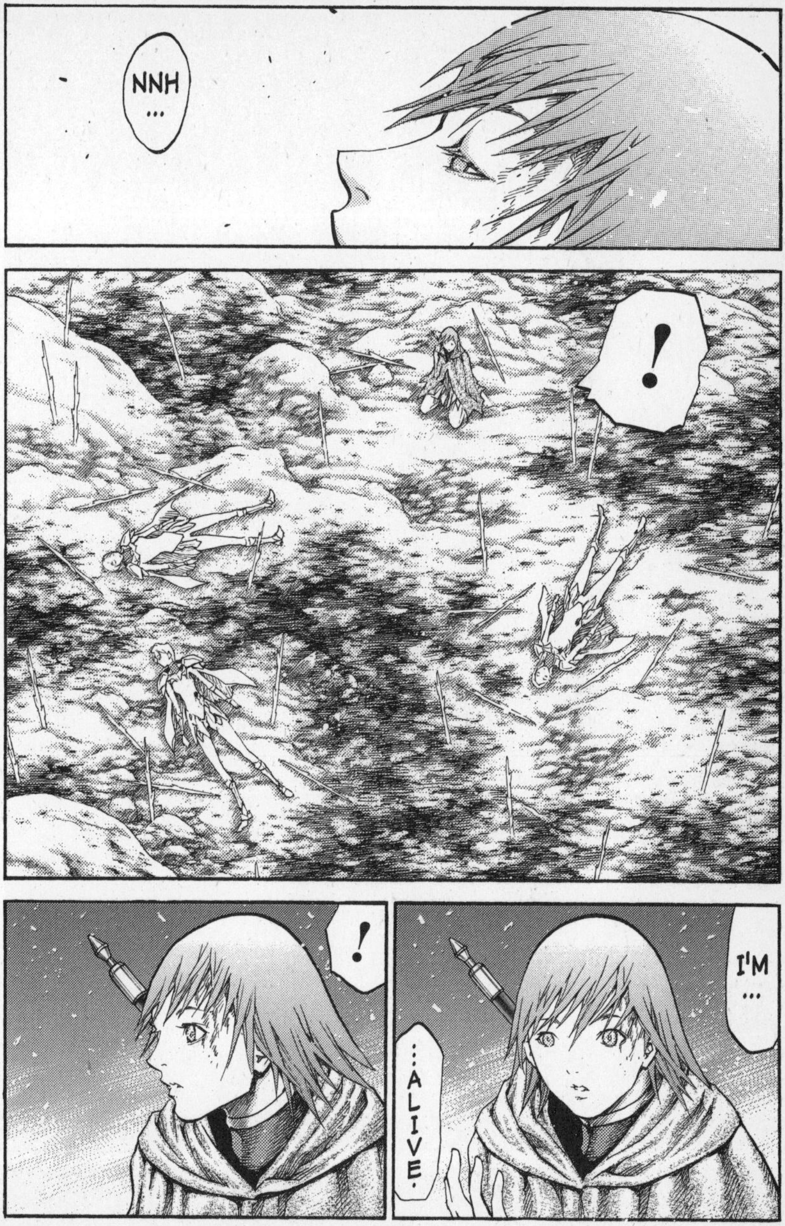
NNH ...
!
I'M ...
...ALIVE.
!

READ THIS WAY

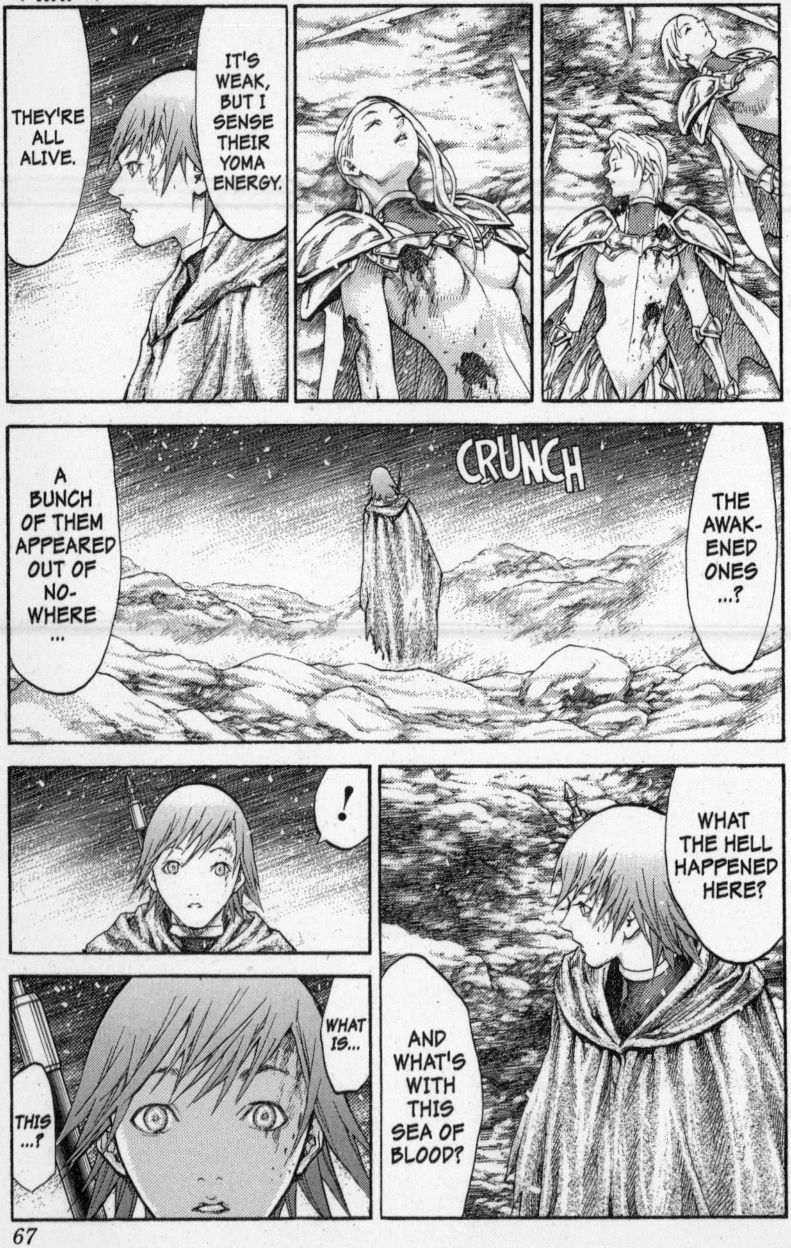
IT'S WEAK, BUT I SENSE THEIR YOMA ENERGY.
THEY'RE ALL ALIVE.
CRUNCH
THE AWAKENED ONES ...?
A BUNCH OF THEM APPEARED OUT OF NO-WHERE ...
WHAT THE HELL HAPPENED HERE?
AND WHAT'S WITH THIS SEA OF BLOOD?
!
WHAT IS...
THIS ...?

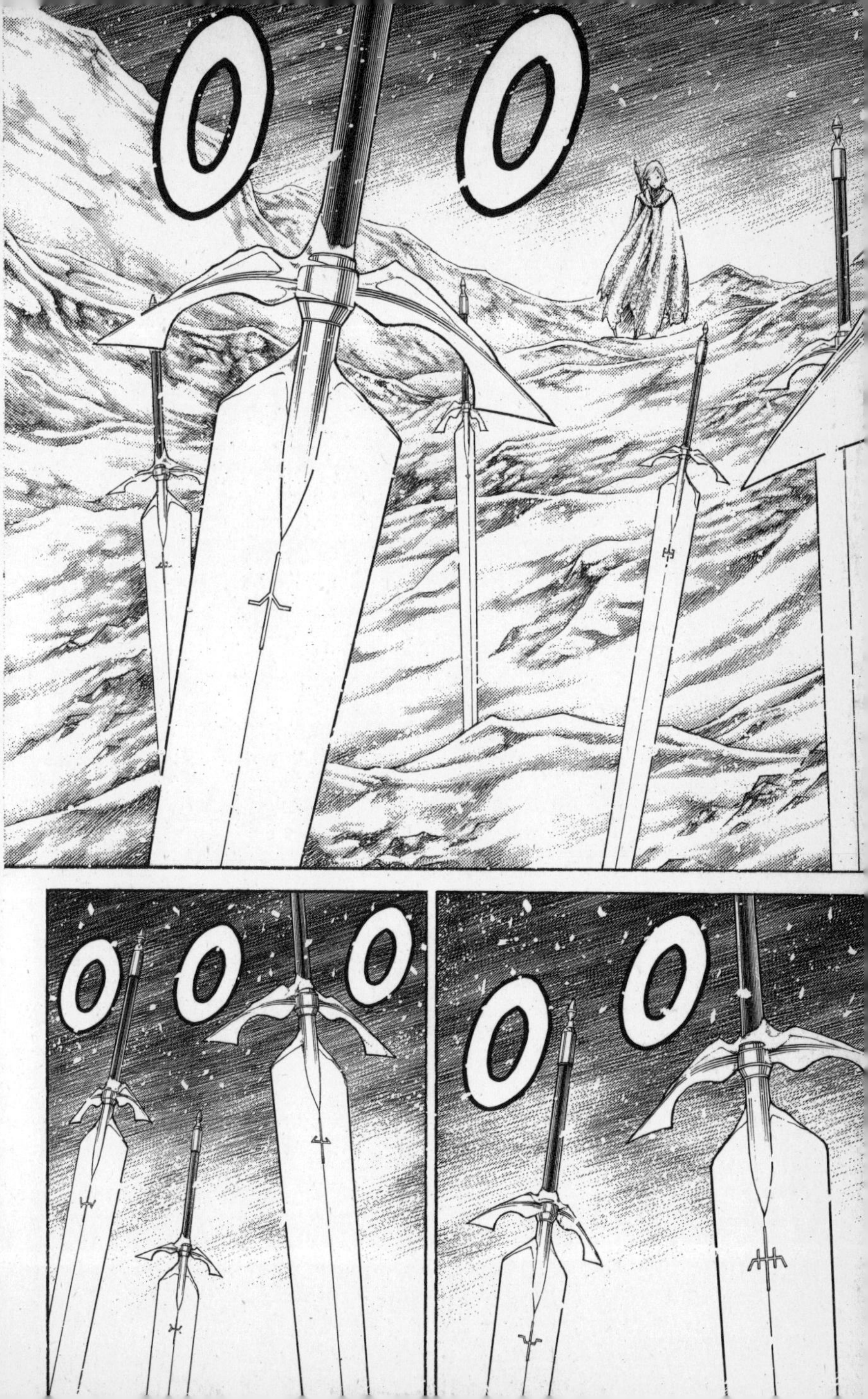
O O
O O
O O O

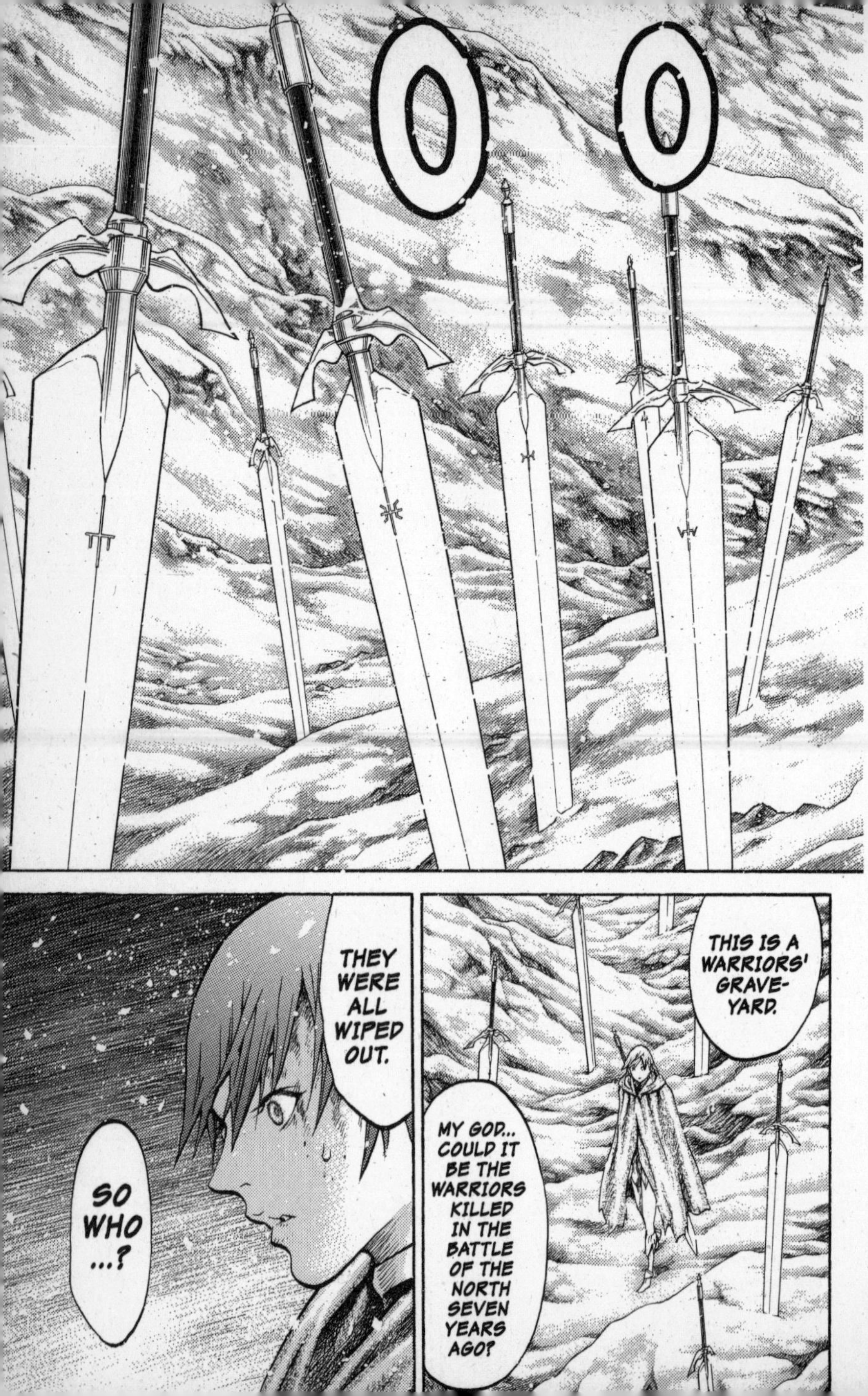
THIS IS A WARRIORS' GRAVEYARD.
MY GOD... COULD IT BE THE WARRIORS KILLED IN THE BATTLE OF THE NORTH SEVEN YEARS AGO?
THEY WERE ALL WIPED OUT.
SO WHO ...?

クレイモア
Claymore

Scene 66: The Souls of the Fallen, Part 2

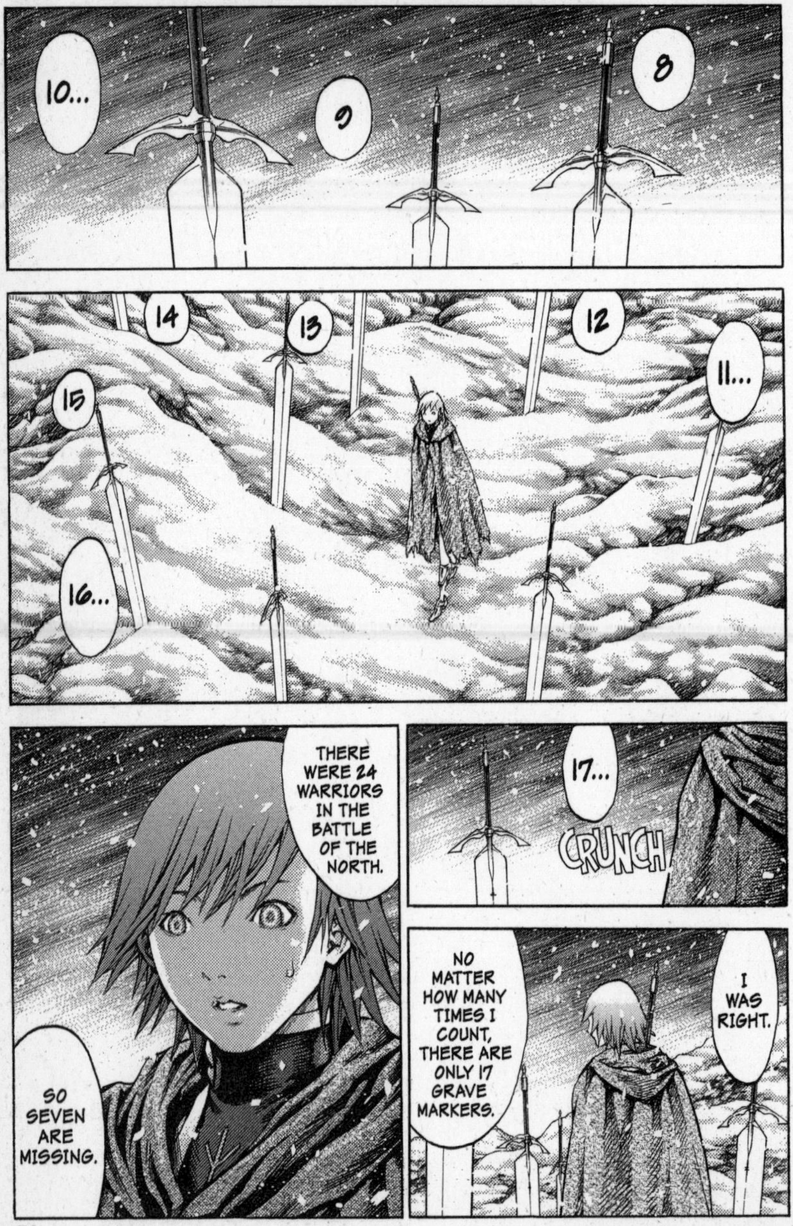
8
9
10...
11...
12
13
14
15
16...
17...
CRUNCH
I WAS RIGHT.
NO MATTER HOW MANY TIMES I COUNT, THERE ARE ONLY 17 GRAVE MARKERS.
THERE WERE 24 WARRIORS IN THE BATTLE OF THE NORTH.
SO SEVEN ARE MISSING.

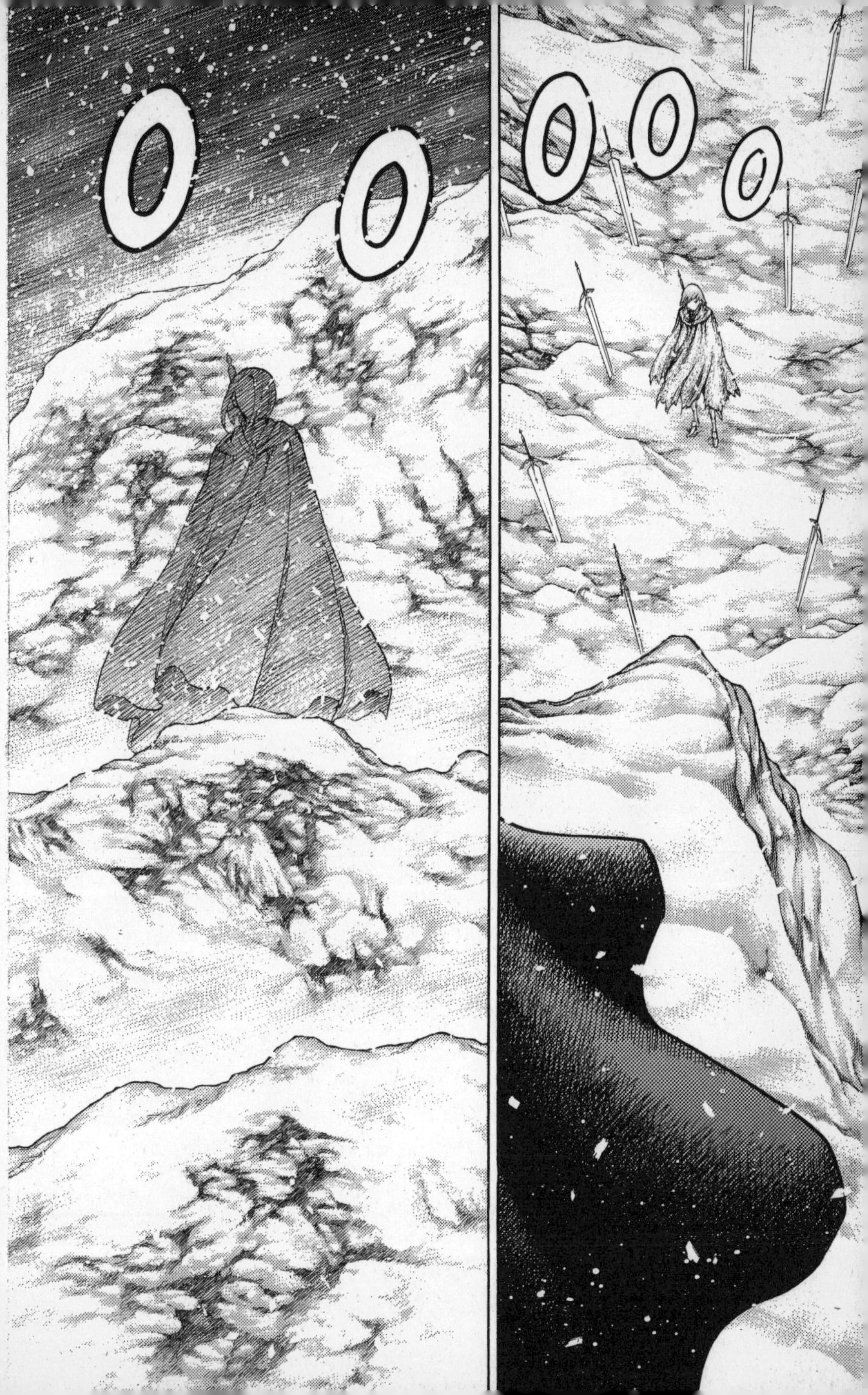
O
O
O
O
O

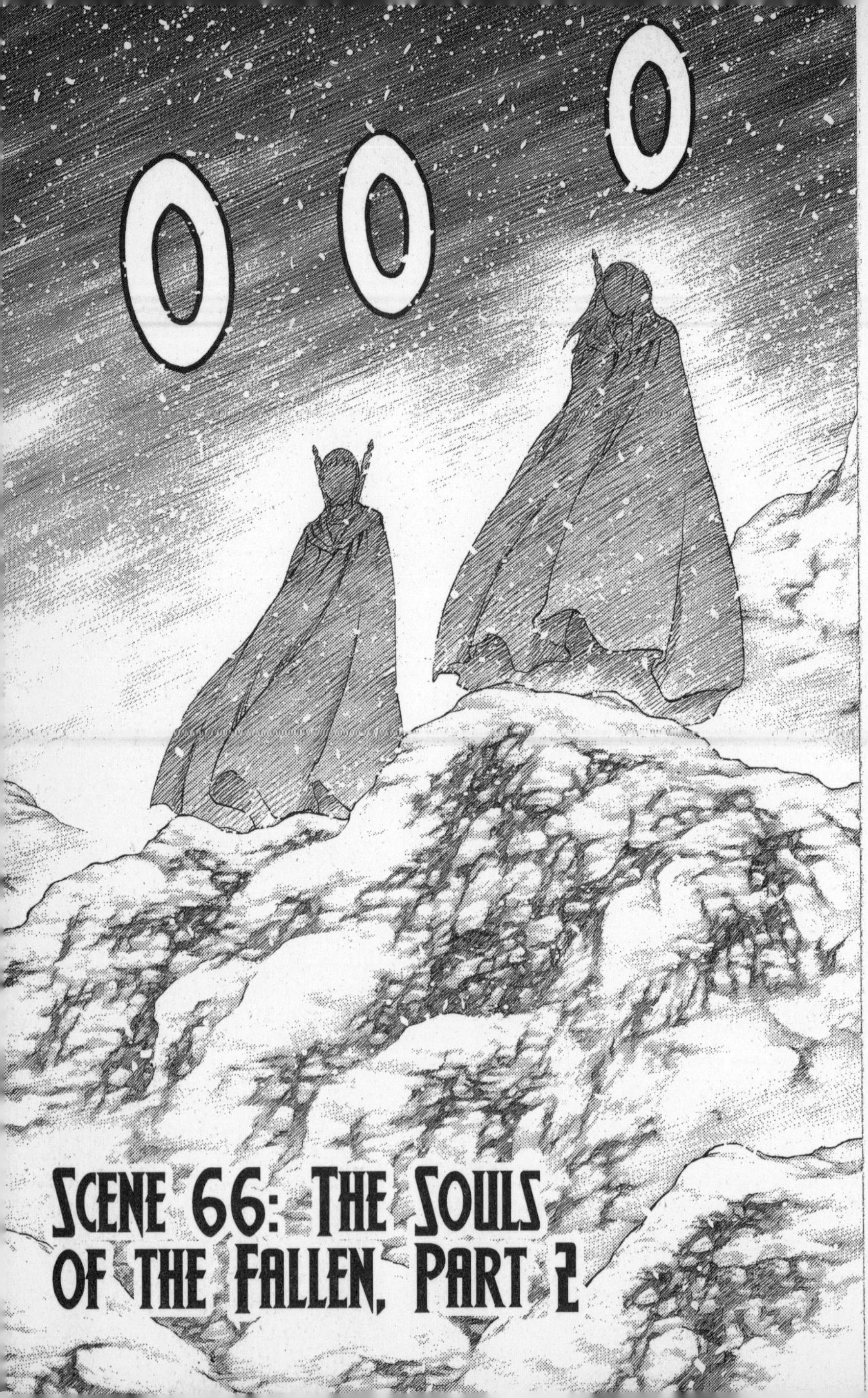
OOO
SCENE 66: THE SOULS OF THE FALLEN, PART 2

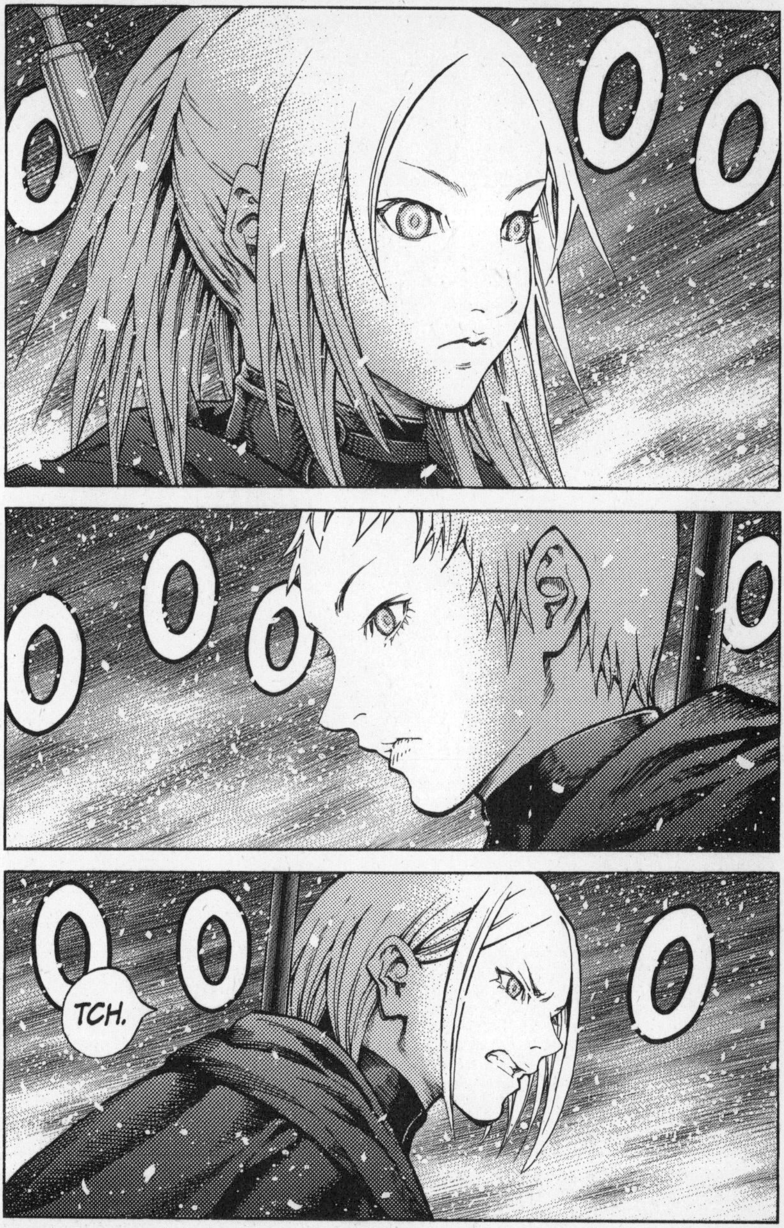
TCH.

READ THIS WAY

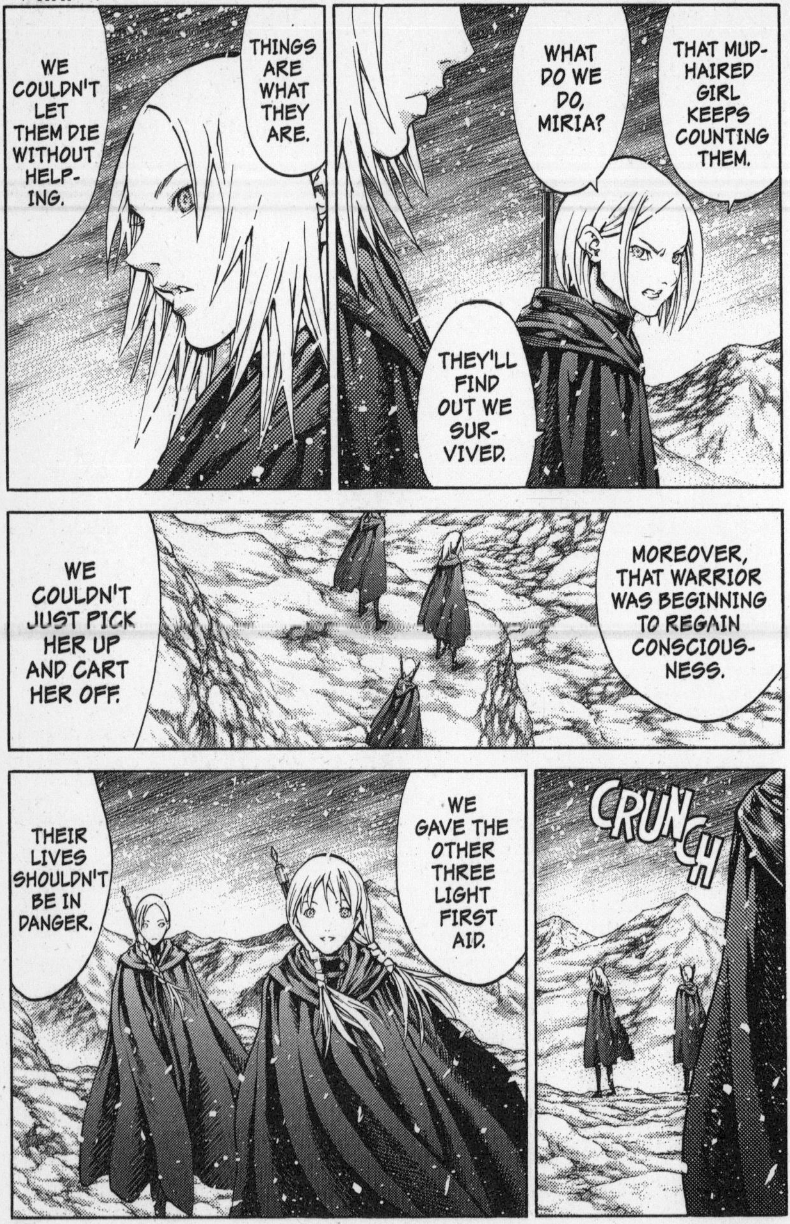
THAT MUD-HAIRED GIRL KEEPS COUNTING THEM.
WHAT DO WE DO, MIRIA?
THEY'LL FIND OUT WE SURVIVED.
THINGS ARE WHAT THEY ARE.
WE COULDN'T LET THEM DIE WITHOUT HELPING.
MOREOVER, THAT WARRIOR WAS BEGINNING TO REGAIN CONSCIOUSNESS.
WE COULDN'T JUST PICK HER UP AND CART HER OFF.
CRUNCH
WE GAVE THE OTHER THREE LIGHT FIRST AID.
THEIR LIVES SHOULDN'T BE IN DANGER.

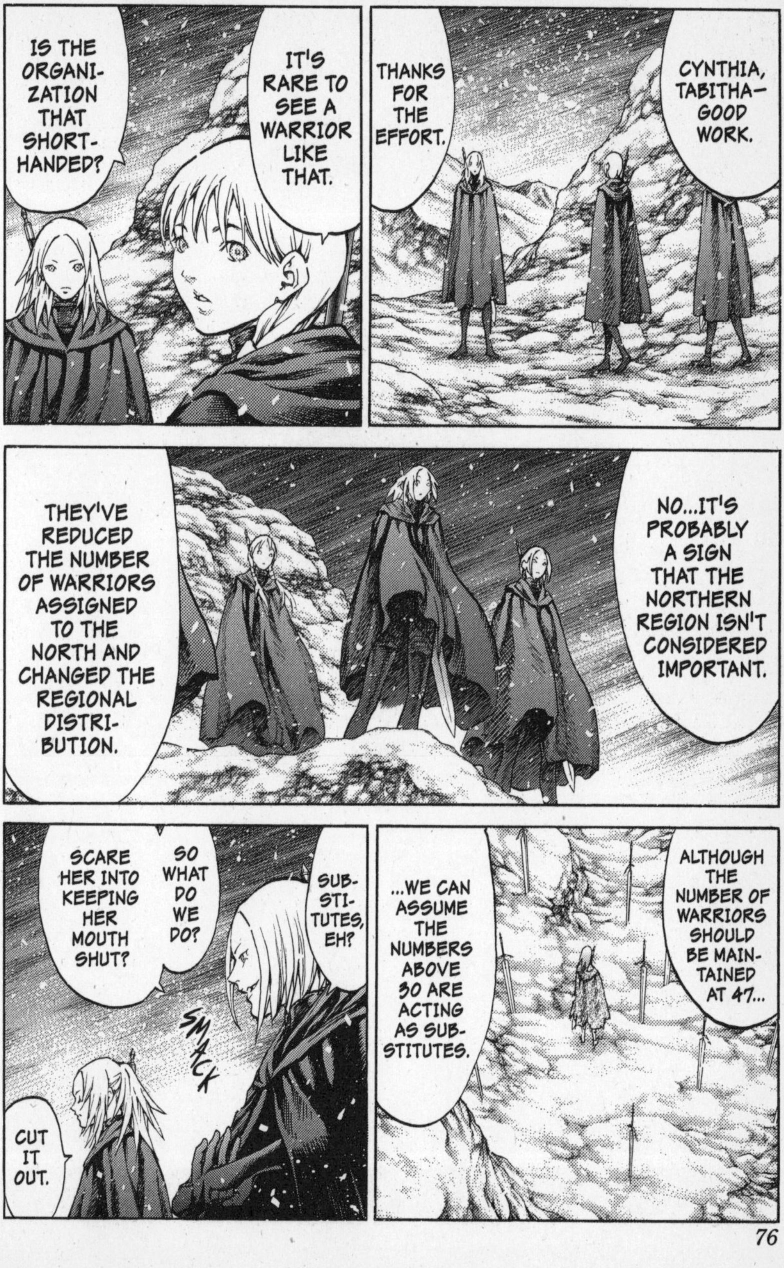
CYNTHIA, TABITHA—GOOD WORK.
THANKS FOR THE EFFORT.
IT'S RARE TO SEE A WARRIOR LIKE THAT.
IS THE ORGANIZATION THAT SHORTHANDED?
NO...IT'S PROBABLY A SIGN THAT THE NORTHERN REGION ISN'T CONSIDERED IMPORTANT.
THEY'VE REDUCED THE NUMBER OF WARRIORS ASSIGNED TO THE NORTH AND CHANGED THE REGIONAL DISTRIBUTION.
ALTHOUGH THE NUMBER OF WARRIORS SHOULD BE MAINTAINED AT 47...
...WE CAN ASSUME THE NUMBERS ABOVE 30 ARE ACTING AS SUBSTITUTES.
SUBSTITUTES, EH?
SO WHAT DO WE DO?
SCARE HER INTO KEEPING HER MOUTH SHUT?
SMACK
CUT IT OUT.

READ THIS WAY

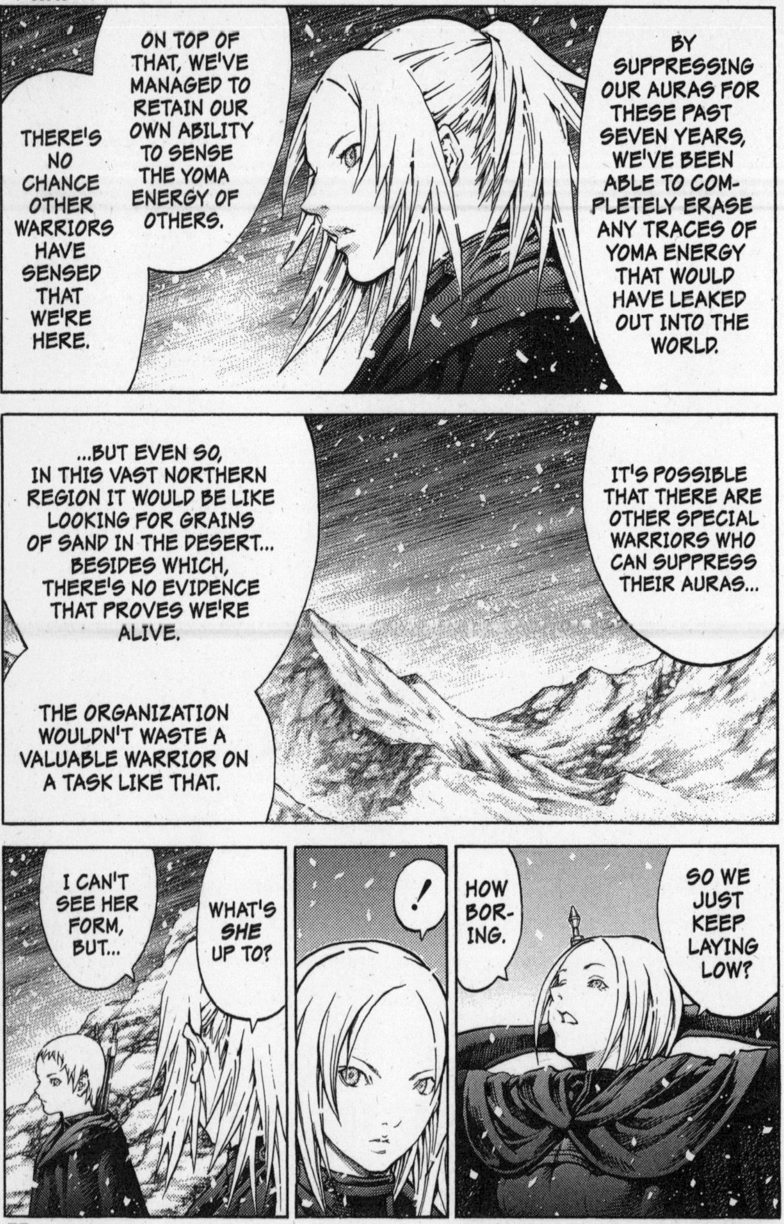
BY SUPPRESSING OUR AURAS FOR THESE PAST SEVEN YEARS, WE'VE BEEN ABLE TO COMPLETELY ERASE ANY TRACES OF YOMA ENERGY THAT WOULD HAVE LEAKED OUT INTO THE WORLD.
ON TOP OF THAT, WE'VE MANAGED TO RETAIN OUR OWN ABILITY TO SENSE THE YOMA ENERGY OF OTHERS.
THERE'S NO CHANCE OTHER WARRIORS HAVE SENSED THAT WE'RE HERE.
IT'S POSSIBLE THAT THERE ARE OTHER SPECIAL WARRIORS WHO CAN SUPPRESS THEIR AURAS...
...BUT EVEN SO, IN THIS VAST NORTHERN REGION IT WOULD BE LIKE LOOKING FOR GRAINS OF SAND IN THE DESERT... BESIDES WHICH, THERE'S NO EVIDENCE THAT PROVES WE'RE ALIVE.
THE ORGANIZATION WOULDN'T WASTE A VALUABLE WARRIOR ON A TASK LIKE THAT.
SO WE JUST KEEP LAYING LOW?
HOW BOR-ING.
!
WHAT'S SHE UP TO?
I CAN'T SEE HER FORM, BUT...

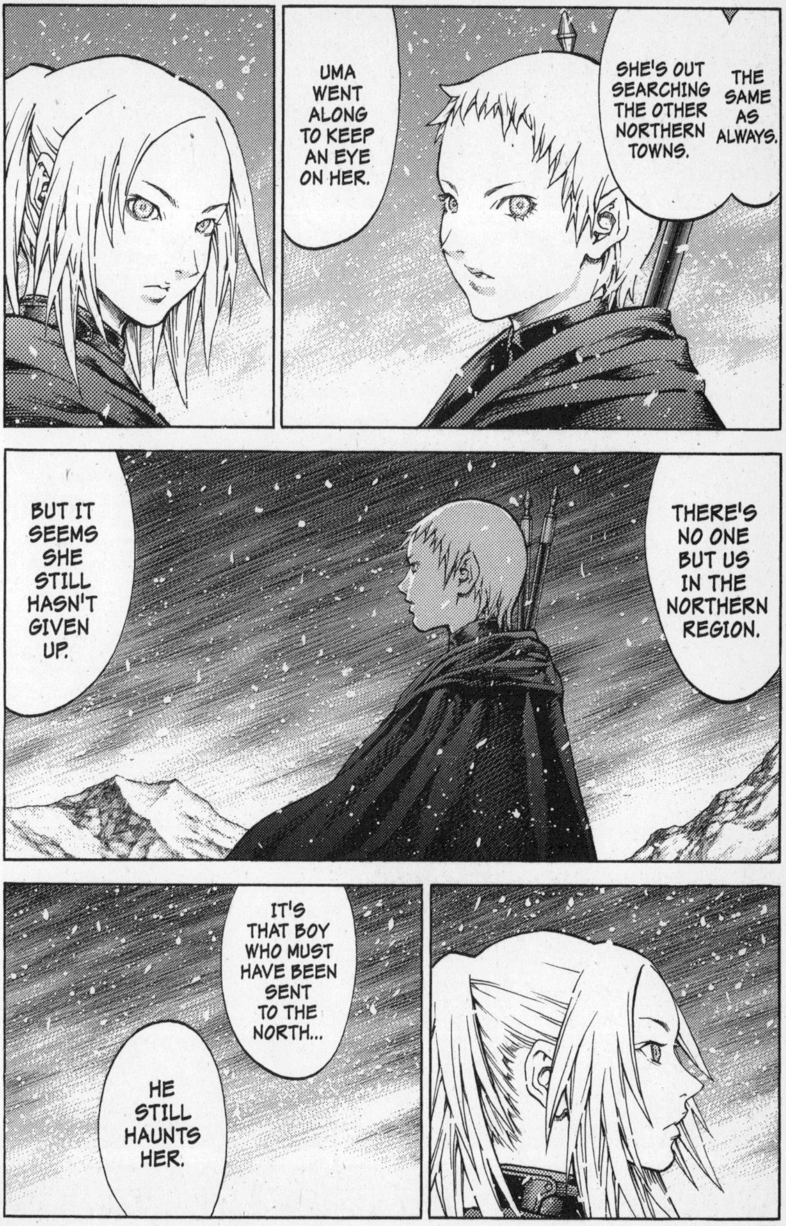
THE SAME AS ALWAYS.
SHE'S OUT SEARCHING THE OTHER NORTHERN TOWNS.
UMA WENT ALONG TO KEEP AN EYE ON HER.
THERE'S NO ONE BUT US IN THE NORTHERN REGION.
BUT IT SEEMS SHE STILL HASN'T GIVEN UP.
IT'S THAT BOY WHO MUST HAVE BEEN SENT TO THE NORTH...
HE STILL HAUNTS HER.

READ THIS WAY

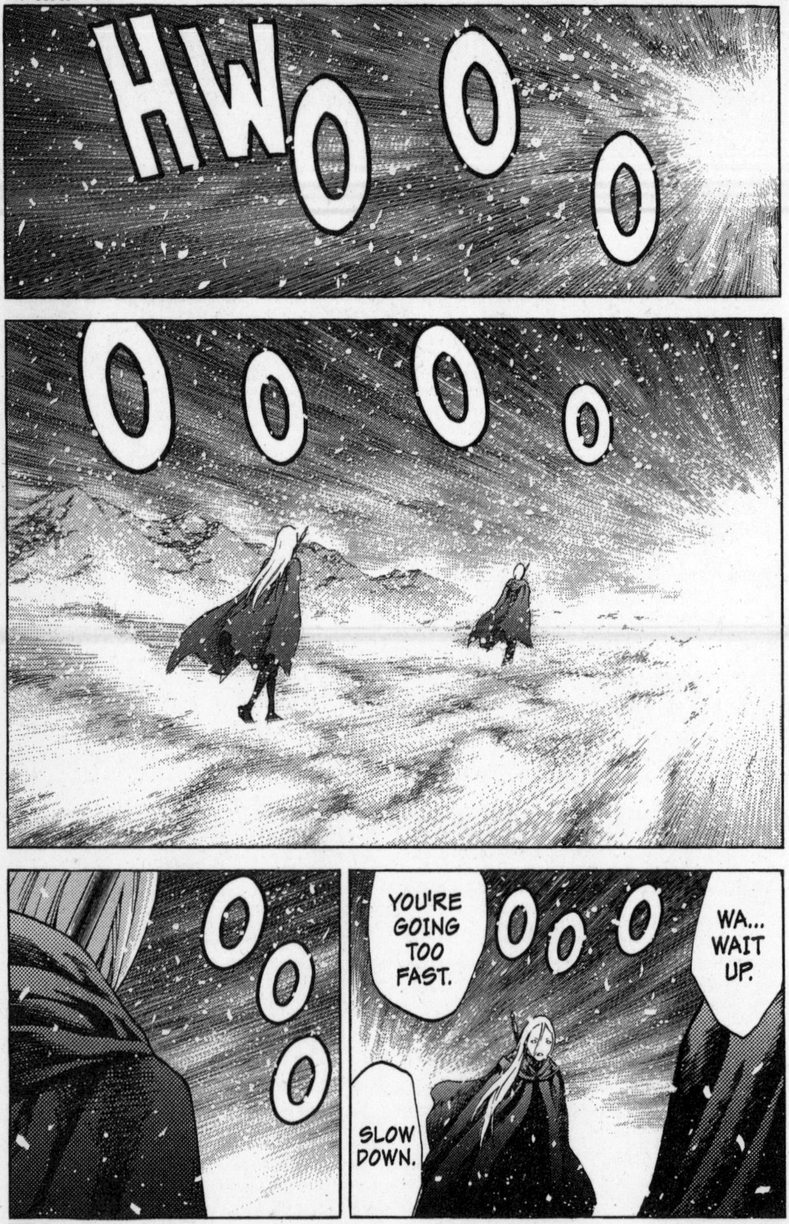
HWOOOO
OOOO
WA... WAIT UP.
YOU'RE GOING TOO FAST.
OOO
SLOW DOWN.
OOO

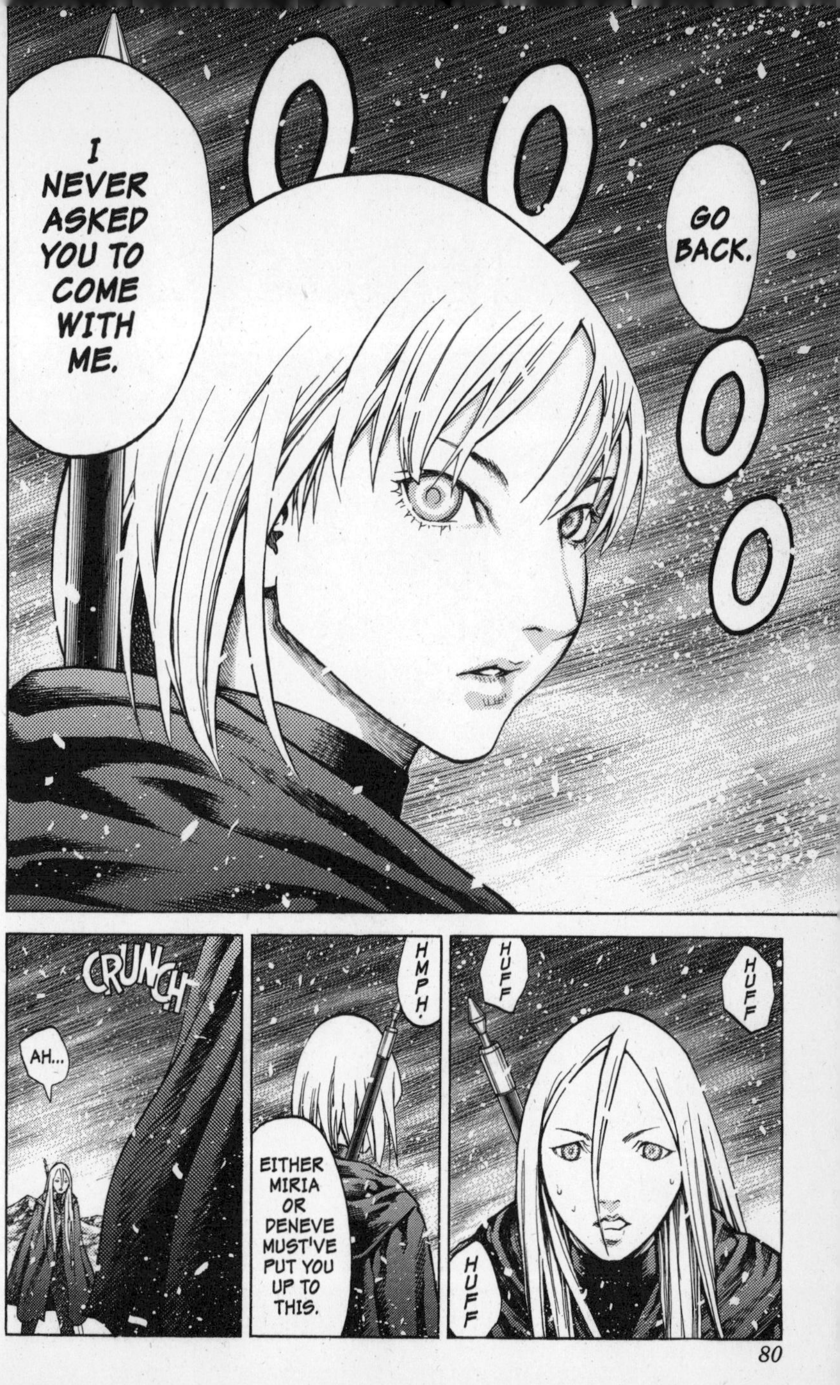
GO BACK.
I NEVER ASKED YOU TO COME WITH ME.
HUFF
HUFF
HUFF
HMPH.
EITHER MIRIA OR DENEVE MUST'VE PUT YOU UP TO THIS.
CRUNCH
AH...

READ THIS WAY

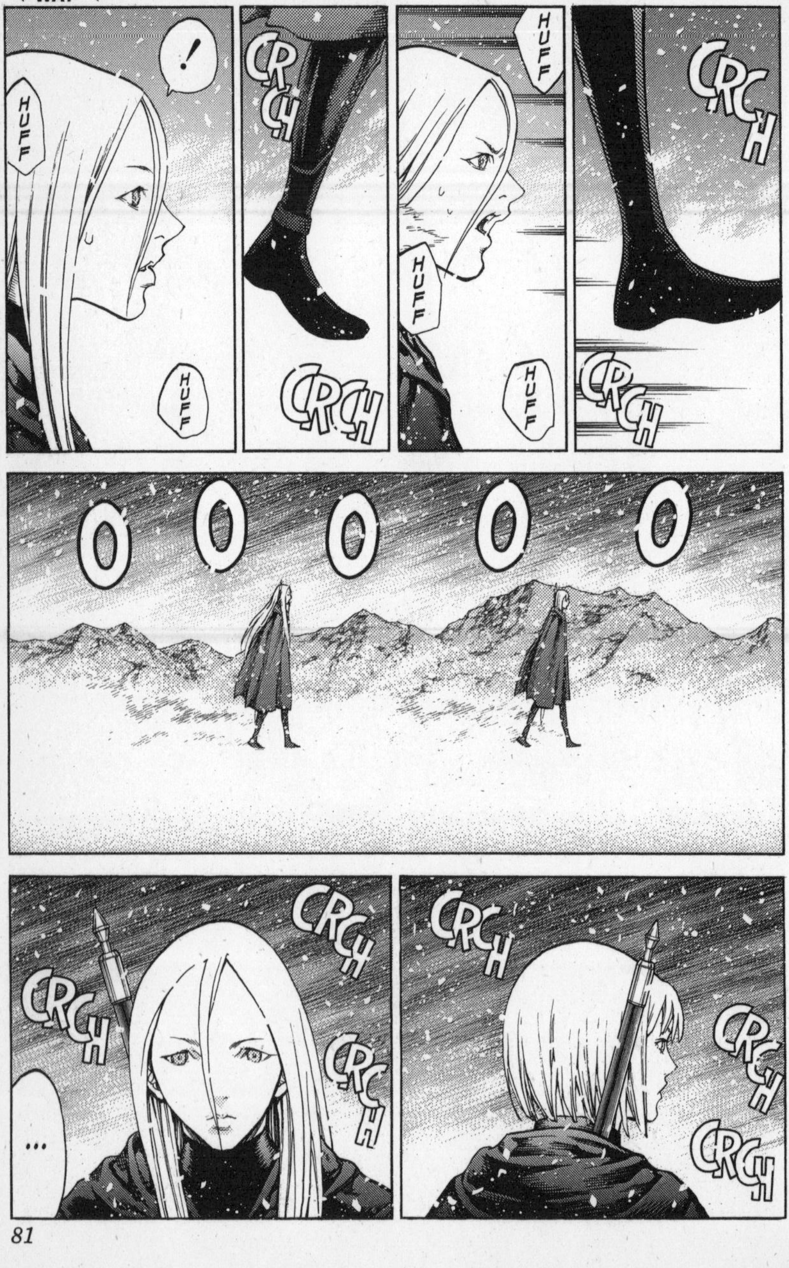

CRCH
CRCH
HUFF
HUFF
HUFF
CRCH
CRCH
!
HUFF
HUFF
OOOOO
CRCH
CRCH
CRCH
CRCH
CRCH
CRCH
CRCH
...

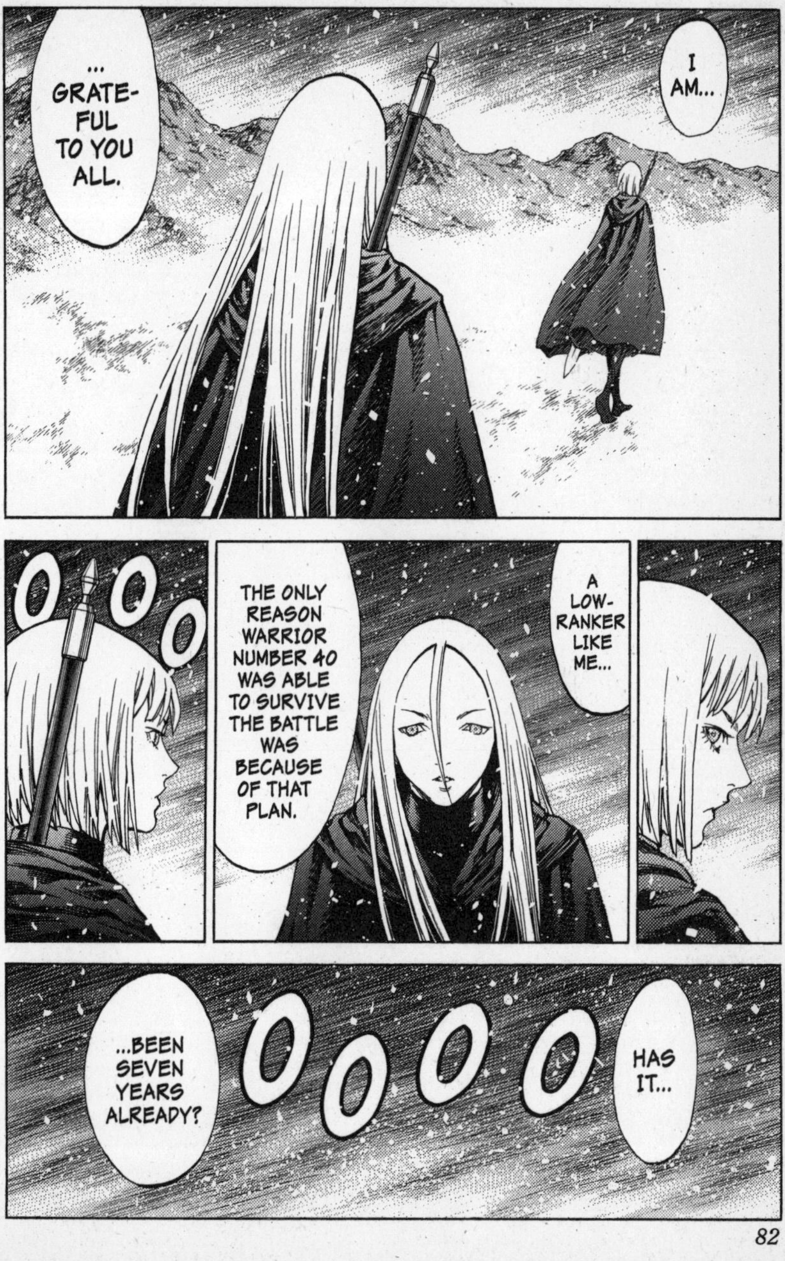
I AM...
... GRATE-FUL TO YOU ALL.
A LOW-RANKER LIKE ME...
THE ONLY REASON WARRIOR NUMBER 40 WAS ABLE TO SURVIVE THE BATTLE WAS BECAUSE OF THAT PLAN.
HAS IT...
...BEEN SEVEN YEARS ALREADY?

READ THIS WAY

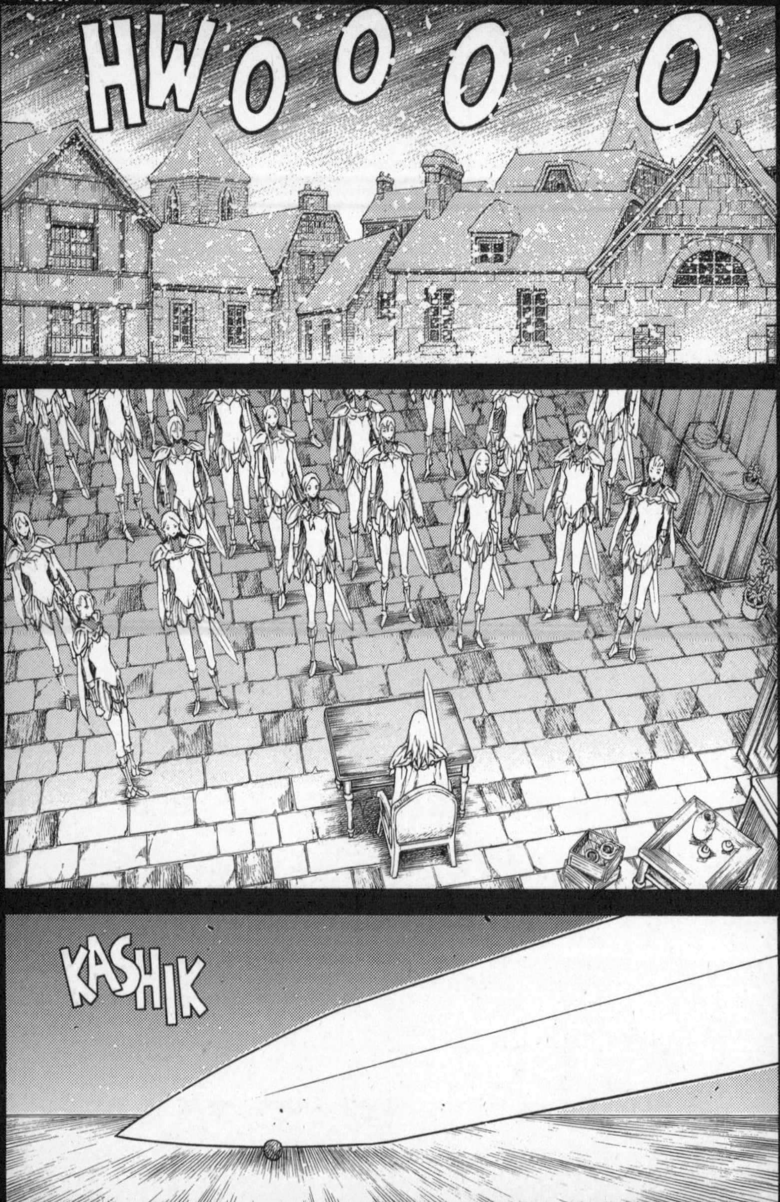
HWOOOO
KASHIK

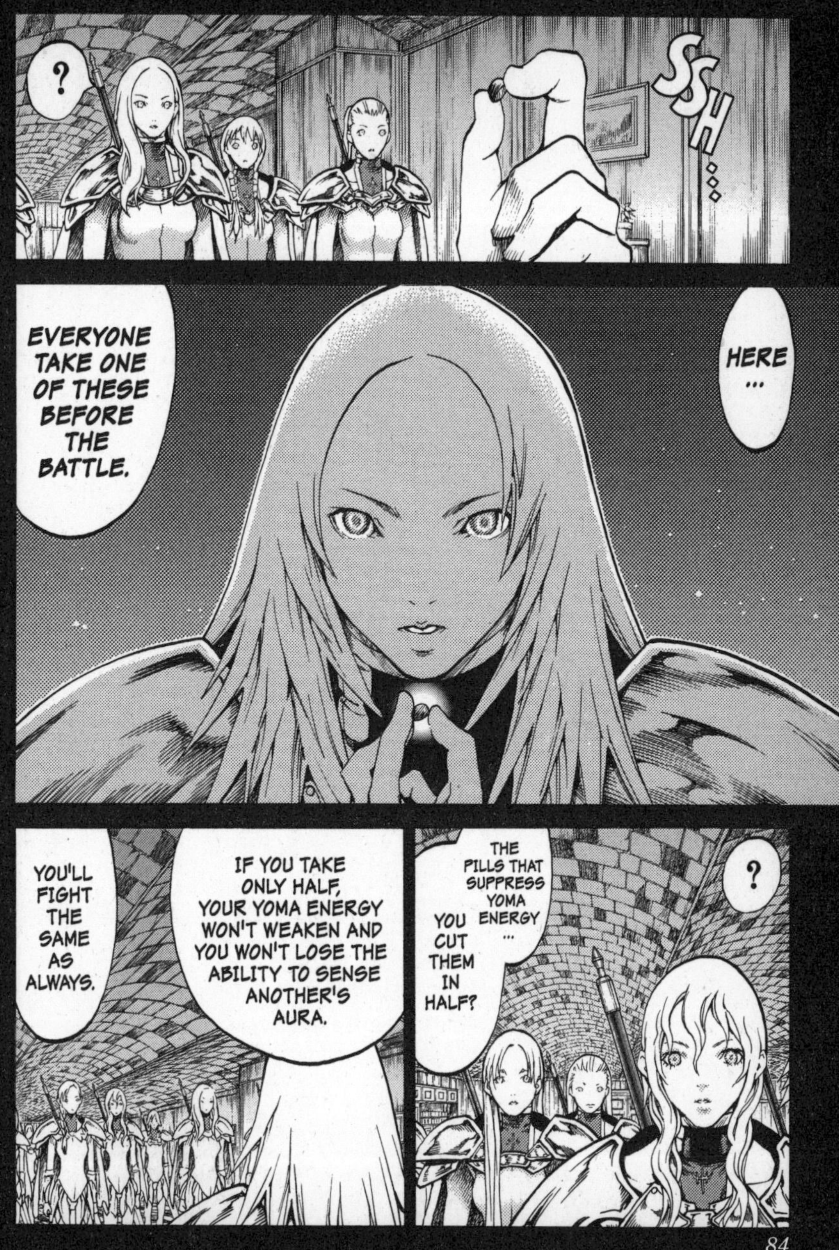
SSH...
?
HERE...
EVERYONE TAKE ONE OF THESE BEFORE THE BATTLE.
?
THE PILLS THAT SUPPRESS YOMA ENERGY...
YOU CUT THEM IN HALF?
IF YOU TAKE ONLY HALF, YOUR YOMA ENERGY WON'T WEAKEN AND YOU WON'T LOSE THE ABILITY TO SENSE ANOTHER'S AURA.
YOU'LL FIGHT THE SAME AS ALWAYS.

READ THIS WAY

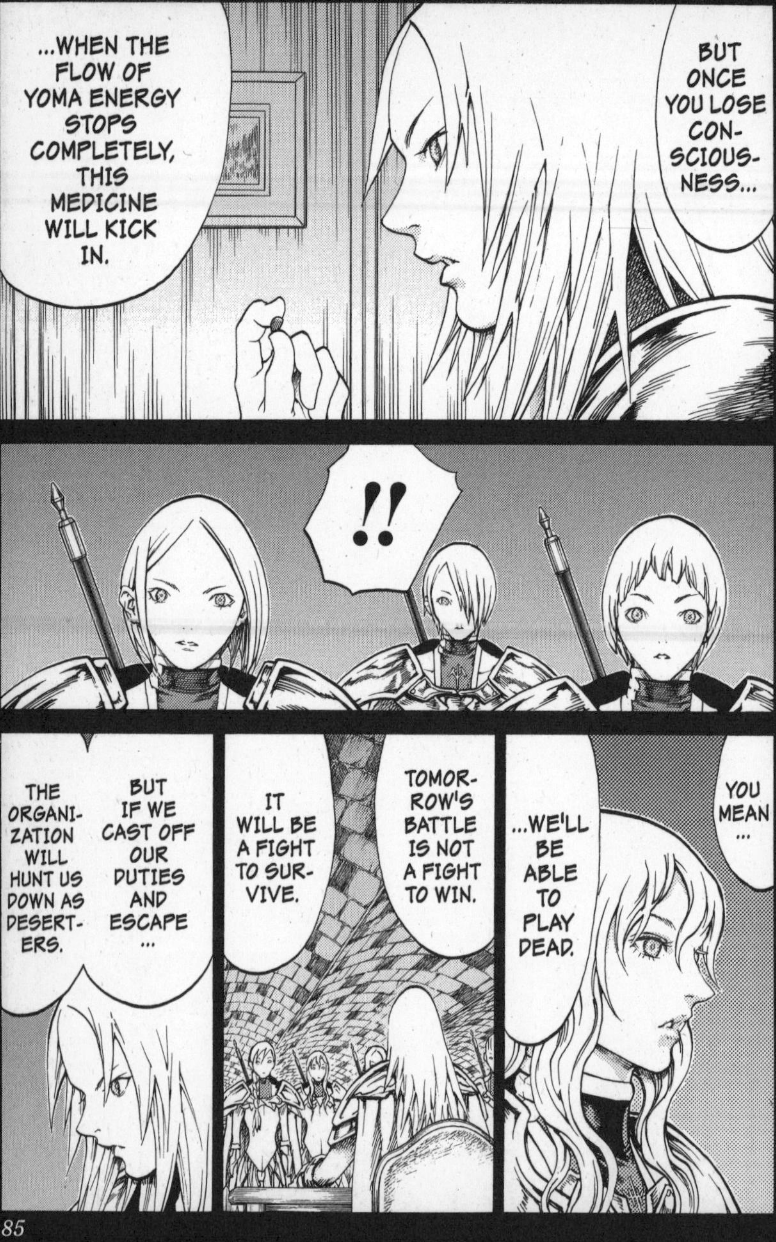
BUT ONCE YOU LOSE CONSCIOUSNESS...
...WHEN THE FLOW OF YOMA ENERGY STOPS COMPLETELY, THIS MEDICINE WILL KICK IN.
!!
YOU MEAN...
...WE'LL BE ABLE TO PLAY DEAD.
TOMORROW'S BATTLE IS NOT A FIGHT TO WIN.
IT WILL BE A FIGHT TO SURVIVE.
BUT IF WE CAST OFF OUR DUTIES AND ESCAPE...
THE ORGANIZATION WILL HUNT US DOWN AS DESERTERS.

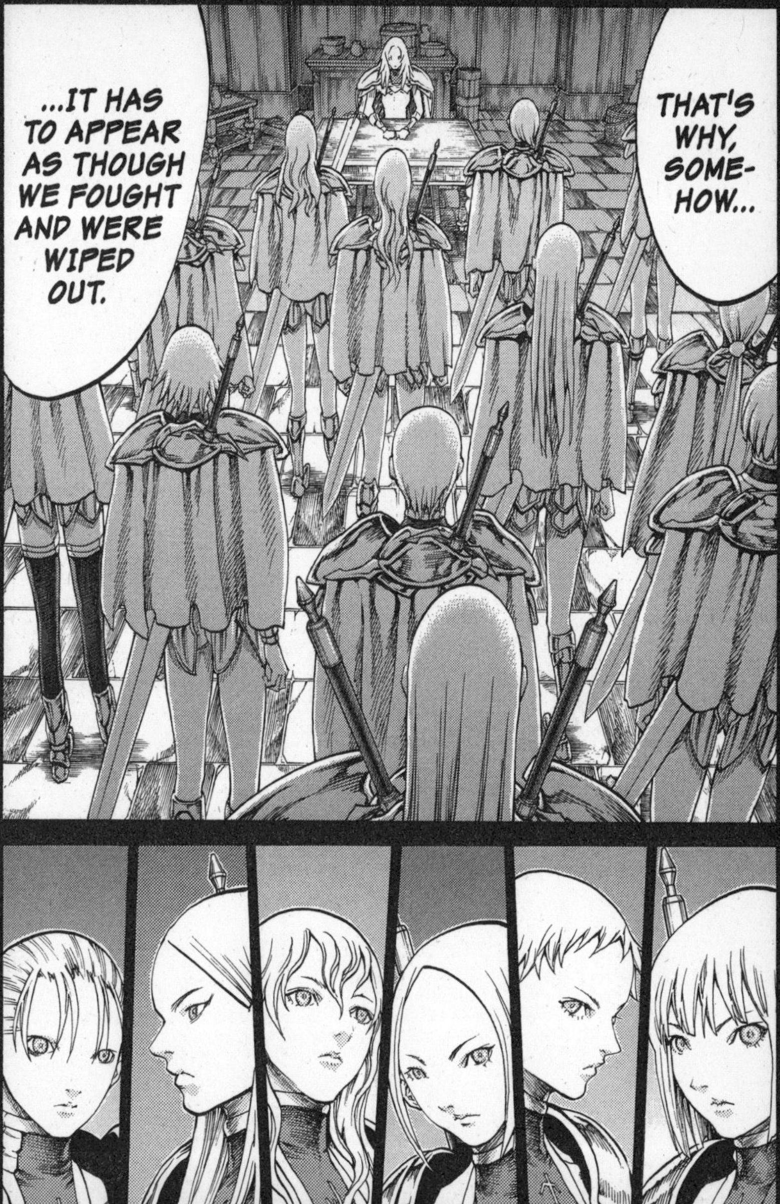
THAT'S WHY, SOME-HOW...
...IT HAS TO APPEAR AS THOUGH WE FOUGHT AND WERE WIPED OUT.

READ THIS WAY

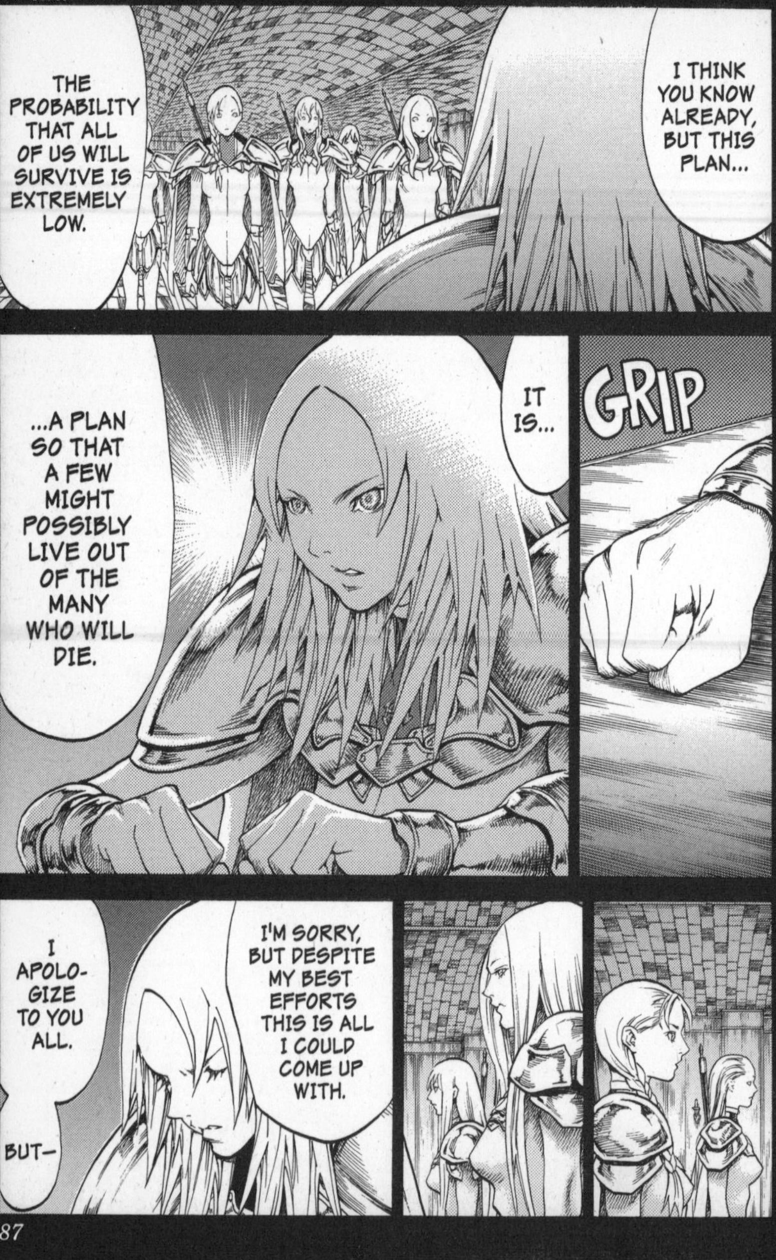

I THINK YOU KNOW ALREADY, BUT THIS PLAN...
THE PROBABILITY THAT ALL OF US WILL SURVIVE IS EXTREMELY LOW.
GRIP
IT IS...
...A PLAN SO THAT A FEW MIGHT POSSIBLY LIVE OUT OF THE MANY WHO WILL DIE.
I'M SORRY, BUT DESPITE MY BEST EFFORTS THIS IS ALL I COULD COME UP WITH.
I APOLO-GIZE TO YOU ALL.
BUT—

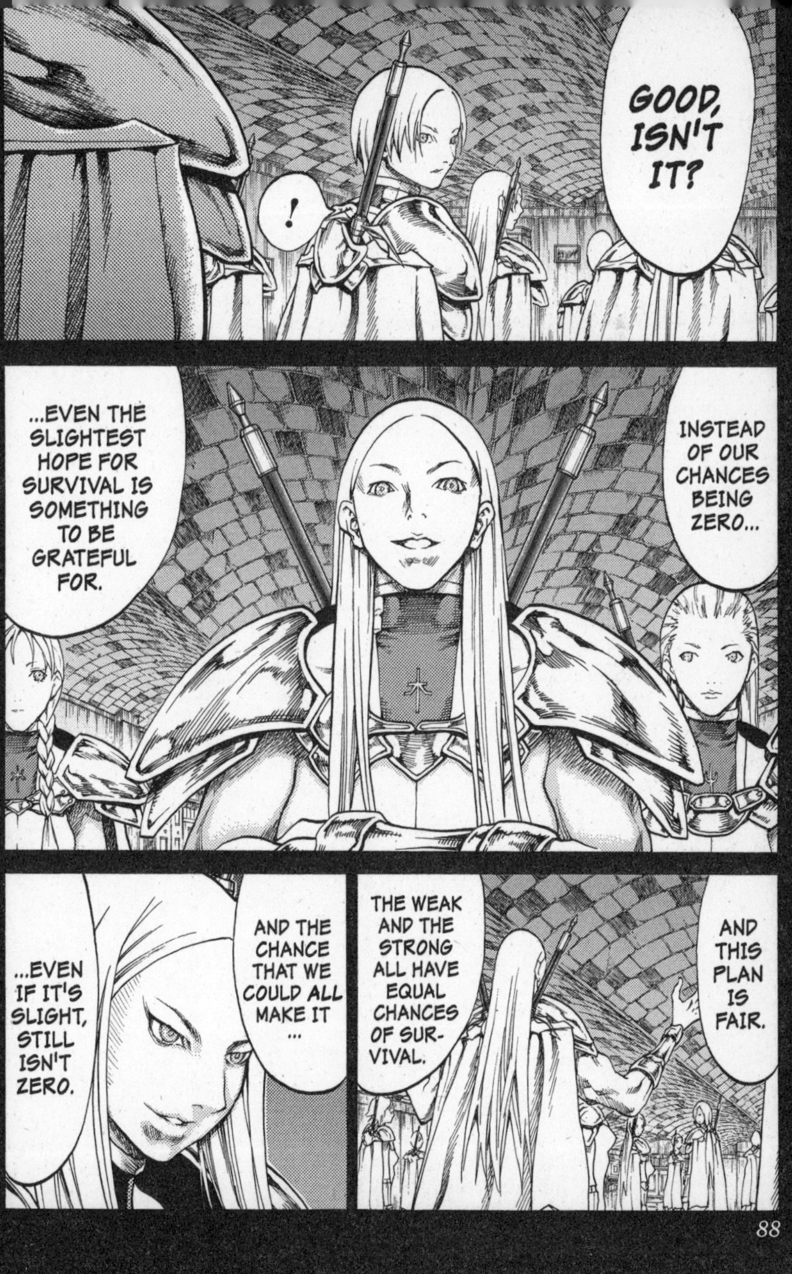
GOOD, ISN'T IT?
!
INSTEAD OF OUR CHANCES BEING ZERO...
...EVEN THE SLIGHTEST HOPE FOR SURVIVAL IS SOMETHING TO BE GRATEFUL FOR.
AND THIS PLAN IS FAIR.
THE WEAK AND THE STRONG ALL HAVE EQUAL CHANCES OF SUR-VIVAL.
AND THE CHANCE THAT WE COULD ALL MAKE IT ...
...EVEN IF IT'S SLIGHT, STILL ISN'T ZERO.

READ THIS WAY

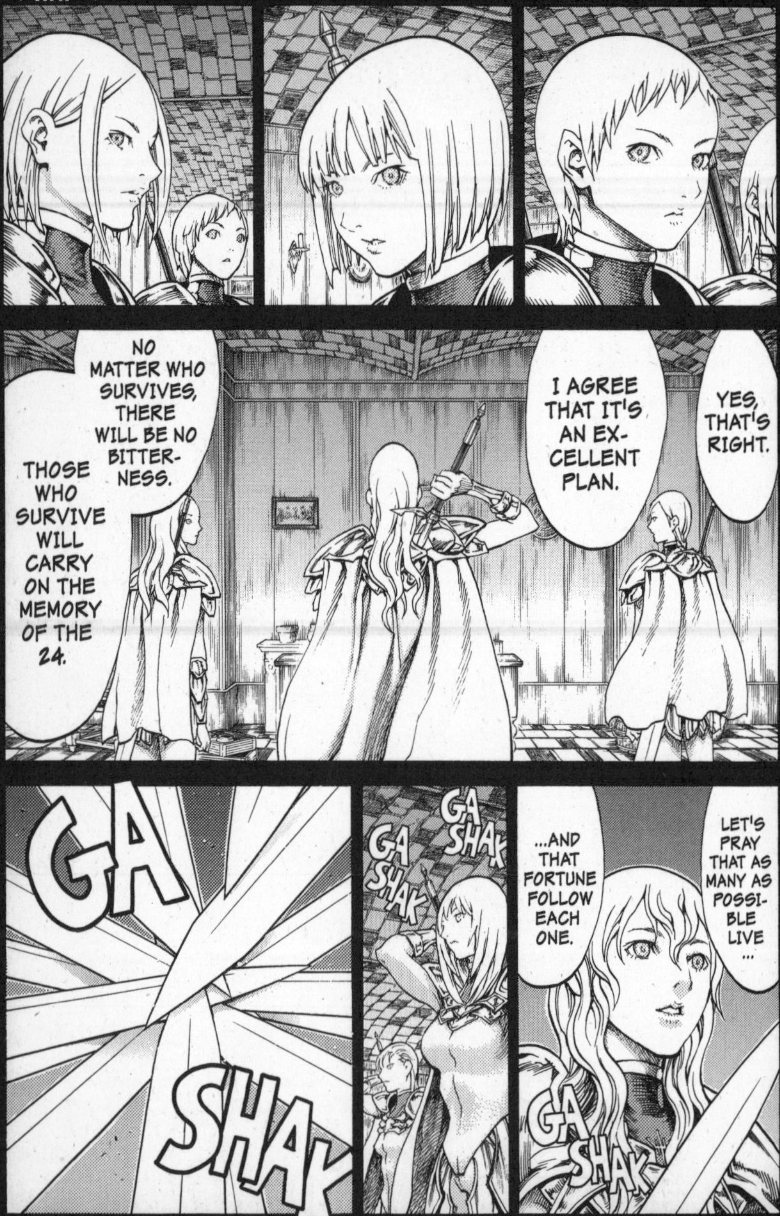
YES, THAT'S RIGHT.
I AGREE THAT IT'S AN EX-CELLENT PLAN.
NO MATTER WHO SURVIVES, THERE WILL BE NO BITTER-NESS.
THOSE WHO SURVIVE WILL CARRY ON THE MEMORY OF THE 24.
LET'S PRAY THAT AS MANY AS POSSI-BLE LIVE ...
...AND THAT FORTUNE FOLLOW EACH ONE.
GA SHAK
GA SHAK
GA SHAK
GA SHAK

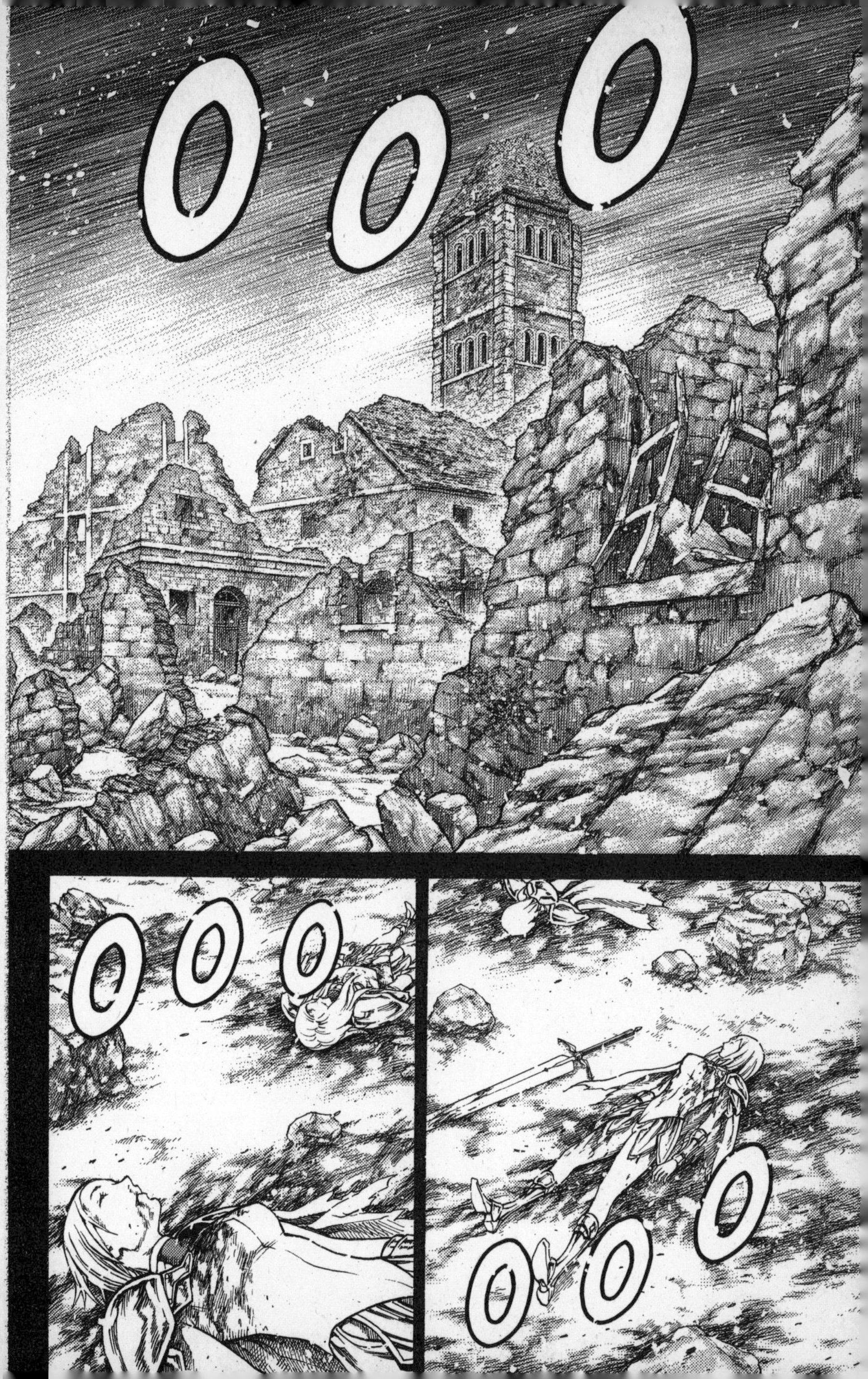
OOO
OOO
OOO

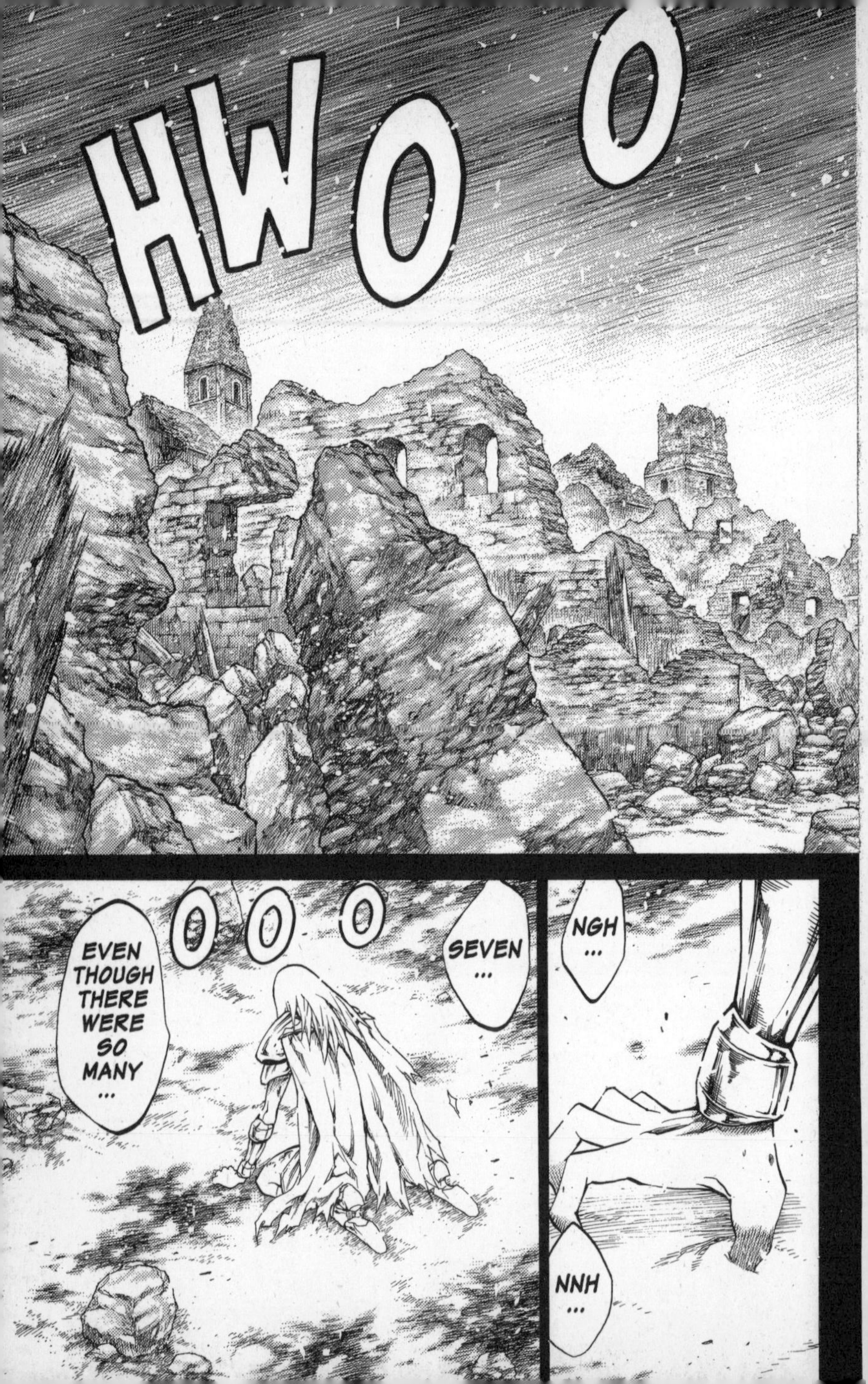
HWO O
NGH ...
NNH ...
OOO
SEVEN ...
EVEN THOUGH THERE WERE SO MANY ...

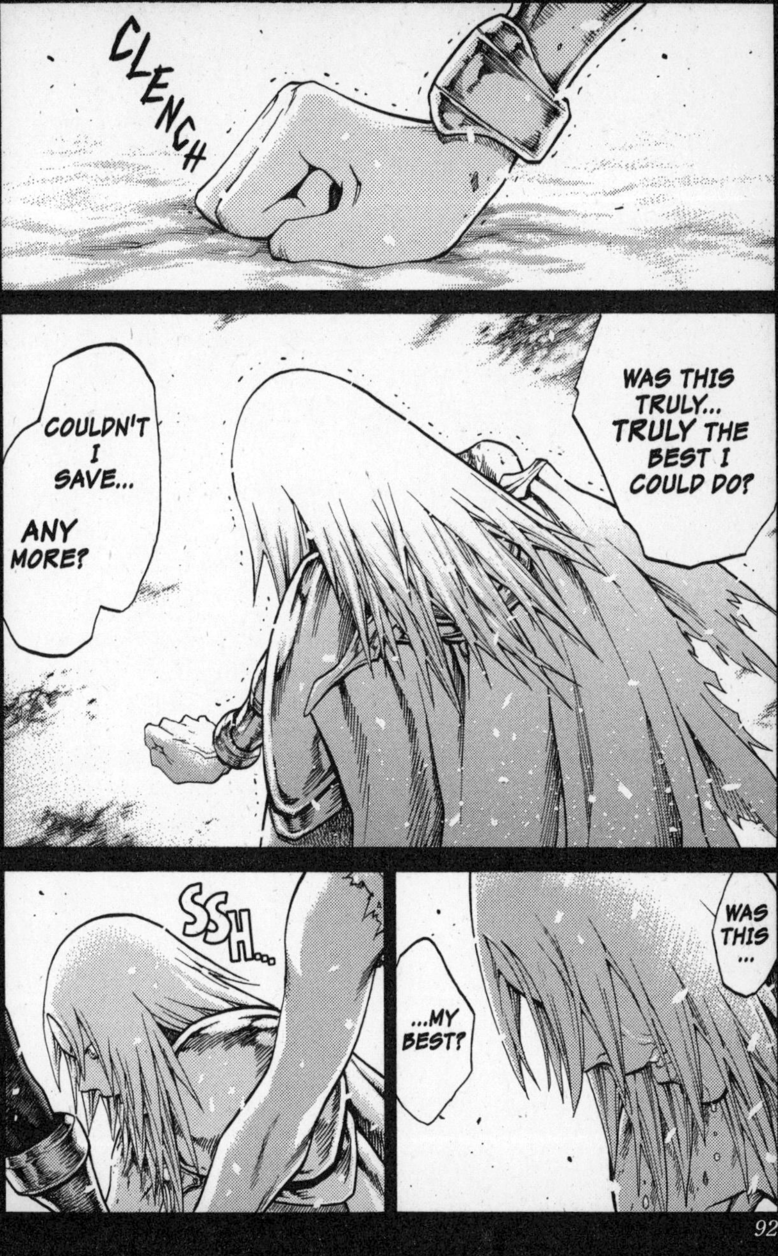
CLENCH
WAS THIS TRULY... TRULY THE BEST I COULD DO?
COULDN'T I SAVE...
ANY MORE?
WAS THIS ...
...MY BEST?
SSH...

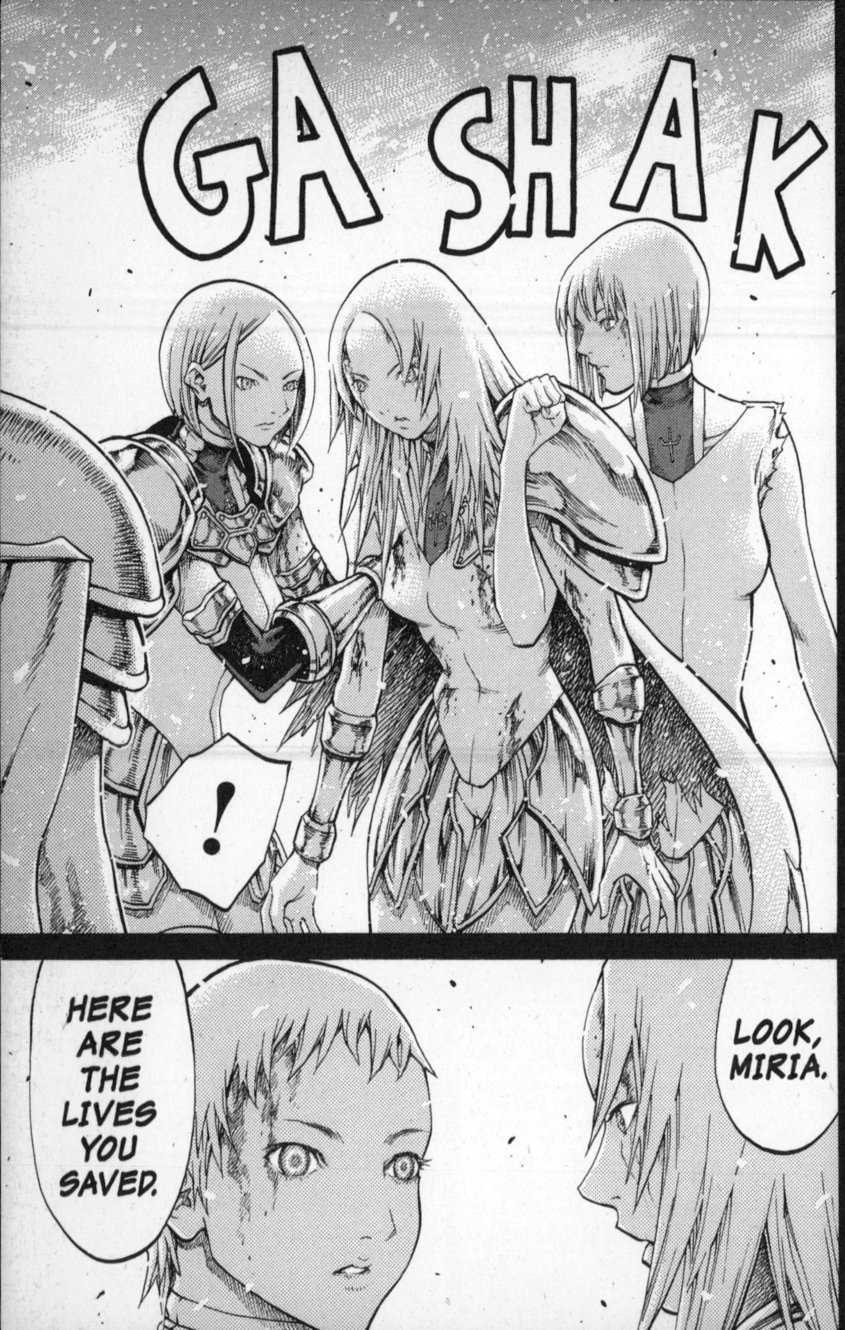
GASHAK
!
LOOK, MIRIA.
HERE ARE THE LIVES YOU SAVED.

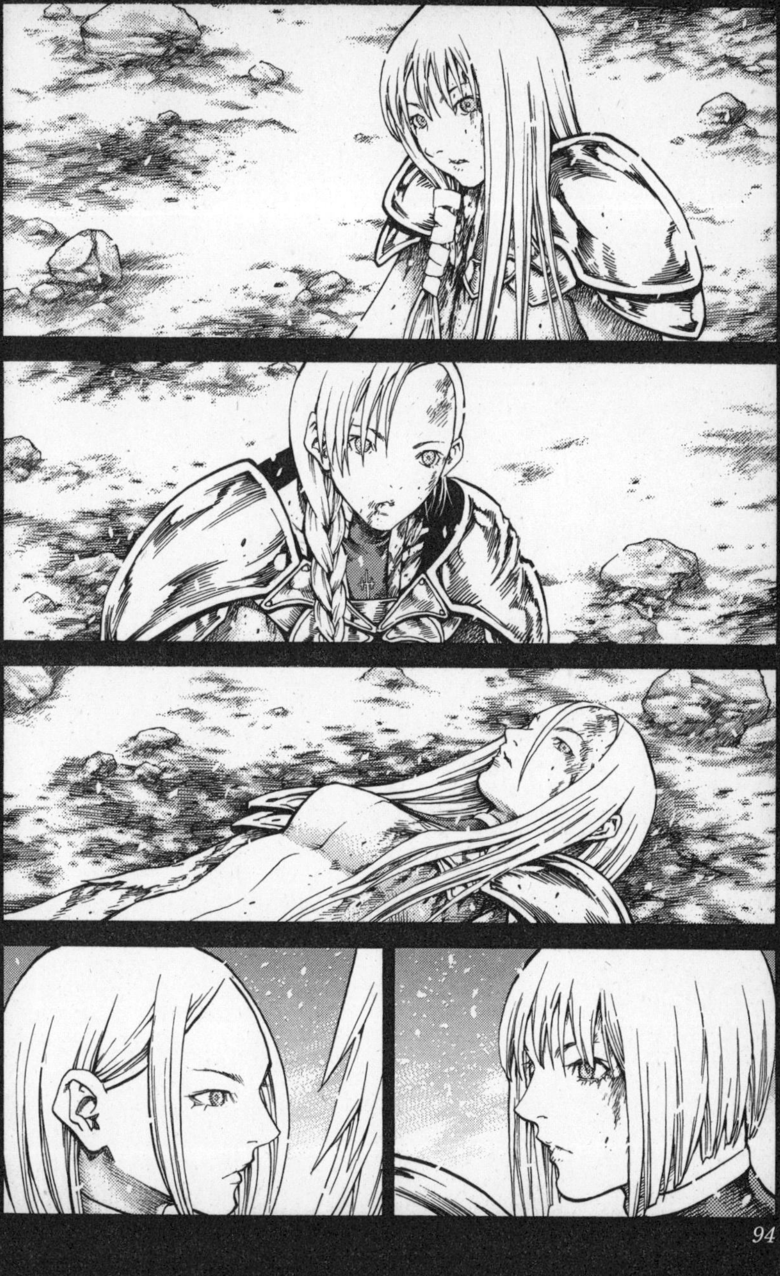

READ THIS WAY

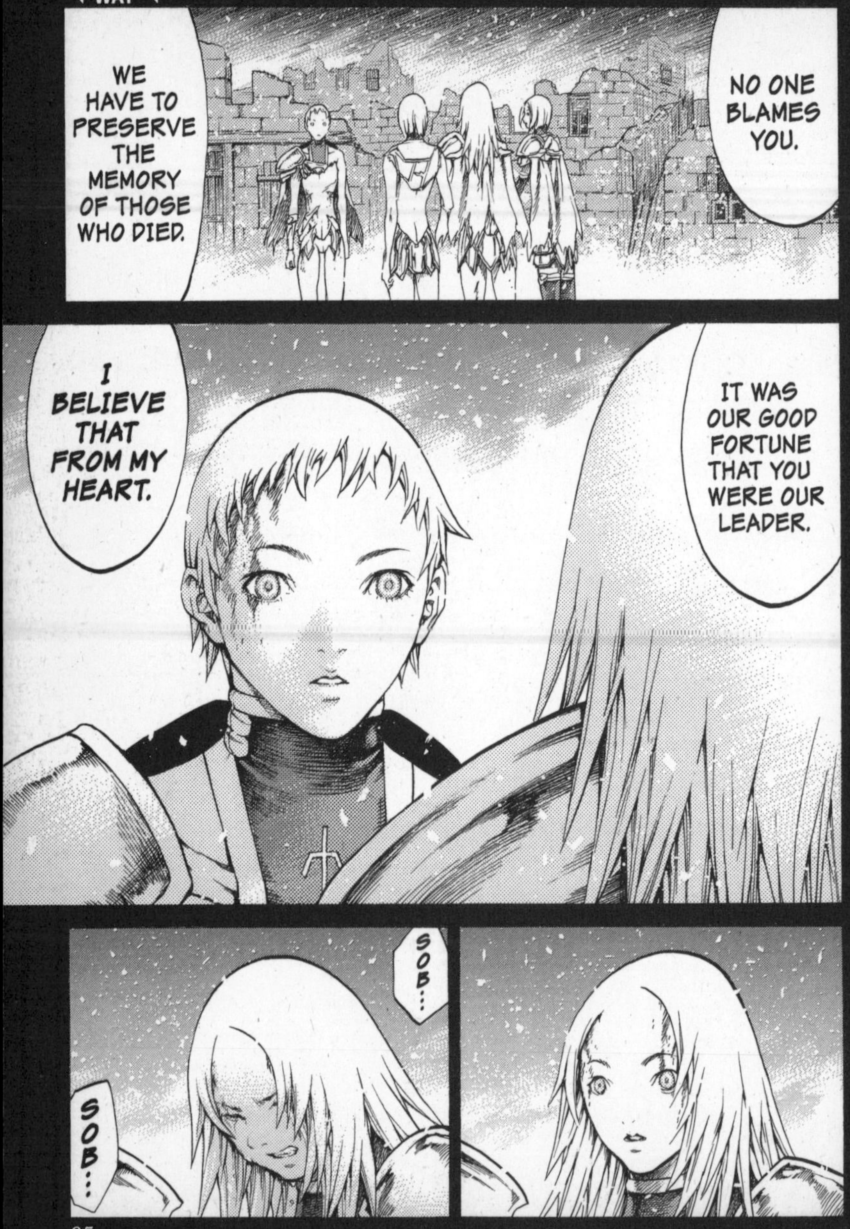
NO ONE BLAMES YOU.
WE HAVE TO PRESERVE THE MEMORY OF THOSE WHO DIED.
IT WAS OUR GOOD FORTUNE THAT YOU WERE OUR LEADER.
I BELIEVE THAT FROM MY HEART.
SOB...
SOB...

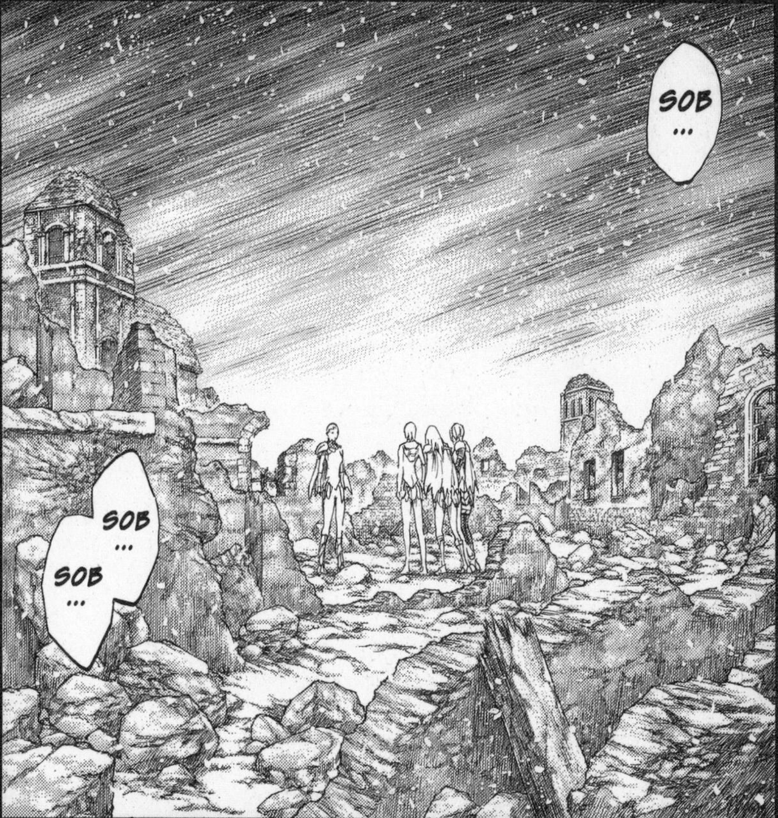
SOB ...
SOB ... SOB ...
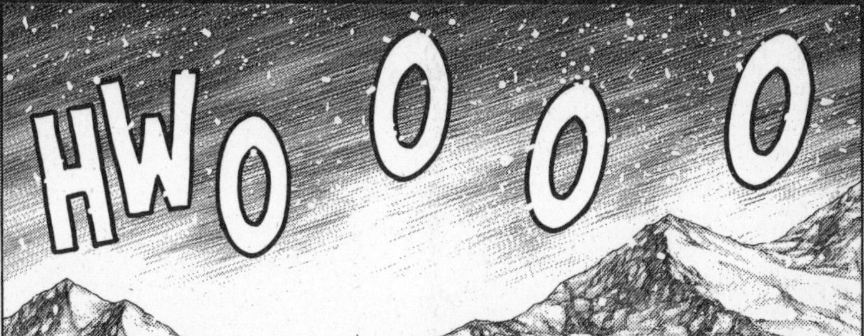
HWOOOO

READ THIS WAY

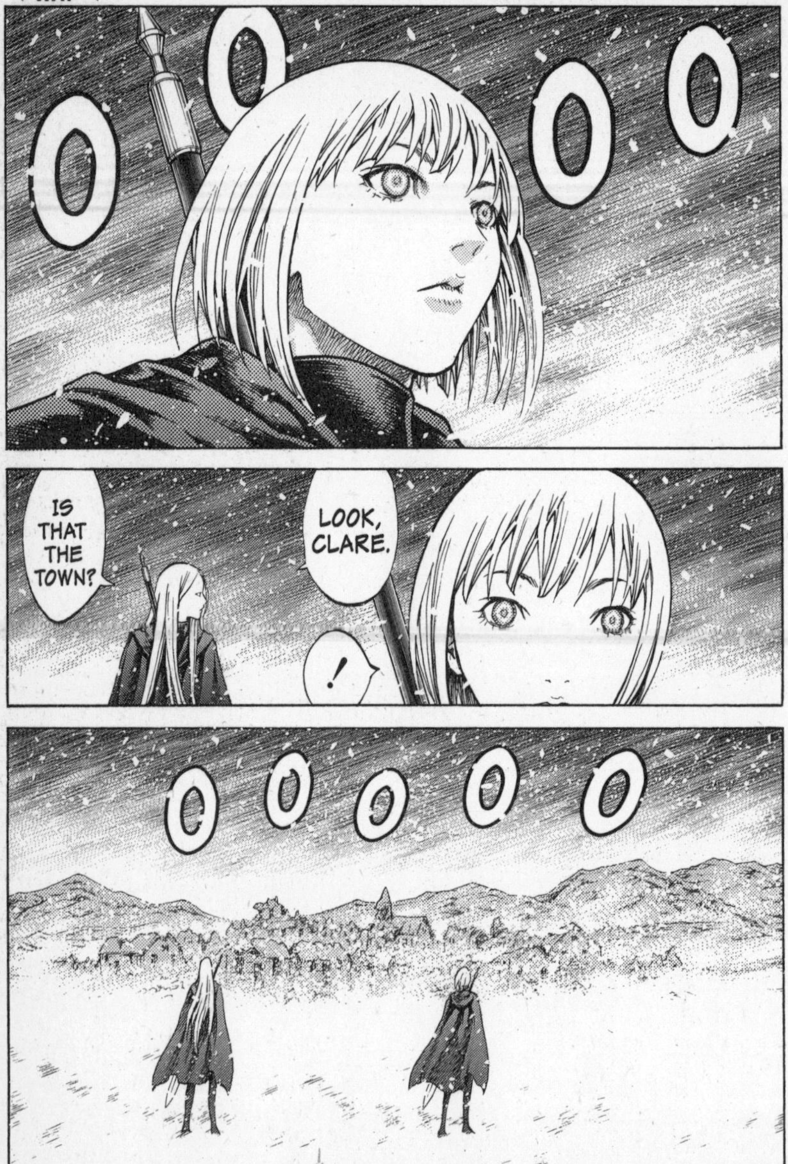
OOOO
LOOK, CLARE.
IS THAT THE TOWN?
!
OOOOO

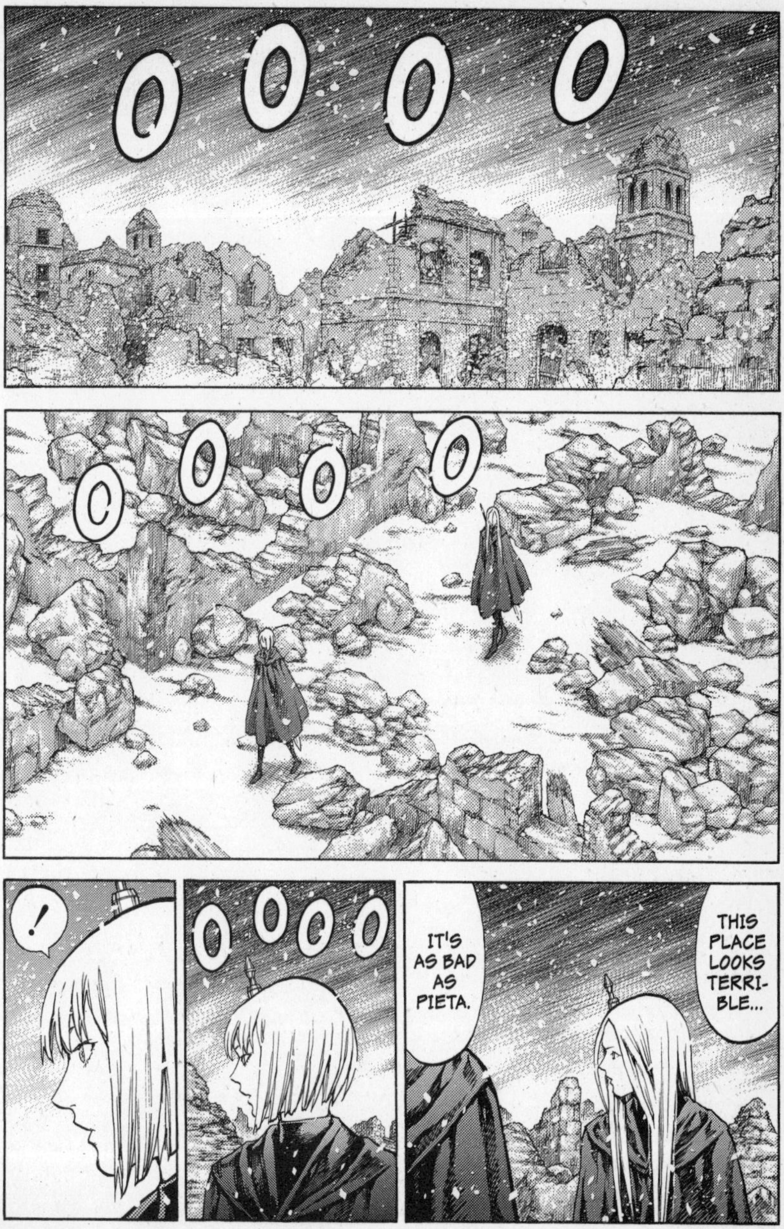
OOOO
OOOO
THIS PLACE LOOKS TERRI-BLE...
IT'S AS BAD AS PIETA.
OOOO
!

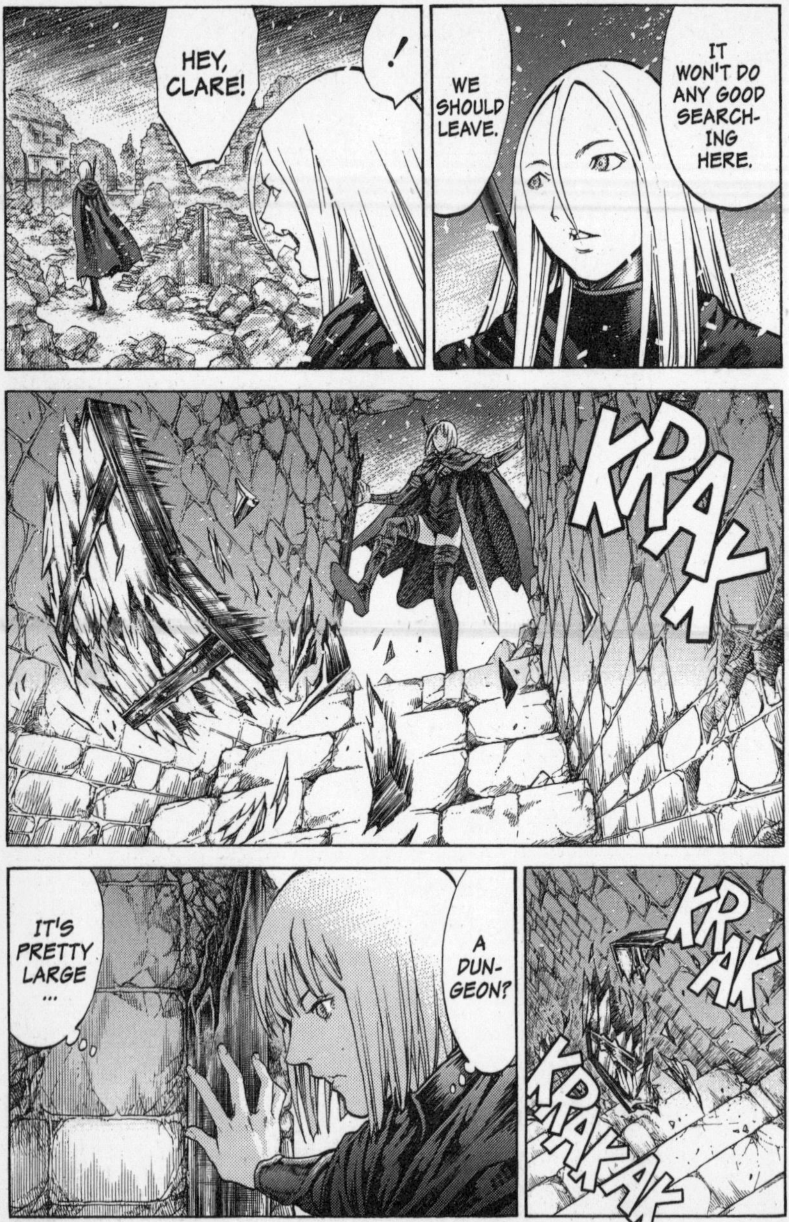

IT WON'T DO ANY GOOD SEARCH-ING HERE.
WE SHOULD LEAVE.
!
HEY, CLARE!
KRAK
KRAK
KRAKAK
A DUN-GEON?
IT'S PRETTY LARGE ...

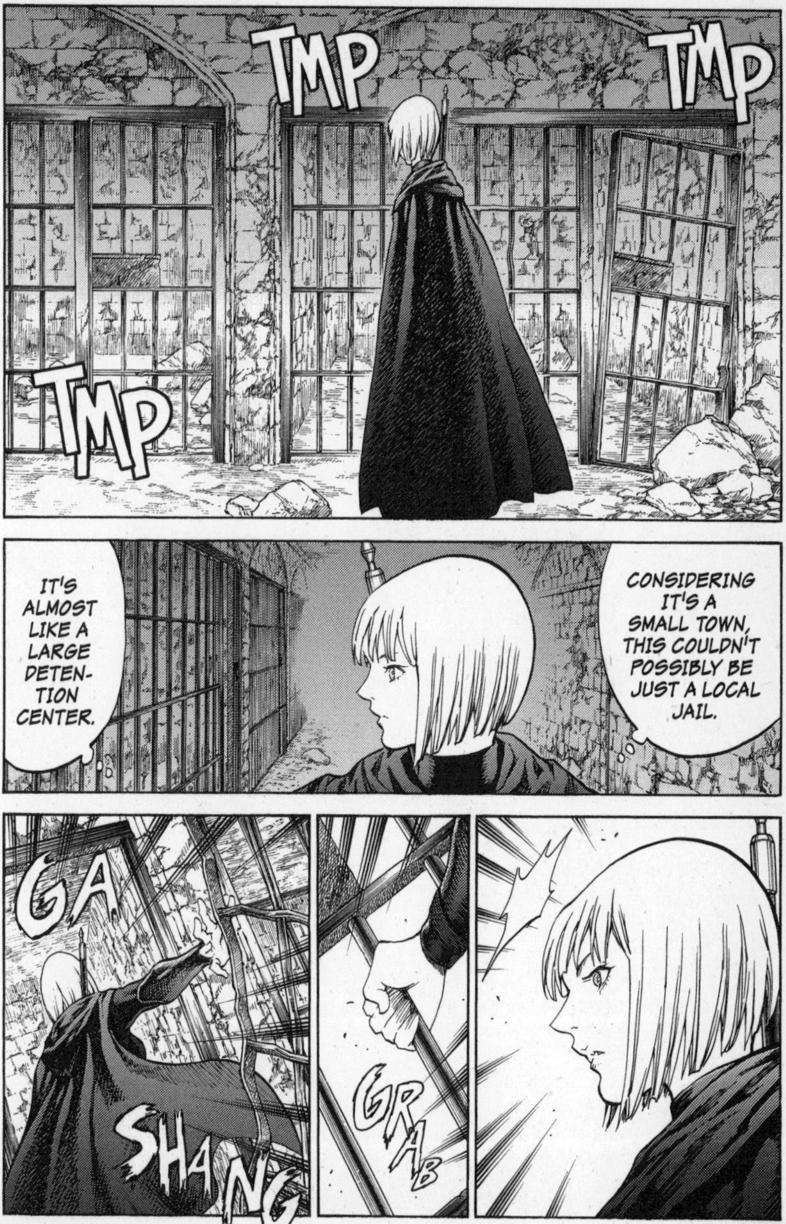
TMP
TMP
TMP
CONSIDERING IT'S A SMALL TOWN, THIS COULDN'T POSSIBLY BE JUST A LOCAL JAIL.
IT'S ALMOST LIKE A LARGE DETEN-TION CENTER.
GRAB
GA
SHANG

READ THIS WAY

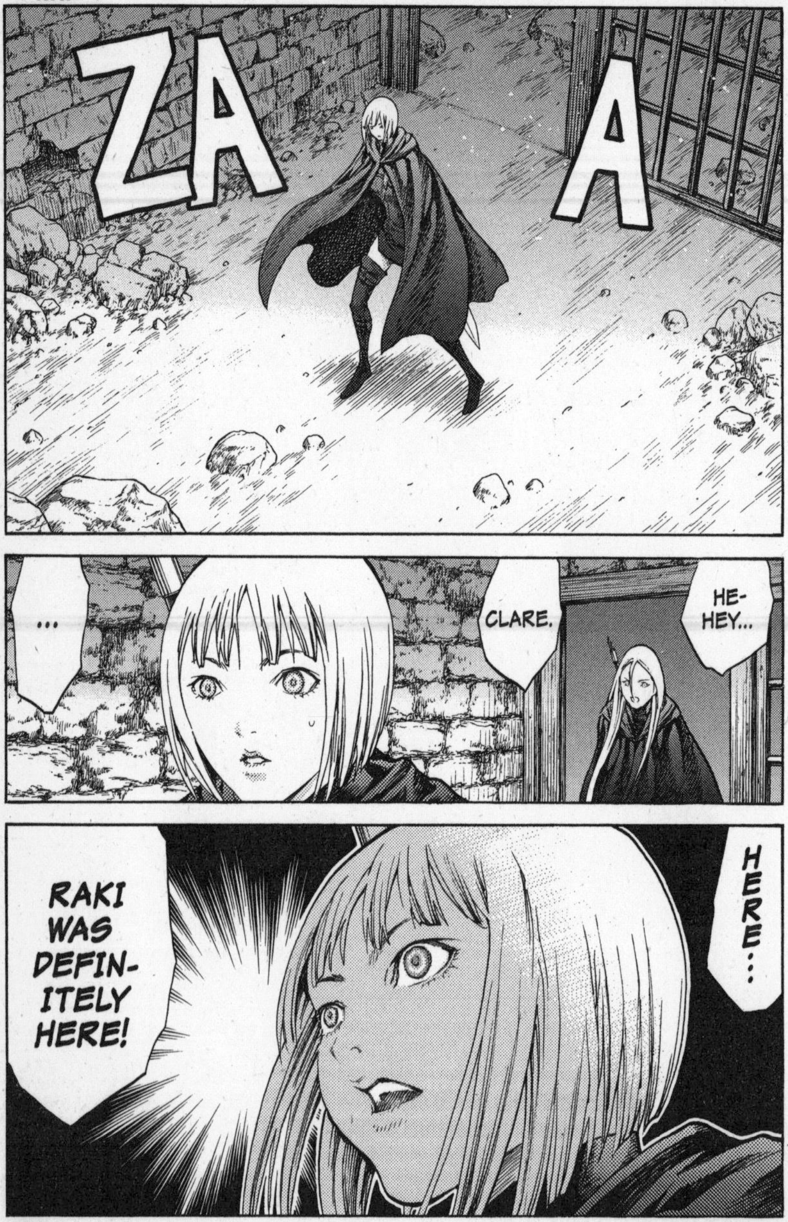
ZAA
HE-HEY...
CLARE.
...
HERE...
RAKI WAS DEFINITELY HERE!

クレイモア
Claymore

Scene 67: The Souls of the Fallen, Part 3

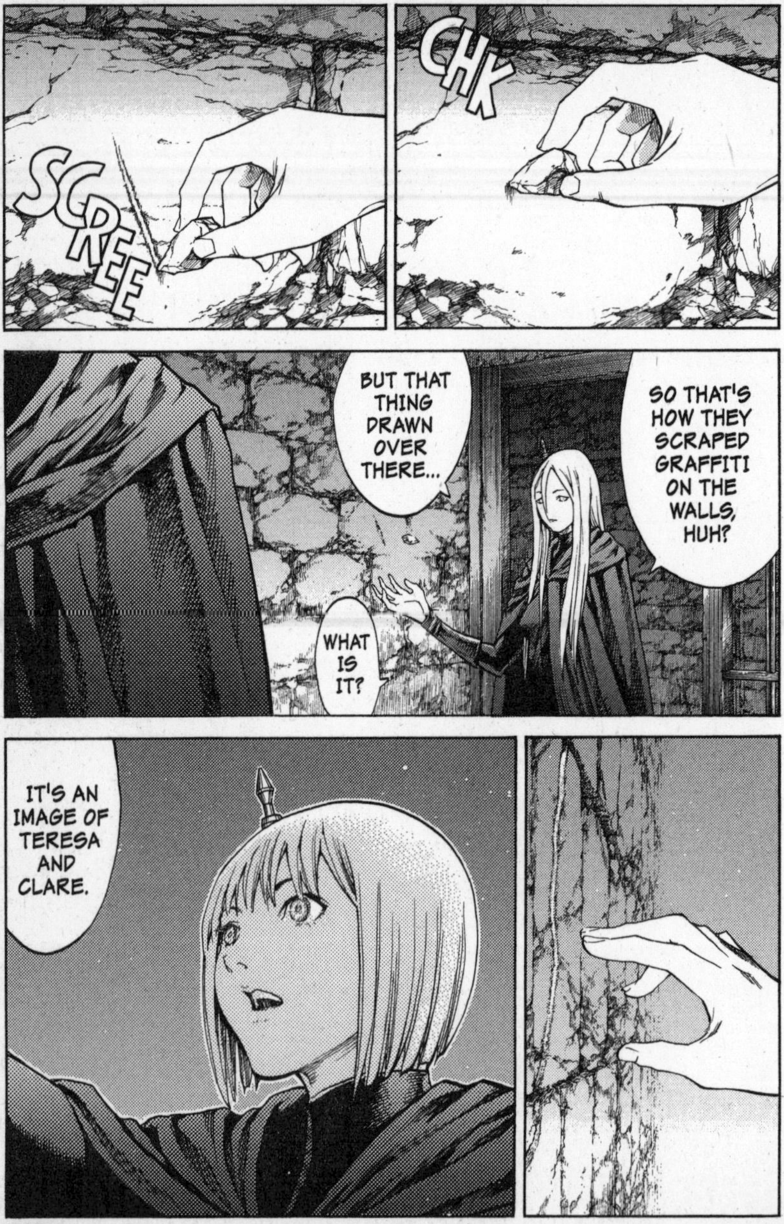
CHK
SCREE
SO THAT'S HOW THEY SCRAPED GRAFFITI ON THE WALLS, HUH?
BUT THAT THING DRAWN OVER THERE...
WHAT IS IT?
IT'S AN IMAGE OF TERESA AND CLARE.

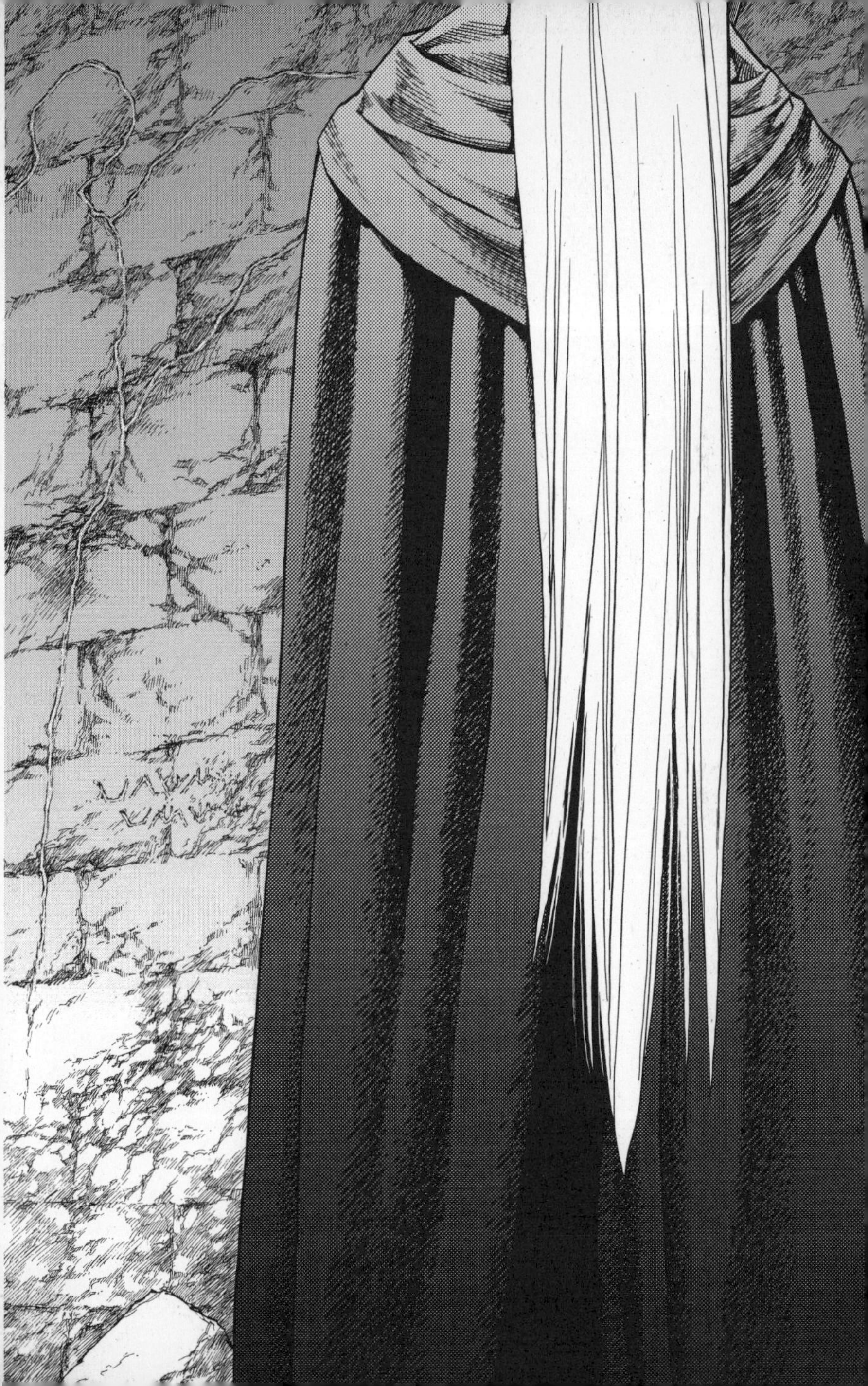

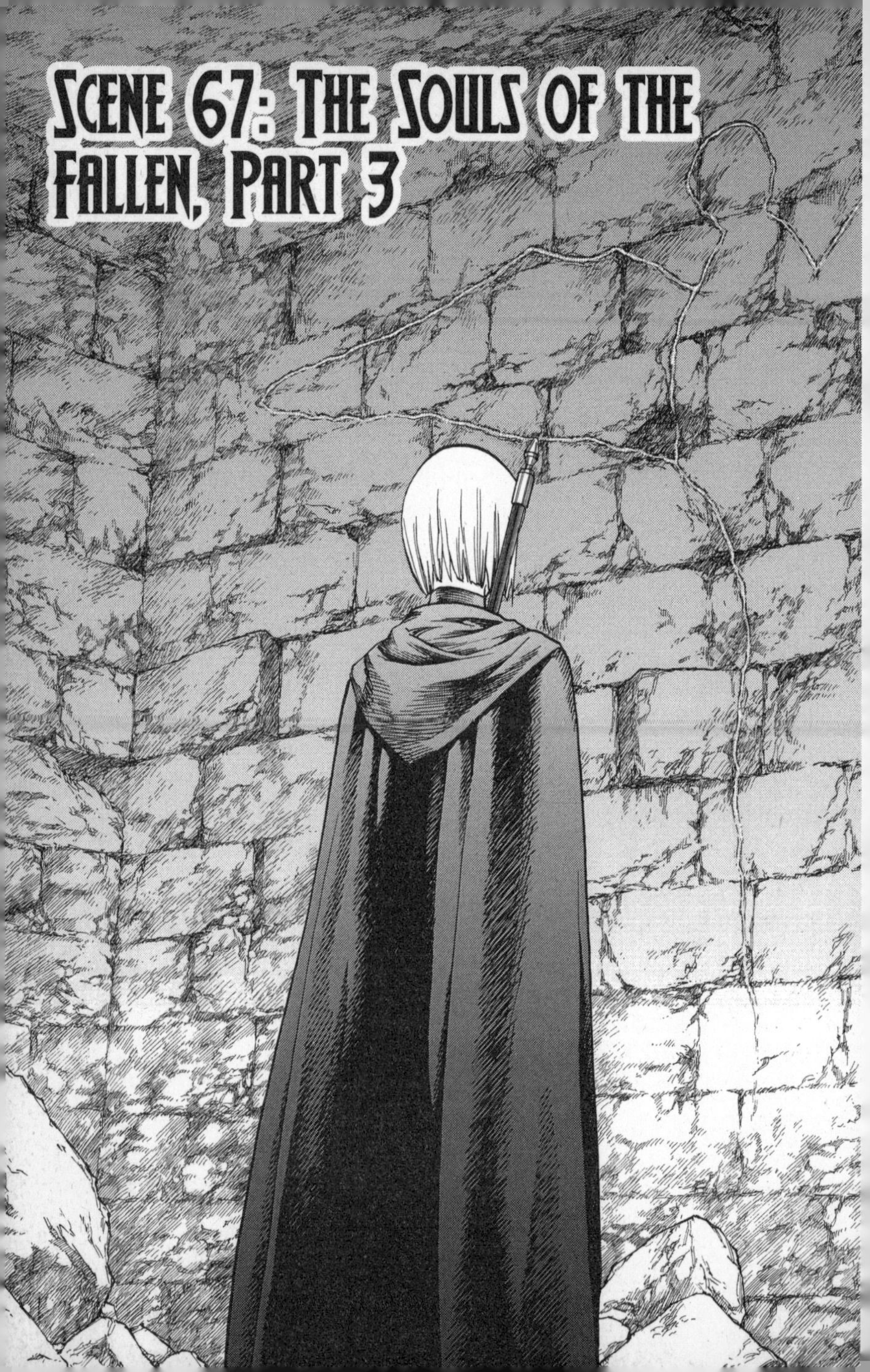
SCENE 67: THE SOULS OF THE FALLEN, PART 3

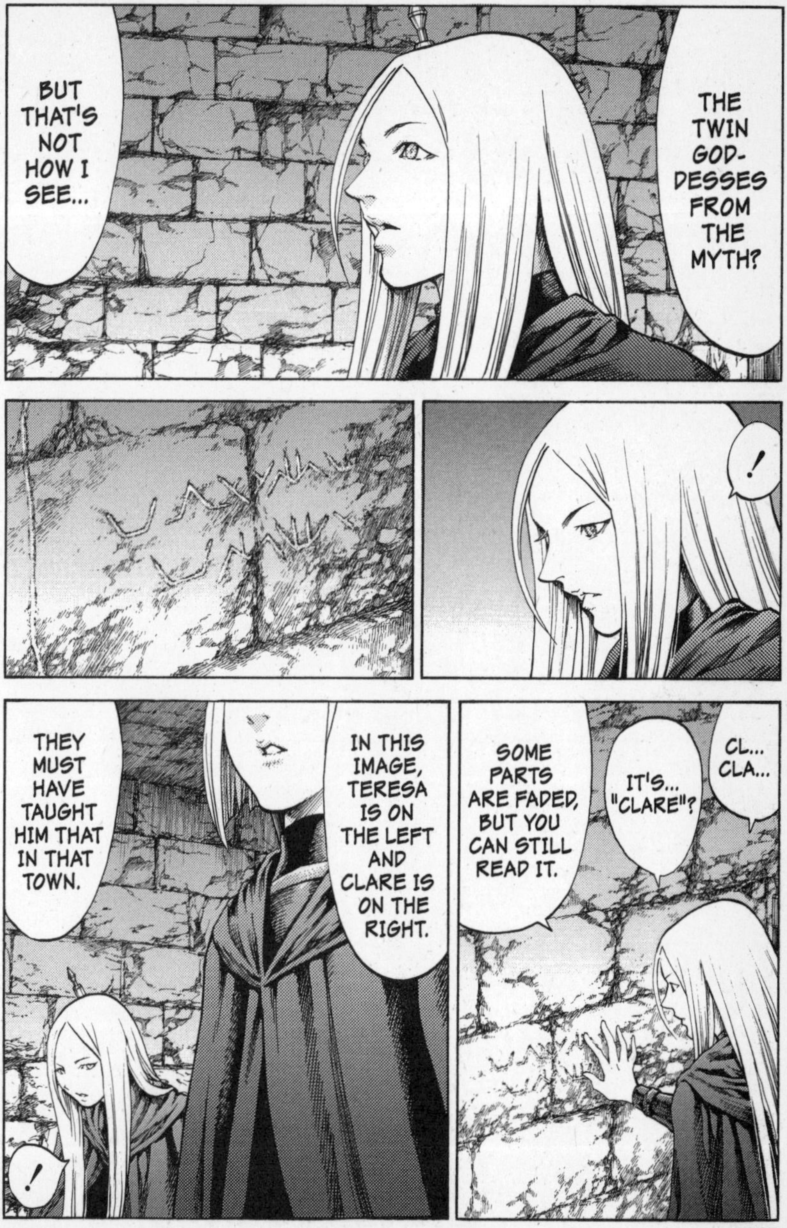
THE TWIN GOD-DESSES FROM THE MYTH?
BUT THAT'S NOT HOW I SEE...
!
CL... CLA...
IT'S... "CLARE"?
SOME PARTS ARE FADED, BUT YOU CAN STILL READ IT.
IN THIS IMAGE, TERESA IS ON THE LEFT AND CLARE IS ON THE RIGHT.
THEY MUST HAVE TAUGHT HIM THAT IN THAT TOWN.
!

READ THIS WAY

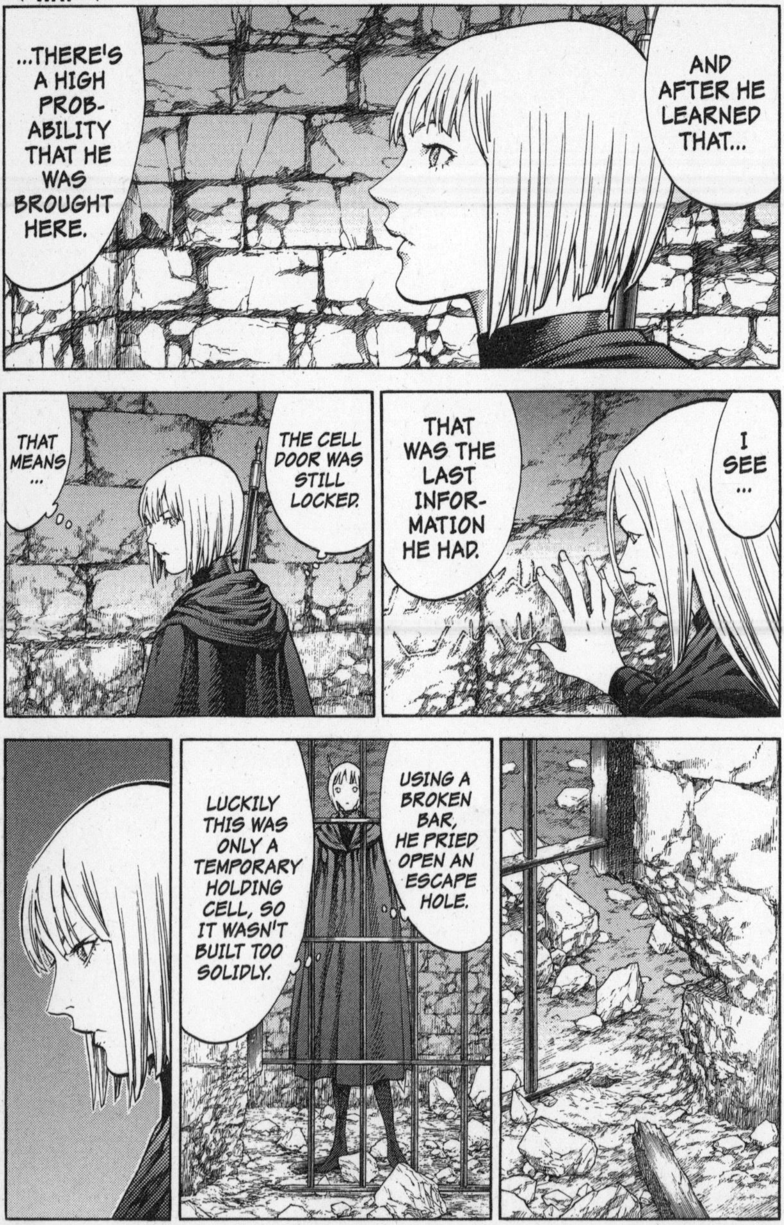
AND AFTER HE LEARNED THAT...
...THERE'S A HIGH PROB-ABILITY THAT HE WAS BROUGHT HERE.
I SEE ...
THAT WAS THE LAST INFOR-MATION HE HAD.
THE CELL DOOR WAS STILL LOCKED.
THAT MEANS ...
USING A BROKEN BAR, HE PRIED OPEN AN ESCAPE HOLE.
LUCKILY THIS WAS ONLY A TEMPORARY HOLDING CELL, SO IT WASN'T BUILT TOO SOLIDLY.

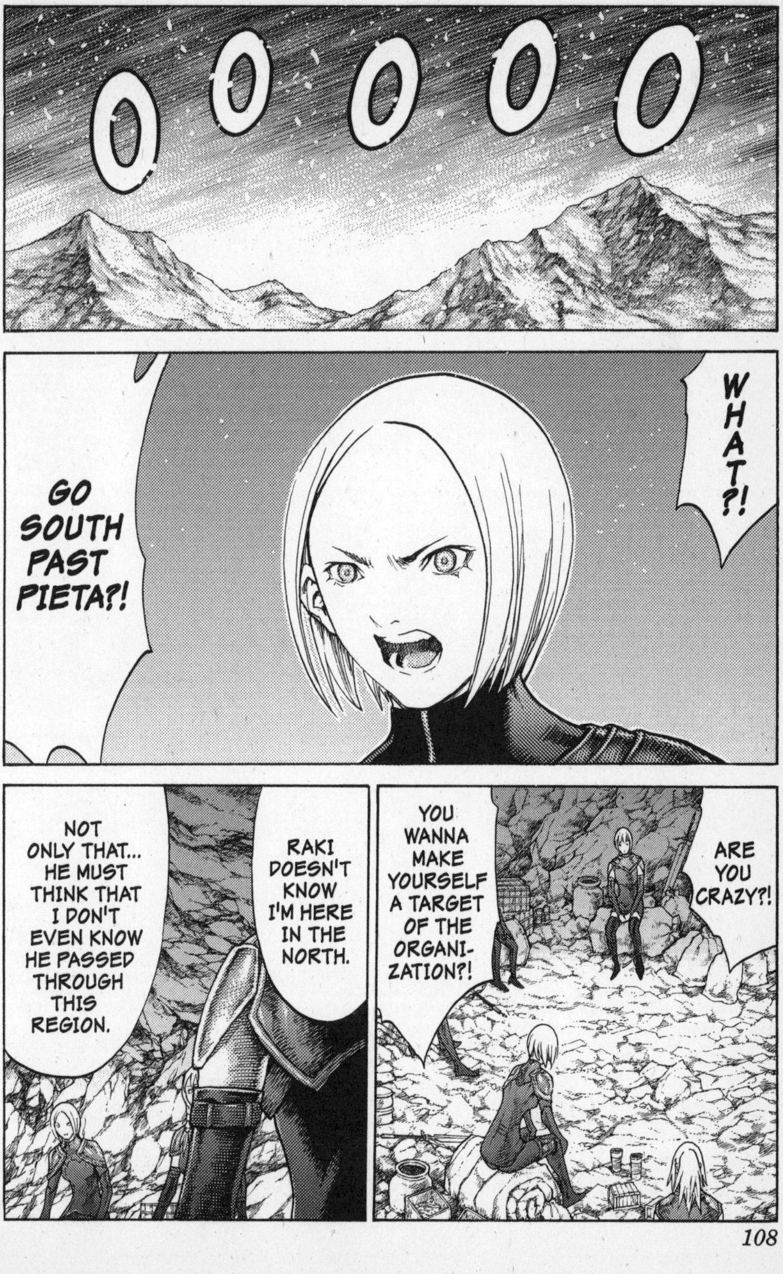
OOOOO
WHAT?!
GO SOUTH PAST PIETA?!
ARE YOU CRAZY?!
YOU WANNA MAKE YOURSELF A TARGET OF THE ORGANIZATION?!
RAKI DOESN'T KNOW I'M HERE IN THE NORTH.
NOT ONLY THAT... HE MUST THINK THAT I DON'T EVEN KNOW HE PASSED THROUGH THIS REGION.

READ THIS WAY

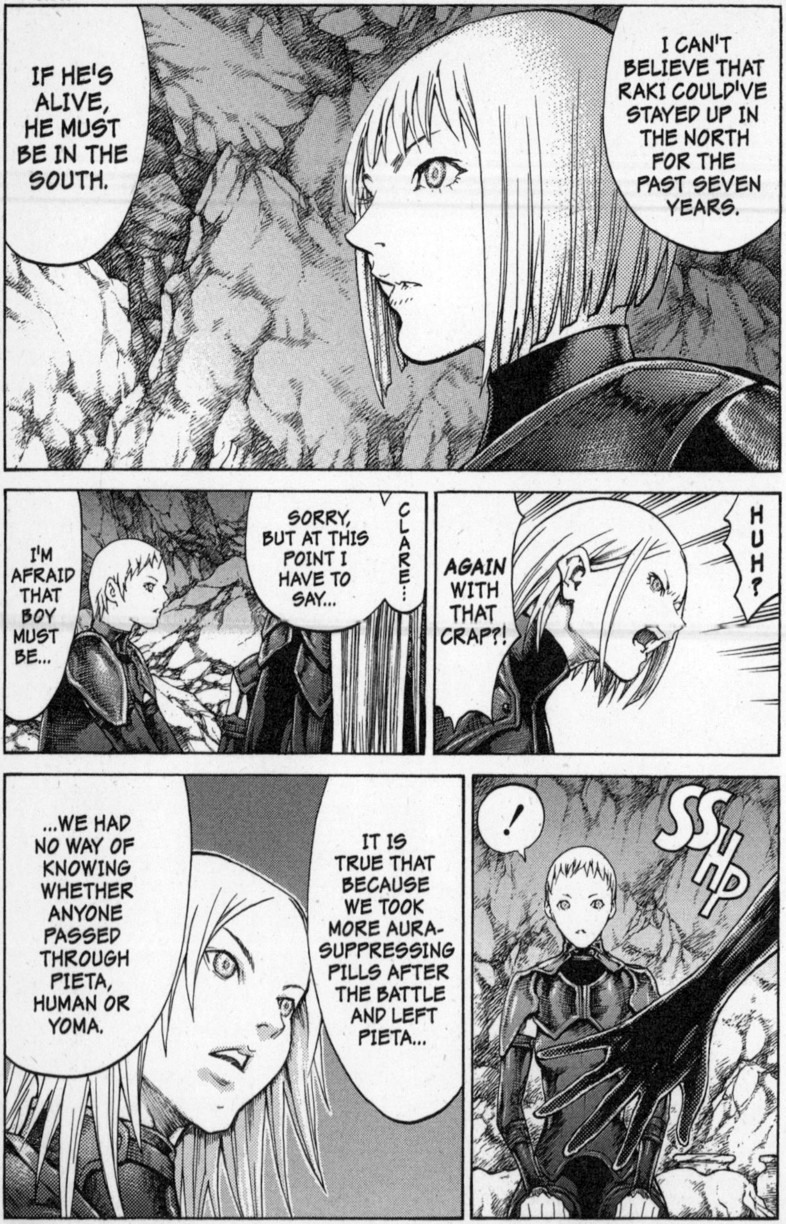
I CAN'T BELIEVE THAT RAKI COULD'VE STAYED UP IN THE NORTH FOR THE PAST SEVEN YEARS.
IF HE'S ALIVE, HE MUST BE IN THE SOUTH.
HUH?
AGAIN WITH THAT CRAP?!
CLARE...
SORRY, BUT AT THIS POINT I HAVE TO SAY...
I'M AFRAID THAT BOY MUST BE...
!
SSHP
IT IS TRUE THAT BECAUSE WE TOOK MORE AURA-SUPPRESSING PILLS AFTER THE BATTLE AND LEFT PIETA...
...WE HAD NO WAY OF KNOWING WHETHER ANYONE PASSED THROUGH PIETA, HUMAN OR YOMA.

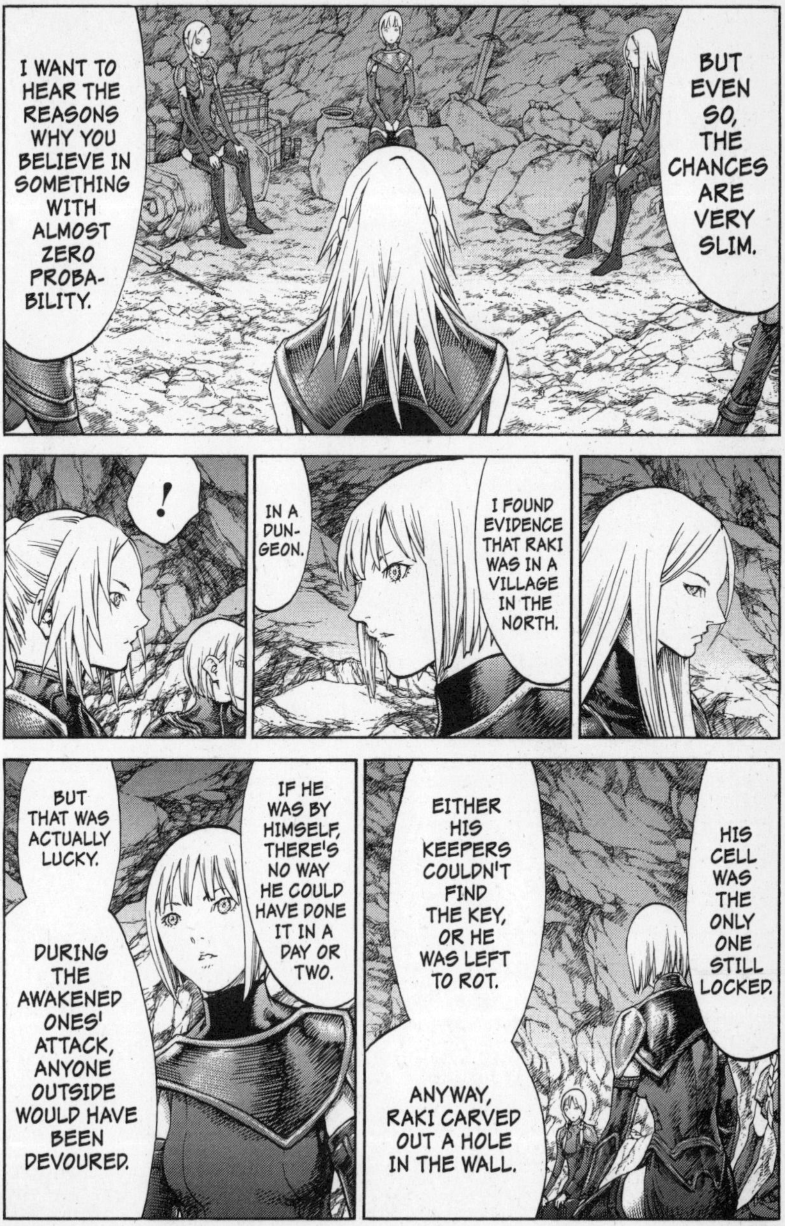
BUT EVEN SO, THE CHANCES ARE VERY SLIM.
I WANT TO HEAR THE REASONS WHY YOU BELIEVE IN SOMETHING WITH ALMOST ZERO PROBA-BILITY.
I FOUND EVIDENCE THAT RAKI WAS IN A VILLAGE IN THE NORTH.
IN A DUN-GEON.
!
HIS CELL WAS THE ONLY ONE STILL LOCKED.
EITHER HIS KEEPERS COULDN'T FIND THE KEY, OR HE WAS LEFT TO ROT.
ANYWAY, RAKI CARVED OUT A HOLE IN THE WALL.
IF HE WAS BY HIMSELF, THERE'S NO WAY HE COULD HAVE DONE IT IN A DAY OR TWO.
BUT THAT WAS ACTUALLY LUCKY.
DURING THE AWAKENED ONES' ATTACK, ANYONE OUTSIDE WOULD HAVE BEEN DEVOURED.

READ THIS WAY

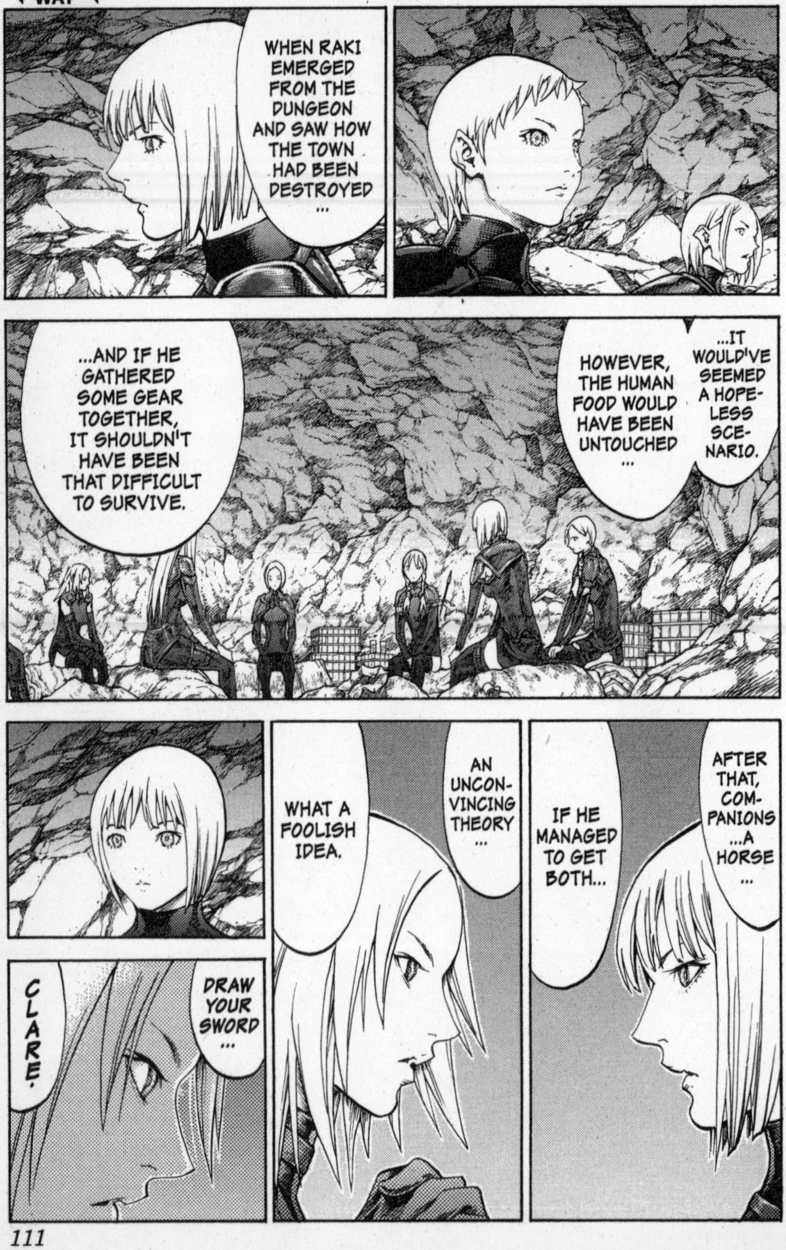
WHEN RAKI EMERGED FROM THE DUNGEON AND SAW HOW THE TOWN HAD BEEN DESTROYED ...
...IT WOULD'VE SEEMED A HOPE-LESS SCE-NARIO.
HOWEVER, THE HUMAN FOOD WOULD HAVE BEEN UNTOUCHED ...
...AND IF HE GATHERED SOME GEAR TOGETHER, IT SHOULDN'T HAVE BEEN THAT DIFFICULT TO SURVIVE.
AFTER THAT, COM-PANIONS ...A HORSE ...
IF HE MANAGED TO GET BOTH...
AN UNCON-VINCING THEORY ...
WHAT A FOOLISH IDEA.
DRAW YOUR SWORD ...
CLARE.

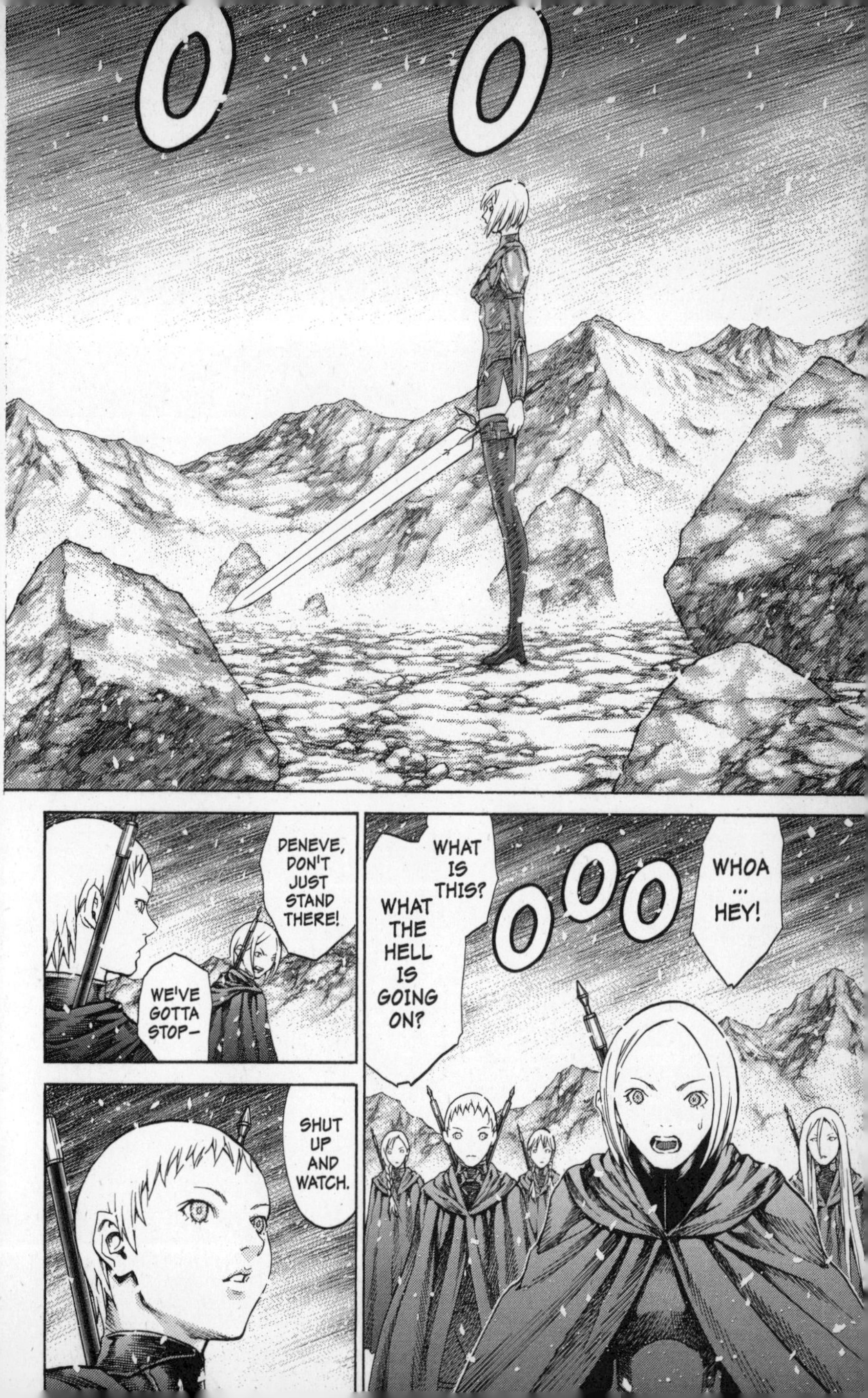
O O
WHOA ... HEY!
OOO
WHAT IS THIS?
WHAT THE HELL IS GOING ON?
DENEVE, DON'T JUST STAND THERE!
WE'VE GOTTA STOP—
SHUT UP AND WATCH.

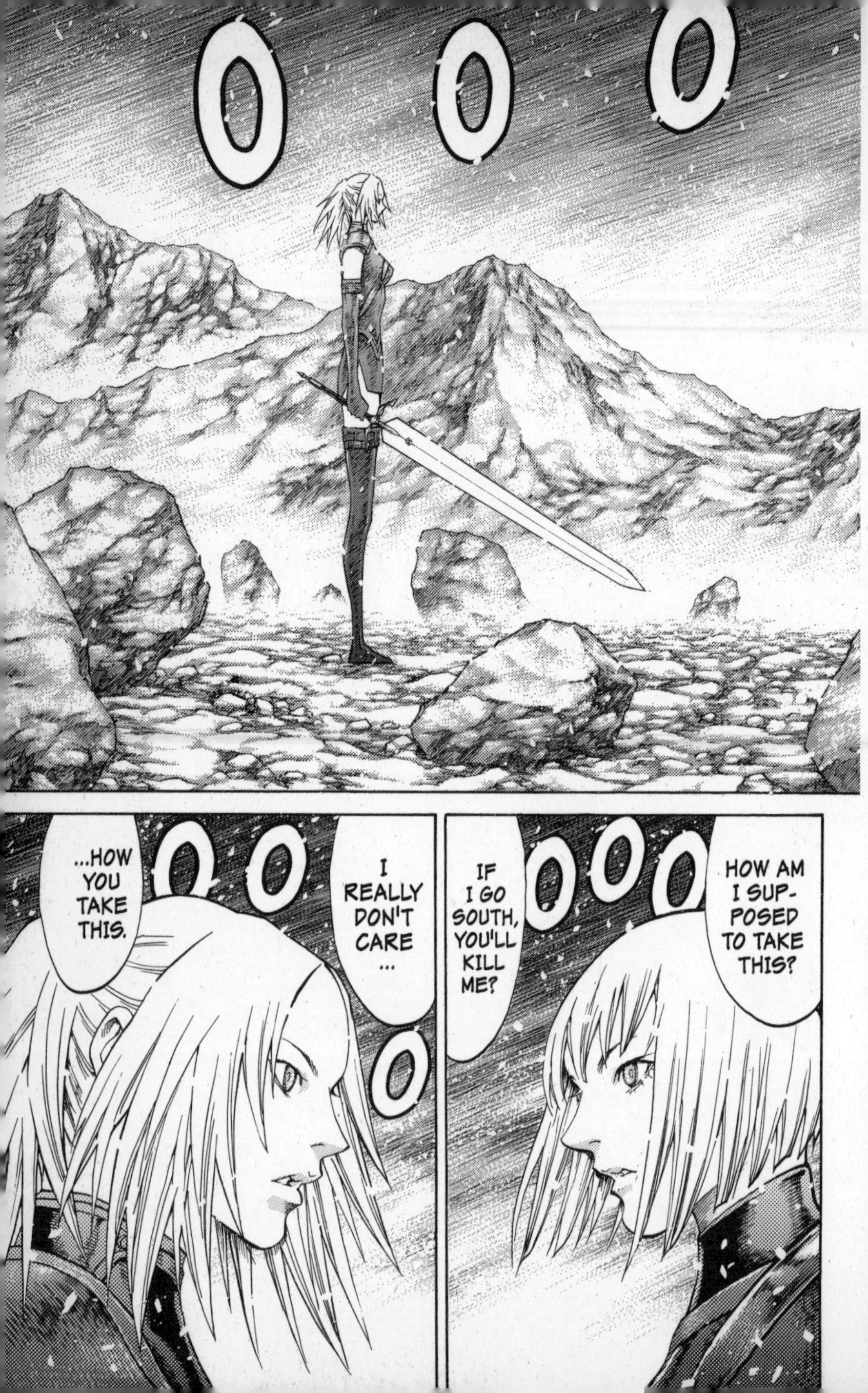
OOO
HOW AM I SUPPOSED TO TAKE THIS?
OOO
IF I GO SOUTH, YOU'LL KILL ME?
OOO
I REALLY DON'T CARE...
...HOW YOU TAKE THIS.

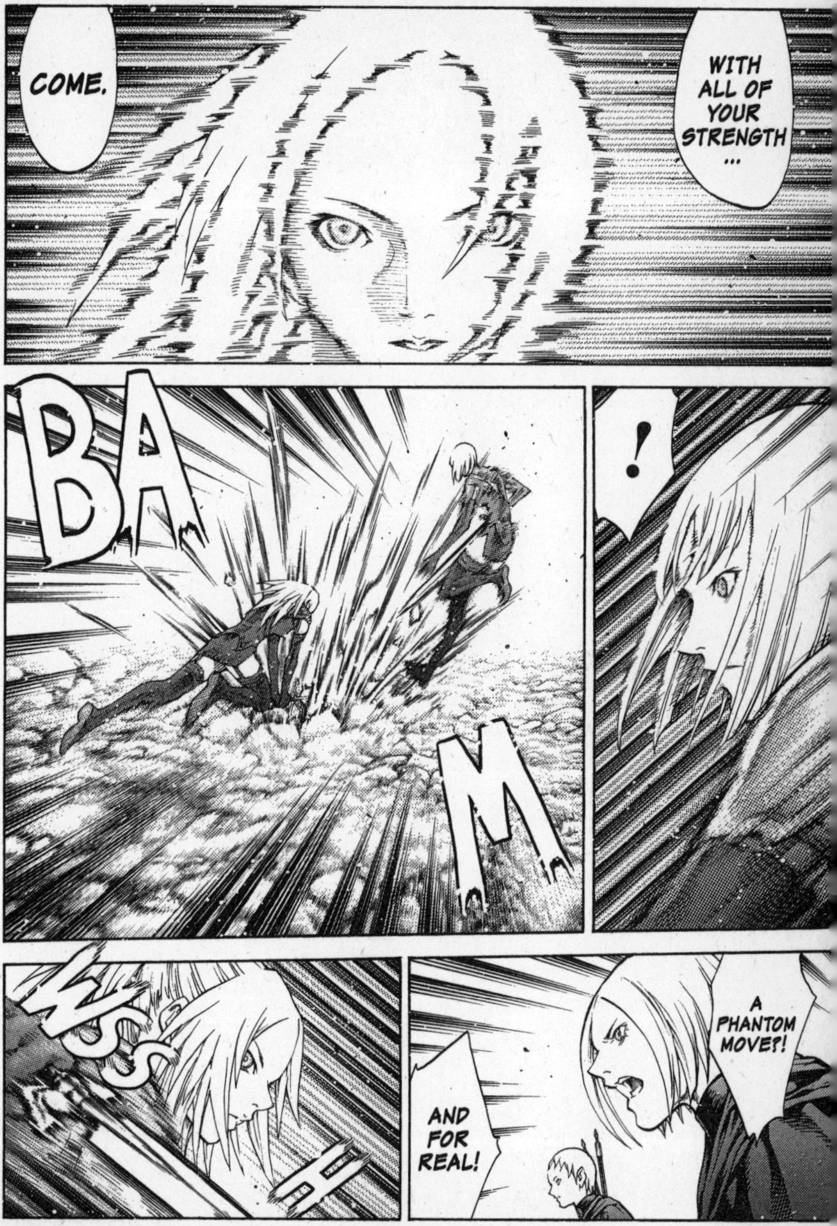
WITH ALL OF YOUR STRENGTH ...
COME.
!
BA
M
A PHANTOM MOVE?!
AND FOR REAL!
WSS
H

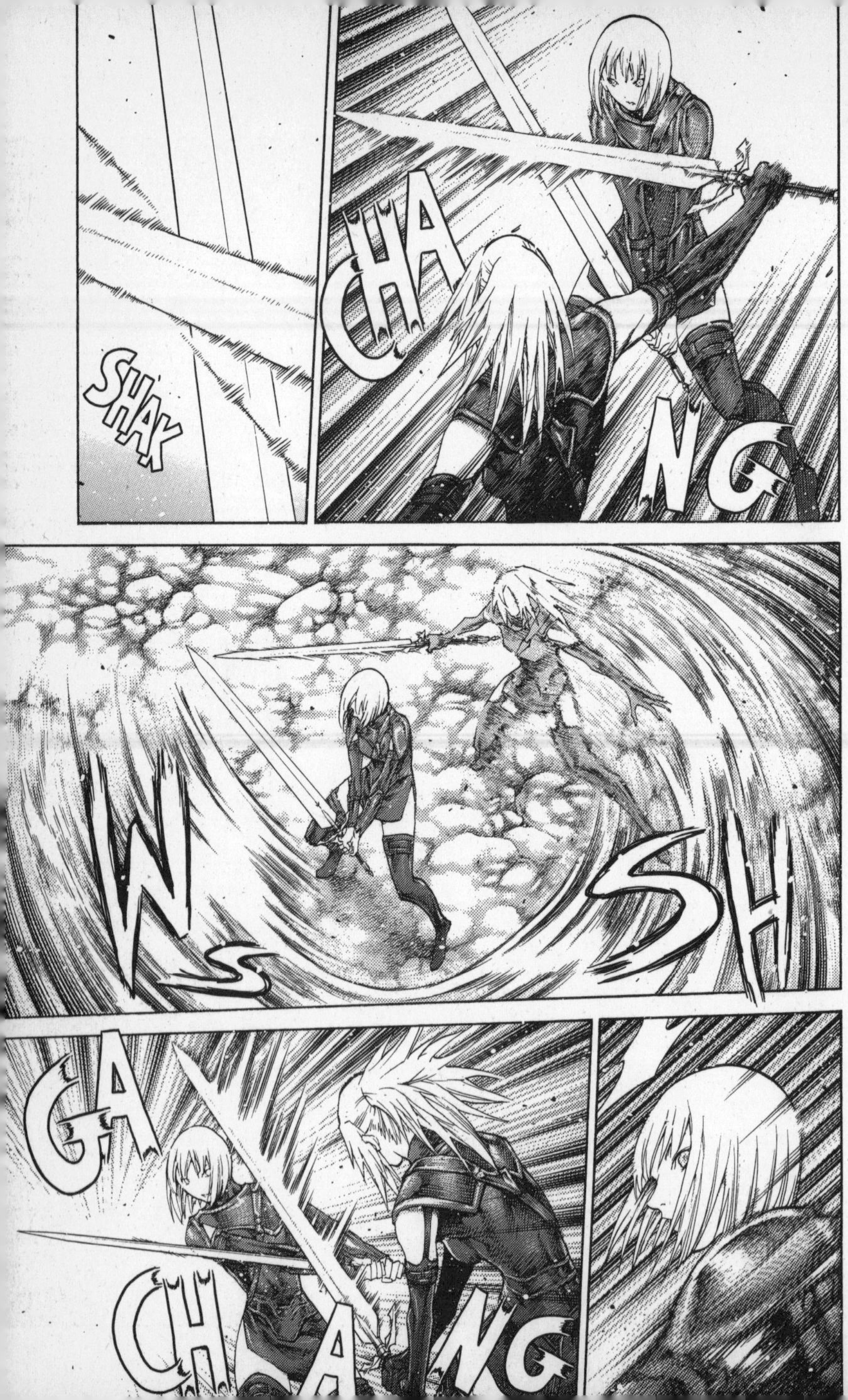
CHANG
SHAK
WSSH
GA
CHANG

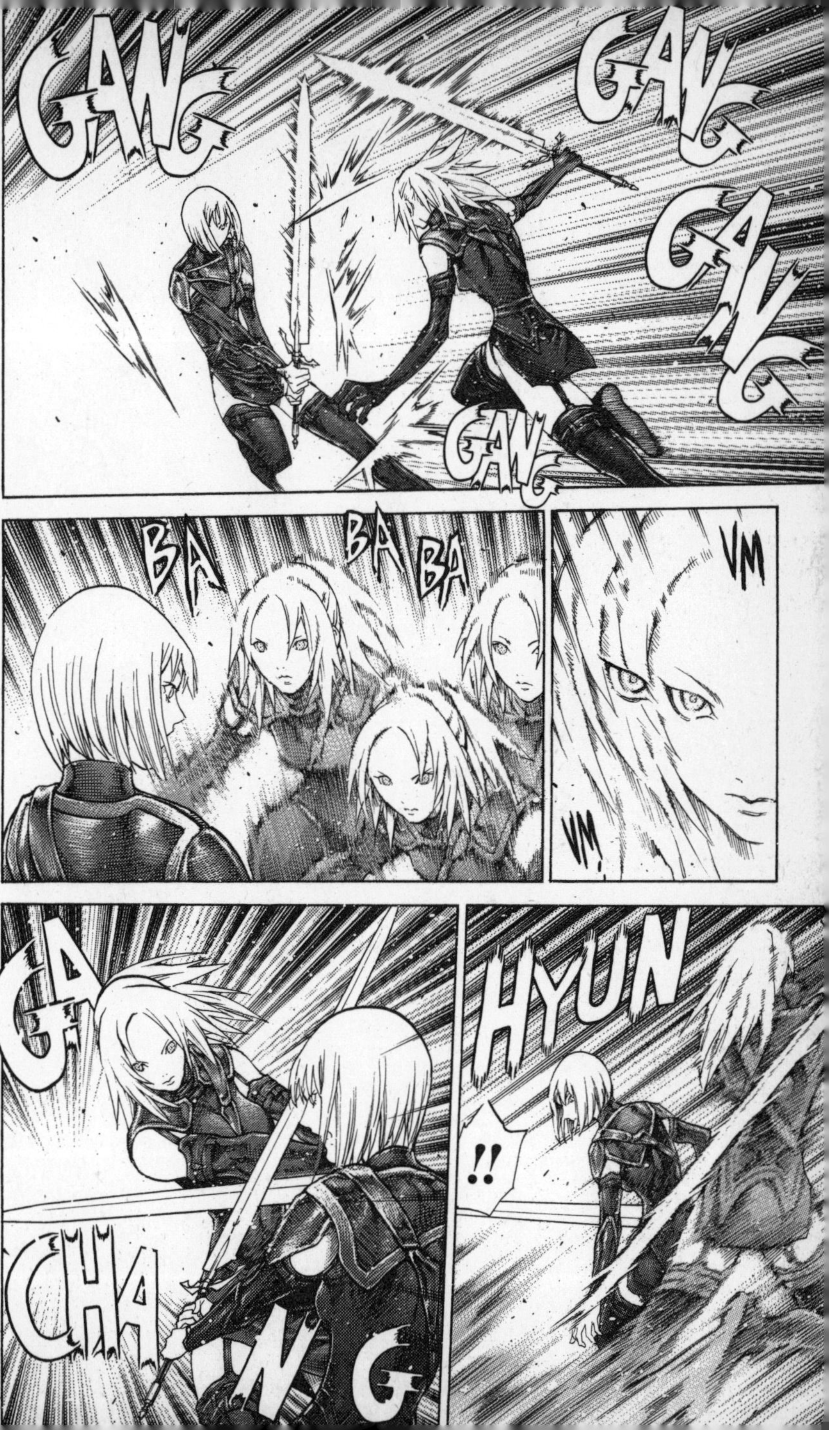
GANG
GANG
GANG
GANG
VM
VM
BA
BA
BA
HYUN
!!
GA
CHANG

READ THIS WAY

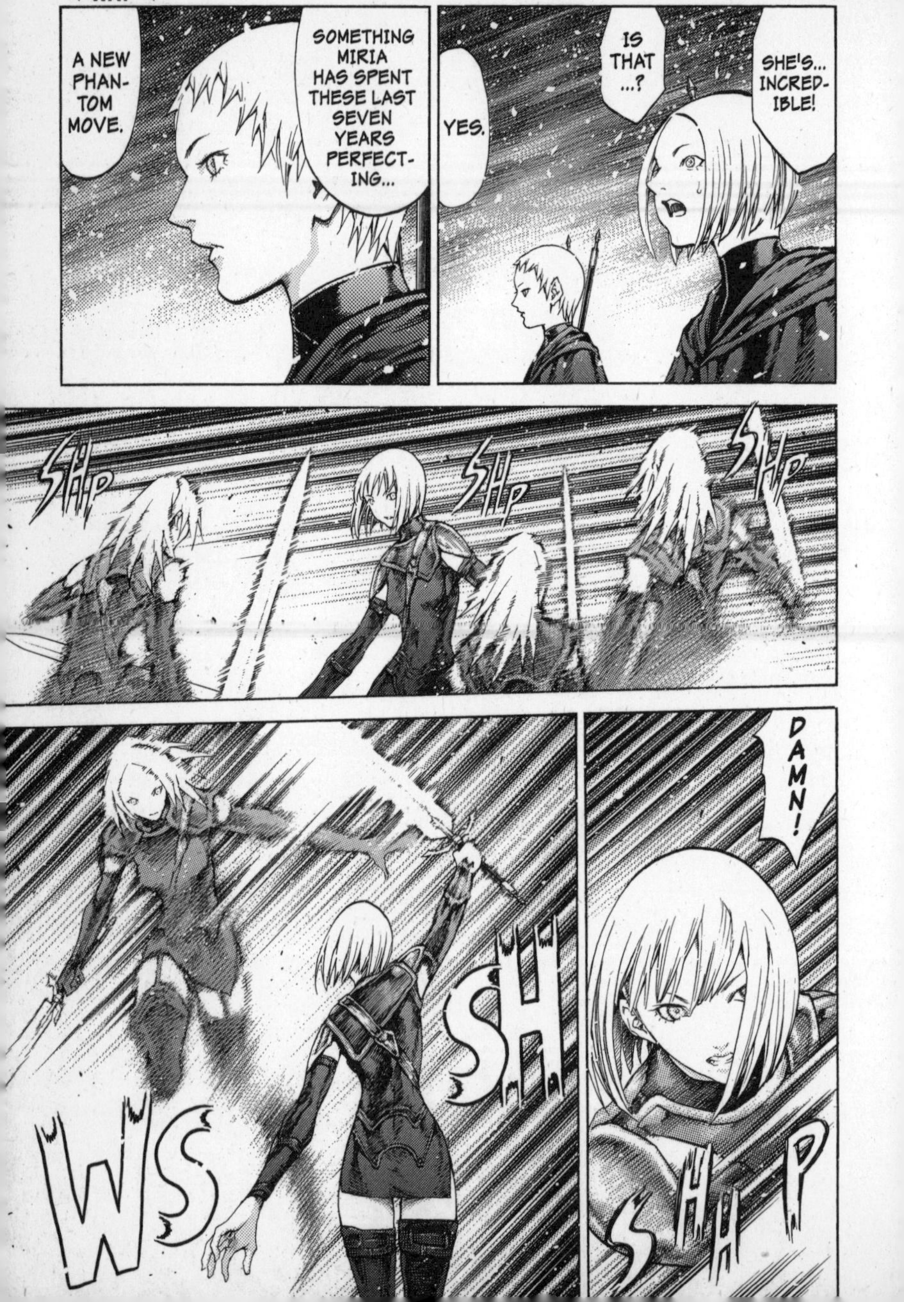
SHE'S... INCREDIBLE!
IS THAT ...?
YES.
SOMETHING MIRIA HAS SPENT THESE LAST SEVEN YEARS PERFECTING...
A NEW PHANTOM MOVE.
SHP
SHP
SHP
DAMN!
SHHP
SH
WS

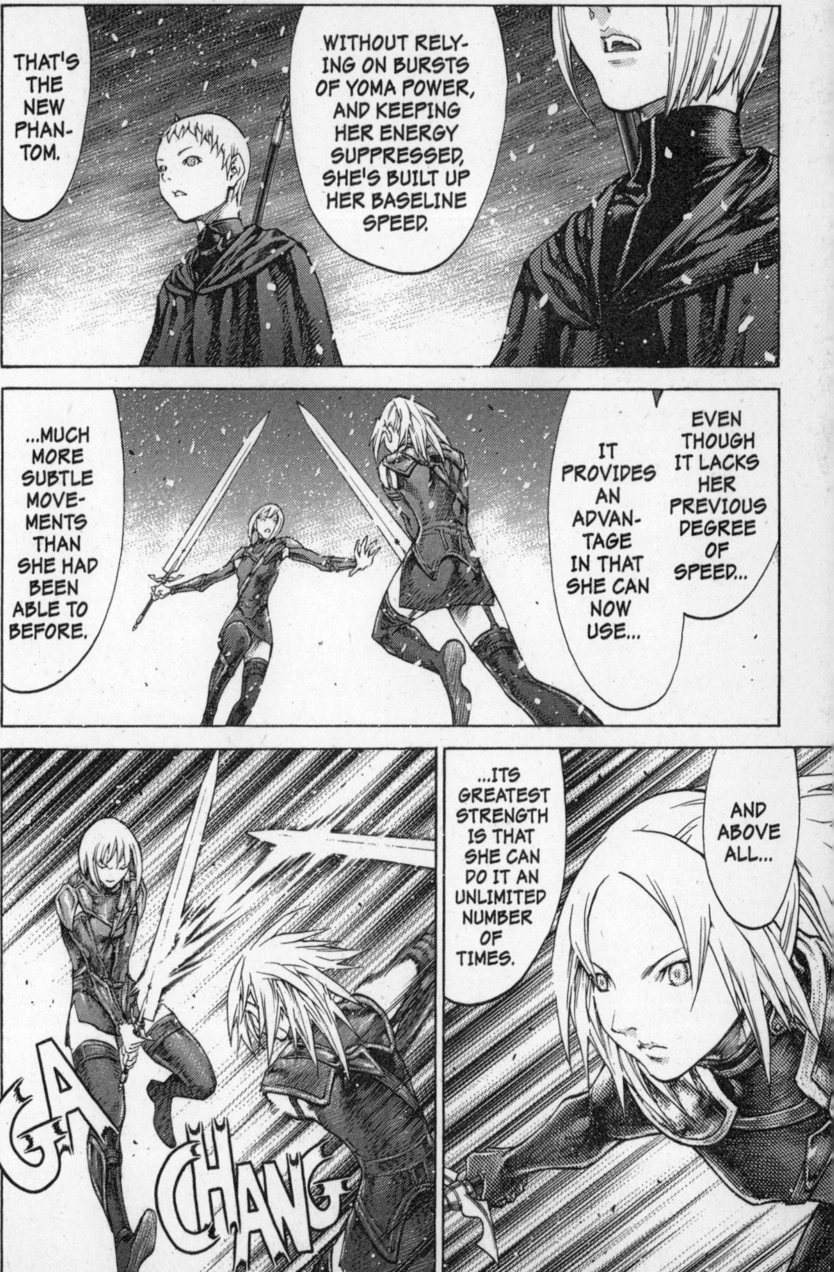
WITHOUT RELYING ON BURSTS OF YOMA POWER, AND KEEPING HER ENERGY SUPPRESSED, SHE'S BUILT UP HER BASELINE SPEED.
THAT'S THE NEW PHANTOM.
EVEN THOUGH IT LACKS HER PREVIOUS DEGREE OF SPEED...
IT PROVIDES AN ADVANTAGE IN THAT SHE CAN NOW USE...
...MUCH MORE SUBTLE MOVEMENTS THAN SHE HAD BEEN ABLE TO BEFORE.
AND ABOVE ALL...
...ITS GREATEST STRENGTH IS THAT SHE CAN DO IT AN UNLIMITED NUMBER OF TIMES.
GA CHANG

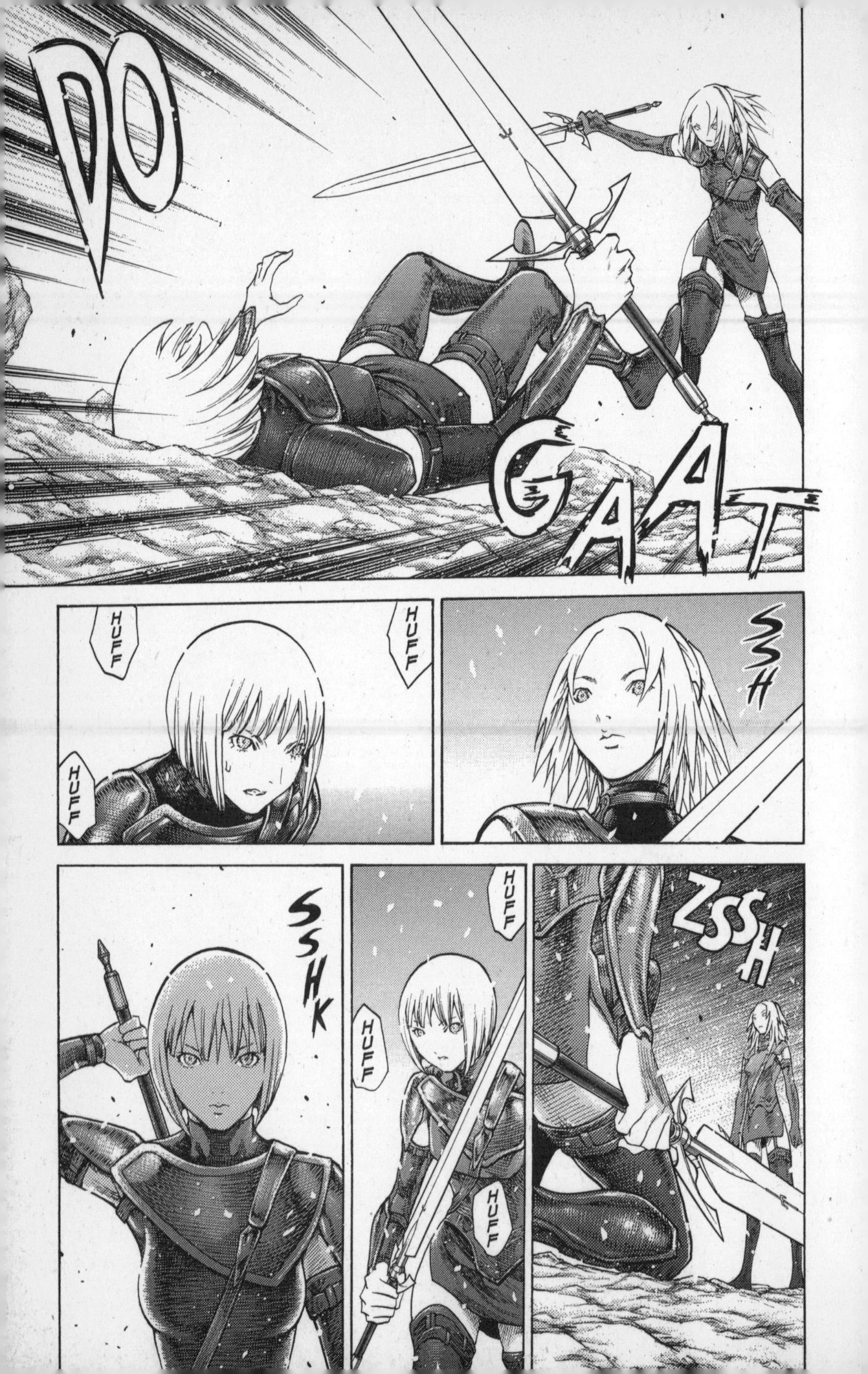
DO
GAAT
SSH
HUFF
HUFF
HUFF
ZSSH
HUFF
HUFF
HUFF
SSHK

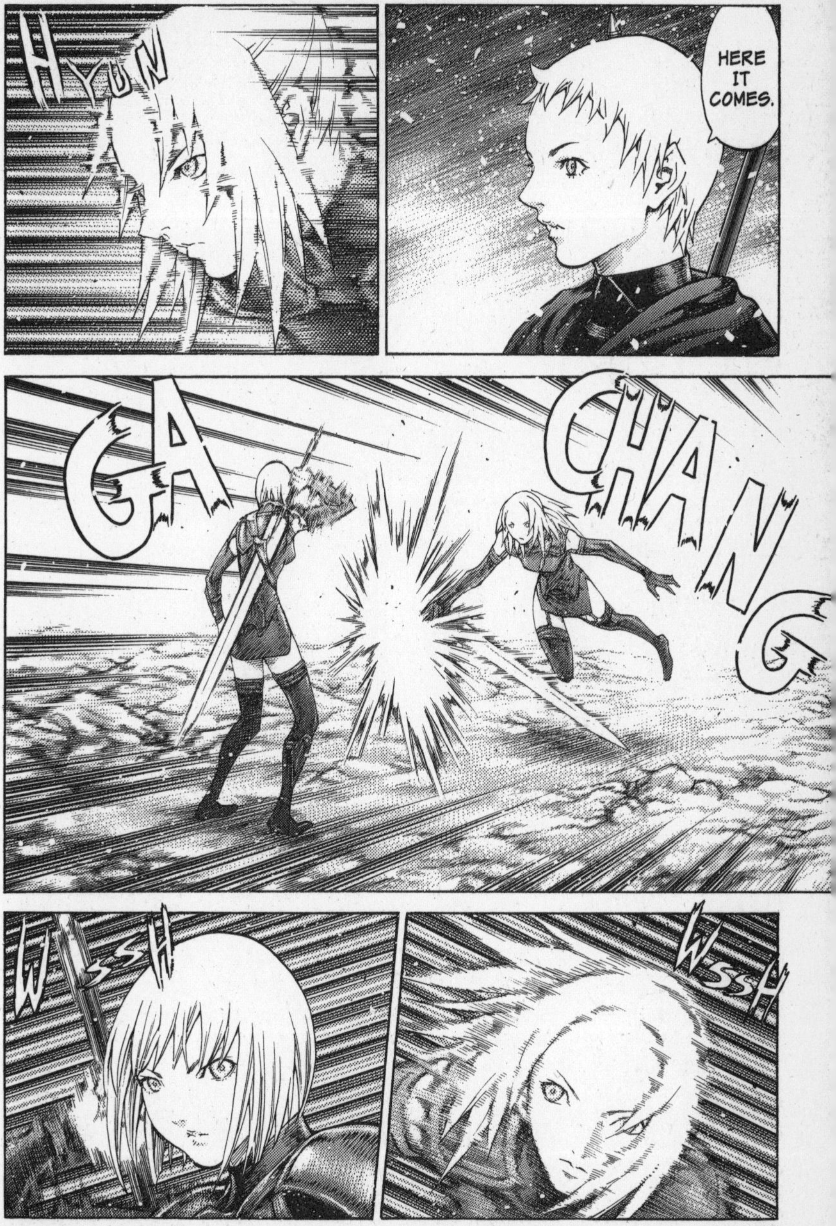
HERE IT COMES.
HYUN
GA CHANG
WSSH
WSSH

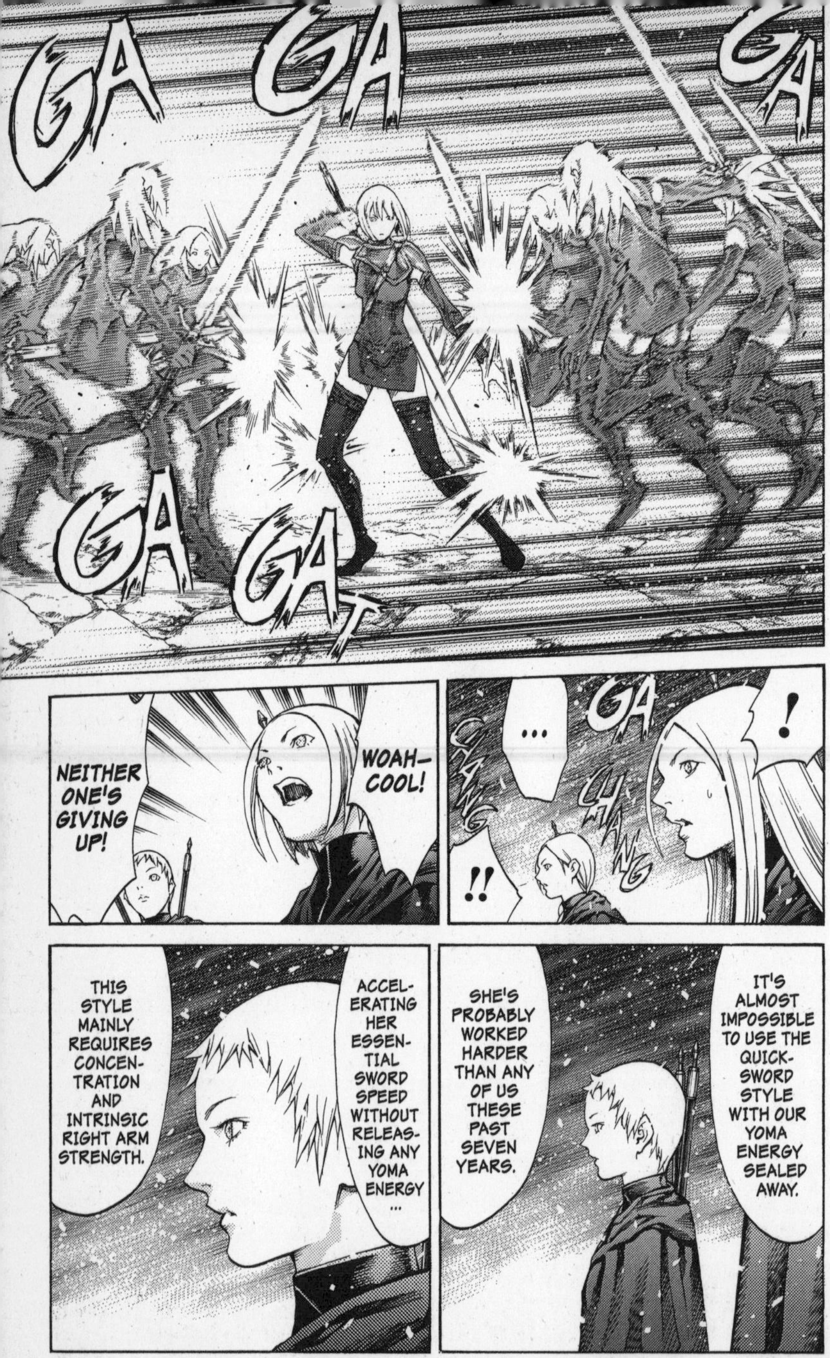
GA
GA
GA
GA
GAT
...
GA
!
CHANG
CHANG
!!
WOAH—COOL!
NEITHER ONE'S GIVING UP!
IT'S ALMOST IMPOSSIBLE TO USE THE QUICK-SWORD STYLE WITH OUR YOMA ENERGY SEALED AWAY.
SHE'S PROBABLY WORKED HARDER THAN ANY OF US THESE PAST SEVEN YEARS.
ACCELERATING HER ESSENTIAL SWORD SPEED WITHOUT RELEASING ANY YOMA ENERGY...
THIS STYLE MAINLY REQUIRES CONCENTRATION AND INTRINSIC RIGHT ARM STRENGTH.

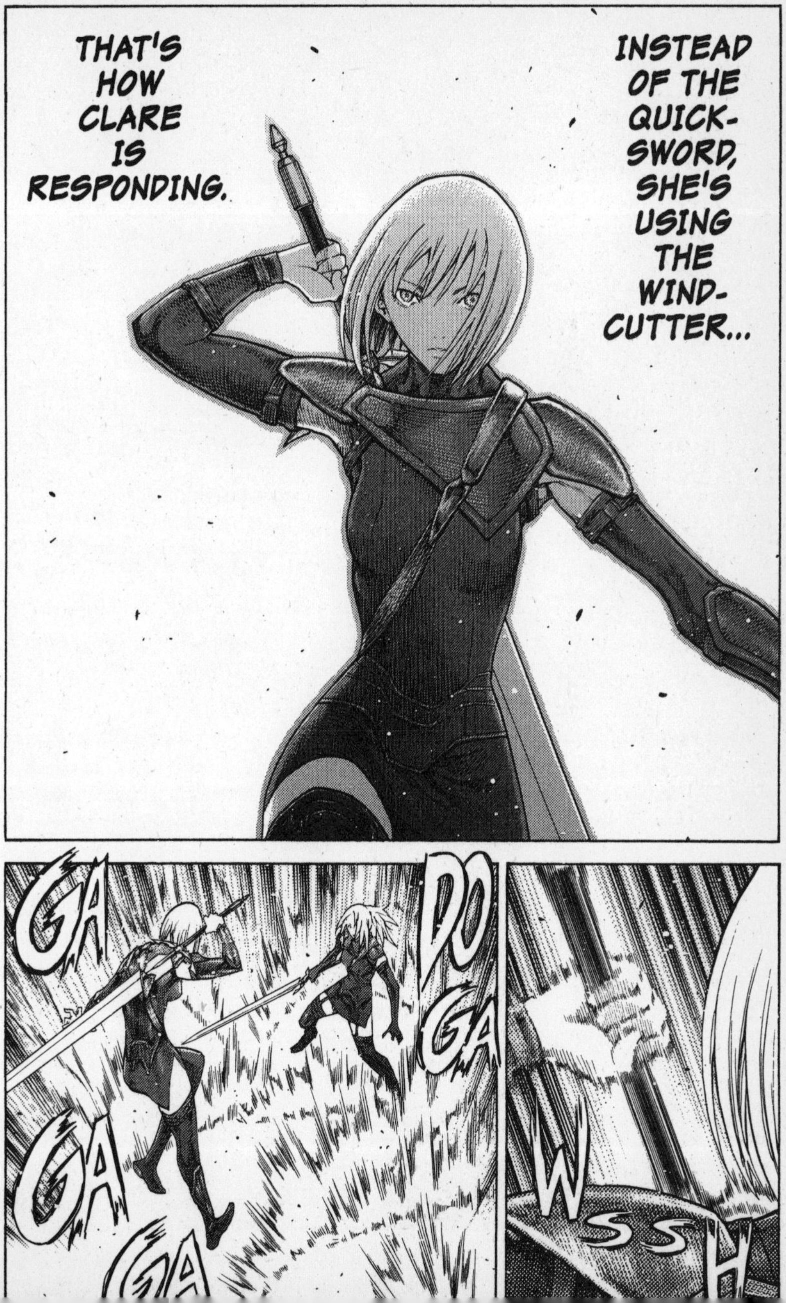
INSTEAD OF THE QUICK-SWORD, SHE'S USING THE WIND-CUTTER...
THAT'S HOW CLARE IS RESPONDING.
WSSH
DOGA
GA
GAGA

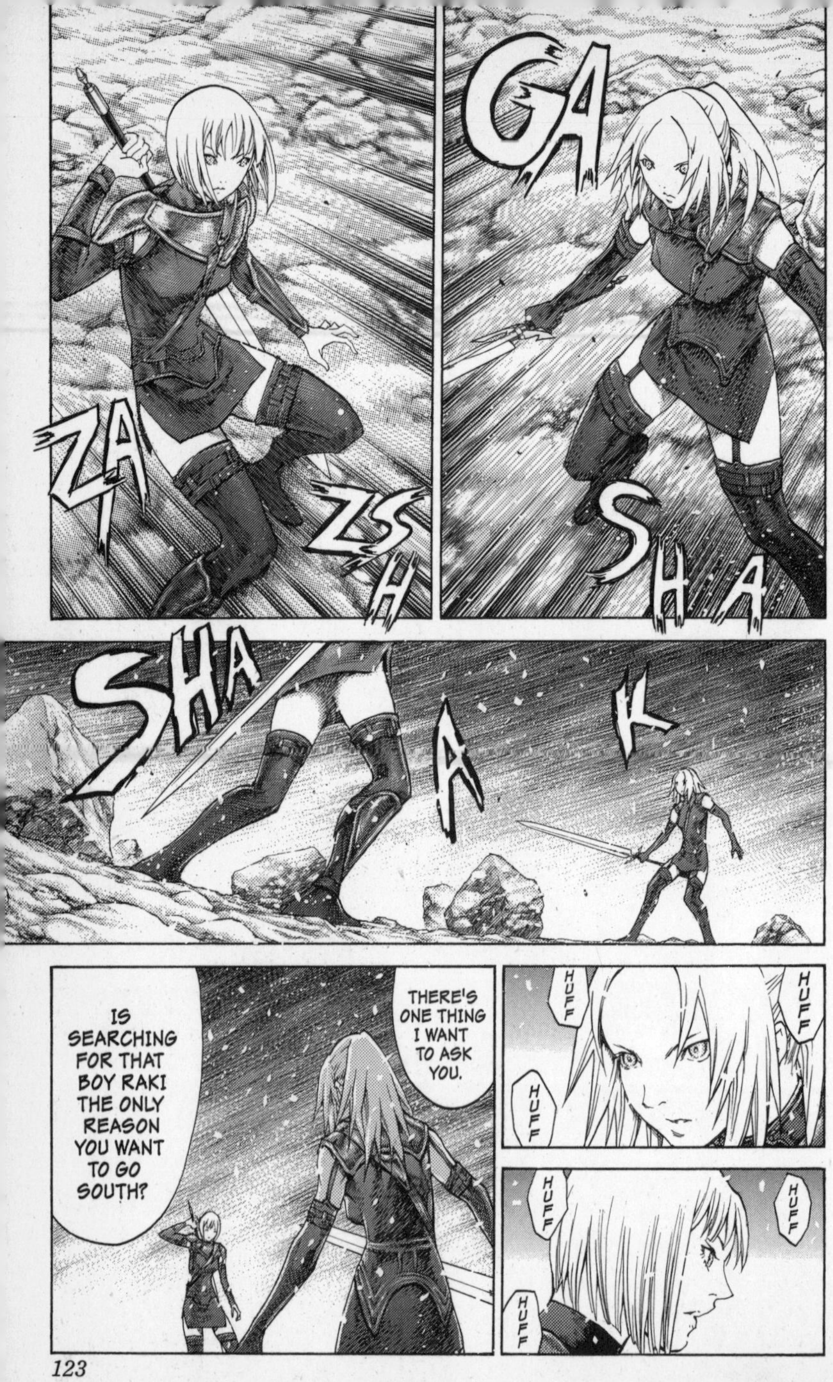
GA
SHA
ZA
ZSSH
SHA
A
K
HUFF
HUFF
HUFF
HUFF
HUFF
HUFF
THERE'S ONE THING I WANT TO ASK YOU.
IS SEARCHING FOR THAT BOY RAKI THE ONLY REASON YOU WANT TO GO SOUTH?

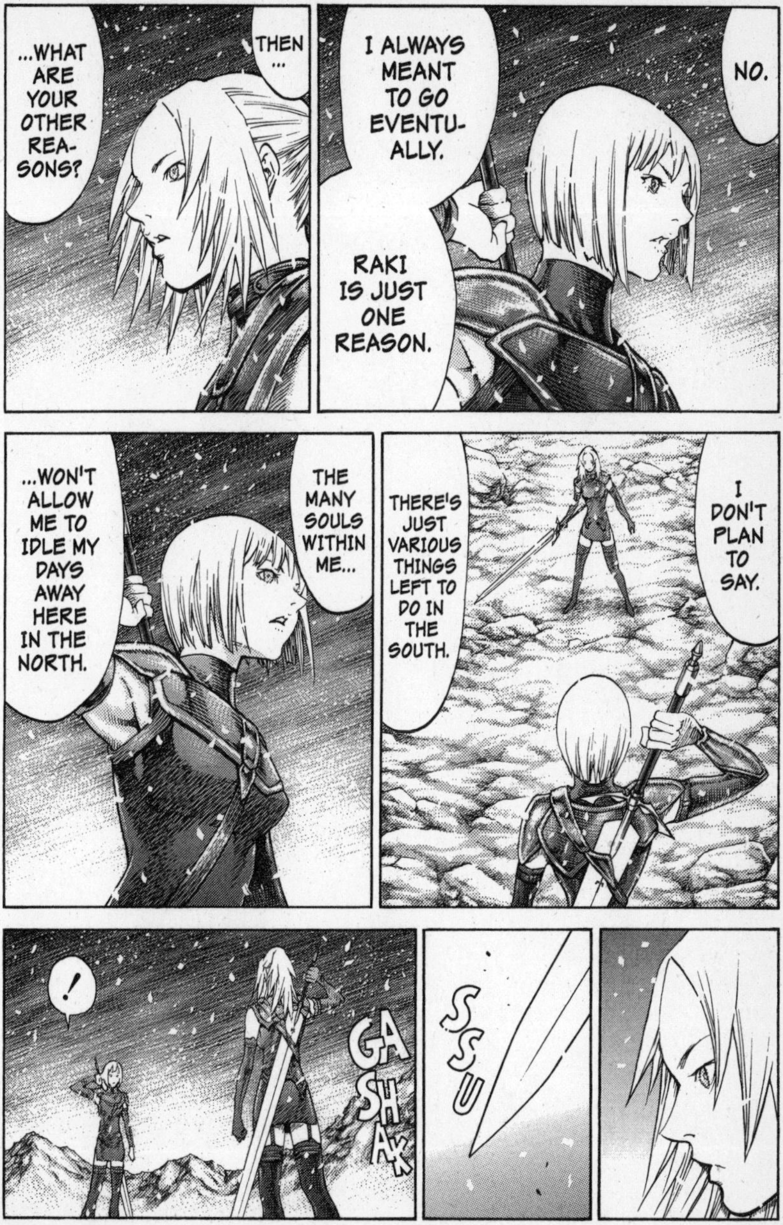
NO.
I ALWAYS MEANT TO GO EVENTUALLY.
RAKI IS JUST ONE REASON.
THEN ...
...WHAT ARE YOUR OTHER REASONS?
I DON'T PLAN TO SAY.
THERE'S JUST VARIOUS THINGS LEFT TO DO IN THE SOUTH.
THE MANY SOULS WITHIN ME...
...WON'T ALLOW ME TO IDLE MY DAYS AWAY HERE IN THE NORTH.
SSU
GASHAK
!

« READ THIS WAY «

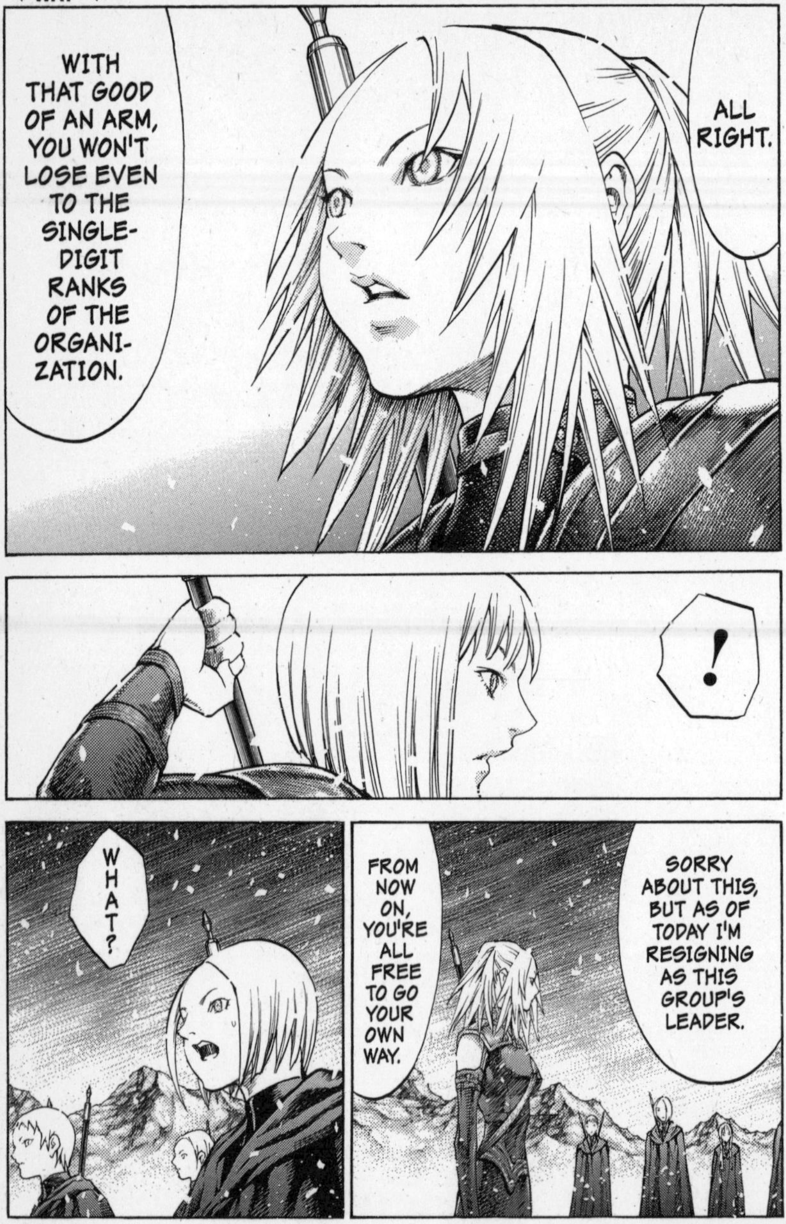
ALL RIGHT.
WITH THAT GOOD OF AN ARM, YOU WON'T LOSE EVEN TO THE SINGLE-DIGIT RANKS OF THE ORGANIZATION.
!
SORRY ABOUT THIS, BUT AS OF TODAY I'M RESIGNING AS THIS GROUP'S LEADER.
FROM NOW ON, YOU'RE ALL FREE TO GO YOUR OWN WAY.
WHAT?

I'M GOING SOUTH WITH HER...
...TO DEFEAT THE ENEMIES OF OUR FRIENDS AND COM-RADES.
!!

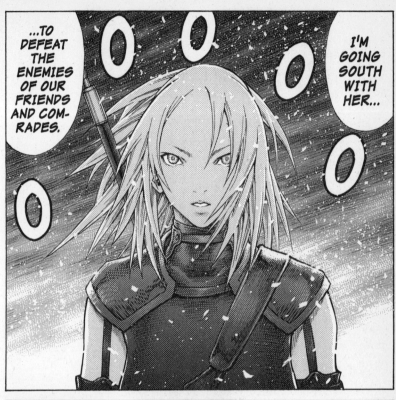

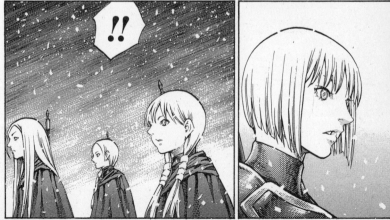

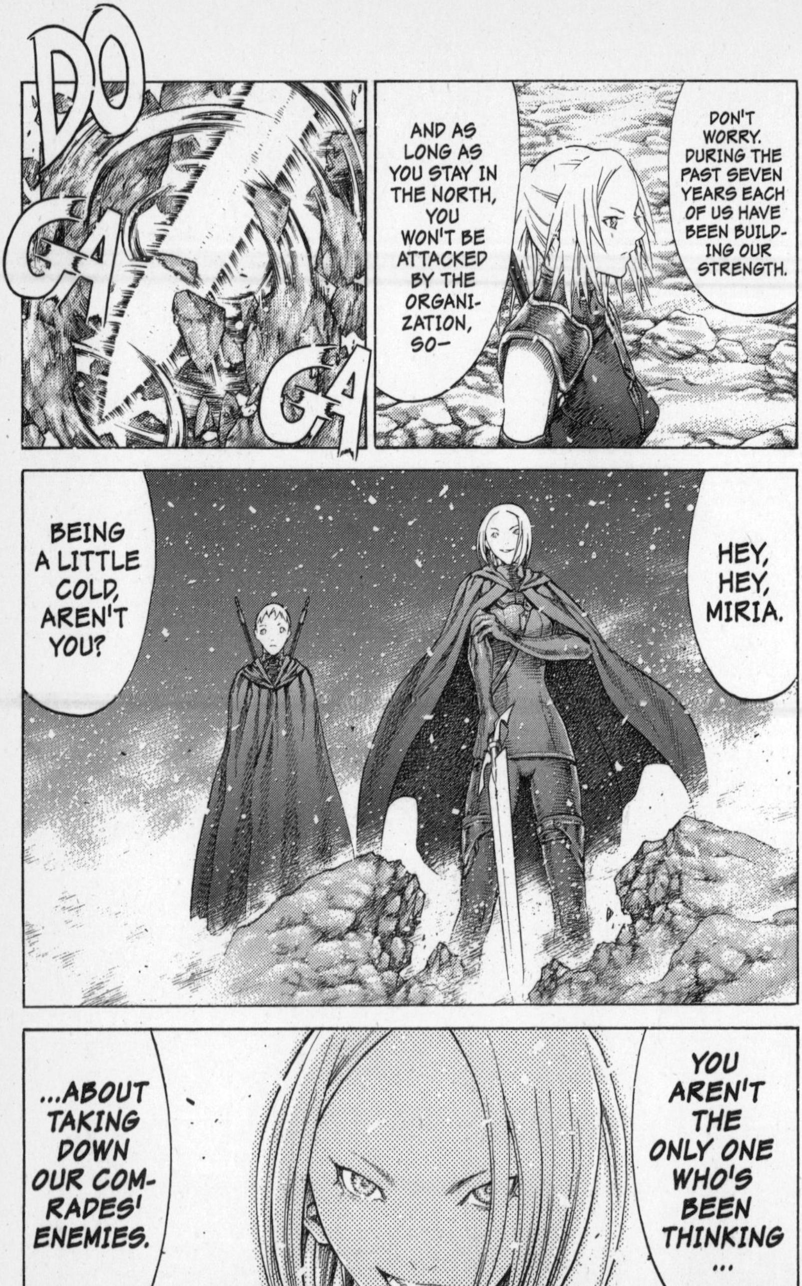
DON'T WORRY. DURING THE PAST SEVEN YEARS EACH OF US HAVE BEEN BUILD-ING OUR STRENGTH.
AND AS LONG AS YOU STAY IN THE NORTH, YOU WON'T BE ATTACKED BY THE ORGANI-ZATION, SO—
DO
GA
GA
HEY, HEY, MIRIA.
BEING A LITTLE COLD, AREN'T YOU?
YOU AREN'T THE ONLY ONE WHO'S BEEN THINKING ...
...ABOUT TAKING DOWN OUR COM-RADES' ENEMIES.

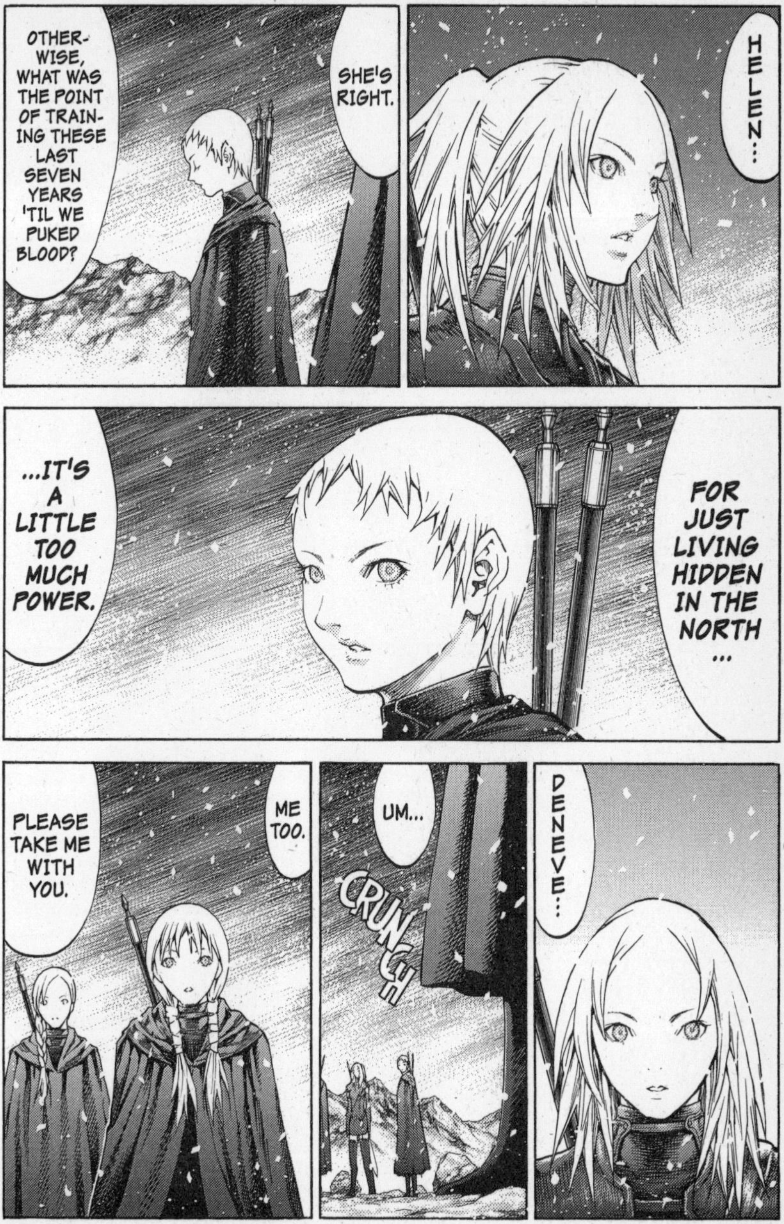
HELEN...
SHE'S RIGHT.
OTHER-WISE, WHAT WAS THE POINT OF TRAINING THESE LAST SEVEN YEARS 'TIL WE PUKED BLOOD?
FOR JUST LIVING HIDDEN IN THE NORTH...
...IT'S A LITTLE TOO MUCH POWER.
DENEVE...
UM...
CRUNCH
ME TOO.
PLEASE TAKE ME WITH YOU.

READ THIS WAY

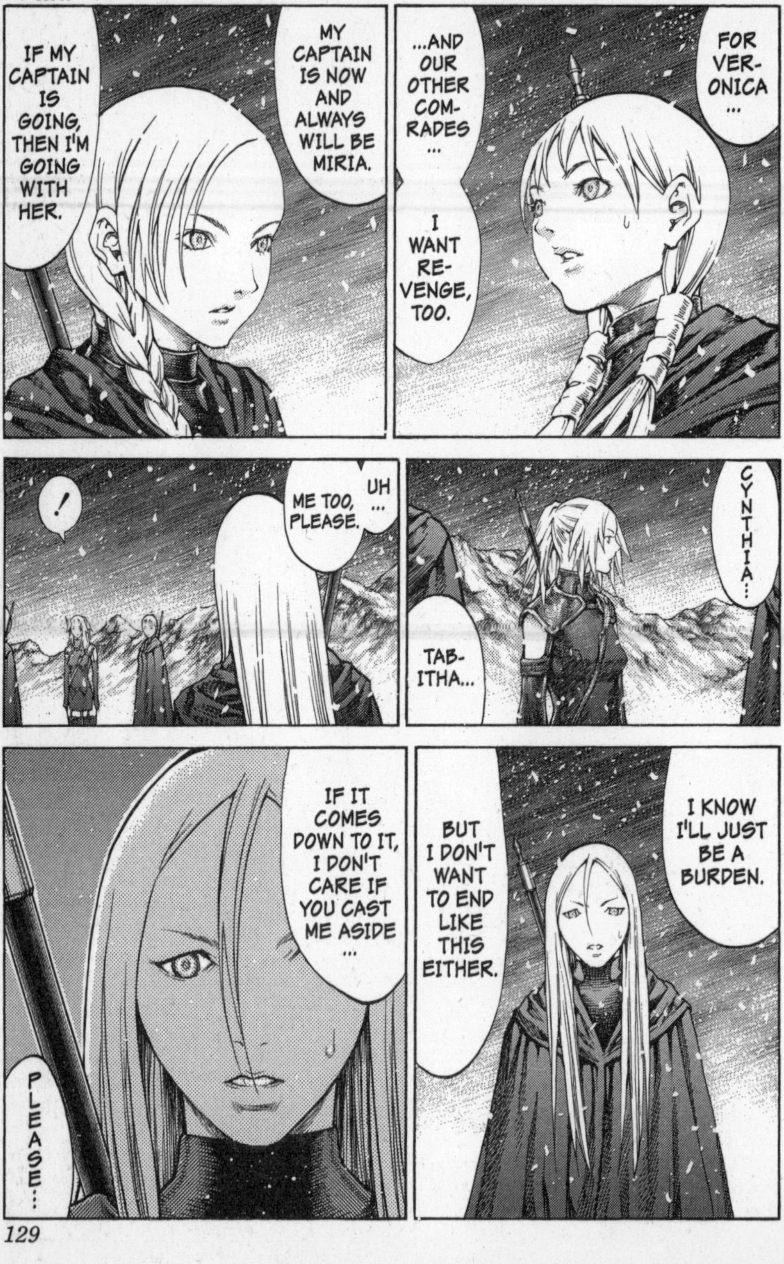

FOR VERONICA ...
...AND OUR OTHER COMRADES ...
I WANT REVENGE, TOO.
MY CAPTAIN IS NOW AND ALWAYS WILL BE MIRIA.
IF MY CAPTAIN IS GOING, THEN I'M GOING WITH HER.
CYNTHIA...
TABITHA...
UH ...
ME TOO, PLEASE.
!
I KNOW I'LL JUST BE A BURDEN.
BUT I DON'T WANT TO END LIKE THIS EITHER.
IF IT COMES DOWN TO IT, I DON'T CARE IF YOU CAST ME ASIDE ...
PLEASE...

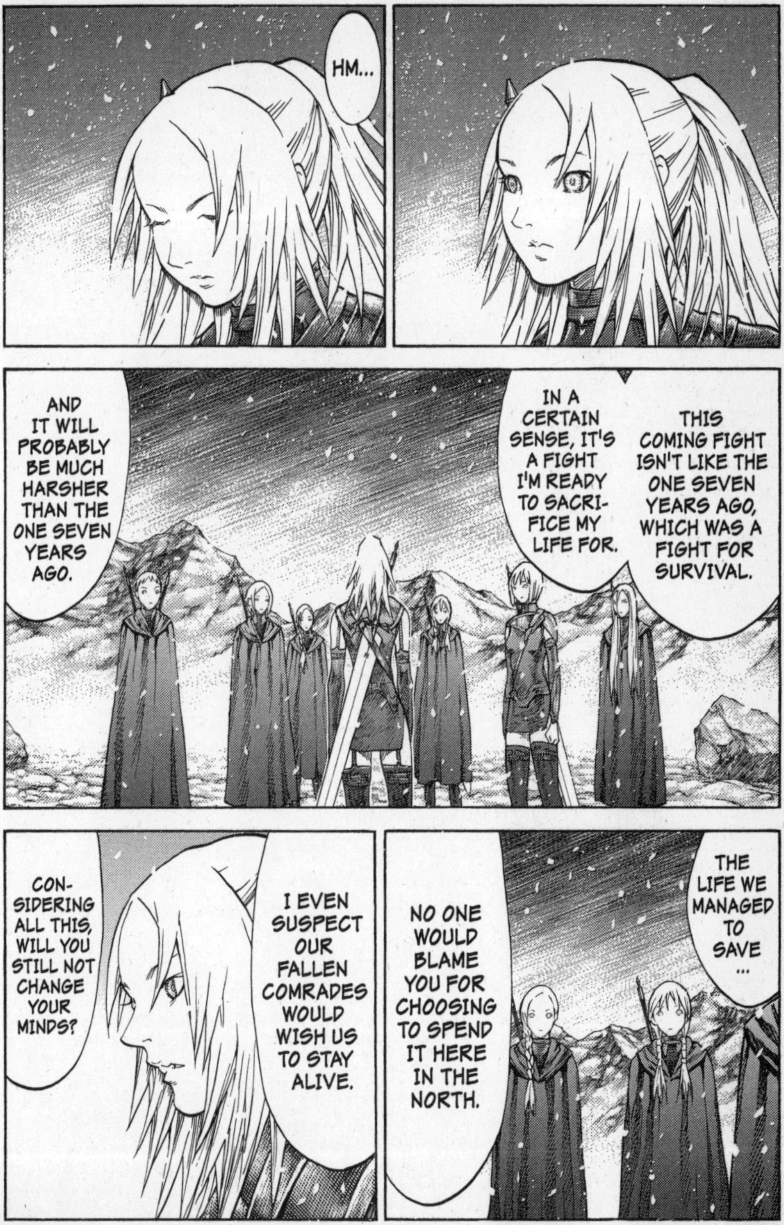
HM...
THIS COMING FIGHT ISN'T LIKE THE ONE SEVEN YEARS AGO, WHICH WAS A FIGHT FOR SURVIVAL.
IN A CERTAIN SENSE, IT'S A FIGHT I'M READY TO SACRI-FICE MY LIFE FOR.
AND IT WILL PROBABLY BE MUCH HARSHER THAN THE ONE SEVEN YEARS AGO.
THE LIFE WE MANAGED TO SAVE ...
NO ONE WOULD BLAME YOU FOR CHOOSING TO SPEND IT HERE IN THE NORTH.
I EVEN SUSPECT OUR FALLEN COMRADES WOULD WISH US TO STAY ALIVE.
CON-SIDERING ALL THIS, WILL YOU STILL NOT CHANGE YOUR MINDS?

READ THIS WAY

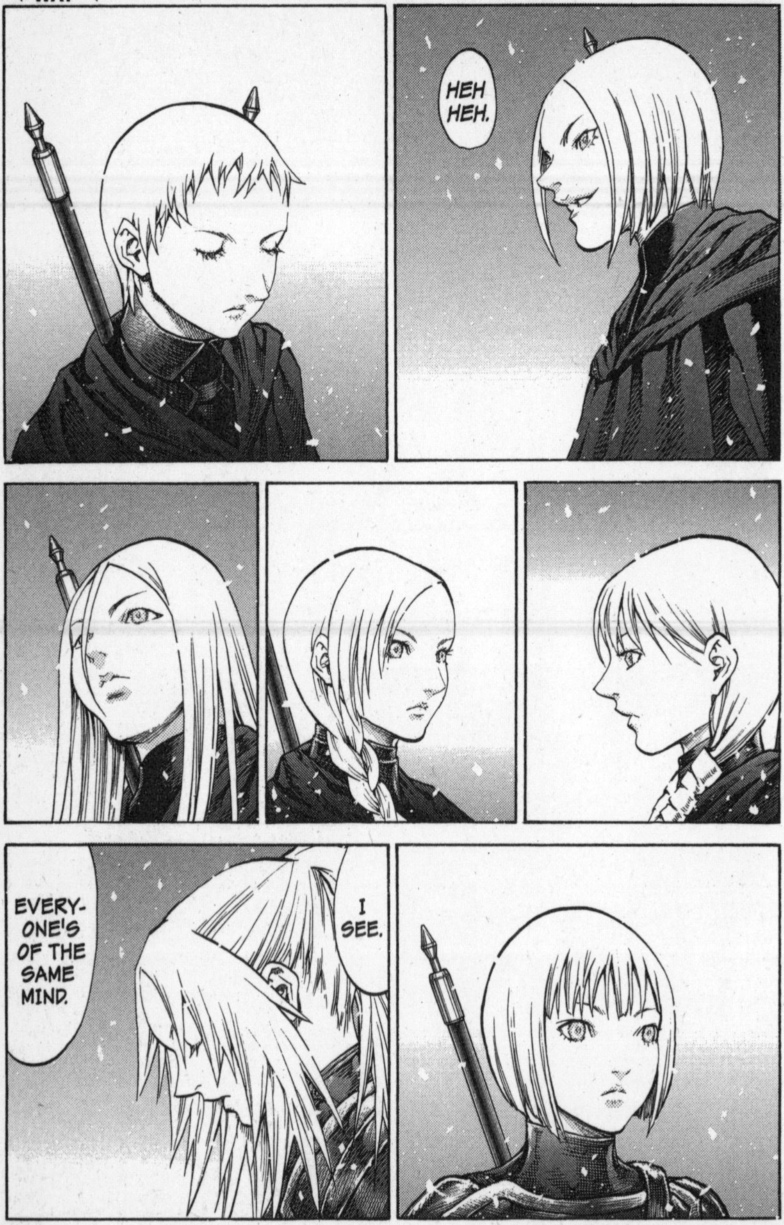
HEH HEH.
I SEE.
EVERY-ONE'S OF THE SAME MIND.

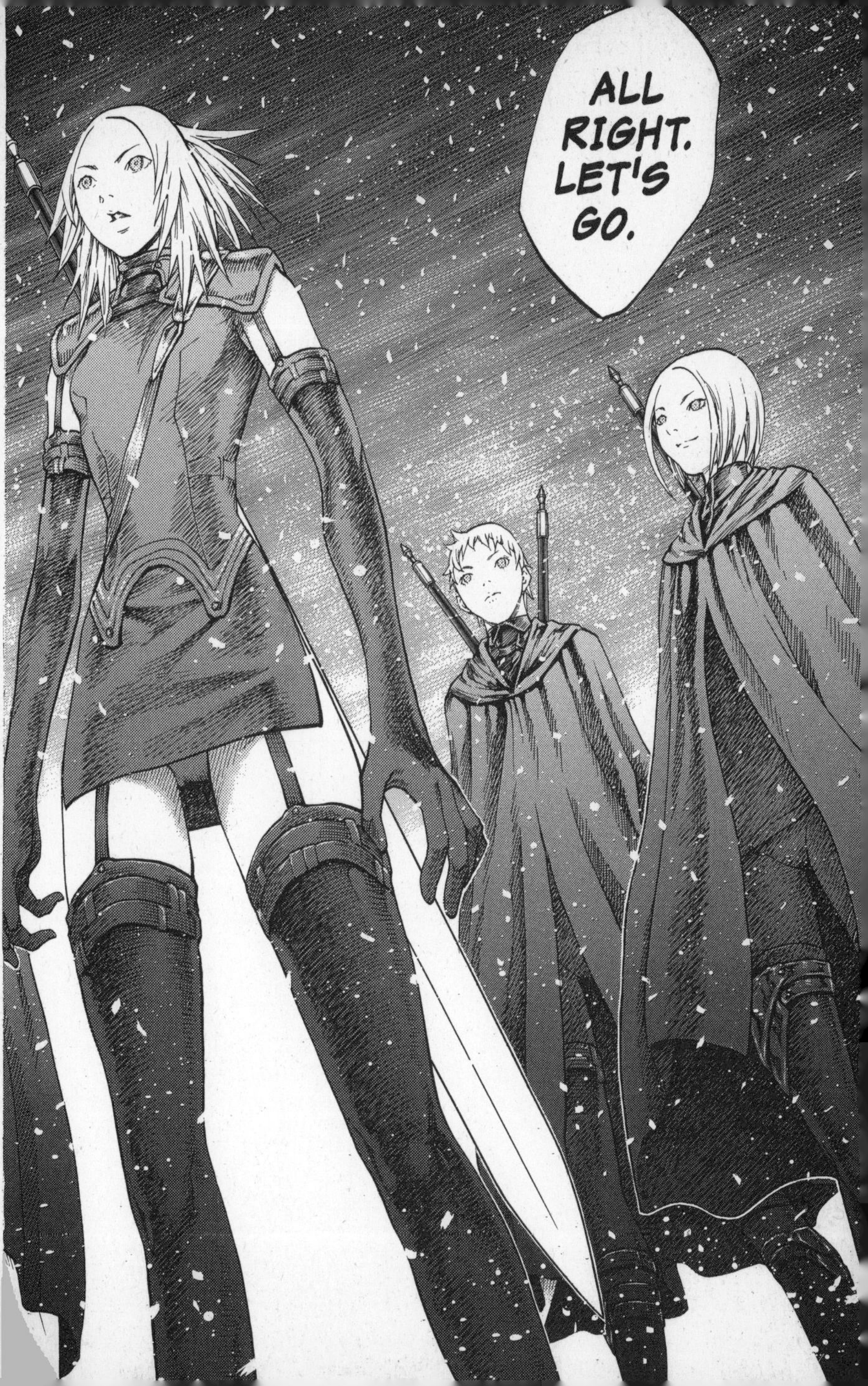
ALL RIGHT. LET'S GO.

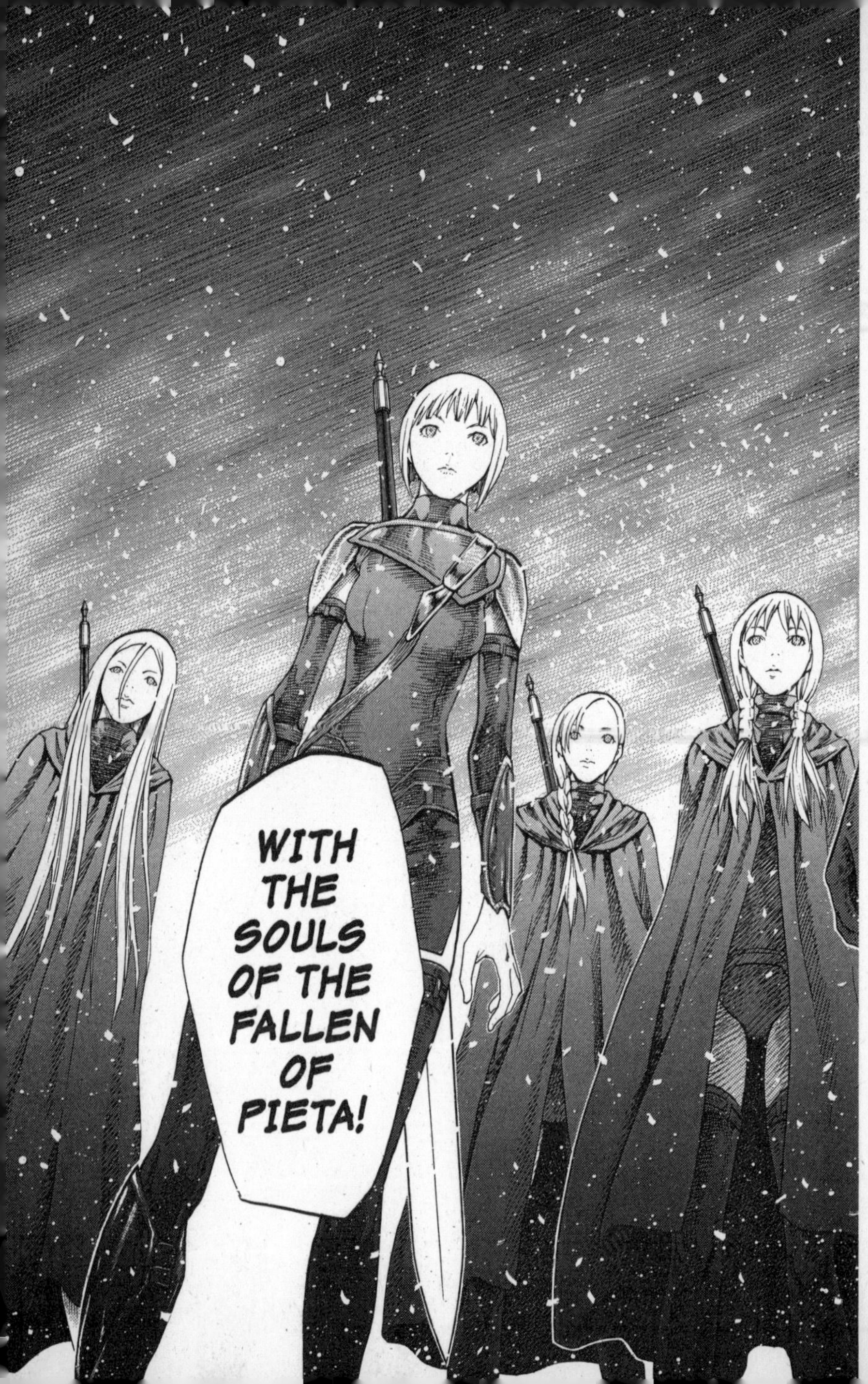
WITH THE SOULS OF THE FALLEN OF PIETA!

クレイモア
Claymore

Scene 68: The Defiant Ones, Part 1

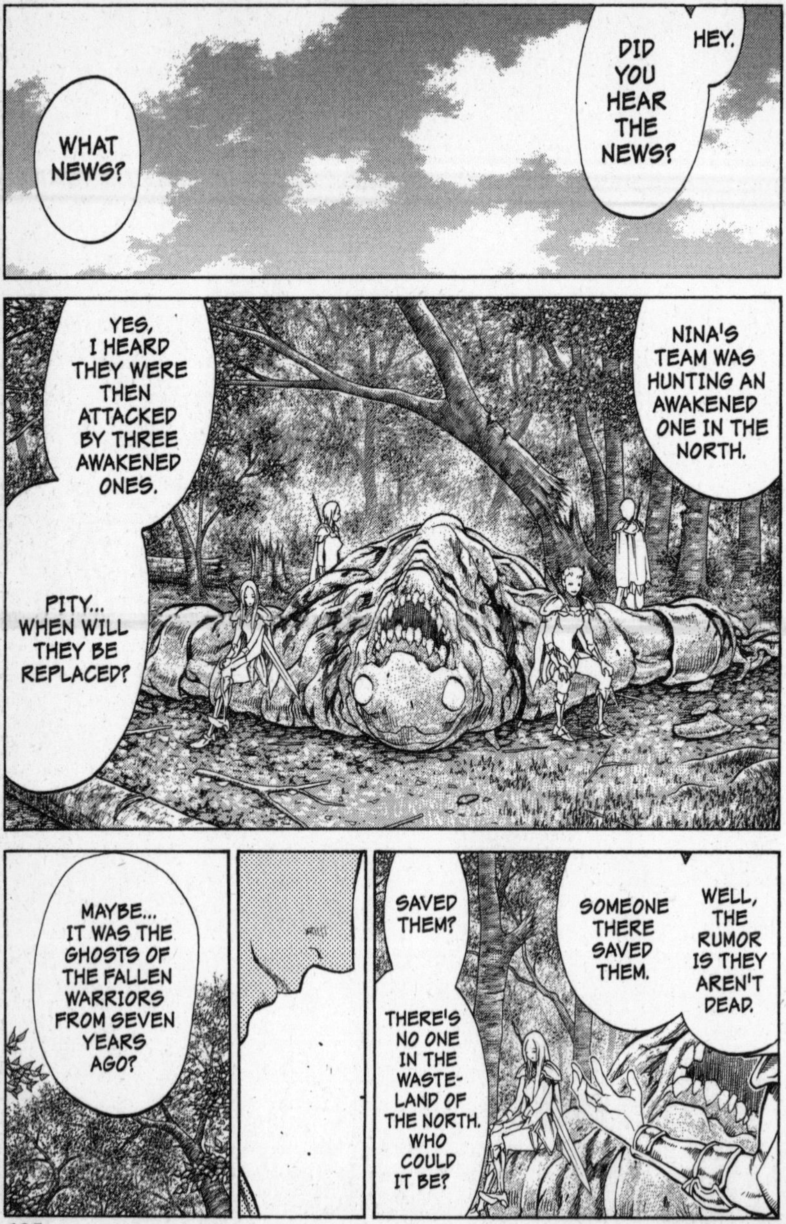
HEY.
DID YOU HEAR THE NEWS?
WHAT NEWS?
NINA'S TEAM WAS HUNTING AN AWAKENED ONE IN THE NORTH.
YES, I HEARD THEY WERE THEN ATTACKED BY THREE AWAKENED ONES.
PITY... WHEN WILL THEY BE REPLACED?
WELL, THE RUMOR IS THEY AREN'T DEAD.
SOMEONE THERE SAVED THEM.
SAVED THEM?
THERE'S NO ONE IN THE WASTE-LAND OF THE NORTH. WHO COULD IT BE?
MAYBE... IT WAS THE GHOSTS OF THE FALLEN WARRIORS FROM SEVEN YEARS AGO?

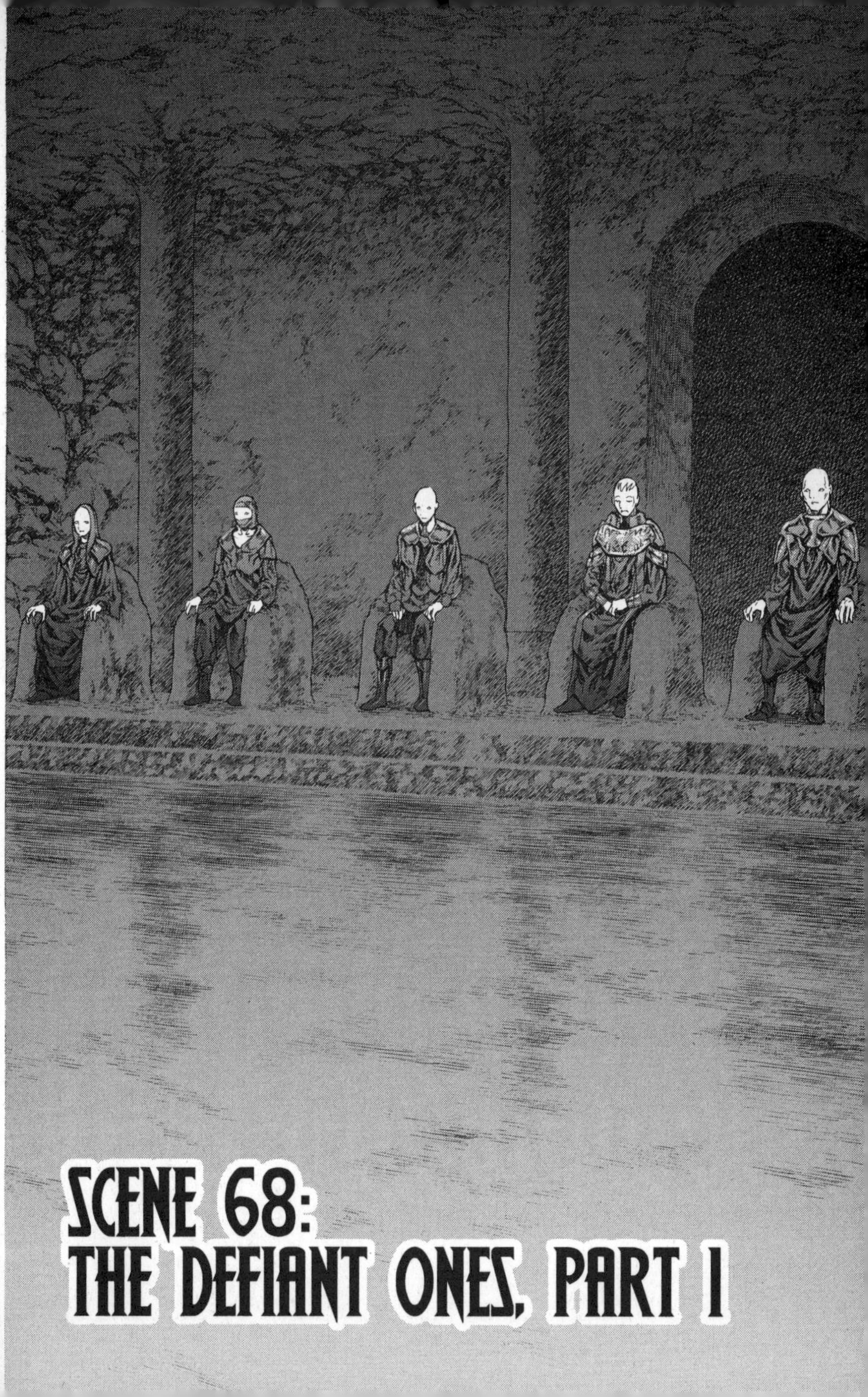
SCENE 68:
THE DEFIANT ONES, PART 1

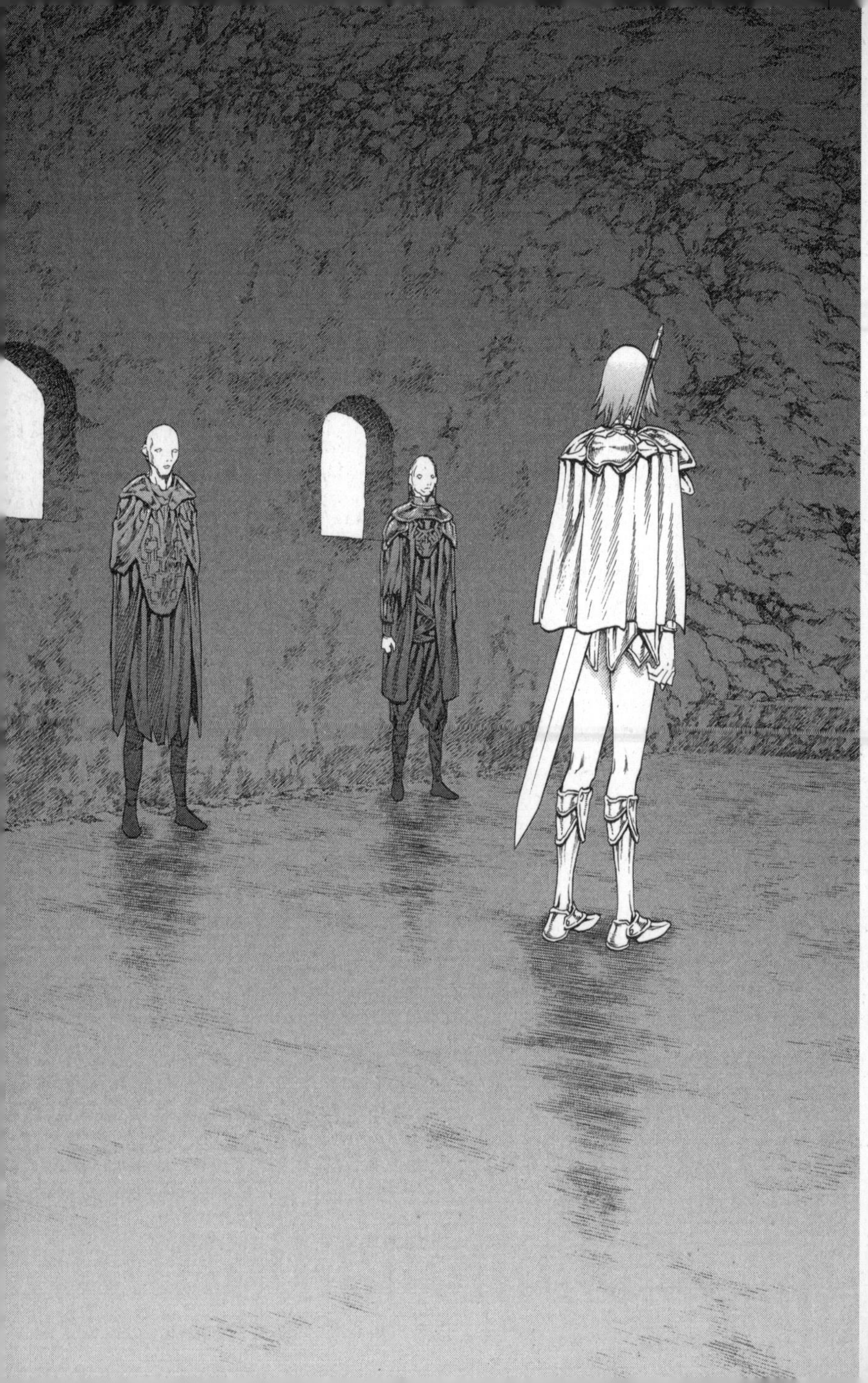

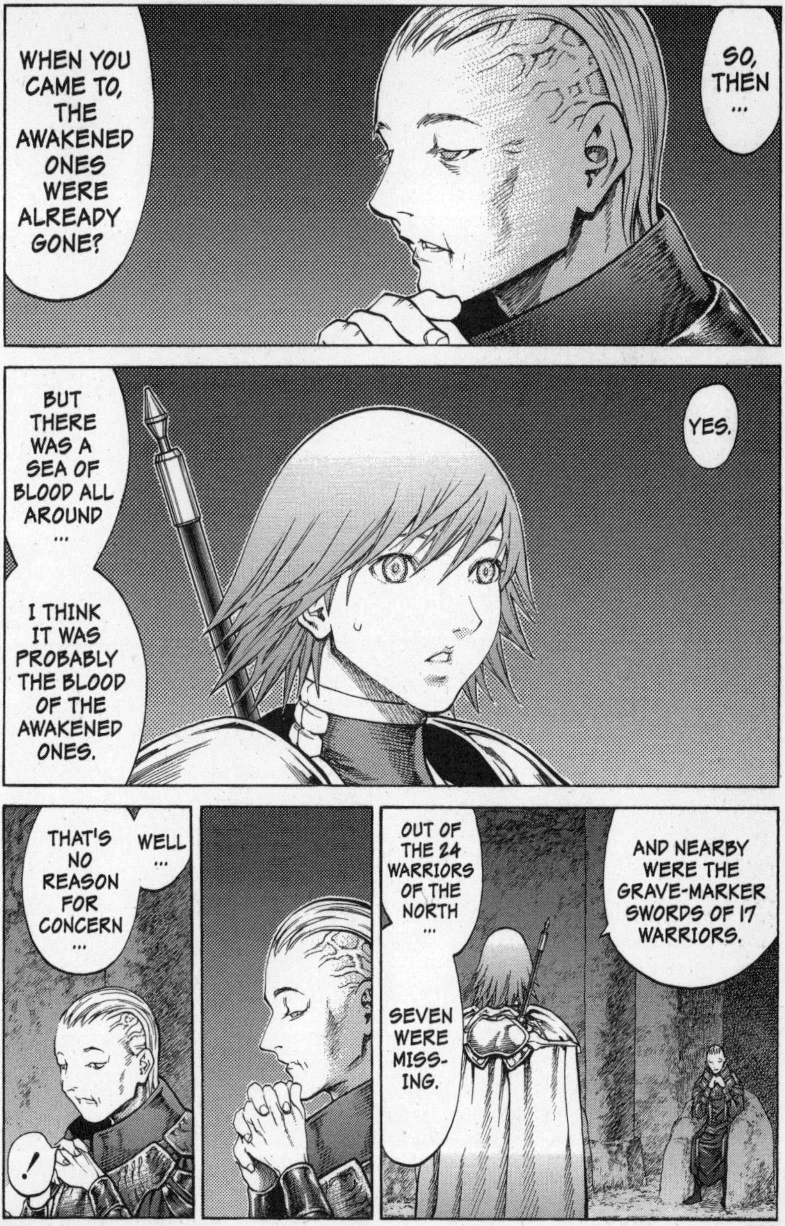
SO, THEN ...
WHEN YOU CAME TO, THE AWAKENED ONES WERE ALREADY GONE?
YES.
BUT THERE WAS A SEA OF BLOOD ALL AROUND ...
I THINK IT WAS PROBABLY THE BLOOD OF THE AWAKENED ONES.
AND NEARBY WERE THE GRAVE-MARKER SWORDS OF 17 WARRIORS.
OUT OF THE 24 WARRIORS OF THE NORTH ...
SEVEN WERE MISS-ING.
WELL ...
THAT'S NO REASON FOR CONCERN ...
!

READ THIS WAY

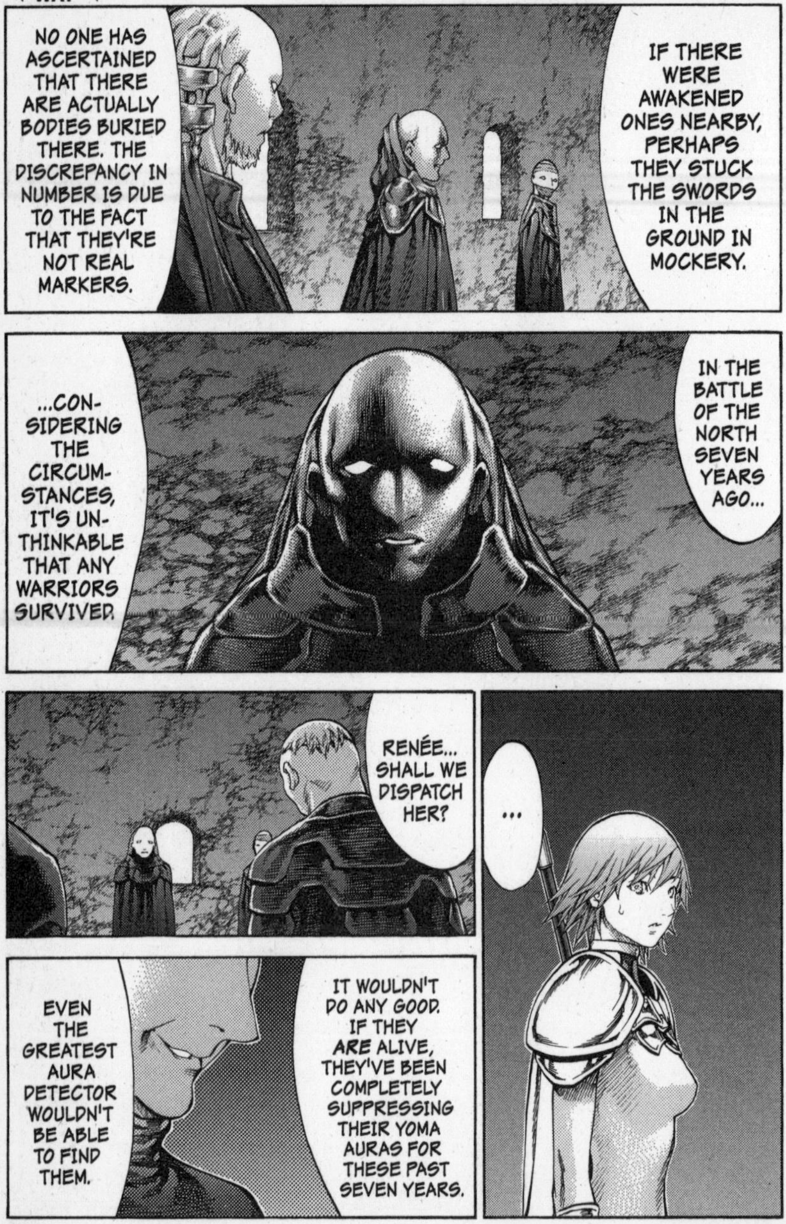
IF THERE WERE AWAKENED ONES NEARBY, PERHAPS THEY STUCK THE SWORDS IN THE GROUND IN MOCKERY.
NO ONE HAS ASCERTAINED THAT THERE ARE ACTUALLY BODIES BURIED THERE. THE DISCREPANCY IN NUMBER IS DUE TO THE FACT THAT THEY'RE NOT REAL MARKERS.
IN THE BATTLE OF THE NORTH SEVEN YEARS AGO...
...CONSIDERING THE CIRCUMSTANCES, IT'S UNTHINKABLE THAT ANY WARRIORS SURVIVED.
...
RENÉE... SHALL WE DISPATCH HER?
IT WOULDN'T DO ANY GOOD. IF THEY **ARE** ALIVE, THEY'VE BEEN COMPLETELY SUPPRESSING THEIR YOMA AURAS FOR THESE PAST SEVEN YEARS.
EVEN THE GREATEST AURA DETECTOR WOULDN'T BE ABLE TO FIND THEM.

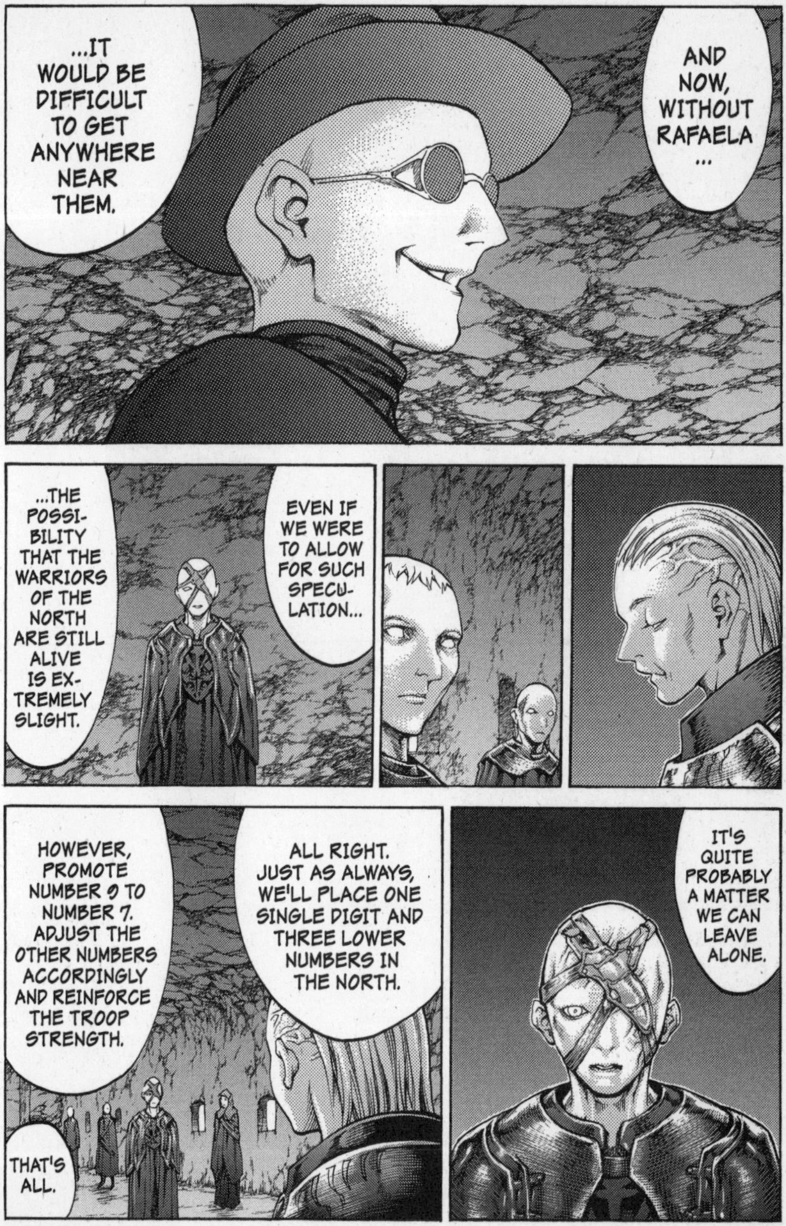
AND NOW, WITHOUT RAFAELA ...
...IT WOULD BE DIFFICULT TO GET ANYWHERE NEAR THEM.
EVEN IF WE WERE TO ALLOW FOR SUCH SPECU-LATION...
...THE POSSI-BILITY THAT THE WARRIORS OF THE NORTH ARE STILL ALIVE IS EX-TREMELY SLIGHT.
IT'S QUITE PROBABLY A MATTER WE CAN LEAVE ALONE.
ALL RIGHT. JUST AS ALWAYS, WE'LL PLACE ONE SINGLE DIGIT AND THREE LOWER NUMBERS IN THE NORTH.
HOWEVER, PROMOTE NUMBER 9 TO NUMBER 7. ADJUST THE OTHER NUMBERS ACCORDINGLY AND REINFORCE THE TROOP STRENGTH.
THAT'S ALL.

READ THIS WAY

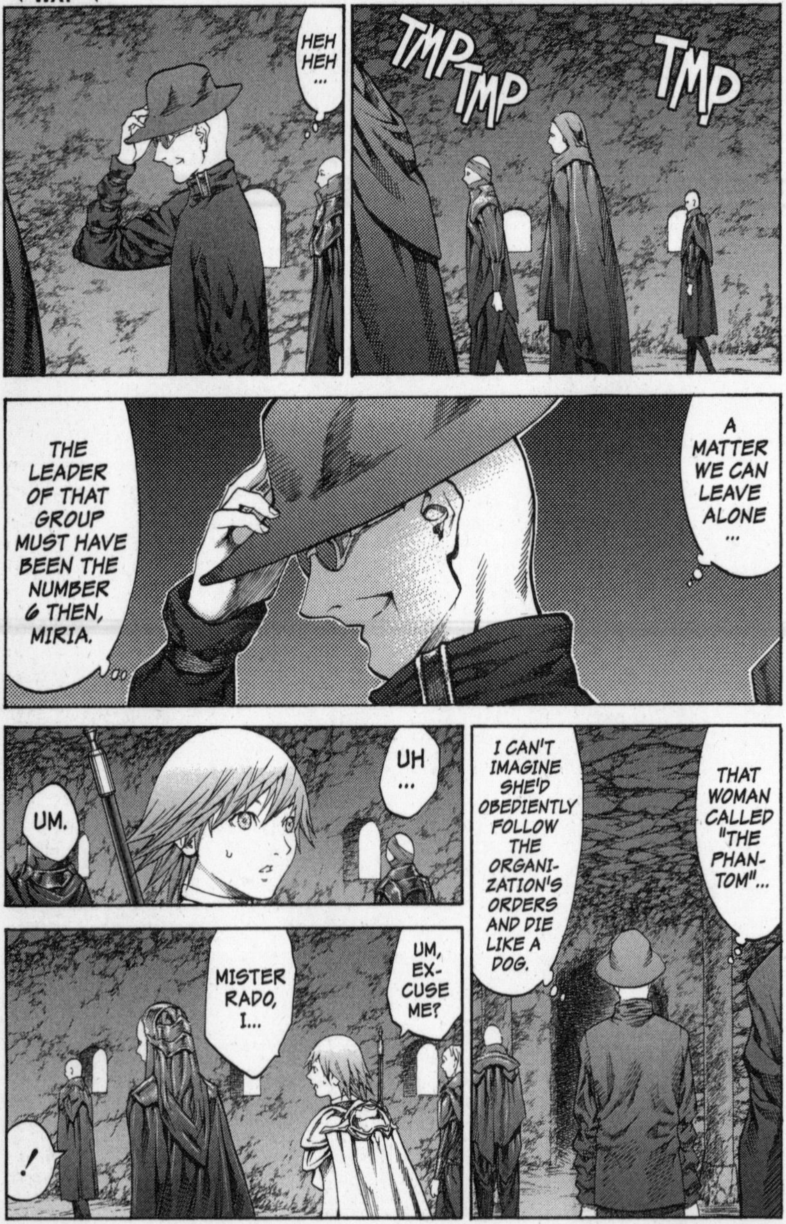
TMP TMP
TMP
HEH HEH ...
A MATTER WE CAN LEAVE ALONE ...
THE LEADER OF THAT GROUP MUST HAVE BEEN THE NUMBER 6 THEN, MIRIA.
THAT WOMAN CALLED "THE PHANTOM"...
I CAN'T IMAGINE SHE'D OBEDIENTLY FOLLOW THE ORGANIZATION'S ORDERS AND DIE LIKE A DOG.
UH ...
UM.
UM, EXCUSE ME?
MISTER RADO, I...
!

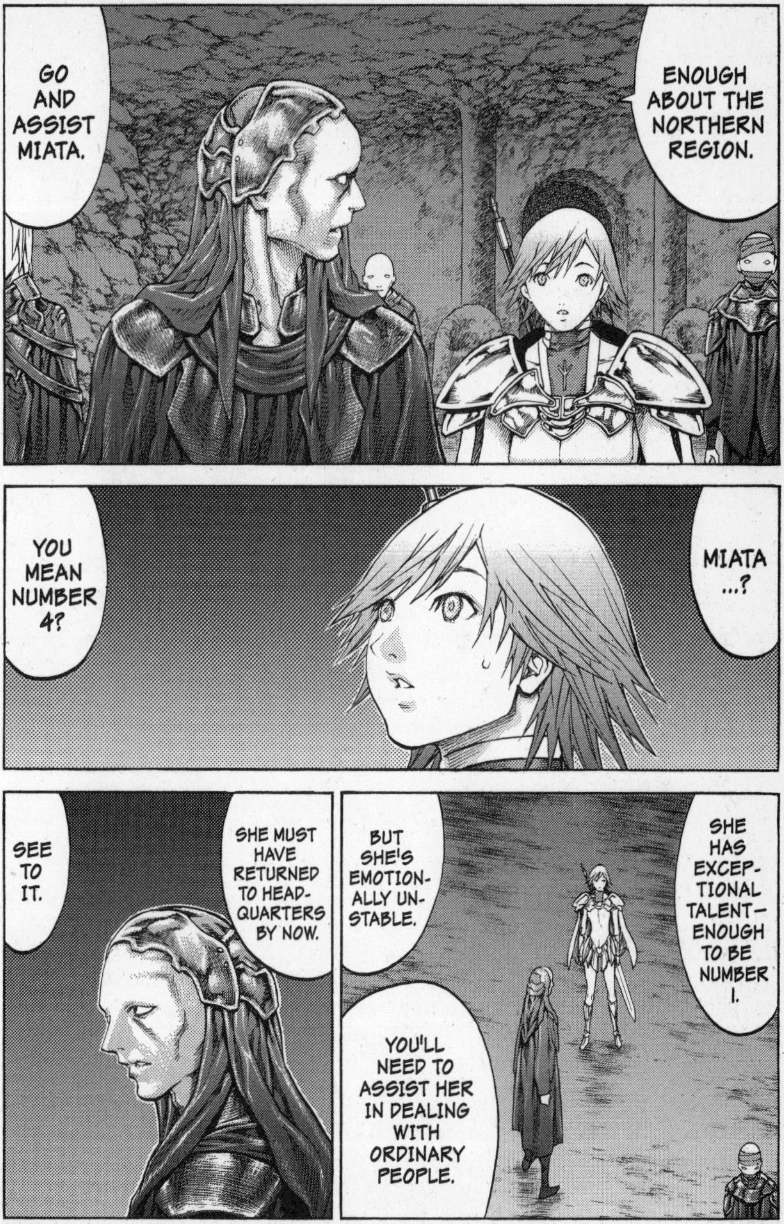
ENOUGH ABOUT THE NORTHERN REGION.
GO AND ASSIST MIATA.
MIATA ...?
YOU MEAN NUMBER 4?
SHE HAS EXCEPTIONAL TALENT—ENOUGH TO BE NUMBER 1.
BUT SHE'S EMOTIONALLY UNSTABLE.
YOU'LL NEED TO ASSIST HER IN DEALING WITH ORDINARY PEOPLE.
SHE MUST HAVE RETURNED TO HEADQUARTERS BY NOW.
SEE TO IT.

READ THIS WAY

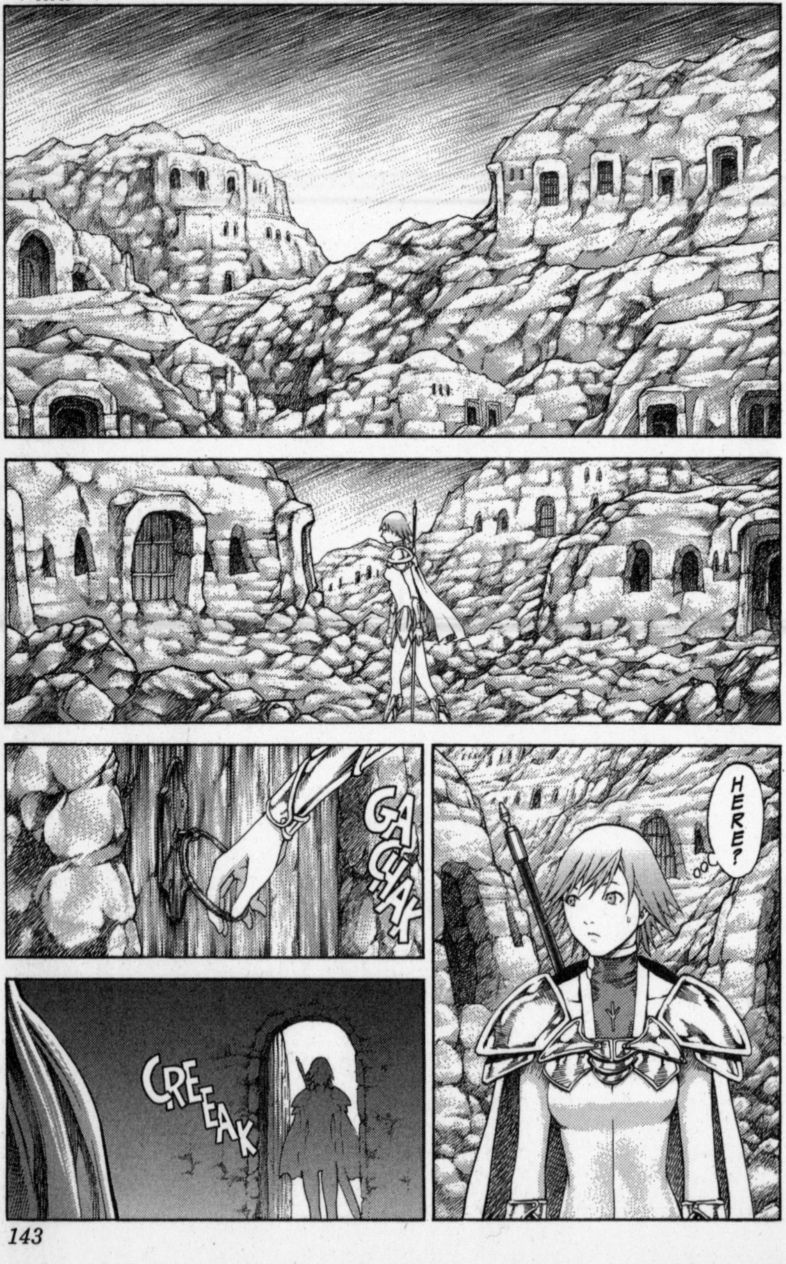
HERE?
GACHAK
CREEAK

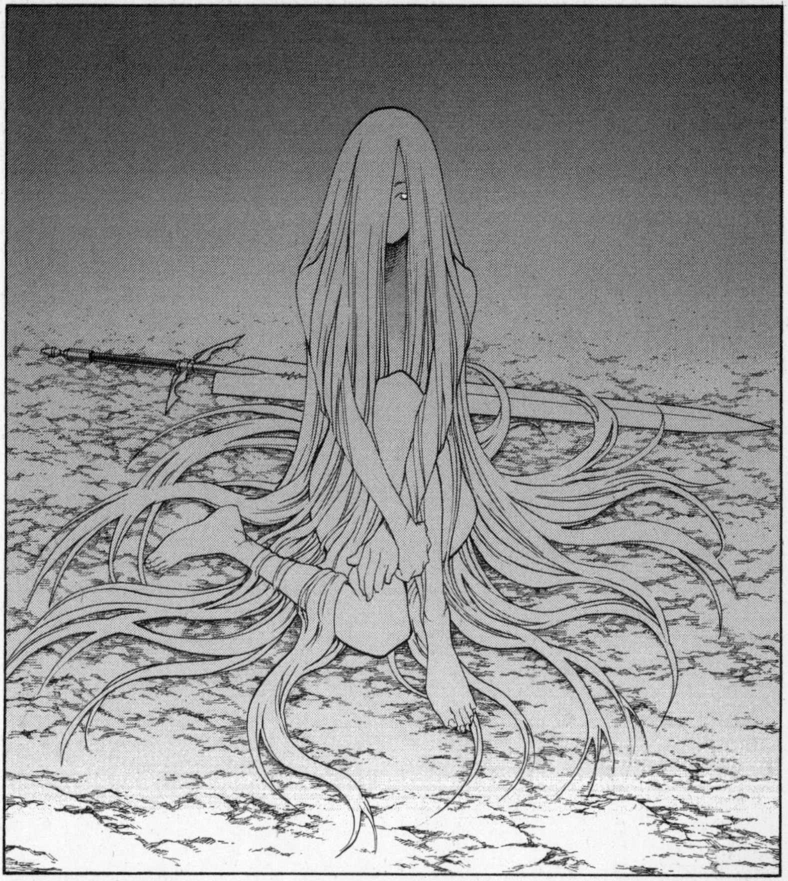

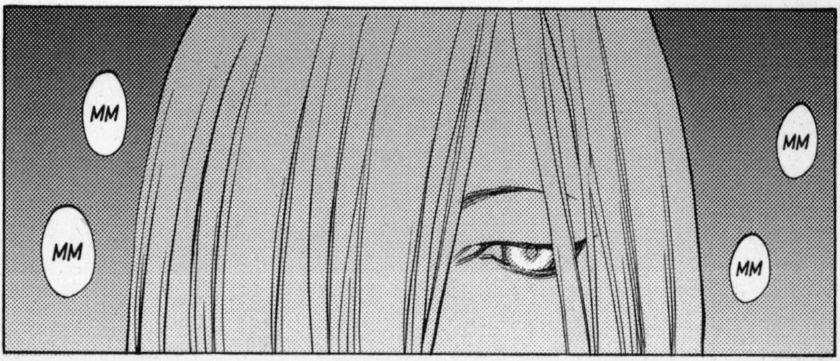
MM
MM
MM
MM

READ THIS WAY

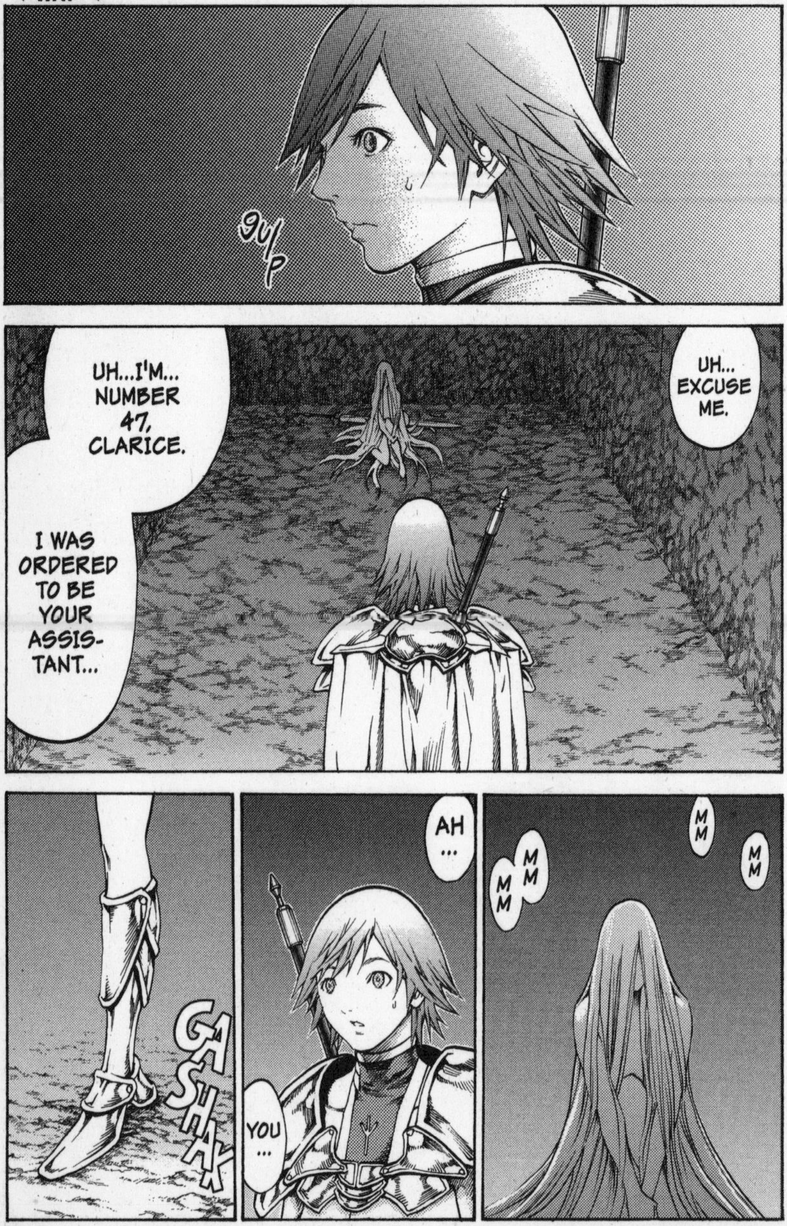

GULP
UH... EXCUSE ME.
UH...I'M... NUMBER 47, CLARICE.
I WAS ORDERED TO BE YOUR ASSISTANT...
MM
MM
MM
MM
MM
AH...
YOU...
GASHAK

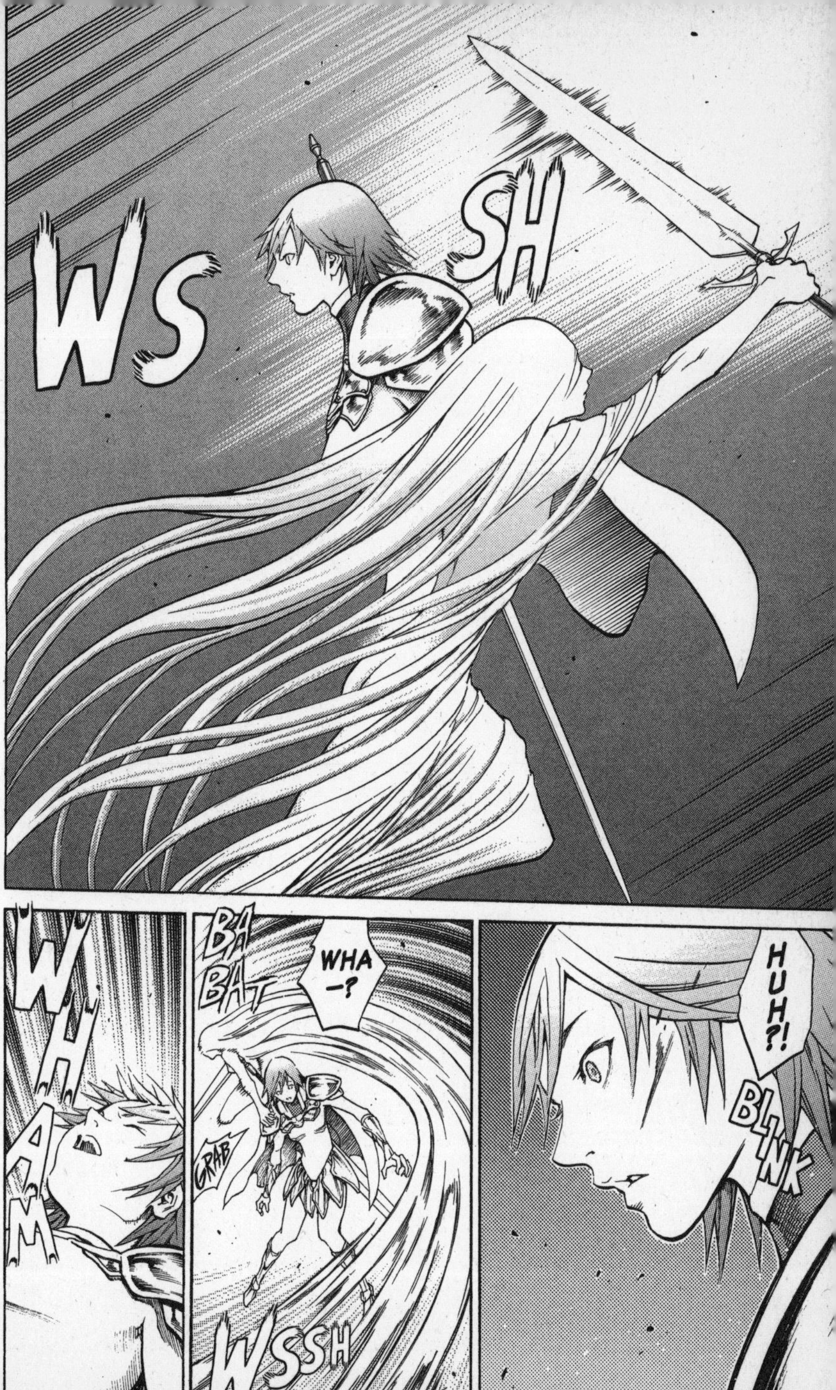
WSSH
HUH?!
BLINK
BA BAT
WHA—?
GRAB
WSSH
WHAM

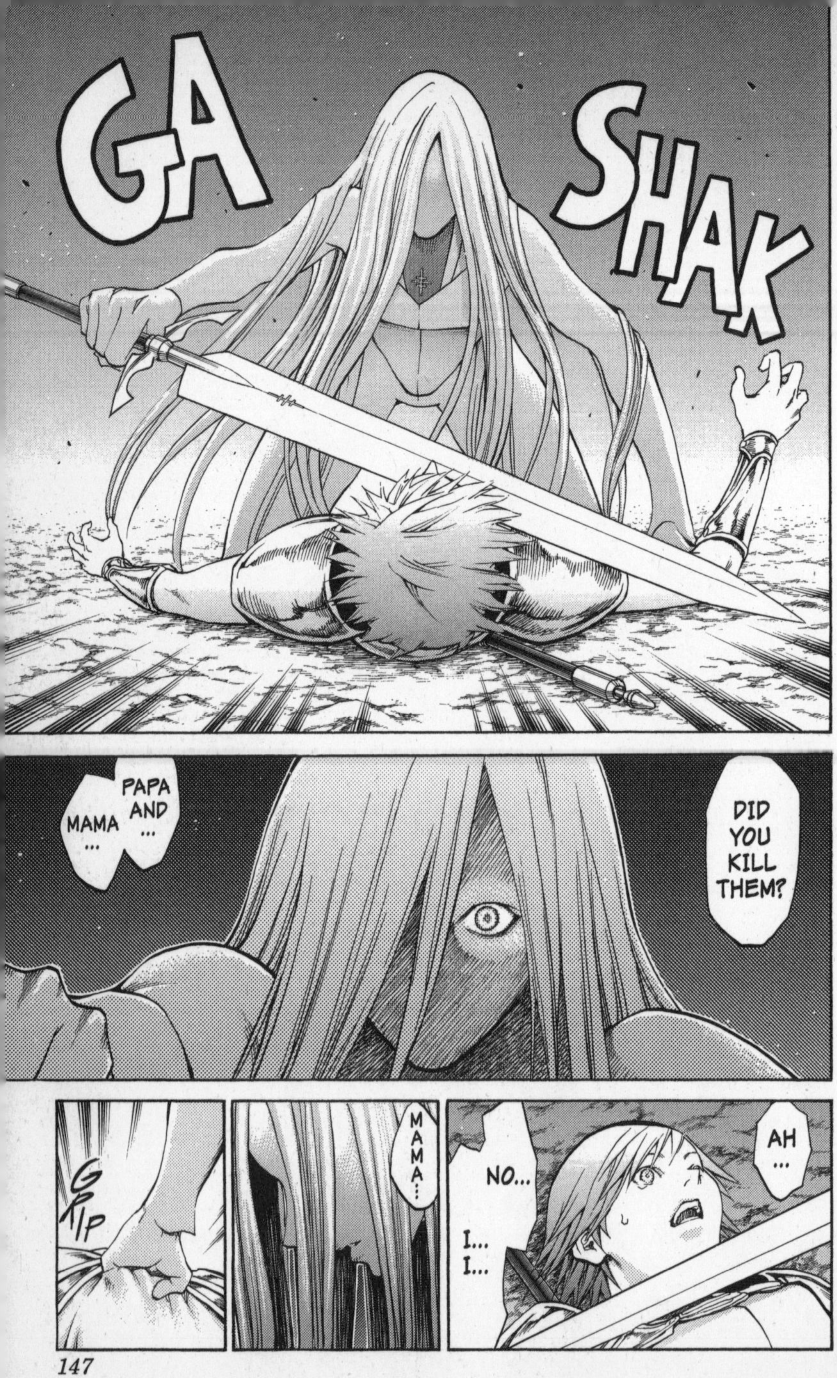
GA
SHAK
DID YOU KILL THEM?
PAPA AND ...
MAMA ...
AH ...
NO...
I... I...
MAMA...
GRIP

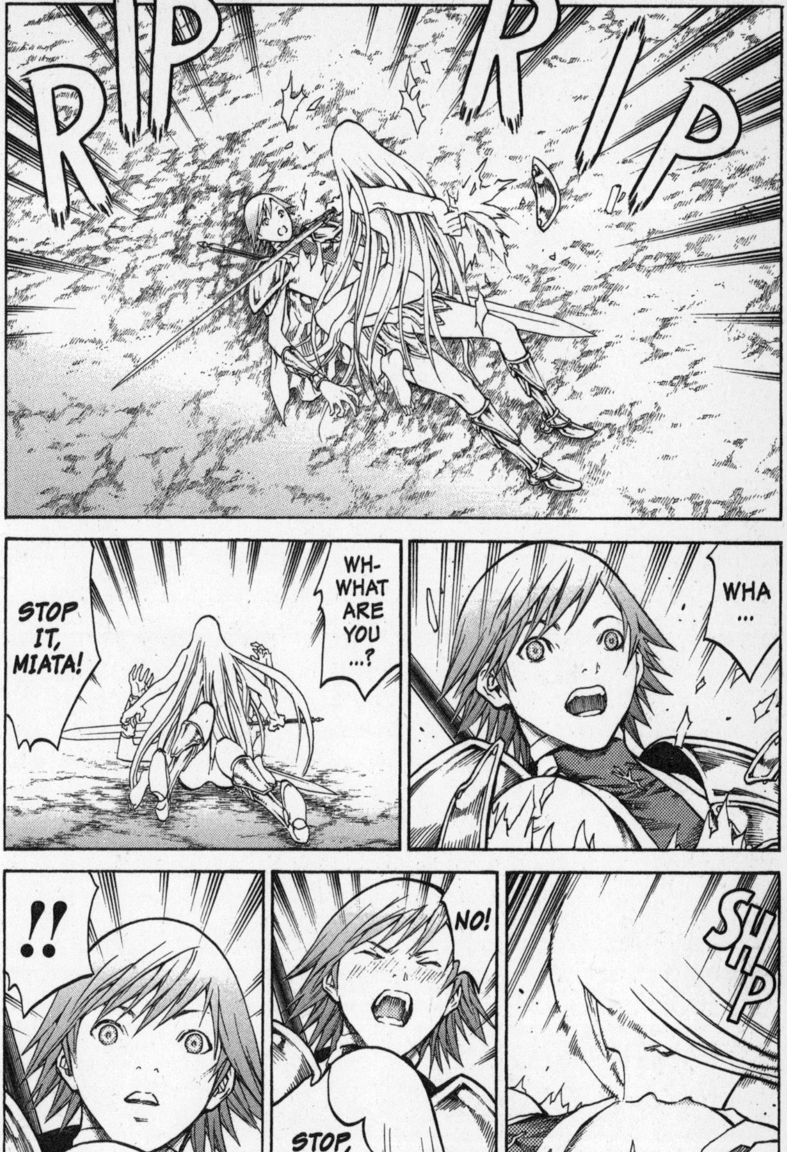
RIP RIP
WHA ...
WH- WHAT ARE YOU ...?
STOP IT, MIATA!
SHP
NO!
STOP, PLEASE!
!!

READ THIS WAY

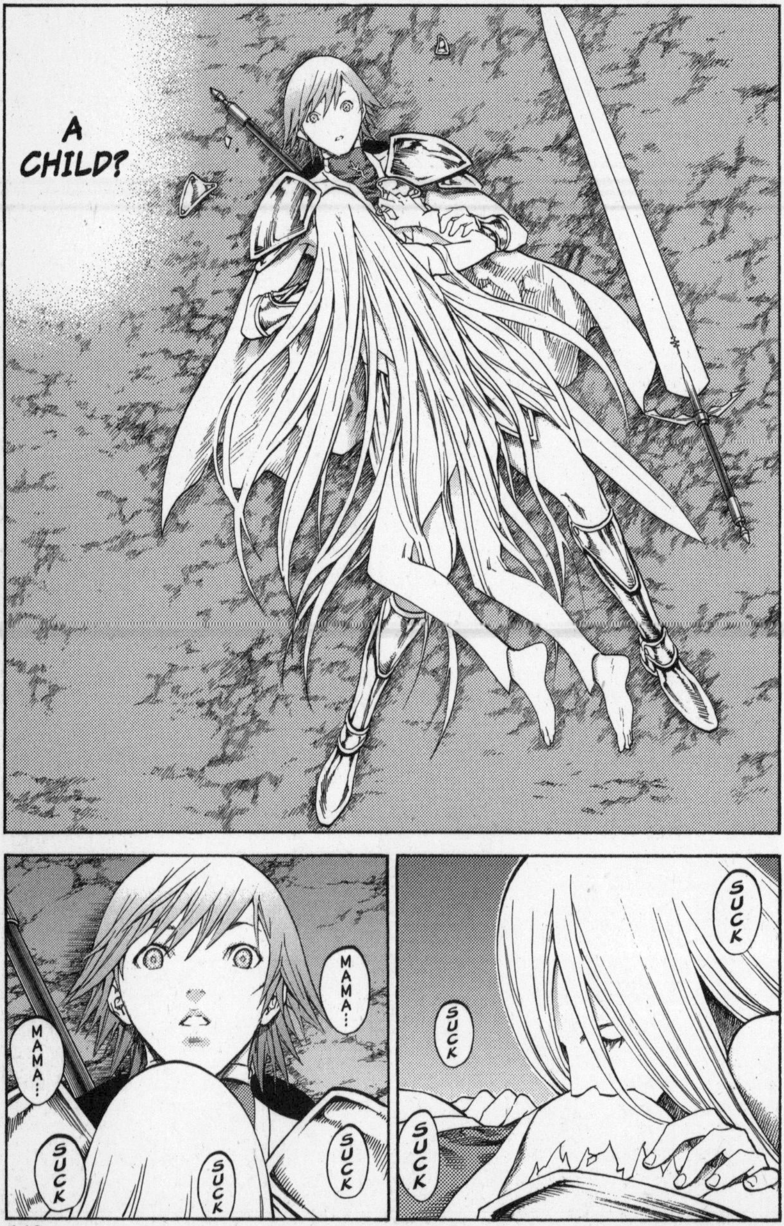
A CHILD?
SUCK
SUCK
SUCK
MAMA...
MAMA...
SUCK
SUCK
SUCK

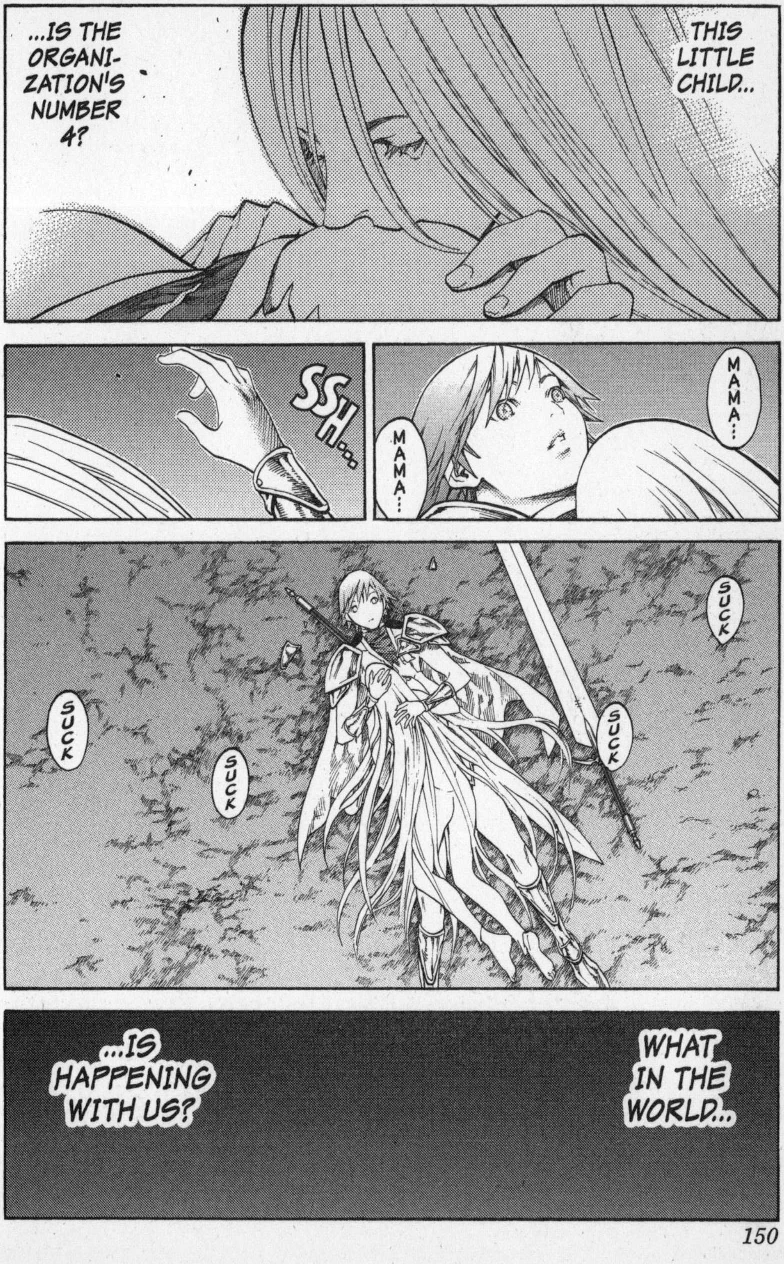
THIS LITTLE CHILD...
...IS THE ORGANIZATION'S NUMBER 4?
MAMA...
MAMA...
SSH...
SUCK
SUCK
SUCK
SUCK
WHAT IN THE WORLD...
...IS HAPPENING WITH US?

READ THIS WAY

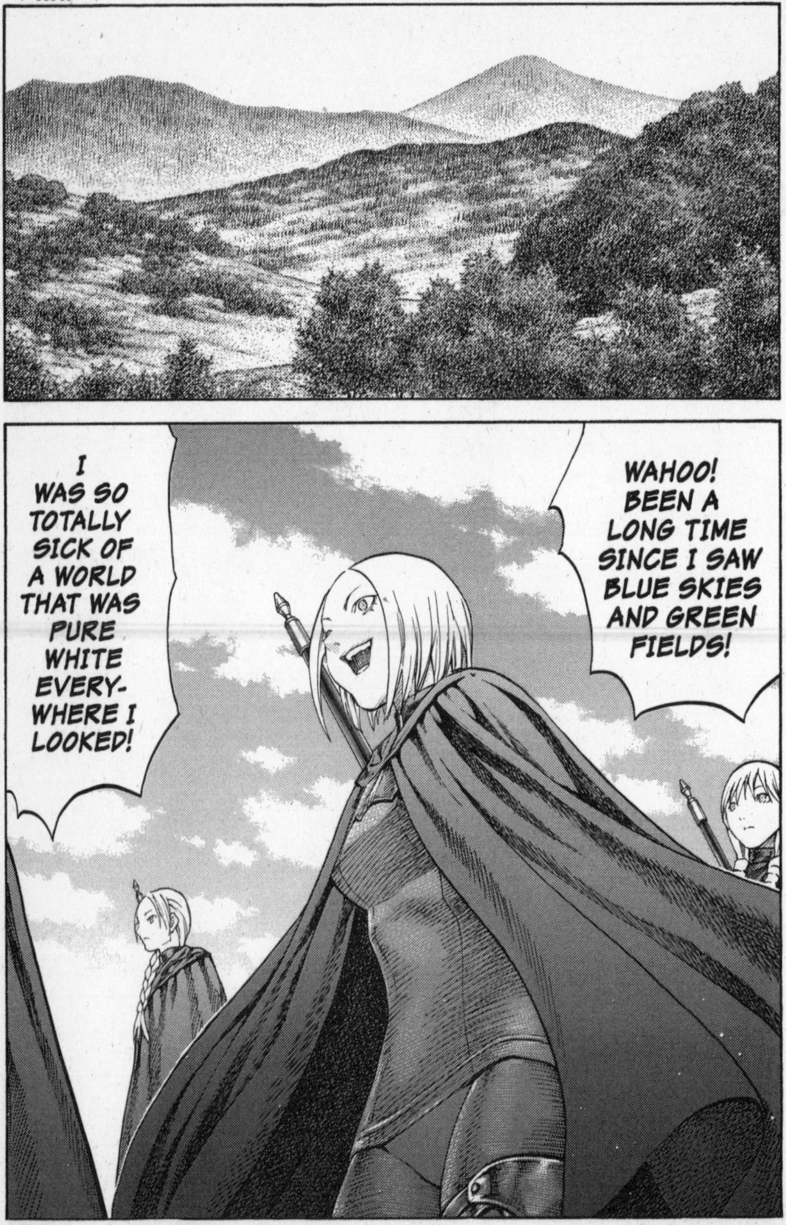
WAHOO! BEEN A LONG TIME SINCE I SAW BLUE SKIES AND GREEN FIELDS!
I WAS SO TOTALLY SICK OF A WORLD THAT WAS PURE WHITE EVERY-WHERE I LOOKED!

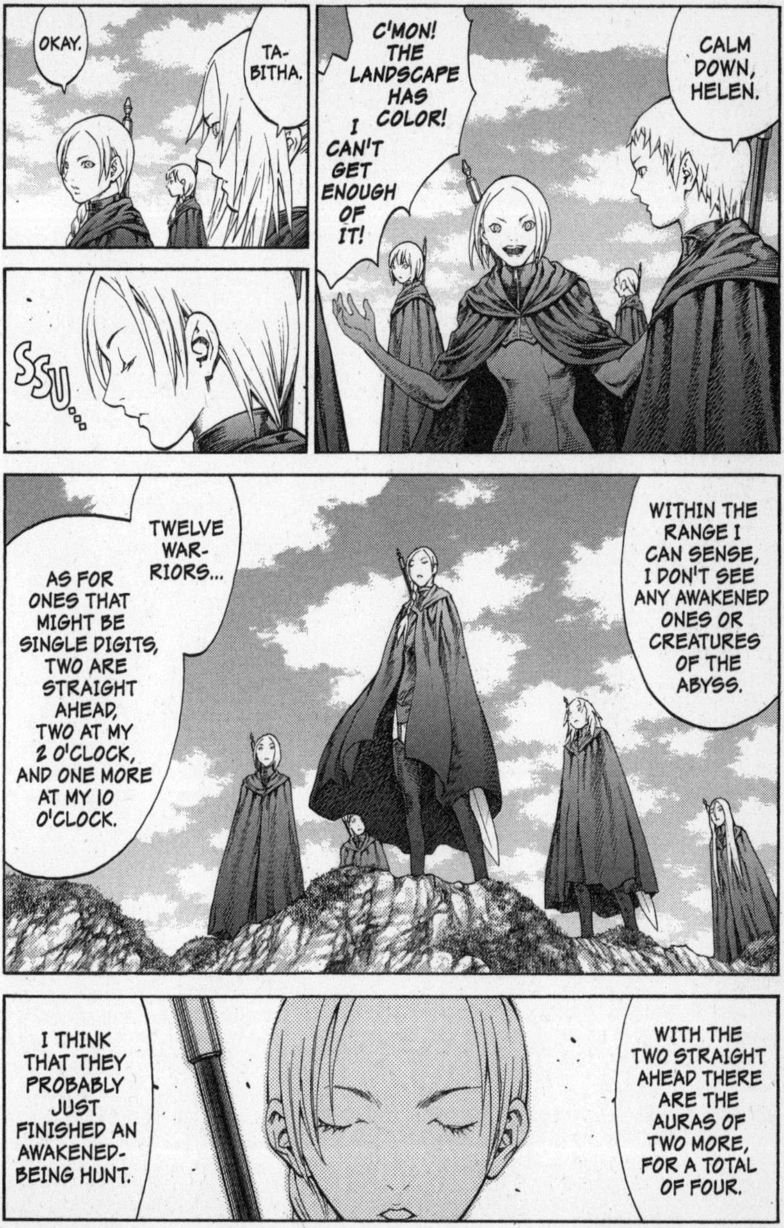
CALM DOWN, HELEN.
C'MON! THE LANDSCAPE HAS COLOR!
I CAN'T GET ENOUGH OF IT!
TA-BITHA.
OKAY.
SSU...
WITHIN THE RANGE I CAN SENSE, I DON'T SEE ANY AWAKENED ONES OR CREATURES OF THE ABYSS.
TWELVE WAR-RIORS...
AS FOR ONES THAT MIGHT BE SINGLE DIGITS, TWO ARE STRAIGHT AHEAD, TWO AT MY 2 O'CLOCK, AND ONE MORE AT MY 10 O'CLOCK.
WITH THE TWO STRAIGHT AHEAD THERE ARE THE AURAS OF TWO MORE, FOR A TOTAL OF FOUR.
I THINK THAT THEY PROBABLY JUST FINISHED AN AWAKENED-BEING HUNT.

READ THIS WAY

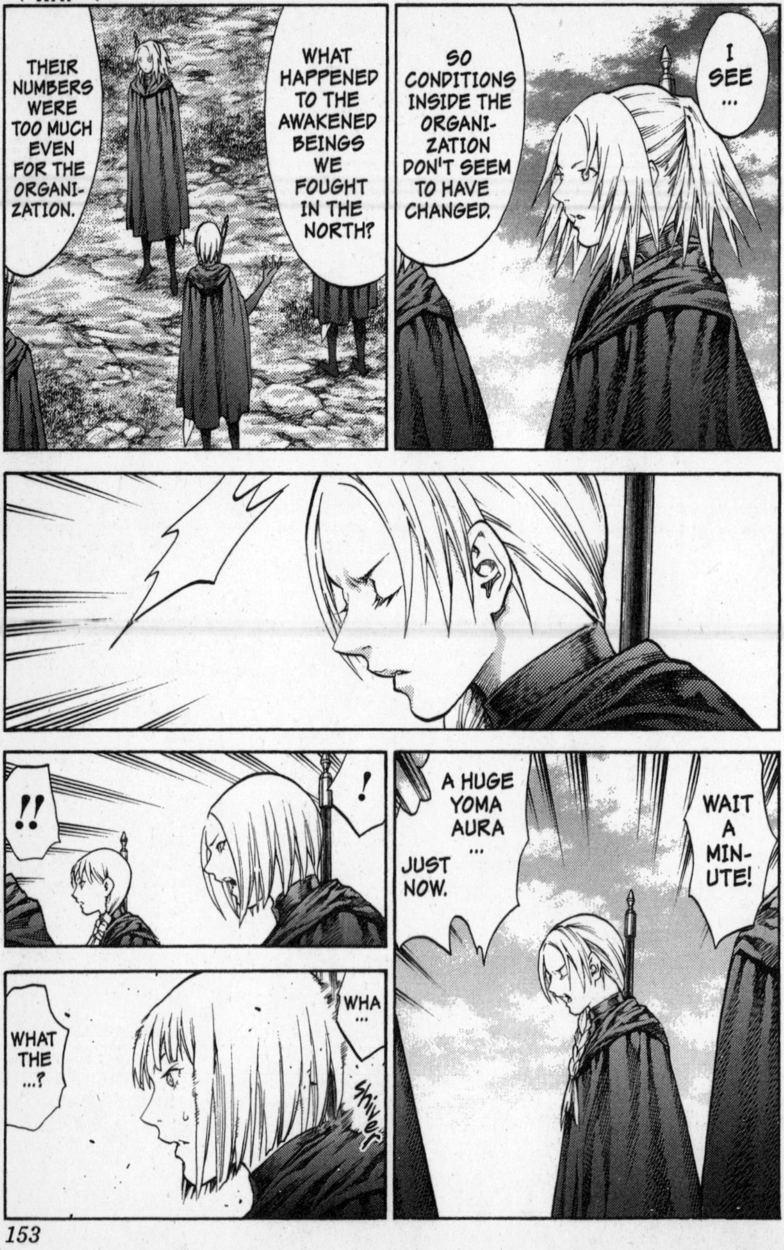
I SEE ...
SO CONDITIONS INSIDE THE ORGANIZATION DON'T SEEM TO HAVE CHANGED.
WHAT HAPPENED TO THE AWAKENED BEINGS WE FOUGHT IN THE NORTH?
THEIR NUMBERS WERE TOO MUCH EVEN FOR THE ORGANIZATION.
WAIT A MINUTE!
A HUGE YOMA AURA ...
JUST NOW.
!
!!
WHA ...
Shiver
WHAT THE ...?

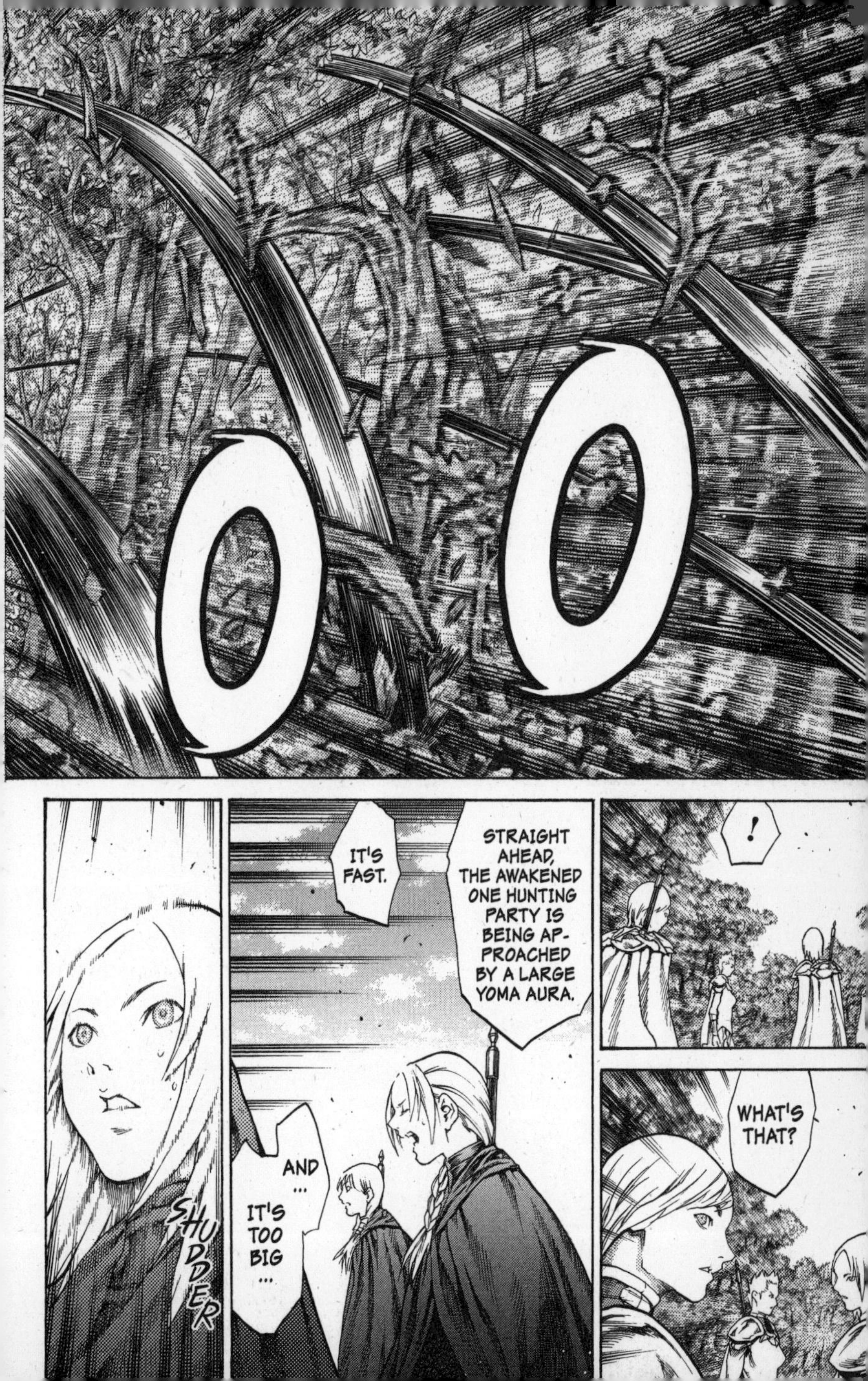
OO
!
WHAT'S THAT?
STRAIGHT AHEAD, THE AWAKENED ONE HUNTING PARTY IS BEING AP-PROACHED BY A LARGE YOMA AURA.
IT'S FAST.
AND ... IT'S TOO BIG ...
SHUDDER

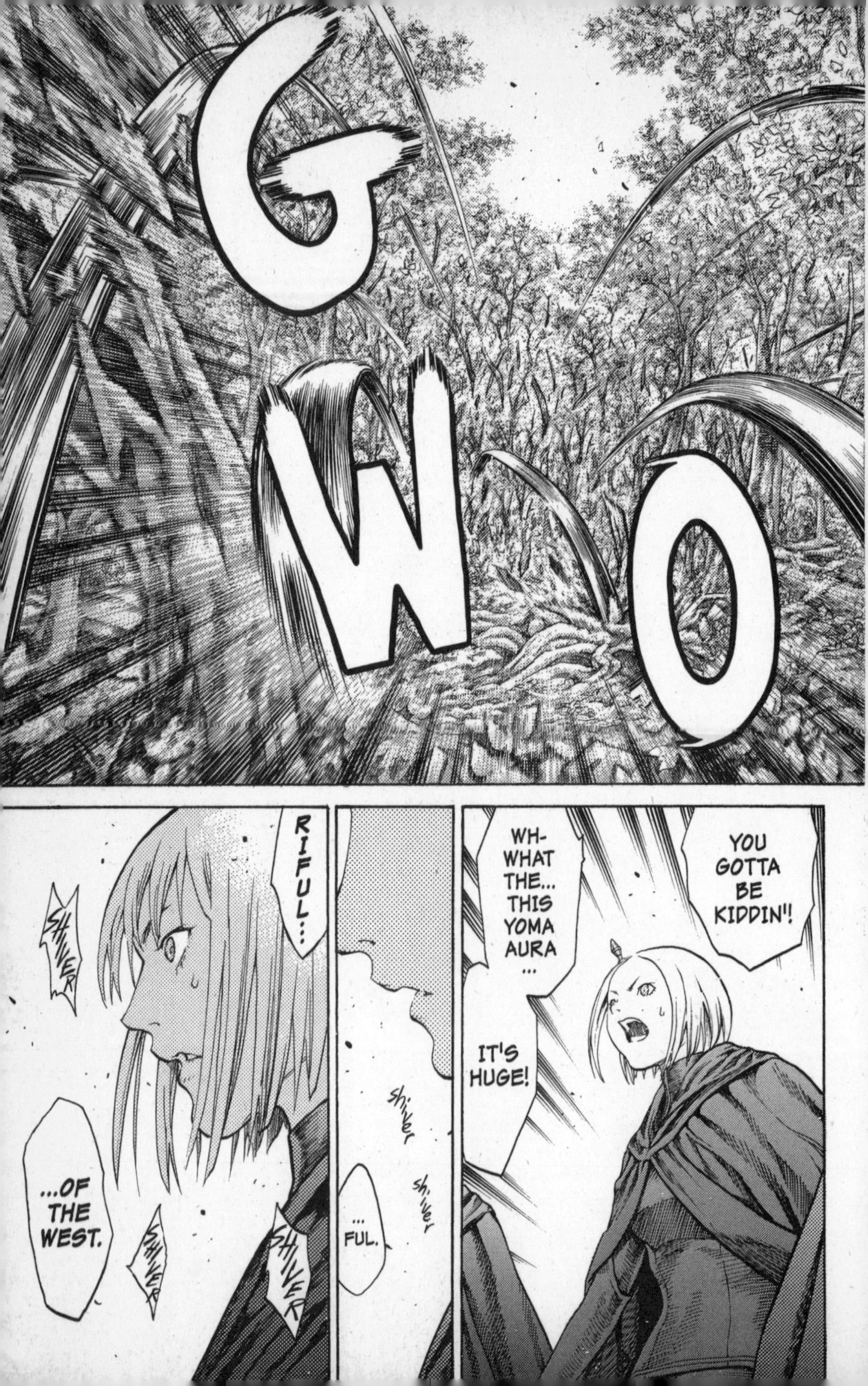
GWO
YOU GOTTA BE KIDDIN'!
WH- WHAT THE... THIS YOMA AURA ...
IT'S HUGE!
shiver
shiver
... FUL.
SHIVER
RIFUL...
SHIVER
...OF THE WEST.
SHIVER

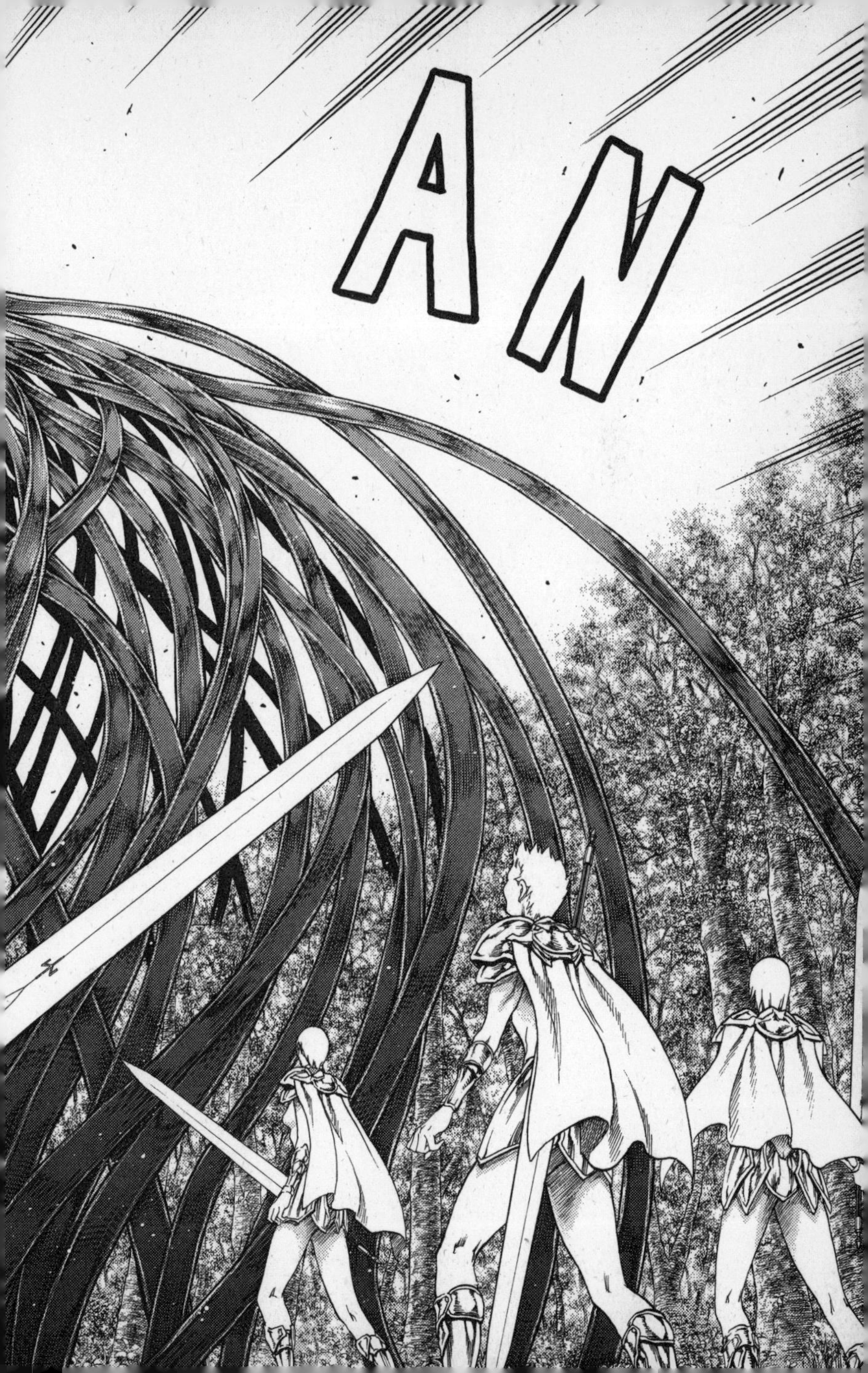
AN

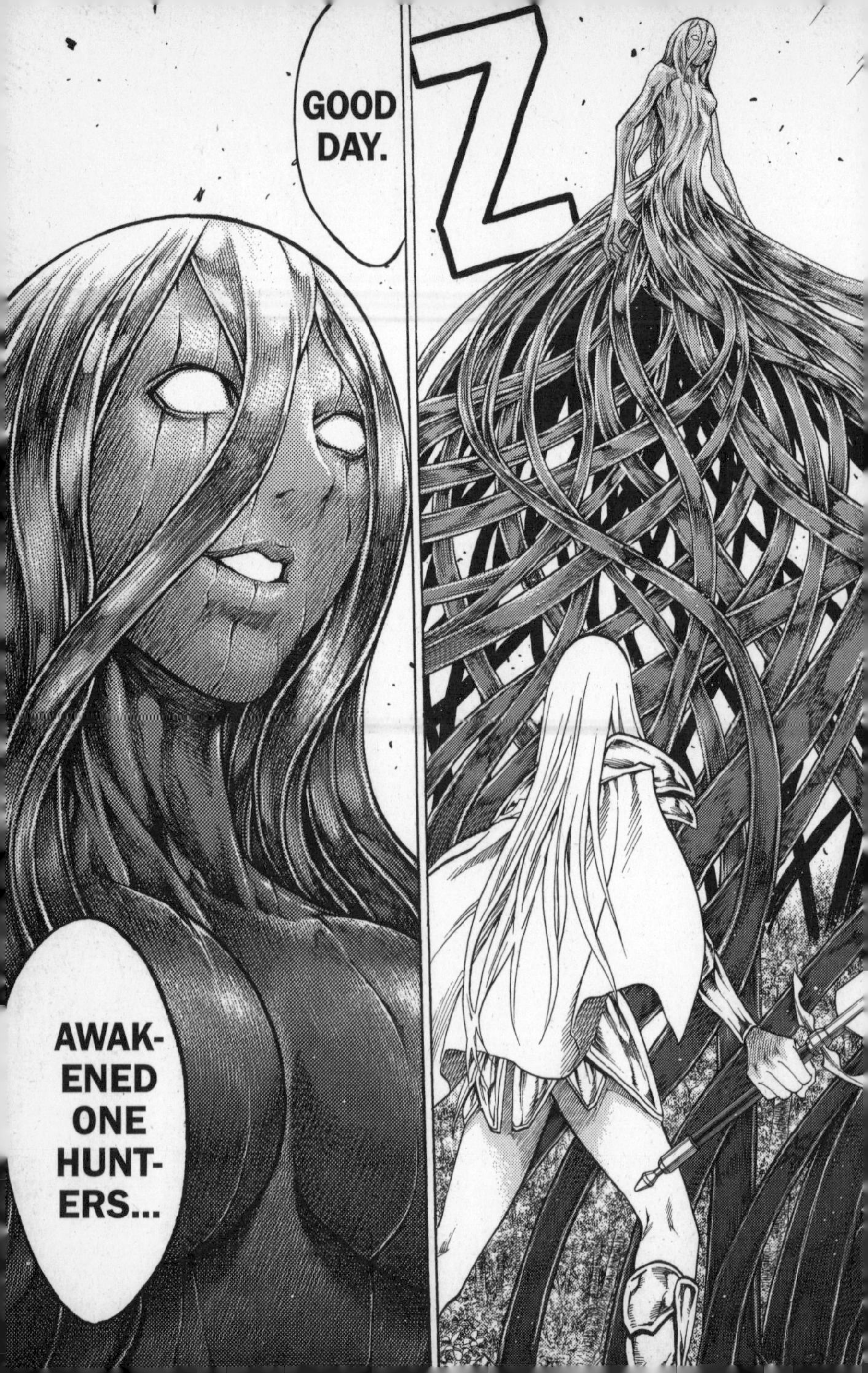
Z
GOOD DAY.
AWAK-ENED ONE HUNT-ERS...

クレイモア
Claymore

Scene 69: The Defiant Ones, Part 2

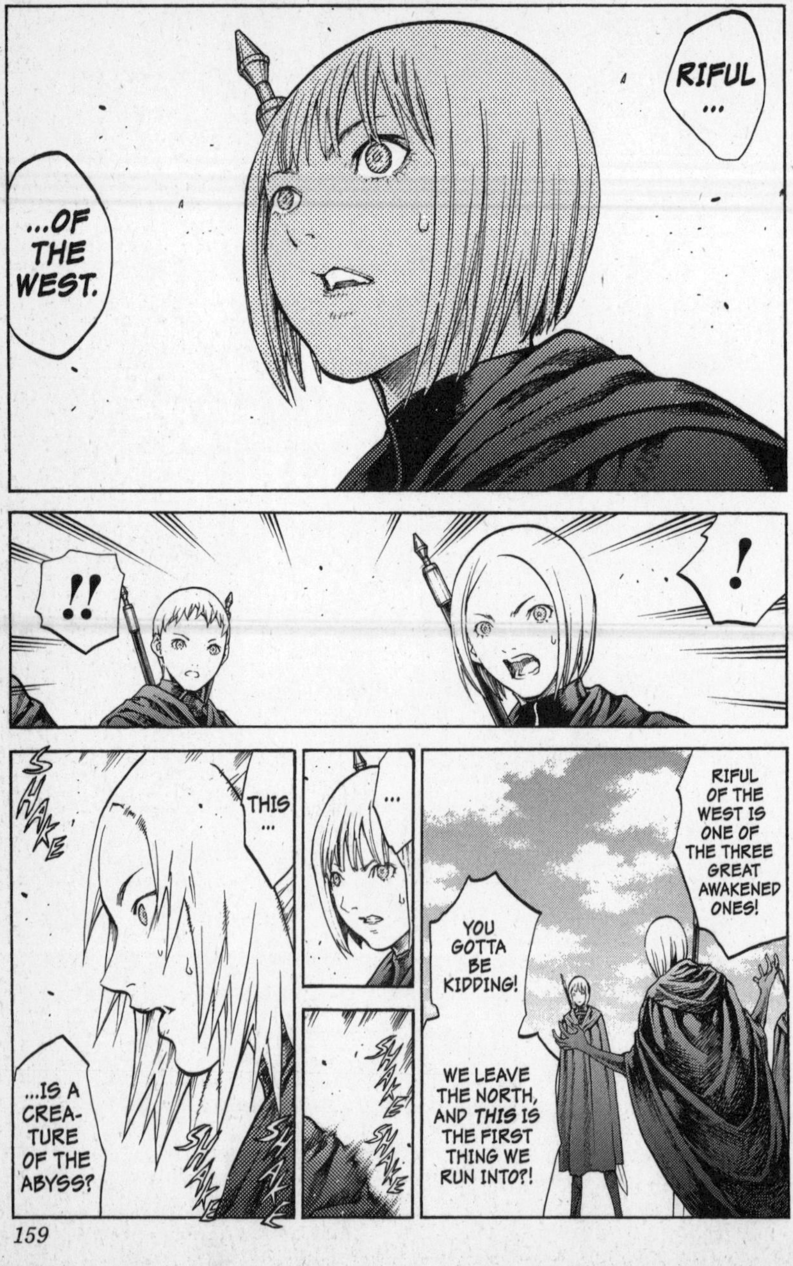
RIFUL ...
...OF THE WEST.
!
!!
RIFUL OF THE WEST IS ONE OF THE THREE GREAT AWAKENED ONES!
YOU GOTTA BE KIDDING!
WE LEAVE THE NORTH, AND *THIS* IS THE FIRST THING WE RUN INTO?!
...
SHAKE SHAKE
SHAKE SHAKE
THIS ...
SHAKE
...IS A CREATURE OF THE ABYSS?
SHAKE SHAKE

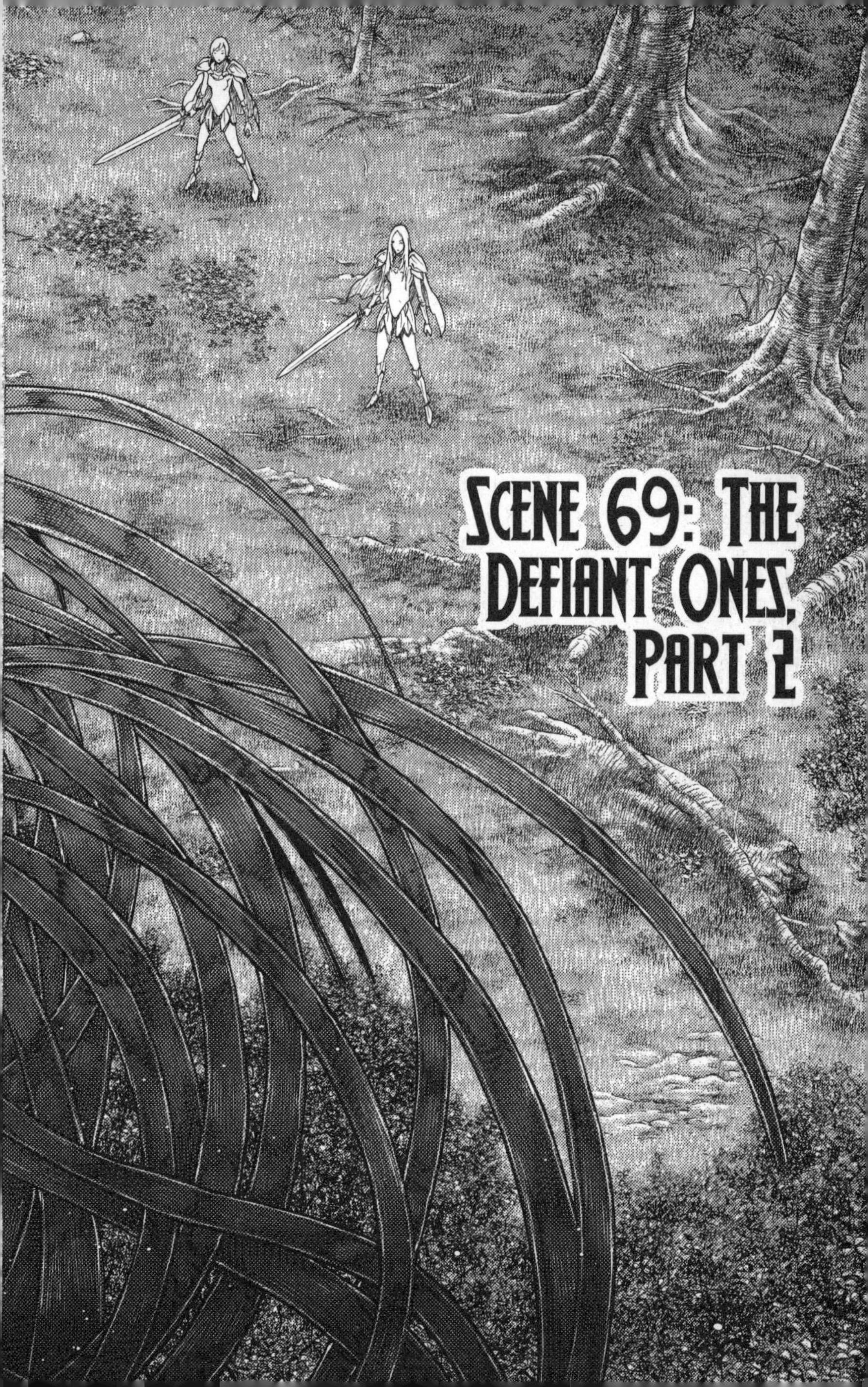
SCENE 69: THE DEFIANT ONES, PART 2

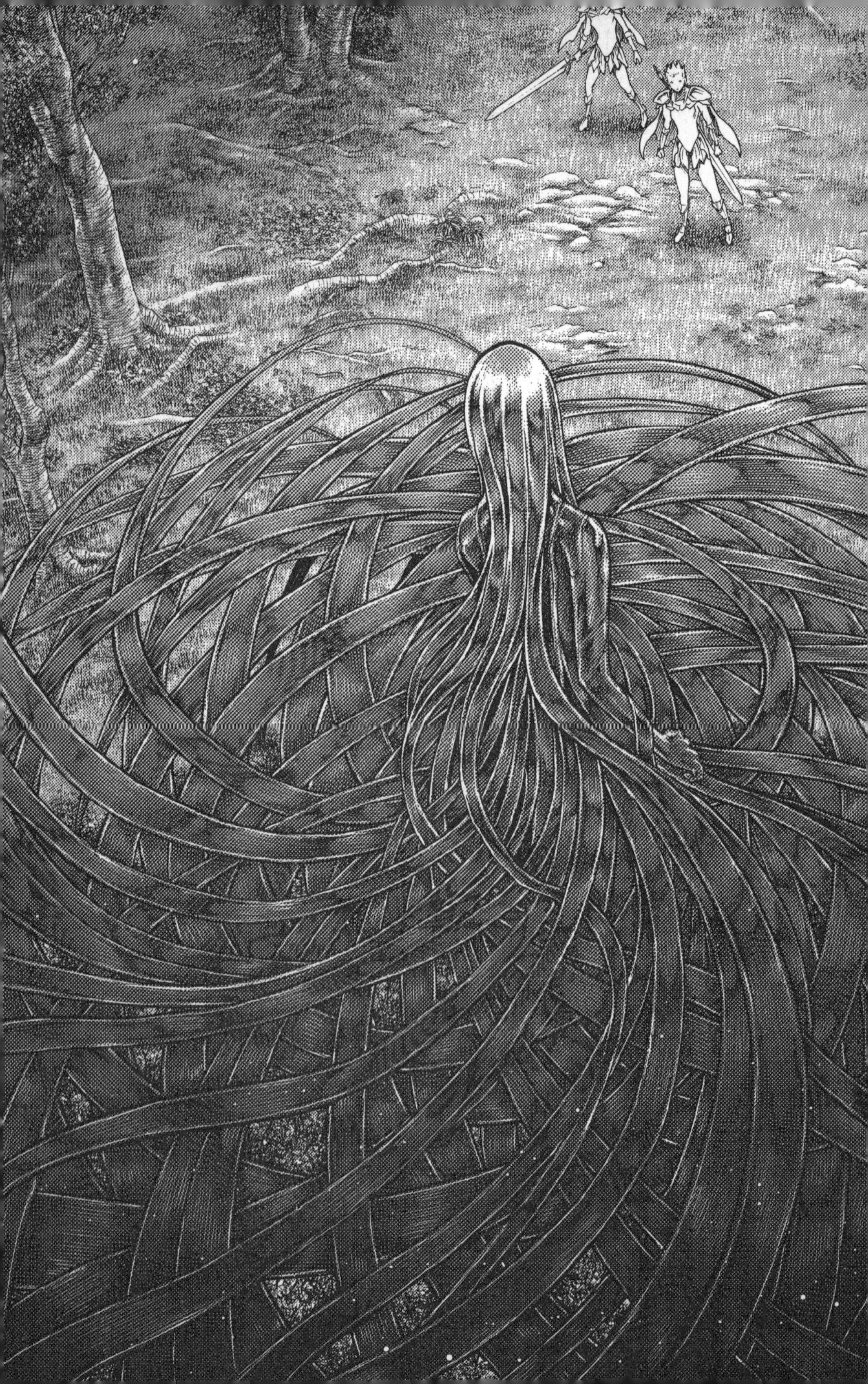

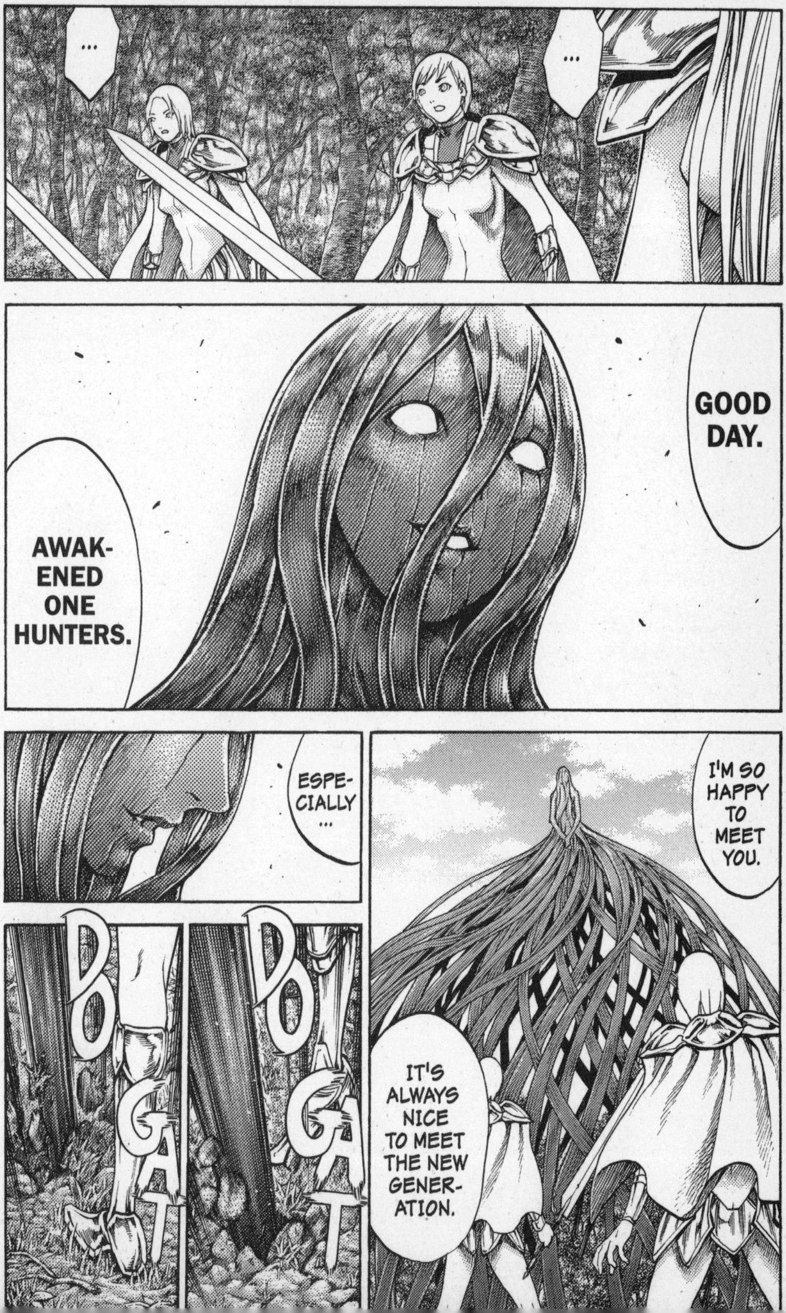
...
...
GOOD DAY.
AWAK-ENED ONE HUNTERS.
I'M SO HAPPY TO MEET YOU.
IT'S ALWAYS NICE TO MEET THE NEW GENER-ATION.
ESPE-CIALLY ...
DOGAT
DOGAT

READ THIS WAY

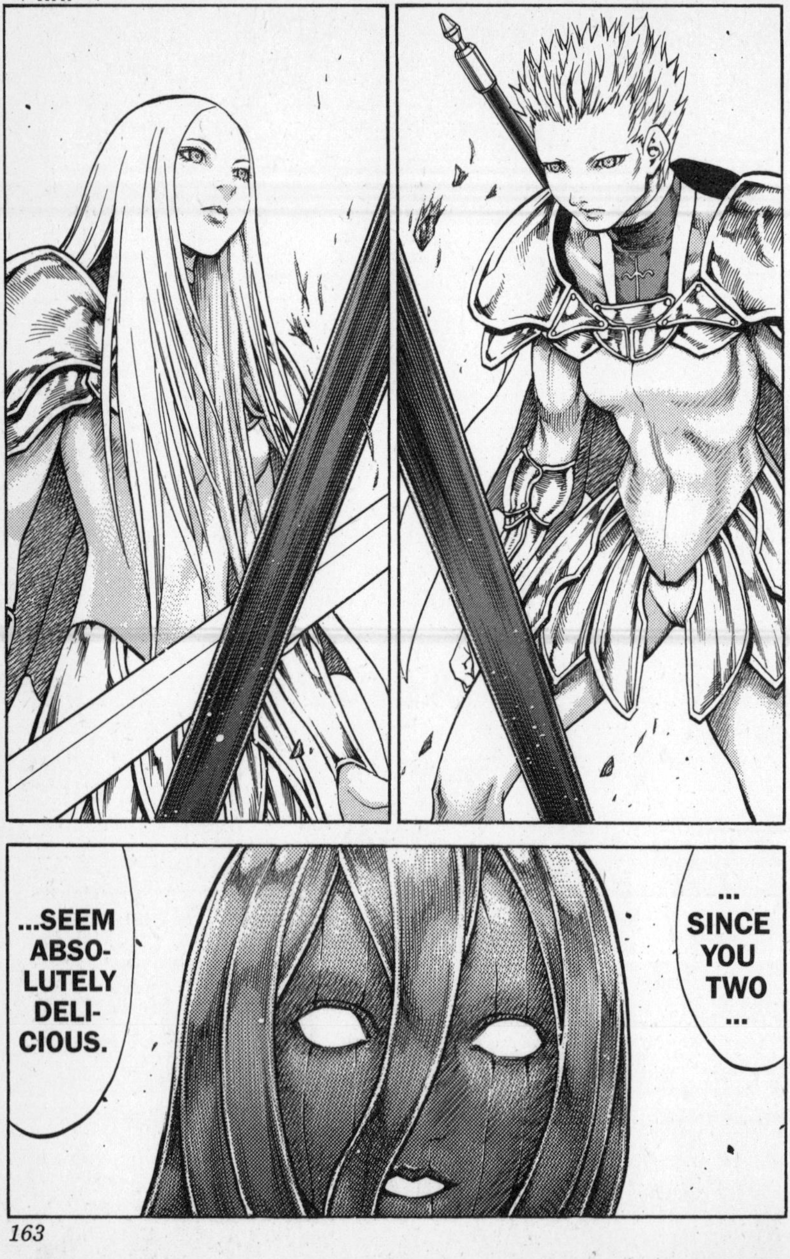
... SINCE YOU TWO ...
...SEEM ABSO-LUTELY DELI-CIOUS.

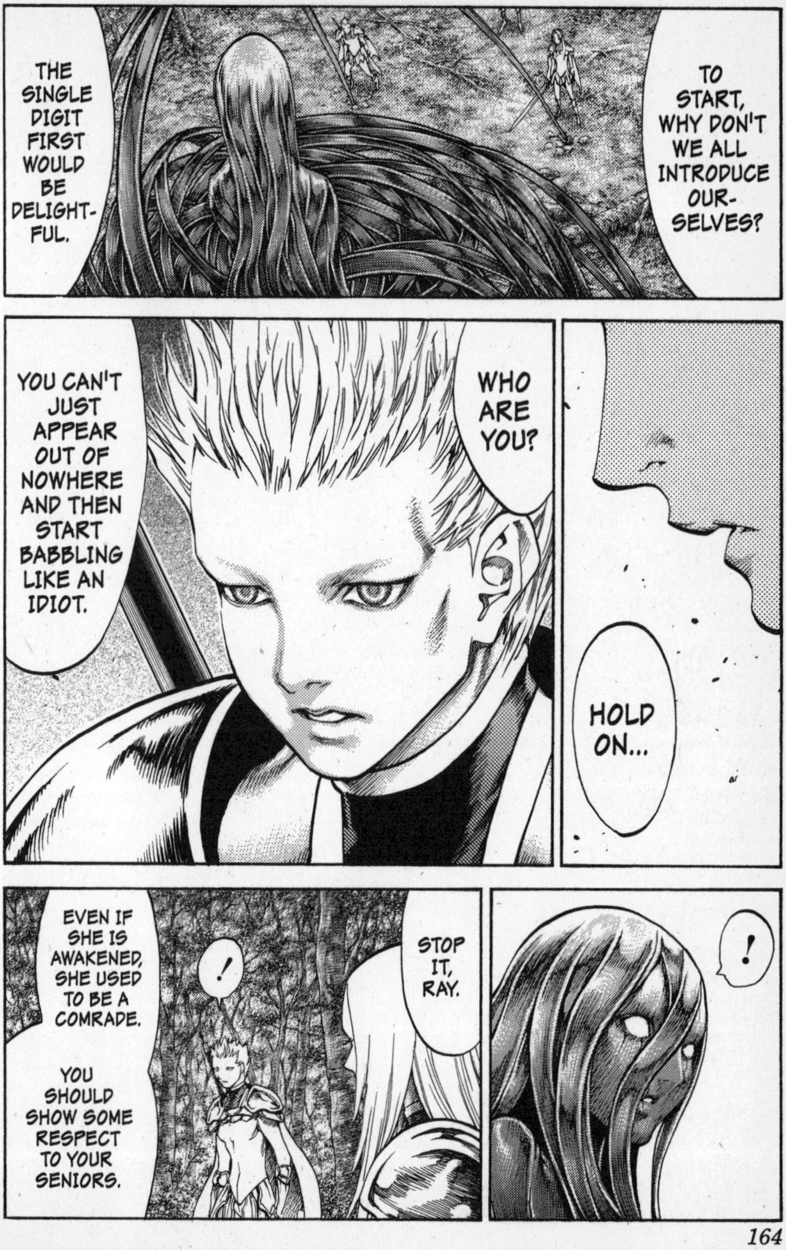
TO START, WHY DON'T WE ALL INTRODUCE OUR-SELVES?
THE SINGLE DIGIT FIRST WOULD BE DELIGHT-FUL.
HOLD ON...
WHO ARE YOU?
YOU CAN'T JUST APPEAR OUT OF NOWHERE AND THEN START BABBLING LIKE AN IDIOT.
!
STOP IT, RAY.
!
EVEN IF SHE IS AWAKENED, SHE USED TO BE A COMRADE.
YOU SHOULD SHOW SOME RESPECT TO YOUR SENIORS.

READ THIS WAY

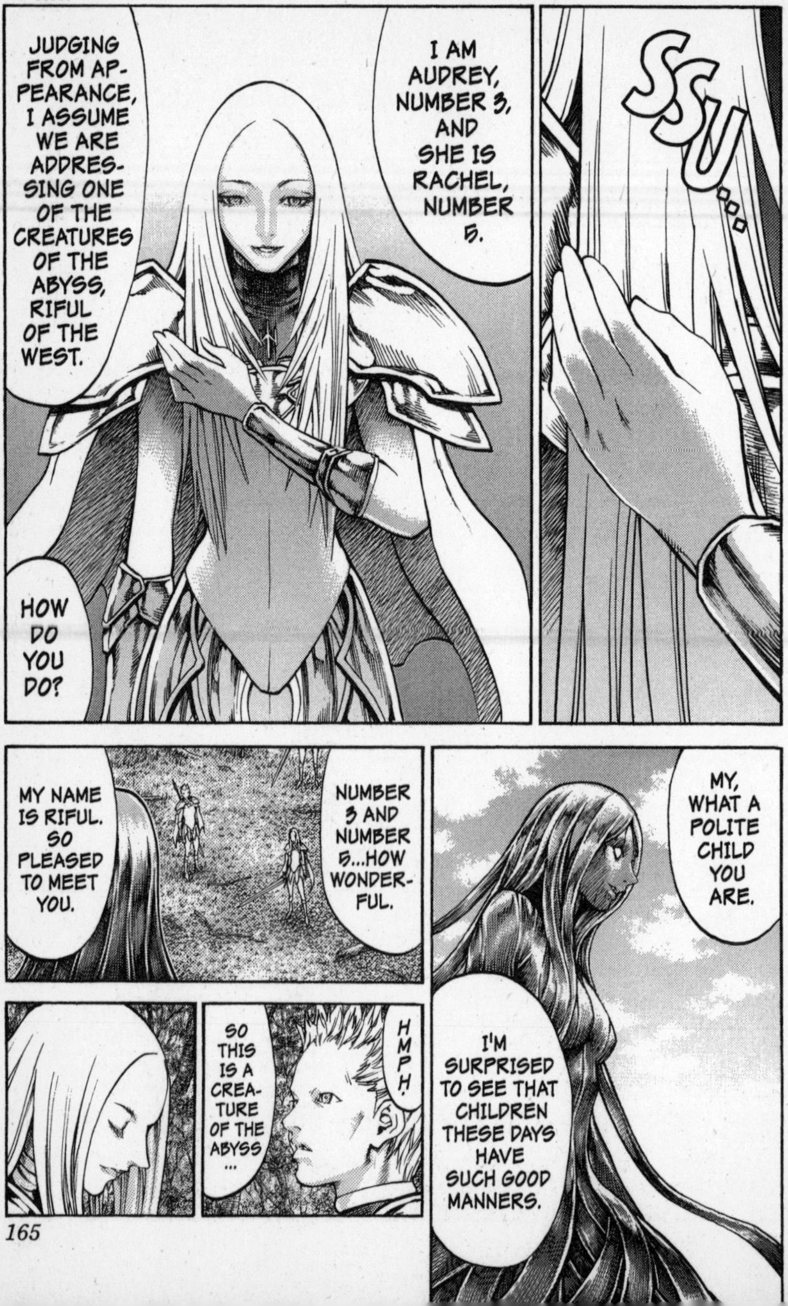
SSU...
I AM AUDREY, NUMBER 3, AND SHE IS RACHEL, NUMBER 5.
JUDGING FROM AP-PEARANCE, I ASSUME WE ARE ADDRES-SING ONE OF THE CREATURES OF THE ABYSS, RIFUL OF THE WEST.
HOW DO YOU DO?
MY, WHAT A POLITE CHILD YOU ARE.
I'M SURPRISED TO SEE THAT CHILDREN THESE DAYS HAVE SUCH GOOD MANNERS.
NUMBER 3 AND NUMBER 5...HOW WONDER-FUL.
MY NAME IS RIFUL. SO PLEASED TO MEET YOU.
HMPH!
SO THIS IS A CREA-TURE OF THE ABYSS...

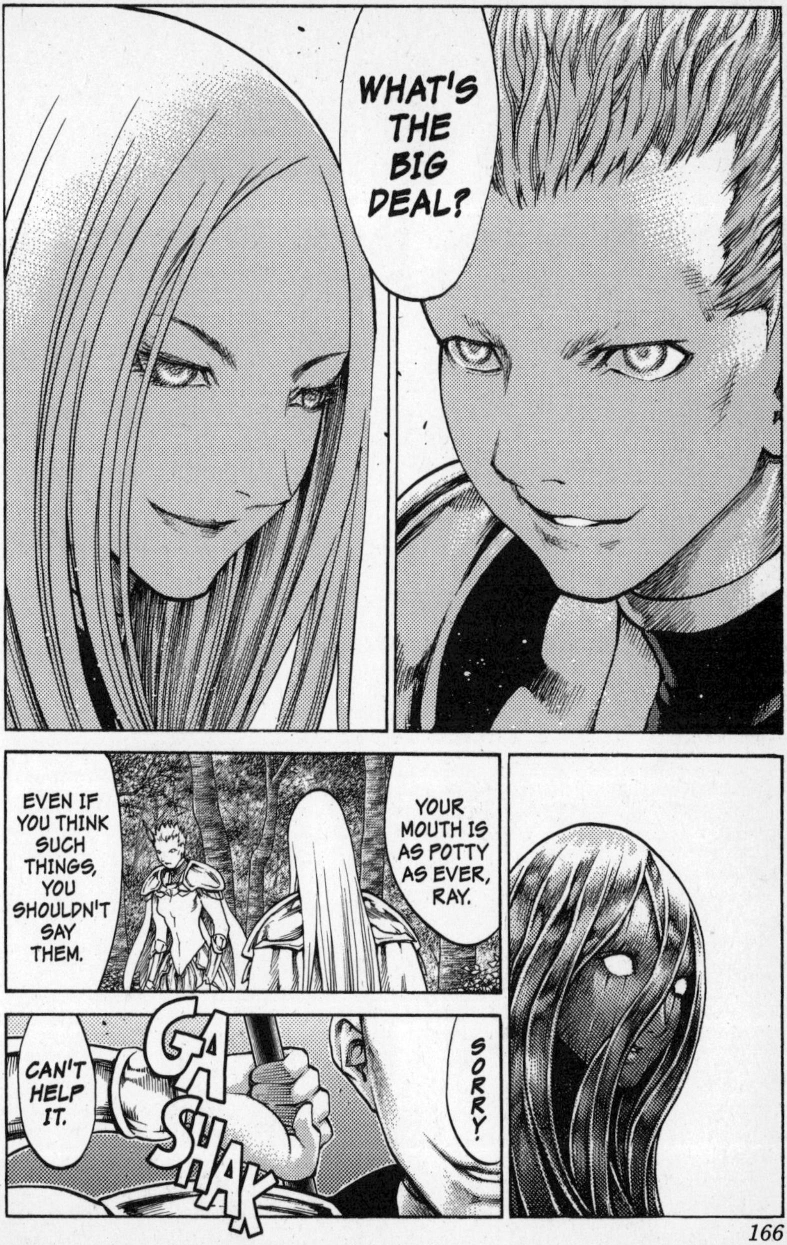
WHAT'S THE BIG DEAL?
YOUR MOUTH IS AS POTTY AS EVER, RAY.
EVEN IF YOU THINK SUCH THINGS, YOU SHOULDN'T SAY THEM.
SORRY.
GA SHAK
CAN'T HELP IT.

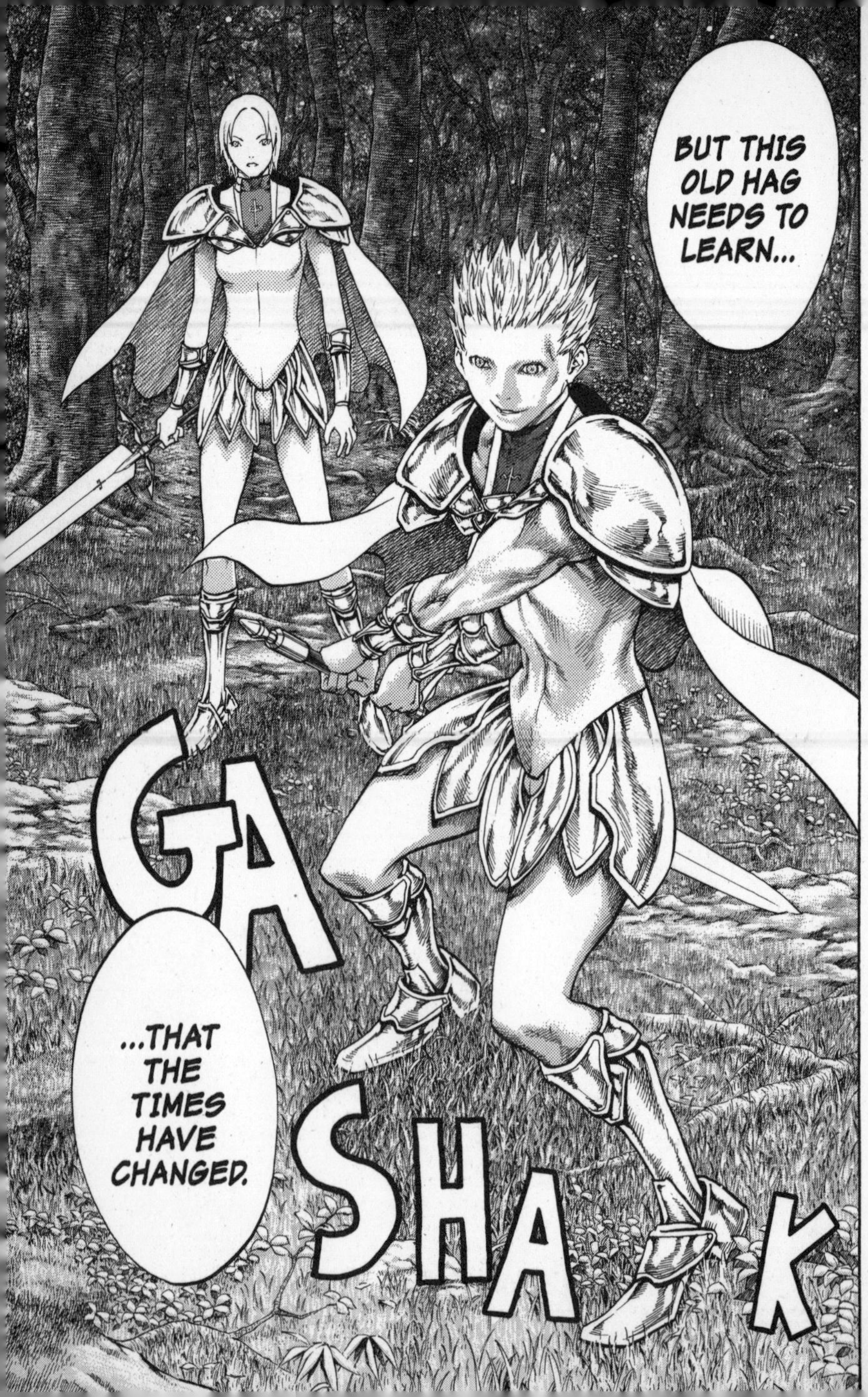
BUT THIS OLD HAG NEEDS TO LEARN...
GASHAK
...THAT THE TIMES HAVE CHANGED.

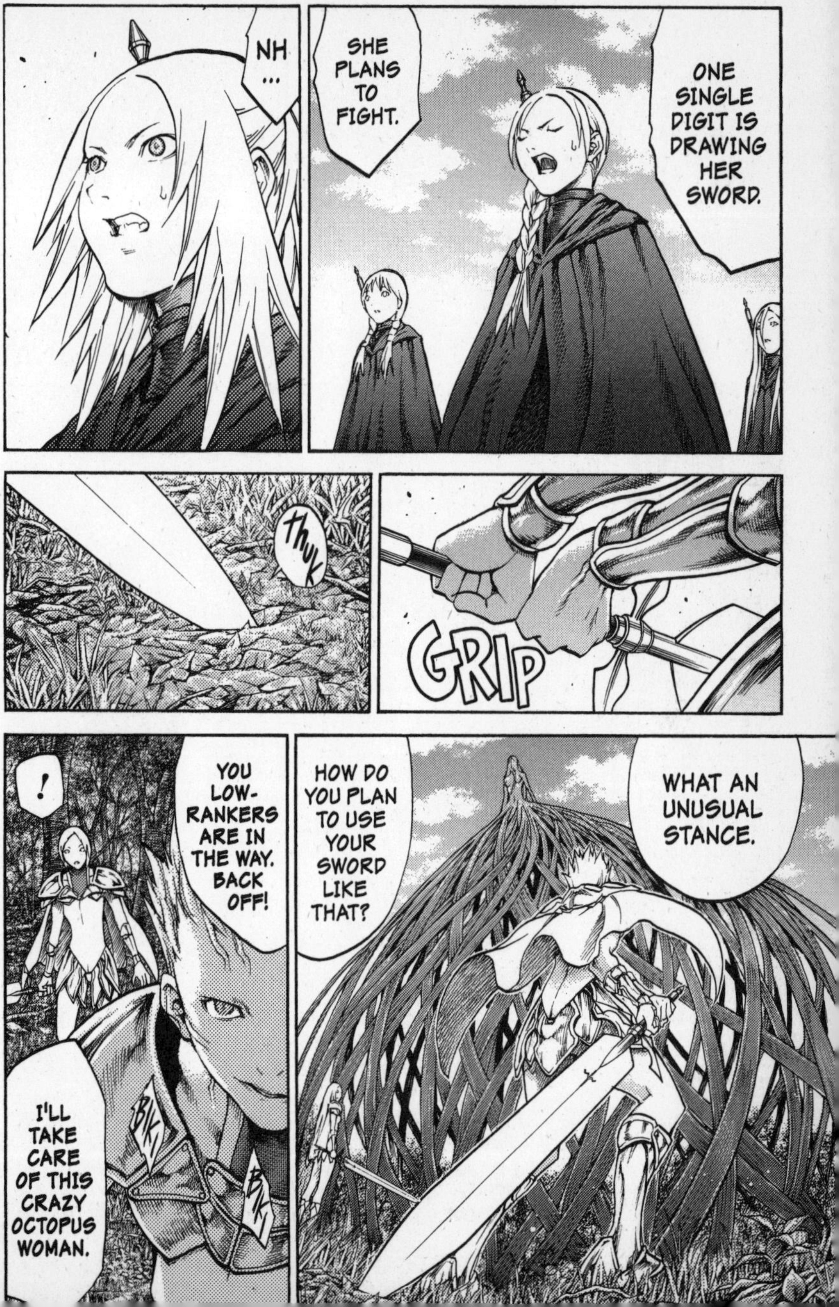
ONE SINGLE DIGIT IS DRAWING HER SWORD.
SHE PLANS TO FIGHT.
NH ...
GRIP
THUK
WHAT AN UNUSUAL STANCE.
HOW DO YOU PLAN TO USE YOUR SWORD LIKE THAT?
YOU LOW-RANKERS ARE IN THE WAY. BACK OFF!
!
I'LL TAKE CARE OF THIS CRAZY OCTOPUS WOMAN.
BIK
BIK

READ THIS WAY

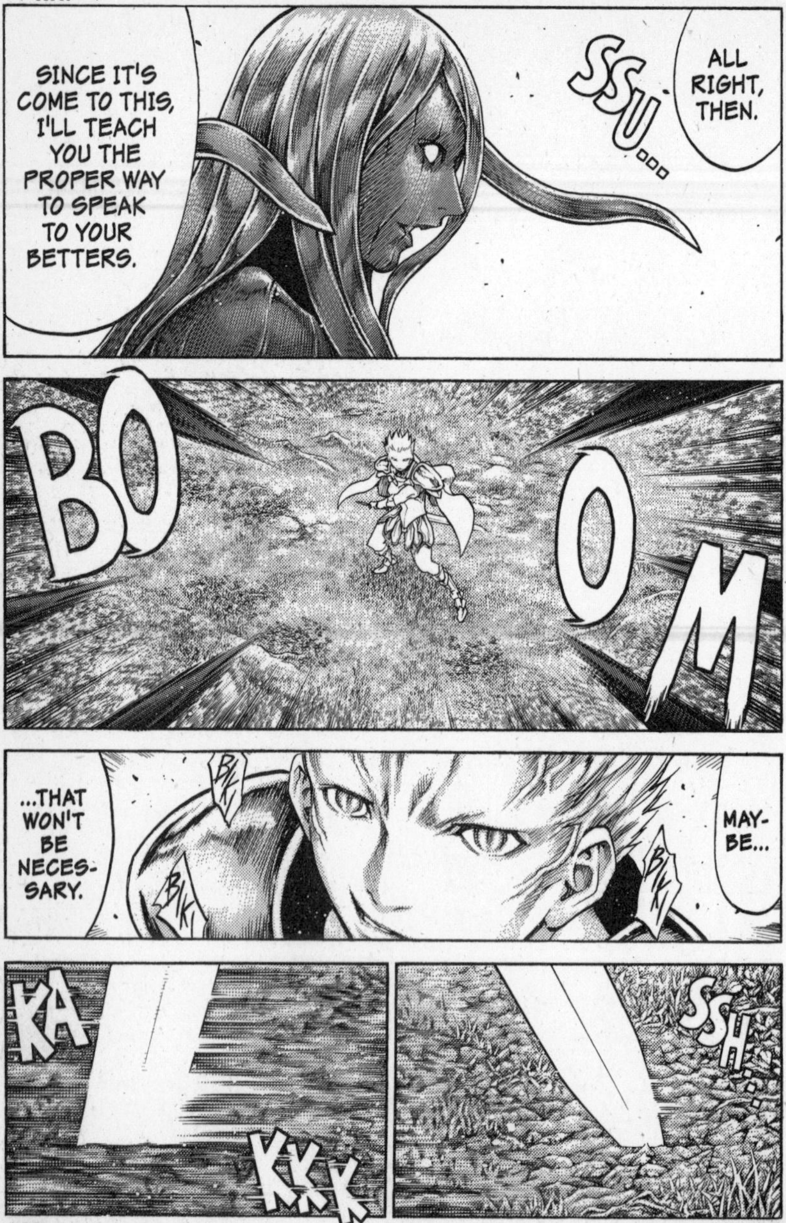
ALL RIGHT, THEN.
SSU...
SINCE IT'S COME TO THIS, I'LL TEACH YOU THE PROPER WAY TO SPEAK TO YOUR BETTERS.
BOOM
MAY-BE...
BIKI
BIKI
BIKI
...THAT WON'T BE NECES-SARY.
SSH..
KAKKK

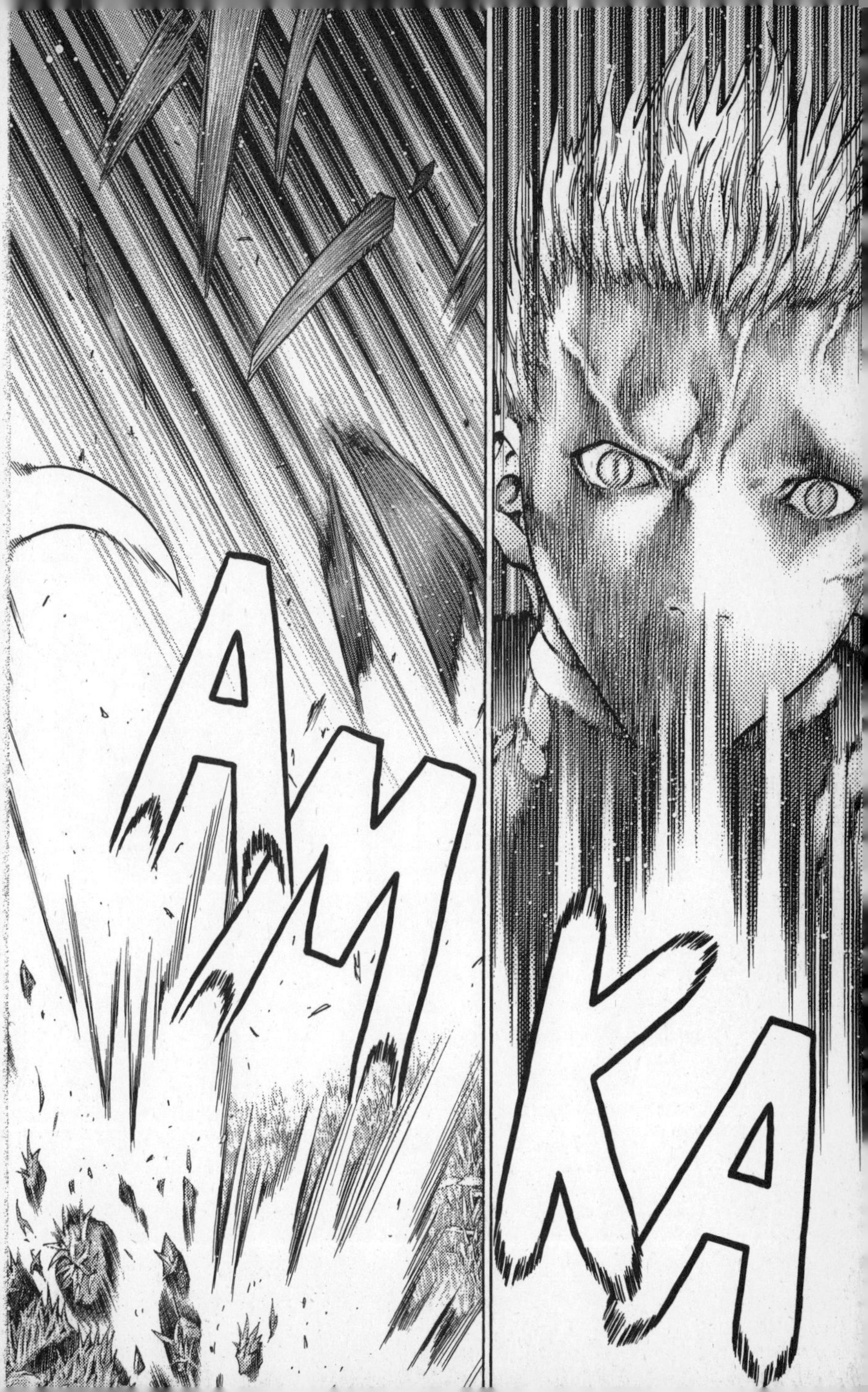
KA
AM

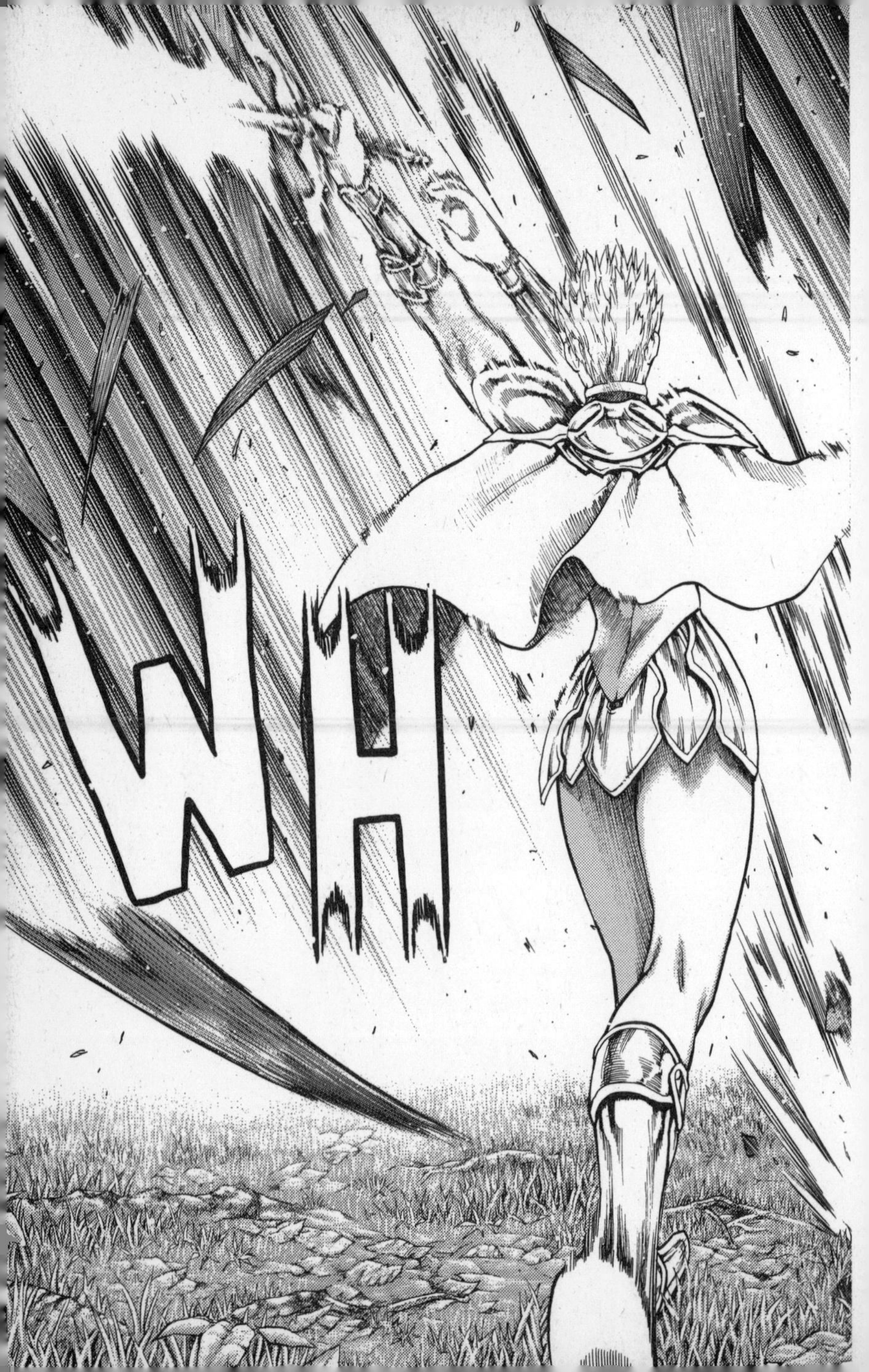
WH

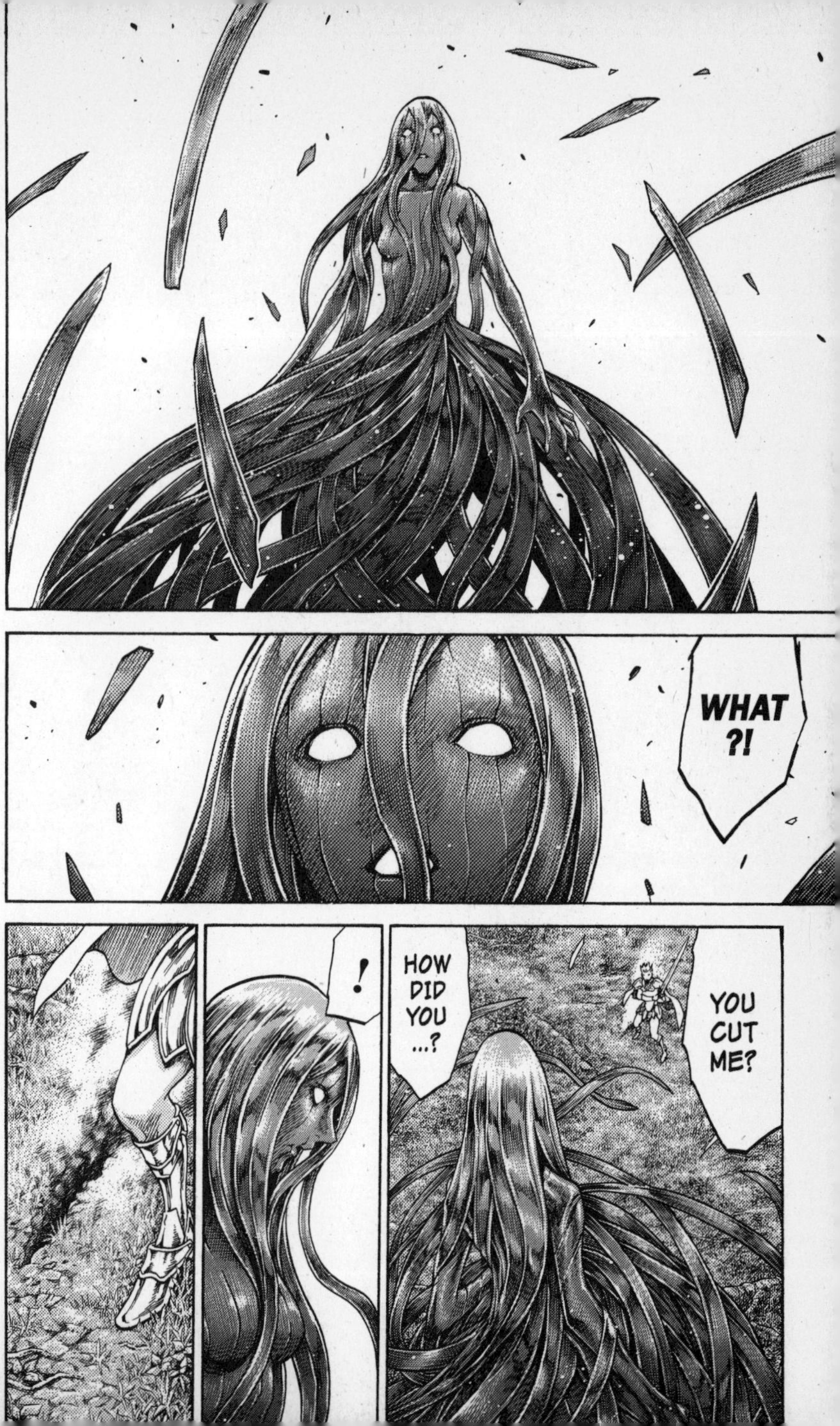
WHAT ?!
YOU CUT ME?
HOW DID YOU ...?
!

READ THIS WAY

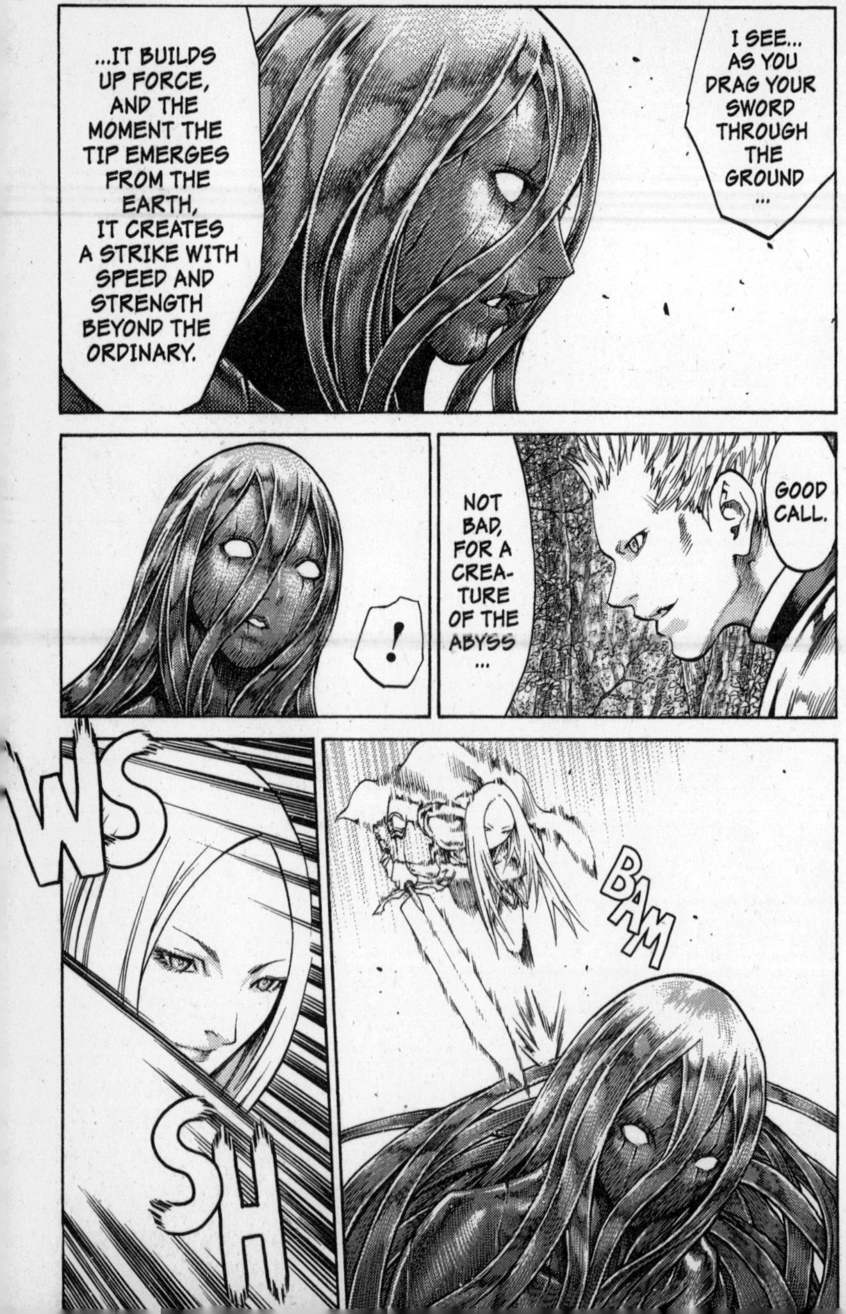
I SEE... AS YOU DRAG YOUR SWORD THROUGH THE GROUND ...
...IT BUILDS UP FORCE, AND THE MOMENT THE TIP EMERGES FROM THE EARTH, IT CREATES A STRIKE WITH SPEED AND STRENGTH BEYOND THE ORDINARY.
GOOD CALL.
NOT BAD, FOR A CREA- TURE OF THE ABYSS ...
!
BAM
WSSH

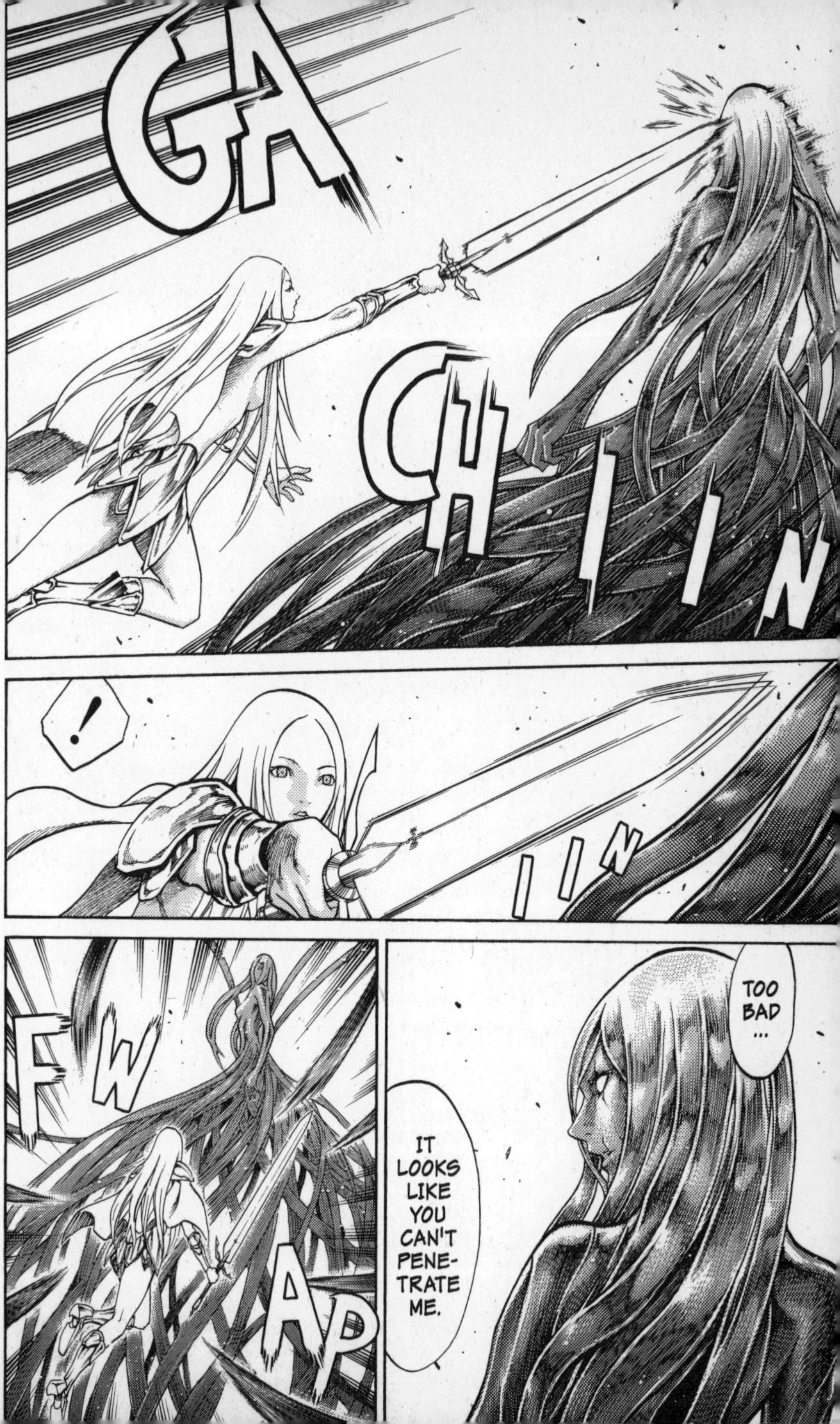
GA
CHIIN
!
IIN
TOO BAD...
IT LOOKS LIKE YOU CAN'T PENETRATE ME.
FWAP

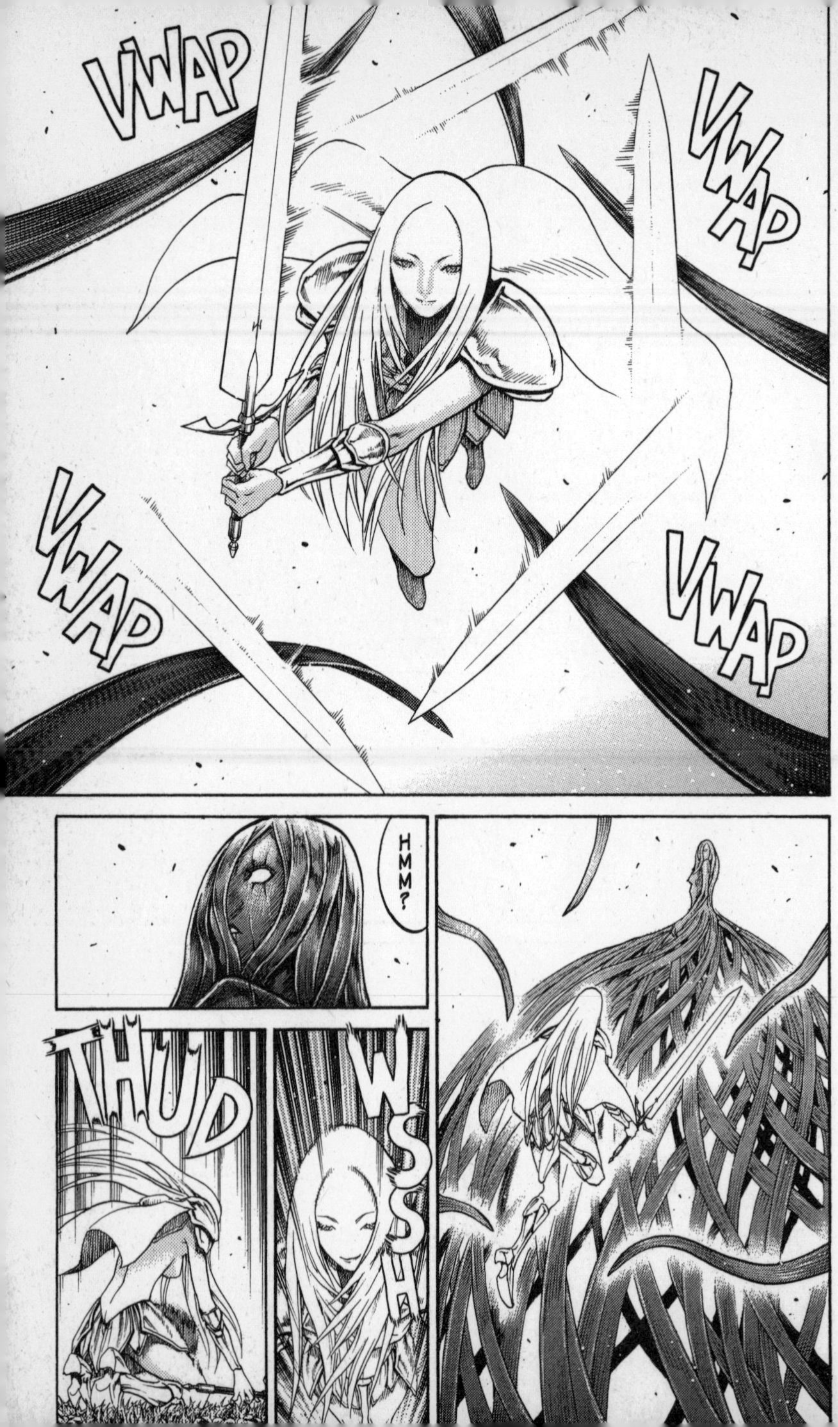
VWAP
VWAP
VWAP
VWAP
HMM?
WSSH
THUD

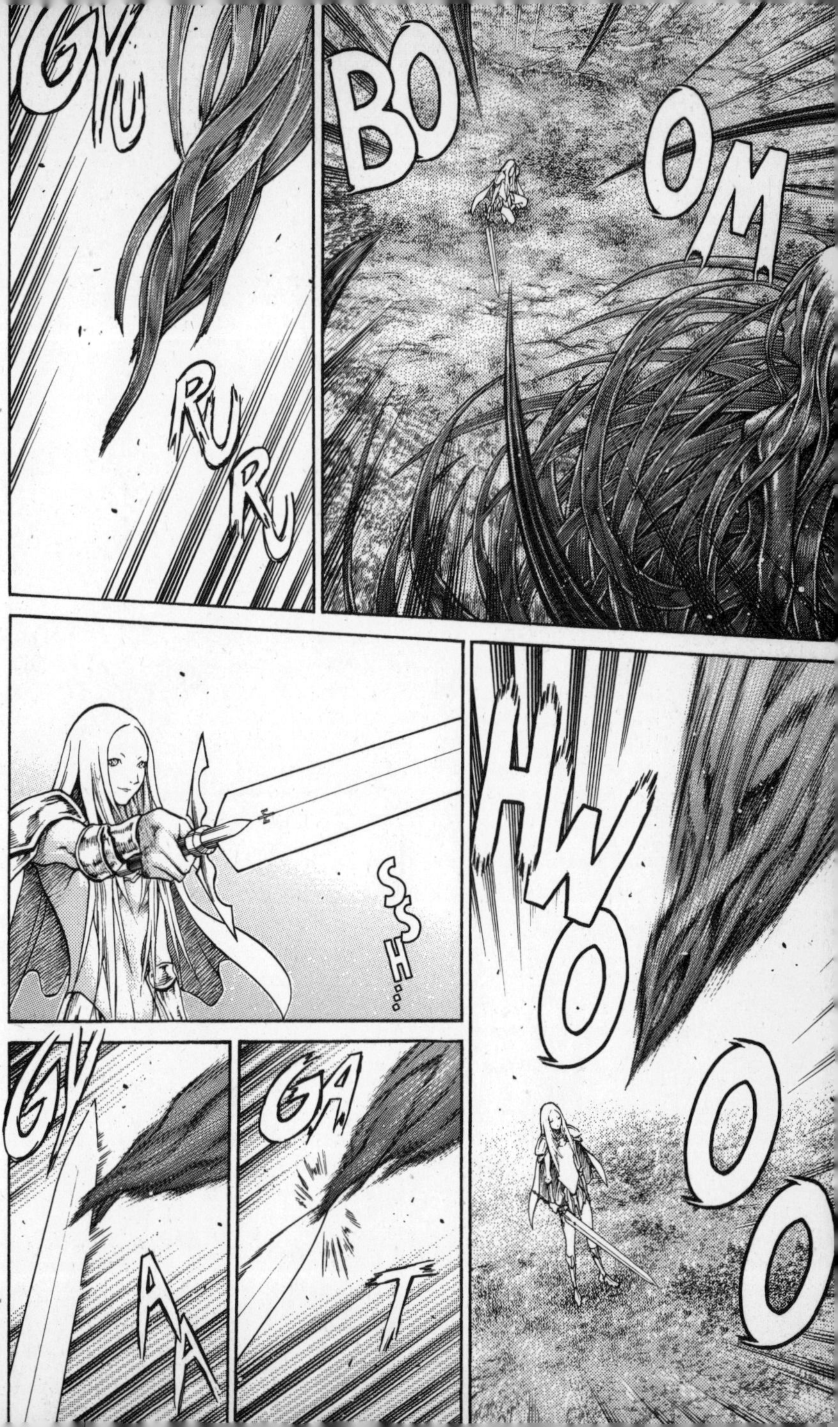
BOOM
GYURURURU
HWOOOOOO
SSSH...
GAT
GYAA

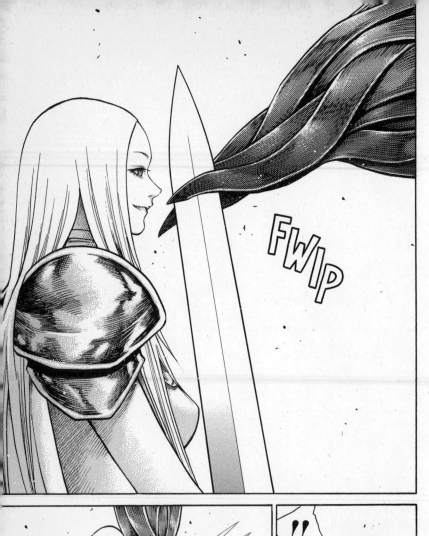

FWIP

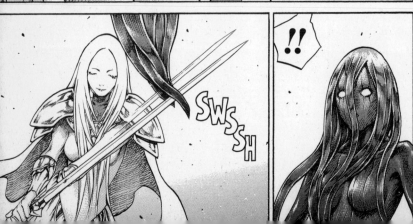

SWSSH

!!

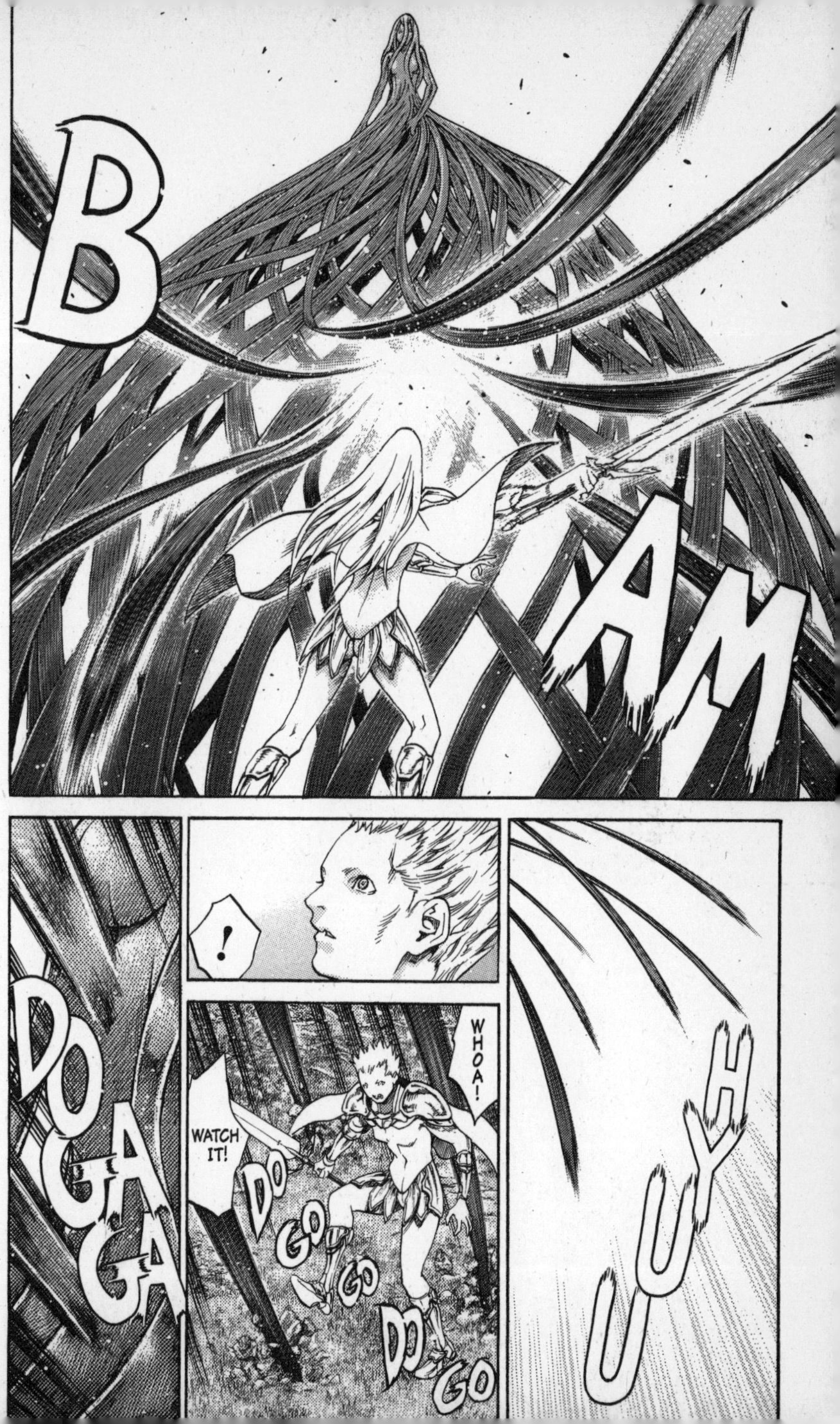
BAM
HYUUU
!
WHOA!
WATCH IT!
DO GO GO
DO GO
DOGAGA

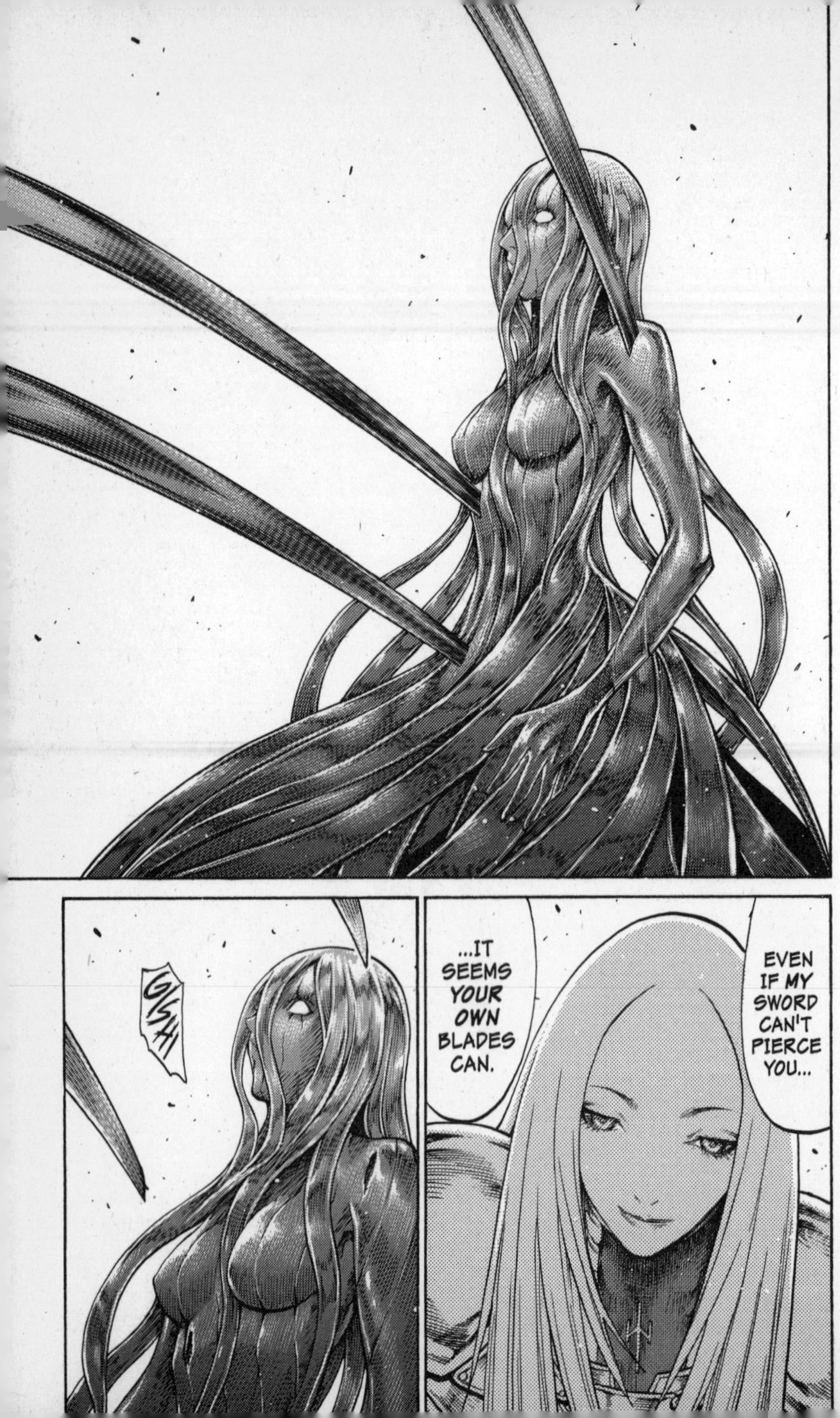
EVEN IF MY SWORD CAN'T PIERCE YOU...
...IT SEEMS YOUR OWN BLADES CAN.
GISHI

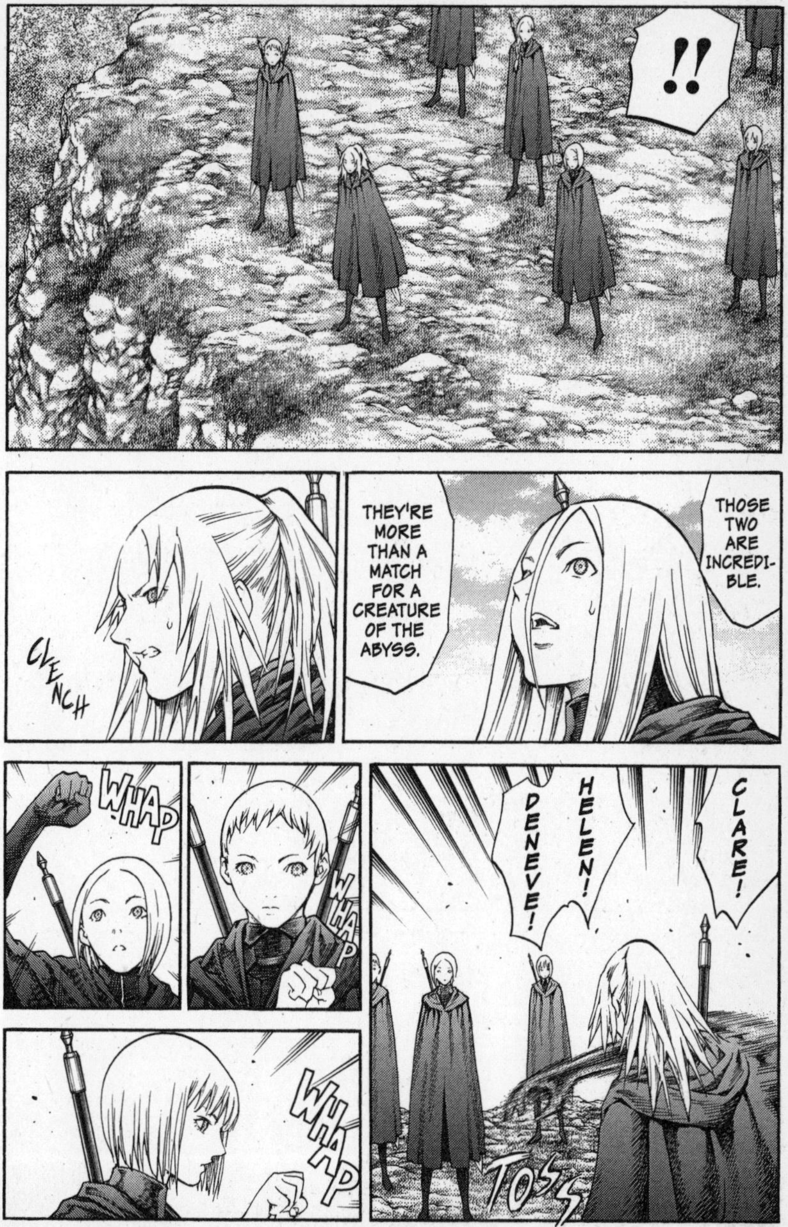

!!
THOSE TWO ARE INCREDIBLE.
THEY'RE MORE THAN A MATCH FOR A CREATURE OF THE ABYSS.
CLENCH
CLARE!
HELEN!
DENEVE!
TOSS
WHAP
WHAP
WHAP

READ THIS WAY

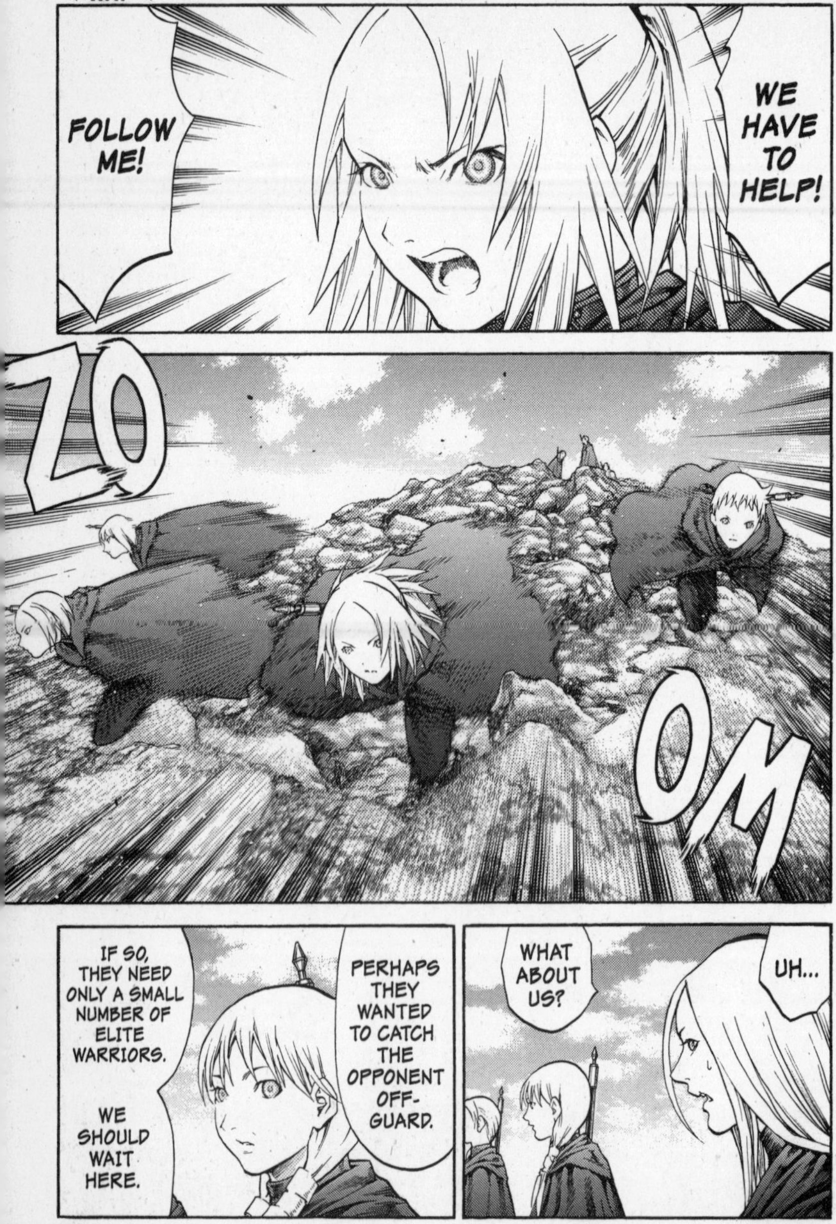
WE HAVE TO HELP!
FOLLOW ME!
ZO
OM
UH...
WHAT ABOUT US?
PERHAPS THEY WANTED TO CATCH THE OPPONENT OFF-GUARD.
IF SO, THEY NEED ONLY A SMALL NUMBER OF ELITE WARRIORS.
WE SHOULD WAIT HERE.

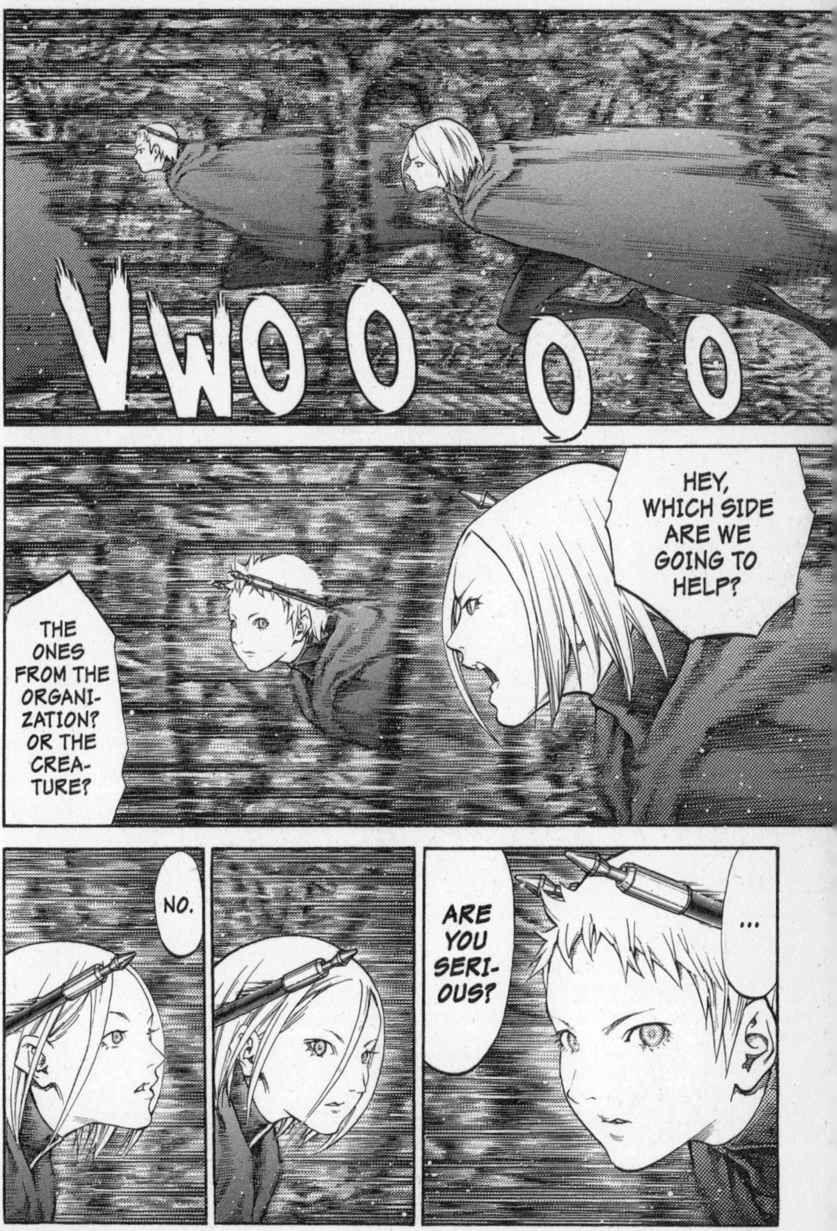
VWOOOOO
HEY, WHICH SIDE ARE WE GOING TO HELP?
THE ONES FROM THE ORGANIZATION? OR THE CREATURE?
...
ARE YOU SERIOUS?
NO.

READ THIS WAY

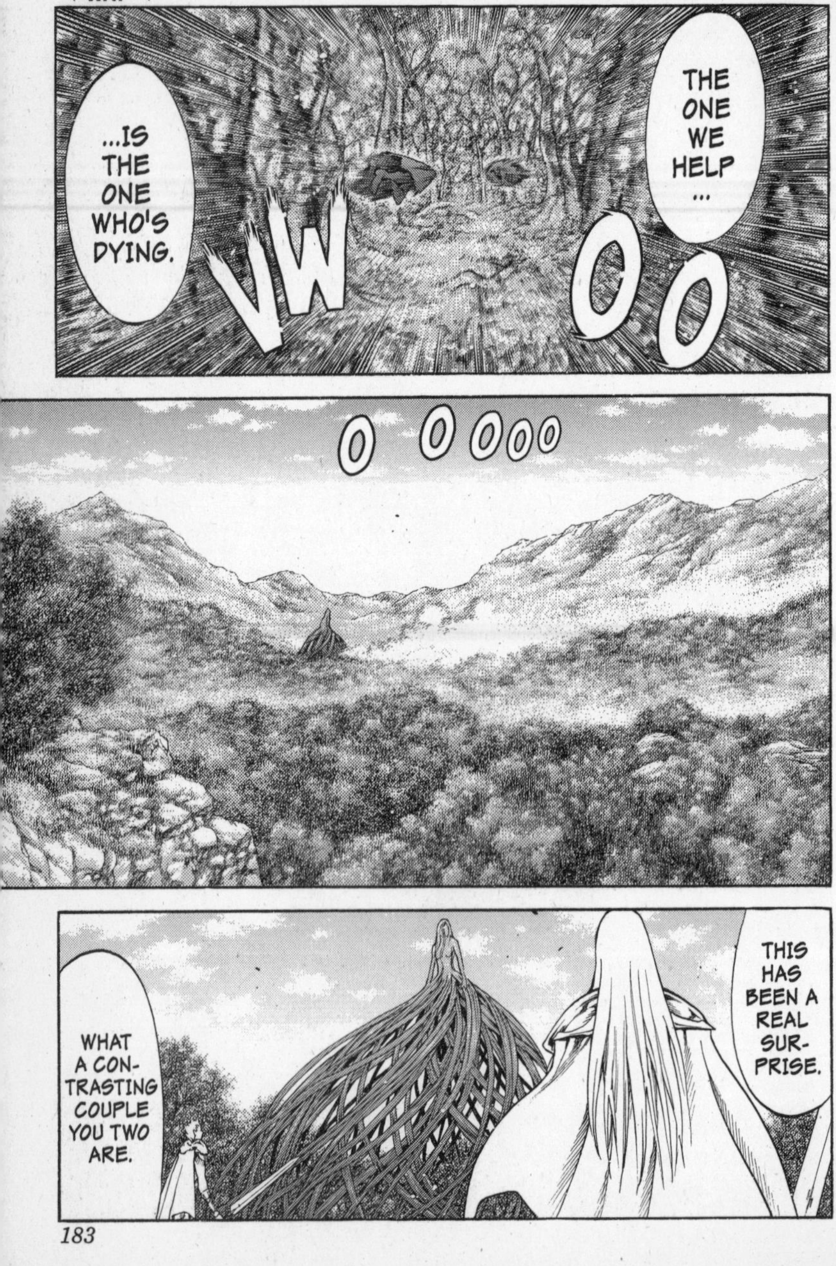
THE ONE WE HELP ...
...IS THE ONE WHO'S DYING.
VWOO
OOOOO
THIS HAS BEEN A REAL SUR-PRISE.
WHAT A CON-TRASTING COUPLE YOU TWO ARE.

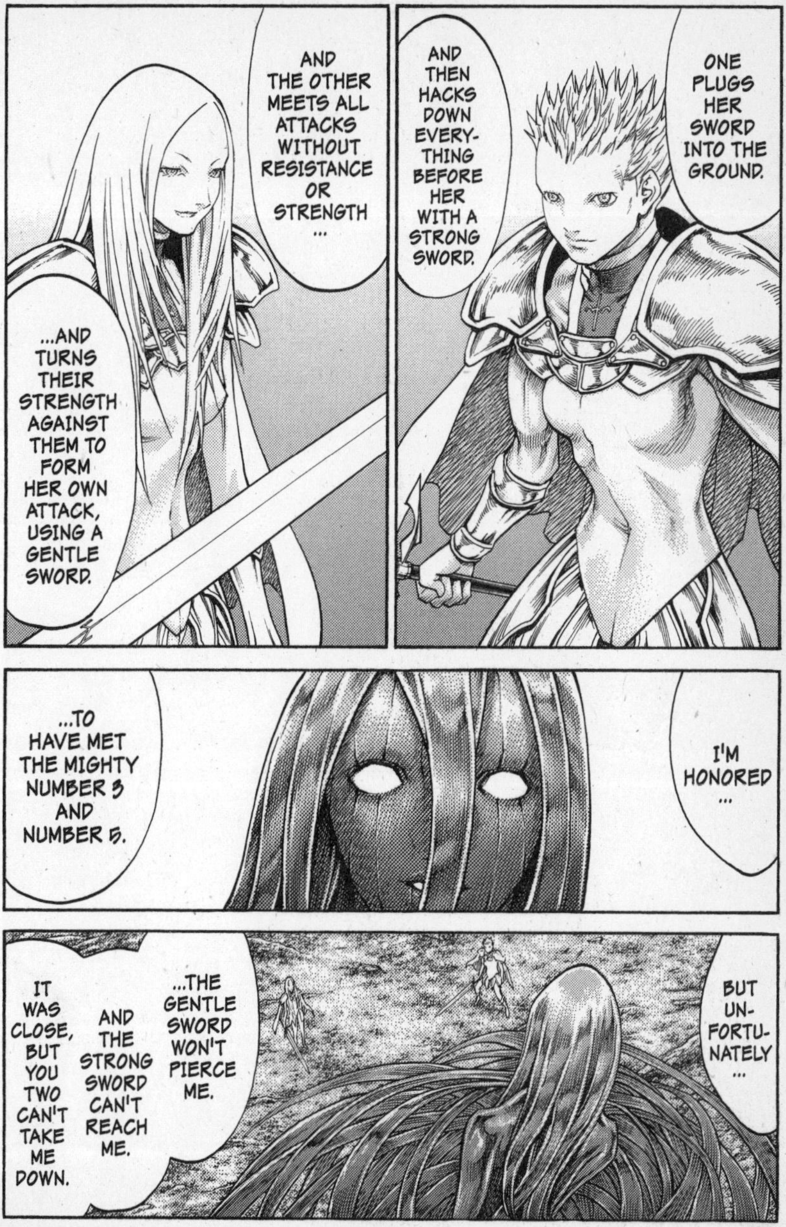
ONE PLUGS HER SWORD INTO THE GROUND.
AND THEN HACKS DOWN EVERY-THING BEFORE HER WITH A STRONG SWORD.
AND THE OTHER MEETS ALL ATTACKS WITHOUT RESISTANCE OR STRENGTH ...
...AND TURNS THEIR STRENGTH AGAINST THEM TO FORM HER OWN ATTACK, USING A GENTLE SWORD.
I'M HONORED ...
...TO HAVE MET THE MIGHTY NUMBER 3 AND NUMBER 5.
BUT UN-FORTU-NATELY ...
...THE GENTLE SWORD WON'T PIERCE ME.
AND THE STRONG SWORD CAN'T REACH ME.
IT WAS CLOSE, BUT YOU TWO CAN'T TAKE ME DOWN.

READ THIS WAY

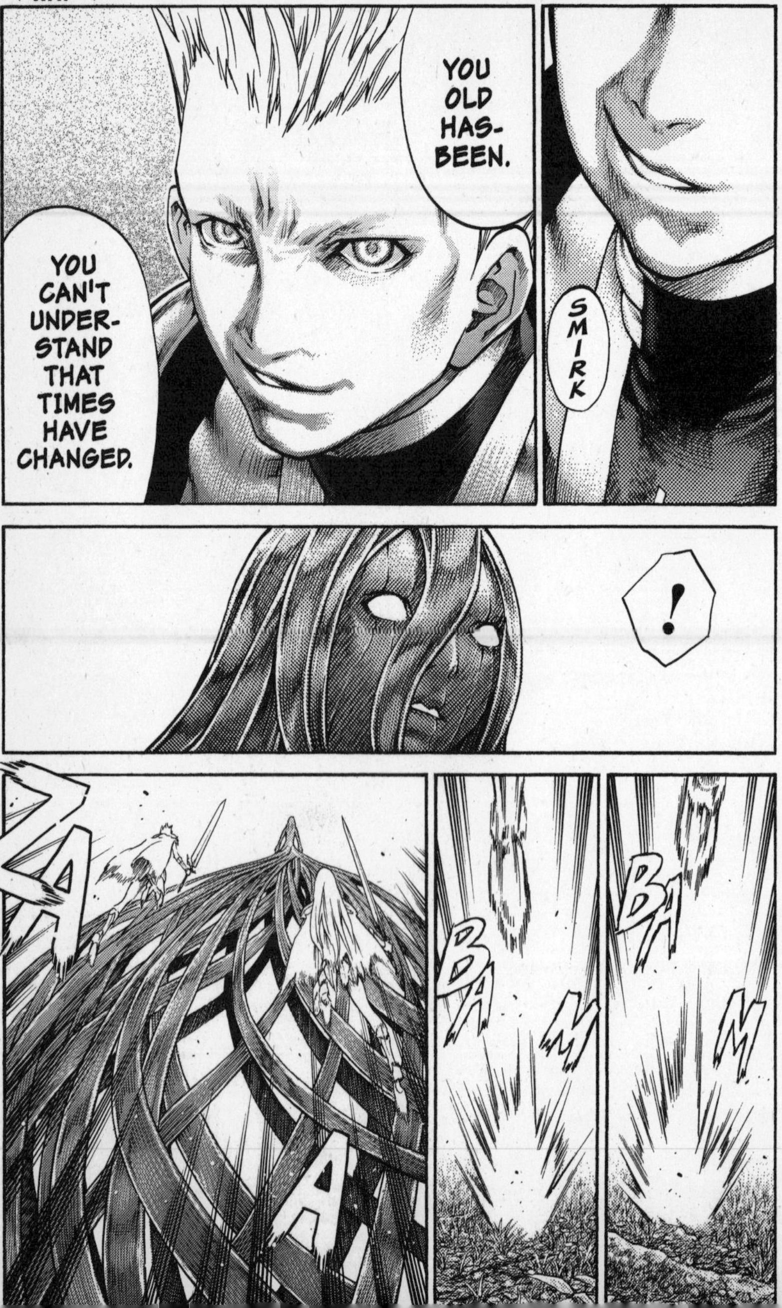
SMIRK
YOU OLD HAS-BEEN.
YOU CAN'T UNDER-STAND THAT TIMES HAVE CHANGED.
!
BAM
BAM
ZA A

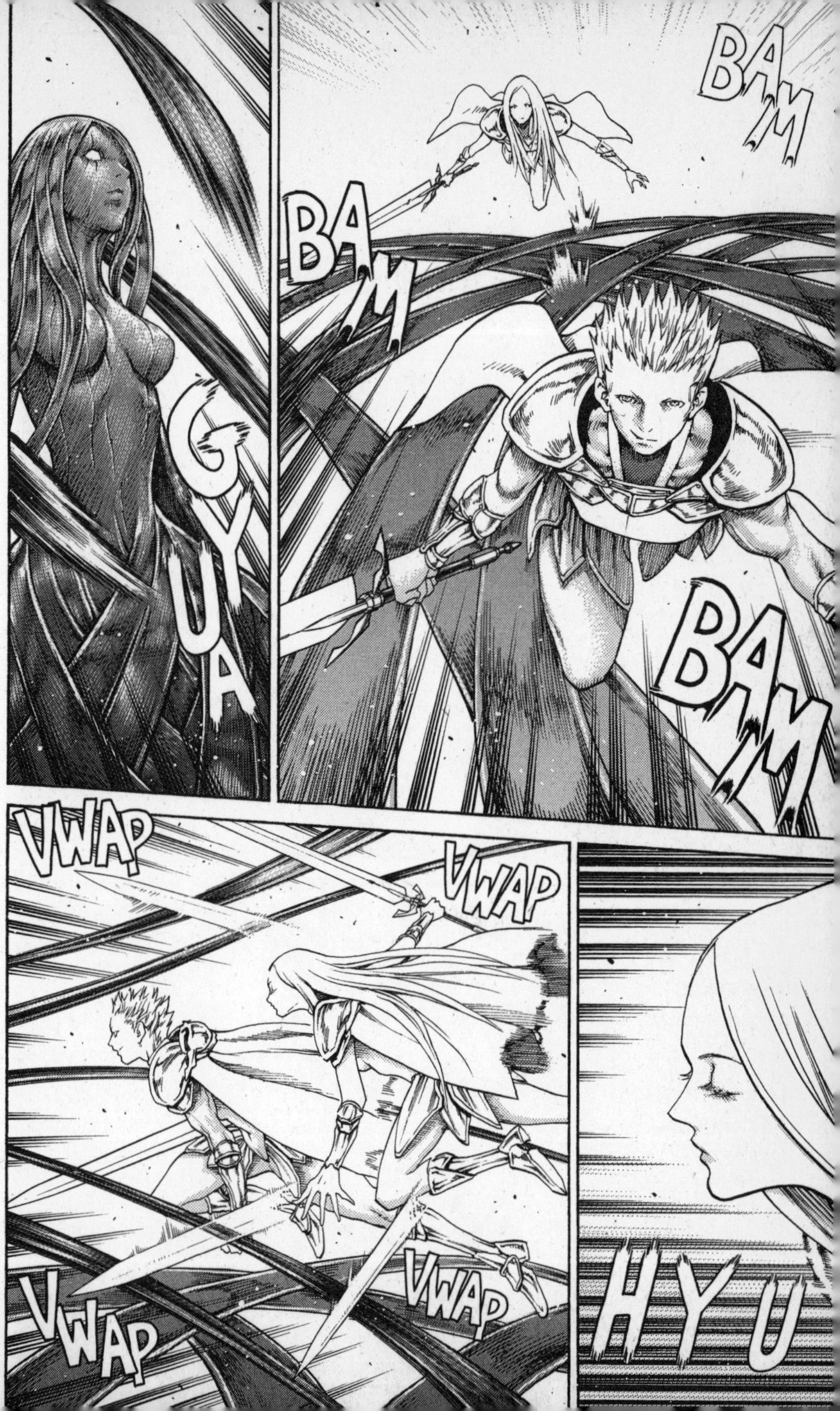
BAM
BAM
BAM
GYUA
HYU
VWAP
VWAP
VWAP
VWAP

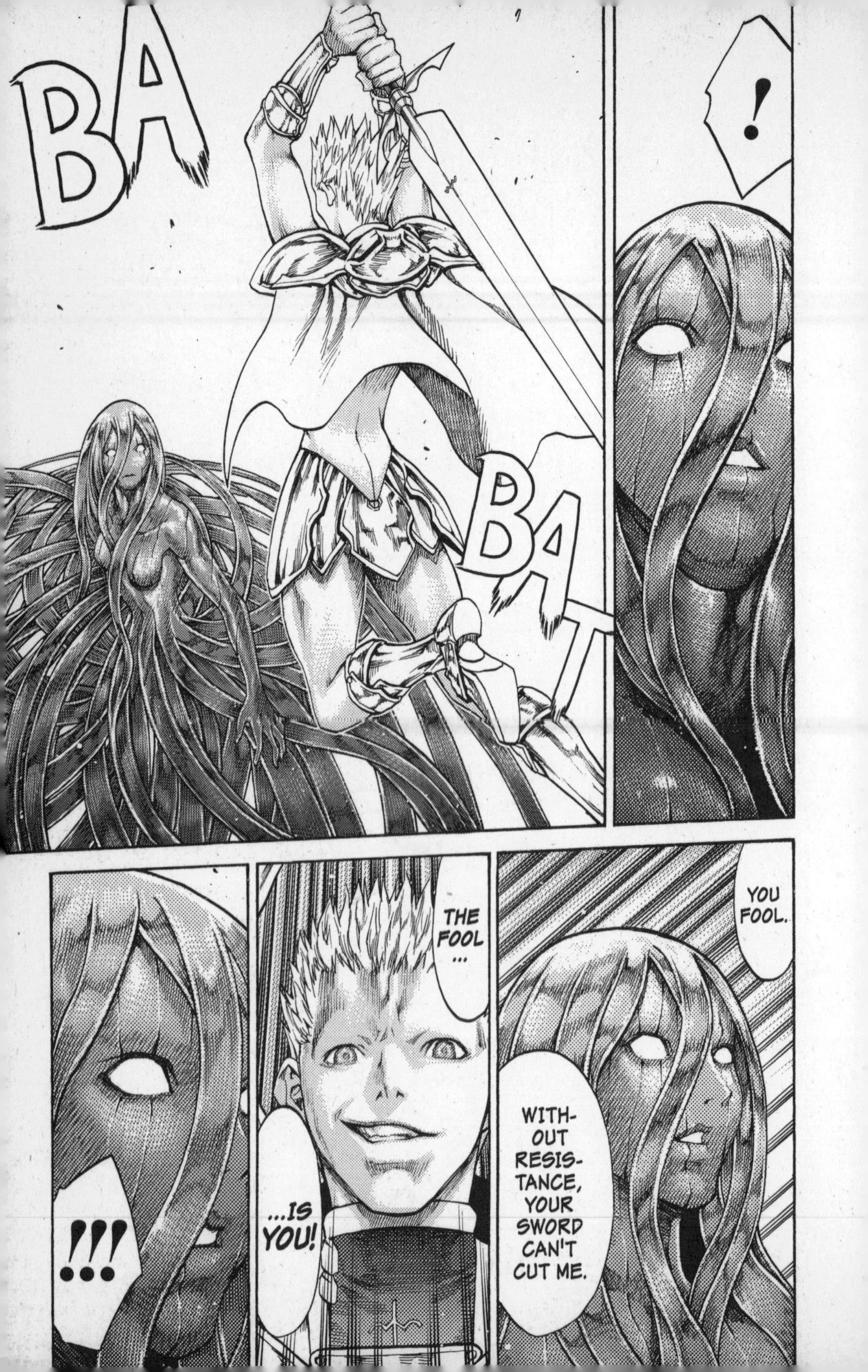
!
BA
BAT
YOU FOOL.
WITHOUT RESISTANCE, YOUR SWORD CAN'T CUT ME.
THE FOOL...
...IS YOU!
!!!

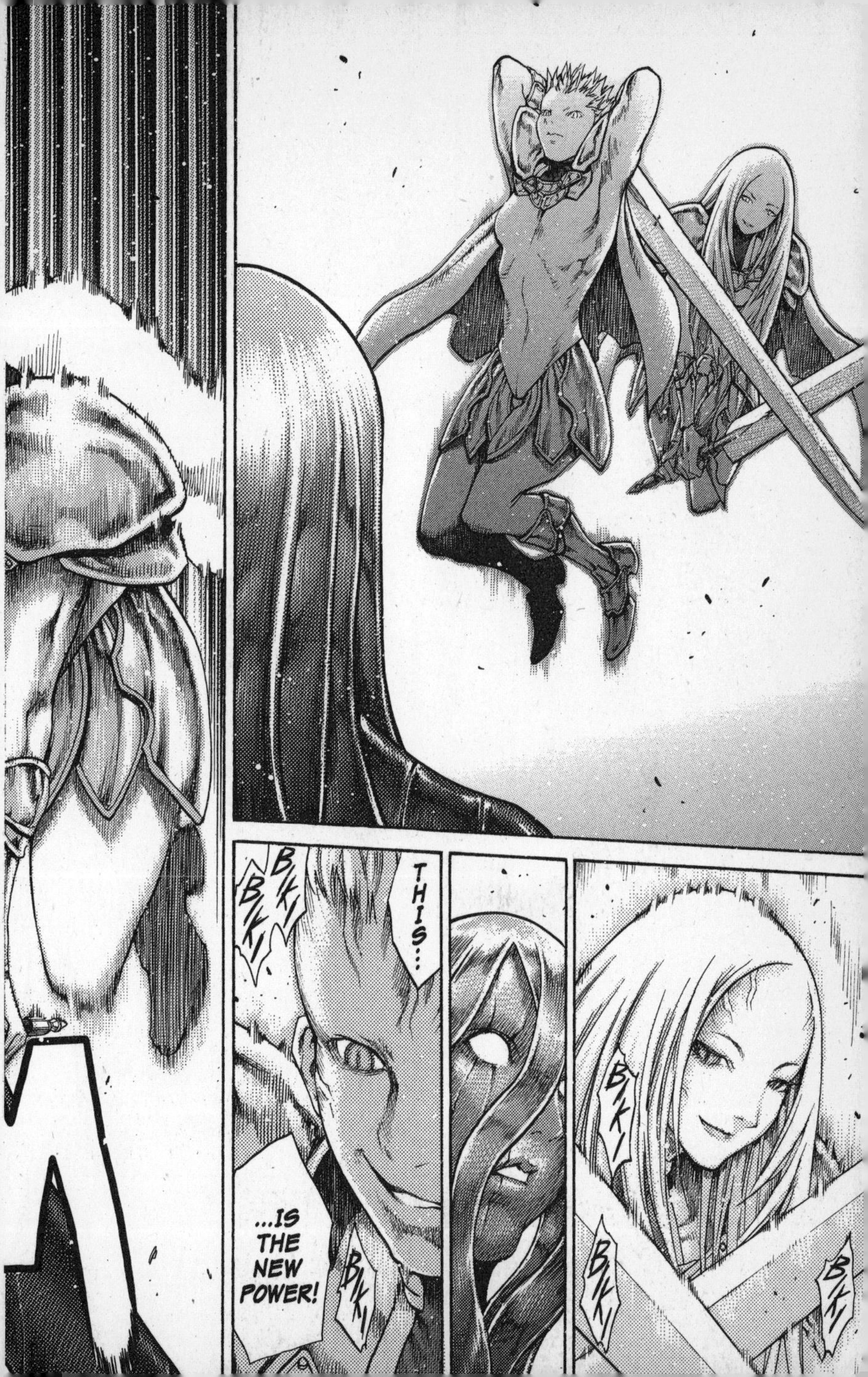
BIKI
BIKI
BIKI
BIKI
BIKI
THIS...
...IS THE NEW POWER!
BIKI

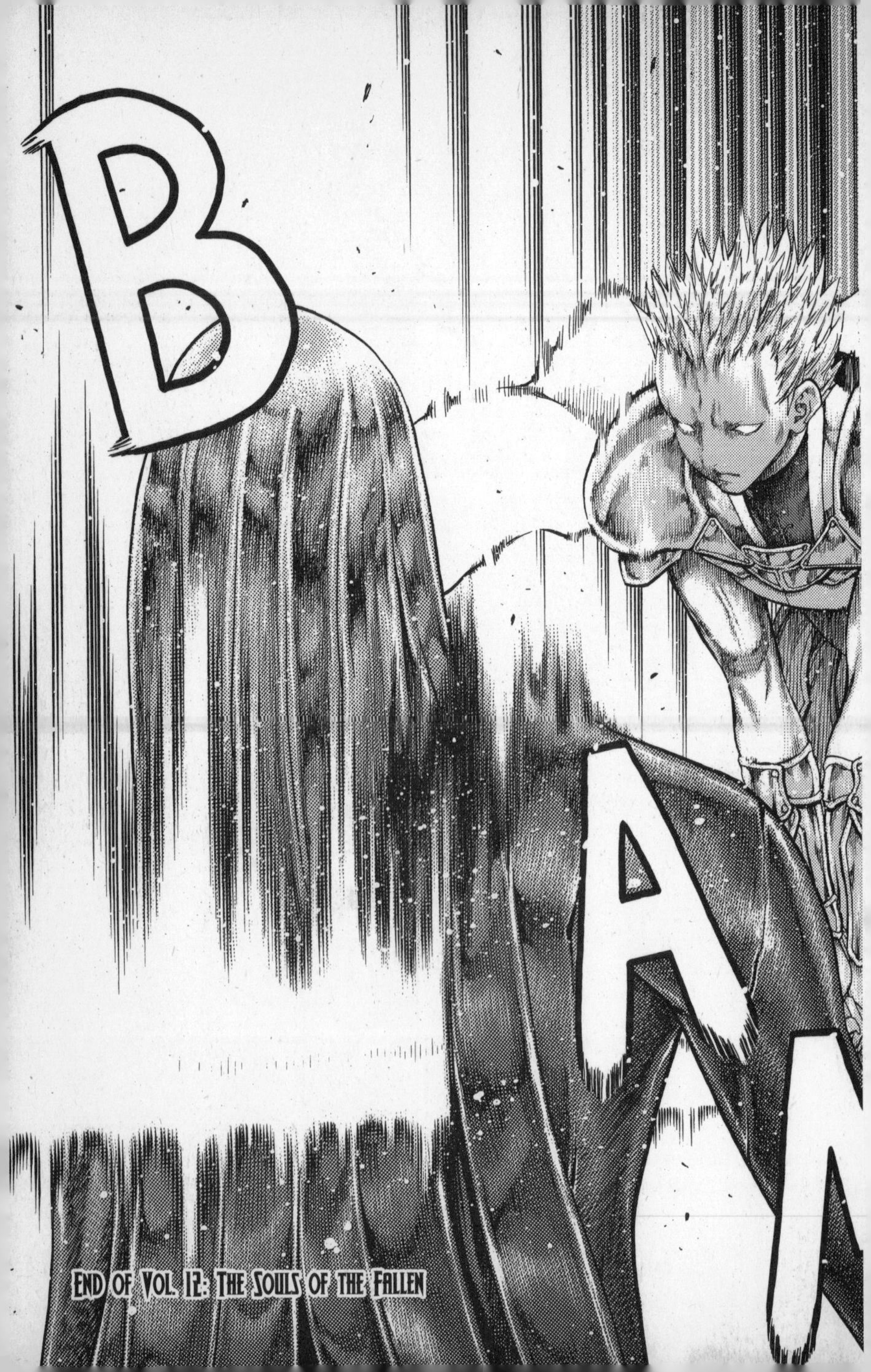
BAM
End of Vol. 12: The Souls of the Fallen

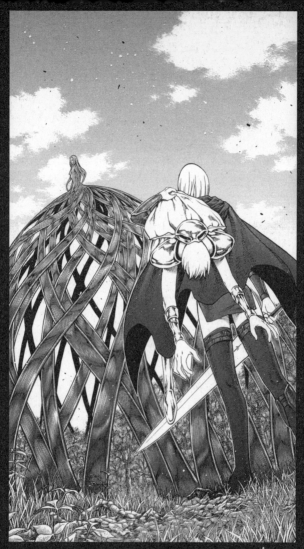

IN THE NEXT VOLUME

Audrey and Rachel continue their battle against Riful of the West, and Clare learns some surprising truths about Priscilla and the Three Great Awakened Ones. Then the Organization sends Miata and Clarice out on an important mission: how will Clarice be able to keep her unstable young charge in line? Also included: two bonus stories of Teresa's and Miria's pasts.

Available in November 2008

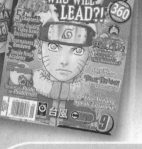
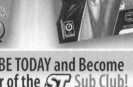

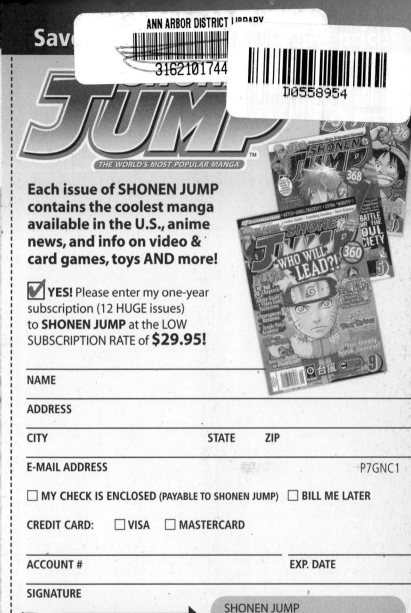